TOUCHSTONE

FUTURE FACTS

A FORECAST OF THE WORLD AS WE WILL KNOW IT
BEFORE THE END OF THE CENTURY

BY

STEPHEN ROSEN

ILLUSTRATIONS BY
THE CHARTMAKERS, INC.

A TOUCHSTONE BOOK
PUBLISHED BY SIMON AND SCHUSTER

Designed by Eve Metz
Manufactured in the United States of America

1 2 3 4 5 6 7 8 9 10

Library of Congress Cataloging in Publication Data

Rosen, Stephen, 1934–
    Future facts: a forecast of the world as we will
know it before the end of the century.

    Includes index.
    1. Technology. 2. Twentieth century—Forecasts.
I. Title.
T20.R58   609′.04   75–15545
ISBN 0–671–22078–0
ISBN 0–671–22756–4 pbk.

Contents

CONTENTS

CONTENTS

CONTENTS

Foreword

Facts I never thought of think of me.

Nine months pass between conception and childbirth while a human mind grows able to think. No one knows precisely when the embryo or fetus thinks, until he becomes a newborn child. Then, the infant tells us: by crying out, his demands change our lives. Organisms become a fact of life, unthought of—even as they begin to think of us.

Whole families of embryonic facts "think" of us: forthcoming products, services, processes and ideas—the offspring of innovators and entrepreneurs. Usually we aren't aware of an innovation until after its conception, or until the developer proudly announces its arrival. But even before the innovator launches a new product, he creates elaborate plans to manufacture, distribute, market and publicize his invention. The inventor and his brainchild truly think of me—before I think of them.

Though familiar to us now, detailed facts about most budding ideas or developments-in-progress were quite unknown, during their incubation period, to the average man-in-the-street: the idea for frozen foods originated in 1908, but the foods themselves weren't introduced to the public until 1923; conceived in 1884, television wasn't seen by most consumers until 1947, a time lag of more than half a century. Here are some other examples:

Innovation	Conception	Realization	Incubation Interval
Antibiotics	1910	1940	30 years
Automatic transmission	1930	1946	16 years
Ball-point pen	1938	1945	7 years

1

Cellophane	1900	1912	12 years
Dry soup mixes	1943	1962	19 years
Filter cigarettes	1953	1955	2 years
Heart pacemaker	1928	1960	32 years
Hybrid corn	1908	1933	25 years
Instant camera	1945	1947	2 years
Instant coffee	1934	1956	22 years
Liquid shampoo	1950	1958	8 years
Long-playing records	1945	1948	3 years
Nuclear energy	1919	1965	46 years
Nylon	1927	1939	12 years
Photography	1782	1838	56 years
Radar	1904	1939	35 years
Roll-on deodorant	1948	1955	7 years
Self-winding wrist-watch	1923	1939	16 years
Video tape recorder	1950	1956	6 years
Xerox copying	1935	1950	15 years
Zipper	1883	1913	30 years

Of course, it takes longer than nine months—usually much longer than the inventor expects—to hatch a worthwhile invention. And successful innovations are those systems-in-motion that will find widespread adoption and application in the marketplace because they fulfill a need.

"The greatest invention of the nineteenth century," said Alfred North Whitehead, "was the invention of the method of invention." Perhaps in the twentieth century we've invented a kind of "birth control" processs for new inventions, or an elaborate obstacle course that allows only the fittest innovations to survive. Great energy and imagination are called for to leap these hurdles —personal struggles, financial barriers, even ridicule by experts:

> *If God had intended that man should fly He would have given him wings. . . . The airship business is a "fake" and has been so since it was started two hundred years ago. . . . Never has the human mind so persistently evaded the issue, begged the question, and, "wrangling resolutely with the facts," insisted upon dreams being accepted as actual performance.*
> —REAR ADMIRAL GEORGE W. MELVILLE, *Chief Engineer of the United States Navy, 1901*

2

Against steep odds the dedicated inventor, entrepreneur or visionary strives to realize his dream—*only* by "wrangling resolutely with the facts." He would certainly agree with H. G. Wells: "Will is stronger than Fact; it can mold and overcome Fact."

It's often said, "Some people see things as they are and ask why; I dream of things that never were and ask why not." This is brave talk, and sometimes reckless talk. But the question "why not" has heroic dimensions. In earlier times the individual who persisted to champion his idea or product in the face of all inhibiting adversity was regarded as a hero. Mythology commemorates Prometheus (whose name in Greek means "foresight") because he stole fire from the sun to bestow upon mankind, but was punished by the gods for his audacity and courage. Theodore Roosevelt spoke of the man "who, if he wins, knows the triumph of high achievement, and who if he fails, at least fails while daring greatly." Today's developers and visionaries are those inventors, scientists, and entrepeneurs who "dare greatly," who ask "why not"—and then do something about it.

It may come as a surprise that the predominant feelings toward science and technology among three fourths of typical American adults are "satisfaction," "hope," "excitement," or "wonder." Yet despite this, a small but vocal minority of debunkers are afflicted with the doomsday syndrome—that gloomy habit of foreseeing the worst aspect of progress. It's not the *inventions* of men that are dangerous, but the *intentions* of men. (For contrary views on science and technology, and on the journalistic notion that "new" is "good," please see the Afterword, page 515.)

However, change does encompass such a vast panorama that a guide to the future is necessary because we're discomforted or shocked by the rapid speed-up of change, the accelerated pace of oncoming events. To decelerate from "future shock" we need a shock absorber—a future *cushion*.

Facts are cushions. Facts enlarge and inform our expectations. Properly selected, facts are an early warning system that gets us ready for the future. Facts may also provide a pleasant preview of things to come. And facts bridge the gap between what we think and what really exists; between what we do and don't

3

know; between the past, present and future. Facts about the future, *future* facts, tell us the way things *will* work.

FUTURE FACTS® are systems-in-motion—products, services, processes or ideas—that are (1) at least one year away from mass-market realization; (2) likely to "succeed" after they appear; (3) probably important future influences on the average man-in-the-street; (4) selected because they're probably "interesting" to read about. They are, in short, facts with a future.

Prophecy, the most gratuitous form of error, is a temptation I could not resist. So in this book forecasts are clearly separated from the facts by setting in a **different typeface.** These forecasts speculate upon the future of the facts.

Unless something special happens, we remember more details from a day last week than from a day last year. Our minds tend to bunch up events of the recent past and to space them out as we think farther back. This "immediacy effect" is probably due to our time-biased memory of the distant past, which we often override when we recall *important* events. By symmetry, our minds create a *forward* immediacy effect, as events imagined *ahead* in time crowd in upon the near-term future and stretch out over the long-range future. Yet facts, I think, override this natural time-bias since facts help us to grasp *vital*—rather than merely *immediate*—things to come. Among countless innovations being created even as you read this, are those vital future facts (at the moment, perhaps, known only to you) whose appearance in a later edition I will welcome.

"My interest is in the future," said Charles F. Kettering, "because I am going to spend the rest of my life there." And my interest is in facts, *future* facts—because we will live among them.

STEPHEN ROSEN

New York, 1975

4

1
Health
and
Medicine

Artificial Life

Evolutionary theory provides a convincing explanation—natural selection—of how life forms evolved from primitive one-celled organisms. Molecular biology, a relatively new discipline, gives us some ideas of how the genetic code enables cells to reproduce themselves. But how did the first living cell come into existence?

A living cell is a complicated organism containing amino acids, building blocks of the protein of the cell. Cells also contain nucleic acids, which embody the genetic code—"instructions" on how to duplicate themselves. Some amino acids may form (from carbon, oxygen, hydrogen, sulfur and nitrogen) under special conditions found on the moon, in meteorites and in interstellar space. But as far as we know, no cells have evolved. Ingredients and conditions existed ages ago on earth to create the first living cell. Some amino acids are formed in the laboratory under conditions that duplicate those we think existed on primitive earth.

Dr. Sidney Fox of the University of Miami has narrowed the gap between amino acids and that first live cell. In the laboratory, he has assembled materials containing chains of amino acids that organized themselves to display some of the attributes of life. Some of these materials are even self-reproducing. The conditions under which these precellular structures are formed indicate that life may be expected to arise by itself on a primordial planet or in interstellar space.

Over a hundred years ago, Louis Pasteur noted that living organisms (for example, maggots) require parents—they cannot arise spontaneously. Dr. Fox addresses the question, "What came before the parents?" There is still a tremendous distance between Fox's primitive self-organizing structures and a "real" living cell, but he and his colleagues have definitely narrowed it.

"The experiments," comments Dr. Fox, "indicate that a microstructure with many of the properties, but not all of the prop-

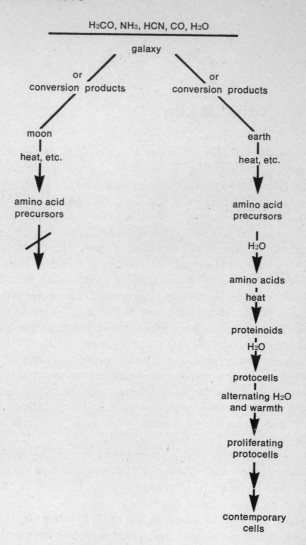

$H_2CO, NH_3, HCN, CO, H_2O$

galaxy

or
conversion products

or
conversion products

moon

heat, etc.

amino acid
precursors

earth

heat, etc.

amino acid
precursors

H_2O

amino acids

heat

proteinoids

H_2O

protocells

alternating H_2O
and warmth

proliferating
protocells

contemporary
cells

A "flowsheet" of spontaneous evolution. Compounds of carbon, nitrogen, hydrogen, and oxygen (top) in interstellar space produce amino acids (center), early prototype cells, and (bottom) the nucleic acid self-replicating cells.

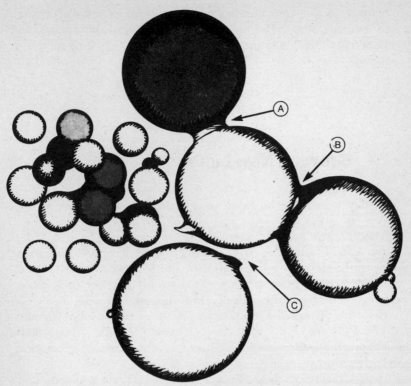

Tiny spheres of proteinlike material (proteinoids) have many properties in common with living cells: they contain fatty substances and huge molecules with information, they are semipermeable, they move spontaneously, and they can proliferate. With other microspheres they also form junctions that are: (A) intact, (B) cracked, and (C) separated. It is possible that across these junctions some form of "communication" takes place.

erties, of the contemporary cell could have arisen with a maximum of simplicity in process. In this respect . . . one needs to recognize that a first structure possessing 'life' was not necessarily a modern cell."

Nucleic-acid "engineering" makes it possible to replicate almost any living substance in the test tube—theoretically. And people are already beginning to wonder about the ethical advisability of such undertakings. But there's another even more prodigious possibility. Chemical engineering could produce species of plants and animals that have never before existed—whole new approaches to life. The fabrication of a single cell might be all that's needed.

Growing New Limbs

Someday a person who loses an arm might simply grow a new one.

Many lower animals are capable of regenerating lost body parts; if a lobster's leg is removed, a new structure will soon appear and develop into a complete and functioning limb. Ordinarily, however, mammals are capable only of very limited regeneration, as when the ends of a broken bone knit together.

Now Dr. Robert O. Becker, an orthopedist at the Upstate Medical Center of the State University of New York, has found that low-amplitude electrical current causes partial regeneration in higher animals.

In previous research Dr. Becker found that direct application of electrical currents could affect the rate and structure of bone growth. Then in 1967 another researcher found that frogs—which are capable of regeneration as tadpoles but not as adults—could grow new legs when electrically stimulated. Dr. Becker modified this technique and tried it on the amputated forelimbs of white rats.

Amazingly, the rats also showed regenerative growth. While no test animal grew a complete limb, most regenerated tissues at least a few millimeters in size. The new legs had the same cell structure and complexity as normal tissues. Bone, cartilage, marrow, muscles, nerves, and blood vessels were all regenerated.

These results, Dr. Becker has written, "were extensive enough to warrant the prediction that similar level currents could have profound clinical implications for humans." He does not anticipate that his work will benefit amputees in the near future, but

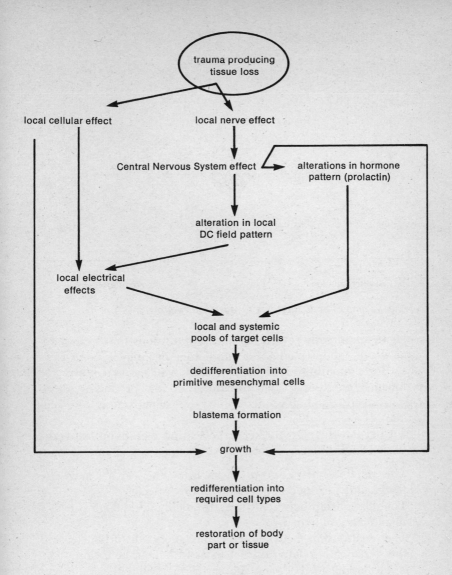

Possible control system of regenerative healing.

he does expect that electromagnetic stimulation will be used to promote healing in a variety of organs. For instance, portions of the heart muscle damaged in a coronary failure might be regenerated.

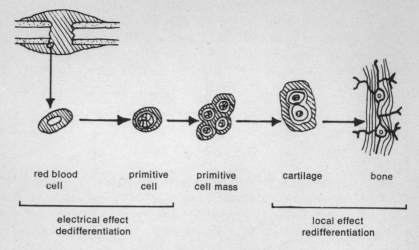

red blood cell   primitive cell   primitive cell mass   cartilage   bone

electrical effect
dedifferentiation

local effect
redifferentiation

Normal healing of bone fractures is regenerative growth.

There are already several medical applications for electromagnetic waves under study: for promoting healing of bone fractures, for promoting rapid healing of skin ulcers and burns, for producing anesthesia (electronarcosis), for producing sleep (electrosleep) and for increasing the effectiveness of acupuncture.

But beyond this, Dr. Becker believes that we are on the verge of understanding such diverse electromagnetic phenomena as

1. The relationship between reversals of the earth's magnetic field and the extinction of various animal species
2. The relationship between the earth's field and biological cycles in animals and in man
3. The relationship between electromagnetic disturbances and the statistically related disturbances in human behavior
4. The relationship between the earth's field and the migratory and homing activities of animals and birds.

Nonetheless, Dr. Becker warns against a rush toward widespread use of electromagnetic medicine, since there may be physical and psychological side effects that have not yet been detected. He is also concerned about the effect that continuous electromagnetic bombardment may be having on the general population, particularly on city dwellers. How does our electrical environment influence the body's own electrical mechanisms?

Dr. Becker says, "What I feel is urgently required is multidisciplinary research on the entire problem of electromagnetic energy and biological systems, covering all areas—the direct injection of electrical currents into living systems, their exposure to radiofrequency fields, and preexisting basic biological electronic control systems. My conviction is that this field holds promise of containing the next great advance in biomedical science."

"More reliance should be placed upon the primordial power of the human skeleton to regenerate injured and missing substance," according to at least one expert. And after this happens successfully for bone growth, what next? Admittedly farfetched, but still a hope—the vital organs: regenerate a stomach, a heart, and although it seems inconceivable with what we now know, perhaps someday a brain.

Human Cells Are Harvested from Mice

An international team of research scientists sponsored by the Brookhaven National Laboratory in Upton, New York, has developed a simple and tiny artificial system in which human blood cells are reproduced and studied outside the body.

A carefully measured amount of human bone marrow and peripheral blood cells is placed in a coin-shaped diffusion chamber made with filters; the chamber is then implanted in the abdominal cavity of a living mouse. Nourished through the filters by elements in the mouse's blood that are identical with basic elements in human blood, the diffusion chamber replenishes red and white blood cells in the same way that bone marrow does in the human body. Human cells have also been harvested from rabbits and goats.

Previous exposure to radiation renders the mouse's tissue unable to reject the foreign substances, which are kept implanted for up to ten days. Ten days is the limit because the radiation usually kills the mouse by that time. But the same diffusion chamber, with the same family of cells, can be continually reimplanted in other mice—theoretically forever.

The diffusion chamber is removed from the "host" for study of its contents at every stage of blood-cell division, differentiation, and maturation. Members of the Brookhaven team have studied blood growth in diffusion chambers over periods of up to thirty days.

The diffusion chamber system provides a window on the intricacies of blood formation in health and disease. Significant findings on the metabolic causes of at least one type of leukemia have already been reported, with more to come. And the system provides a way to investigate the effects of experimental drugs on blood diseases without having to use human patients as guinea pigs.

Dr. Arland L. Carsten, in whose laboratory at Brookhaven most of the diffusion chamber work was done, says, "In addition to obtaining information on the cellular kinetics and the characterization of diseased marrow, it seems reasonable that the system might be used to study the effectiveness of various treatment regimens on modifying the growth of human marrow within the chambers."

If human blood cells can grow outside the human body, why not human bone cells, muscle cells, and nerve cells? And eventually all of them together, functioning as a single living organism created in the "image of its maker"—as Mary Shelley envisioned long ago in her novel *Frankenstein: A Modern Prometheus.* . . . Meanwhile a way has been opened to understand and eventually to treat complex, widespread, and often dangerous blood diseases.

Airborne Intensive Care for Infants

A recent study found that the United States ranks fourteenth among all nations in the prevention of infant mortality (19.8 deaths per 1000 births). Too many babies die or are neurologically crippled who could be saved by existing techniques. Dr. Sprague Gardiner, chairman of the American Medical Association's committee on maternal and child care, estimates that the infant mortality rate could be cut by as much as one half if intensive care were available for high-risk newborns throughout the country.

The solution is farsighted contingency planning for bringing an infant in trouble to the lifesaving facilities.

In six mountain states this sort of planning is in effect. Ailing newborns are flown in specially equipped planes and helicopters to a regional intensive care center in Salt Lake City. While airborne, an infant rests in an incubator, under the constant care of a doctor-and-nurse team. The system makes intensive care available in a large and thinly populated area, where local hospitals cannot afford the space-age technology needed to handle a rare emergency.

The Intermountain Newborn Intensive Care Center has all the latest equipment to care for infants struggling to stay alive: a device that constantly measures the baby's skin temperature and adjusts the incubator heat accordingly; sensors that monitor heartbeat, breathing, and blood pressure, sounding an alarm in case of trouble; oxygen analyzers and regulators to keep the child's oxygen intake at prescribed levels; machines that administer glucose, water, salts, proteins and antibiotics intravenously into the baby's system. It's not unusual to have as much as $15,000 worth of equipment tending a single sick child.

They also have the personnel to give the young patients constant attention. While an ordinary hospital nursery may assign a single nurse to care for ten babies, the center maintains a ratio of two babies per nurse in its newcomer ward.

The majority of the babies at the center are premature, and because their lungs are not fully developed, many suffer from

INTERMOUNTAIN NEWBORN INTENSIVE CARE CENTER
UNIVERSITY MEDICAL CENTER   SALT LAKE CITY, UTAH

1972

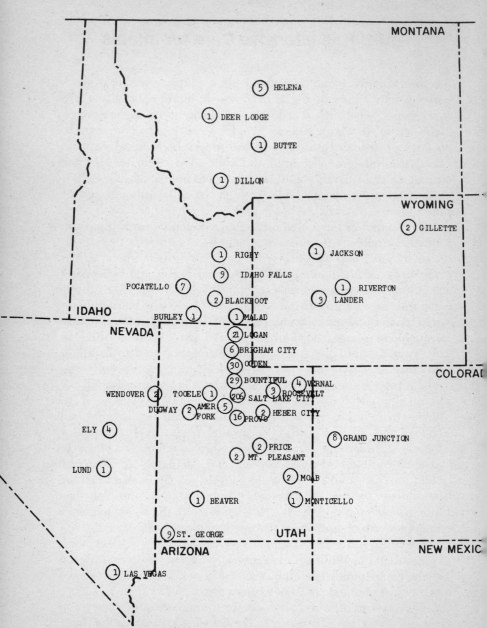

Areas and number of patients served by the center in 1972.

respiratory difficulties. These babies are placed in incubators filled with nearly 100 percent oxygen and treated with special respirators.

The center tries to prepare for trouble before it arrives. Ninety percent of high-risk babies are born to the 10 percent of pregnant women classified as "high risk." These include women under 18 and over 35, diabetics, those with heart disease, those carrying breech babies or twins, and those with a history of miscarriages or other problems that call for precautions. The center encourages these women to come to a Salt Lake City hospital for delivery, so they will be near the intensive care facilities if trouble does develop.

The success of this kind of advanced planning shows up in the statistics: The Intermountain unit has cut the first-month mortality rate for infants in local hospitals from 20 to 10 per 1000 births.

Dr. August L. Jung, director of the center, says, "We're saving babies who would have died. And those babies by and large are intact, normal babies. What's more, we're saving babies who might have suffered brain damage—and they are now whole human beings, not retarded."

The future may see airborne intensive care in rural areas for adults.

Synthetic Blood

A substitute for blood is urgently needed. All too often, natural blood isn't available where and when it's required. People are frequently injured in out-of-the-way places where facilities are lacking for storing blood or administering transfusions. Then, too, the blood administered must be of the right type and it must be free of disease or it can be dangerous to life. For these reasons and more, the medical world was greatly heartened in 1966 when Dr. Leland C. Clark, Jr., of the University of Cincinnati's College

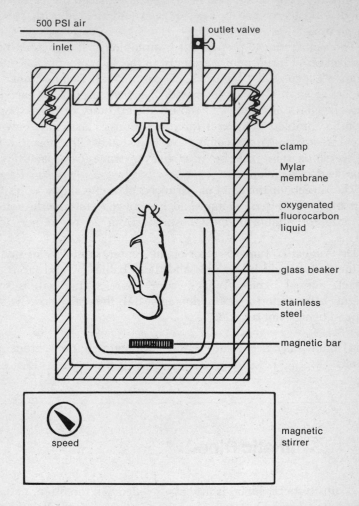

500 PSI air

inlet

outlet valve

clamp

Mylar membrane

oxygenated fluorocarbon liquid

glass beaker

stainless steel

magnetic bar

speed

magnetic stirrer

Mice immersed in fluorocarbon liquid survived, suggesting larger creatures could safely subsist on oxygenated liquids.

of Medicine, reported he had substituted certain liquids for natural blood in experimental animals for a limited time and the animals had survived in apparent good health.

The liquids used by Dr. Clark and his associates are fluorocarbon emulsions. These emulsions have a remarkable property—they're able to carry oxygen to the body cells, absorb carbon dioxide from them, and transport it to the lungs. These are major tasks that are performed by the hemoglobin in natural blood.

The ultimate aim of the experiments, of course, is to develop emulsions that will have an oxygen-carrying capacity resembling that of human blood. Before that day can come, however, the researchers must produce better emulsions and learn all they can about their long-range, as well as their immediate, effects on experimental animals.

"We hope that it may be possible to prepare a type of artificial blood which will function for a few hours, long enough perhaps to do an open-heart surgical procedure, long enough to get an accident victim to a hospital, long enough to save the prize animal in the zoo," according to Dr. Clark.

Someday liquids made in a laboratory may take the place of natural blood in emergency transfusions.

Blood Test for Gonorrhea

A blood test to detect gonorrhea is a vital necessity. Now scientists at American medical institutions are developing one that they believe will reveal many "hidden" cases of the disease.

Venereal disease, especially gonorrhea, has reached epidemic proportions in recent years, largely as a result of increasing sexual freedom. Gonorrhea is particularly difficult to control because, although men have obvious symptoms, women can become infected and not always know it. They then "carry" it symptom-free, and can infect any man they have sexual relations with, who in turn may infect other women. Thus a diagnostic blood test would be an invaluable aid to control of the disease.

There is a twenty-year history of unsuccessful attempts to discover such a blood test. Experiments failed because there are many types of gonococci and closely related bacteria. Not all of these cause gonorrhea, and previous tests weren't selective enough to respond just to the virulent type. However, a few years ago, simultaneous discoveries in Denmark and the United States indicated that the disease-causing germ can be distinguished by little hairlike structures, or "pili" (see page 22).

Dr. Thomas M. Buchanan of Rockefeller University is confident he has found a way to make a reliable test using this discovery. In the test, antibodies to the gonococcal pili are sought in the blood serum as a clue to the presence of the disease. So far the results are very encouraging. A drug firm, Organon, has a quick blood test that detects gonorrhea.

Dr. Buchanan emphasizes the need for the new test by citing evidence that present procedures for detecting gonorrhea are unreliable. "In a collaborative study with the New York City Bureau of Venereal Disease Control, 248 consecutive women presenting to a New York City venereal disease clinic were cultured and questioned according to ordinary clinic operation, but in addition . . . serum was tested for antibody to pili. We found evidence that a significant proportion, possibly up to one third of the infected women, were not being detected."

The development of this blood test and a vaccine against gonorrhea (see below) could virtually stamp out the disease.

Weapons Against Gonorrhea

Promising new weapons are being investigated in the fight against gonorrhea, including a vaccine that may wipe out the disease.

Man has developed effective drugs to treat the two major venereal diseases, syphilis and gonorrhea, but still they continue to spread like wildfire. Of the two, gonorrhea represents the more prevalent threat. Eighty to 90 percent of all venereal infections are caused by gonorrhea. The U.S. Public Health Service says the disease is out of control in the United States.

New weapons are constantly being tried against gonorrhea, but the perfect one has yet to be found. The prime drug in the fight is penicillin. However, *Neisseria gonorrhoeae*, the gonococcus—the germ that causes gonorrhea—is now producing strains resistant to this antibiotic as well as other kinds. The ideal solution to the problem is a vaccine. Researchers at the Canadian Communicable Disease Centre in Ottawa, Ontario, have developed one. Tests are well under way to determine its effectiveness.

Gonococcal cells seen with an electron microscope. The arrows point to the pili, by which the germs attach themselves to their host.

Much of the difficulty in producing a vaccine can be blamed on our lack of knowledge of the biology of the infecting bacterium. The gonococcus is being studied intensively by scientists, and many new things are being learned about it. Dr. John Swanson of the Utah College of Medicine in Salt Lake City has found, for example, that some types of gonococcus are covered with pili (hairlike growths) and others are not. The first type produces severe cases of gonorrhea, the second mild ones. At Mount Sinai School of Medicine in New York, doctors have discovered a possible new weapon against the germs. They have demonstrated that minute amounts of copper inhibit the growth of the bacteria. A new type of intrauterine device containing copper may do an effective job in helping to prevent the disease. Eliminate the disease in one sex and you eliminate it almost entirely.

But tests take time and the results must be painstakingly scrutinized. "It would be easy to detect vaccine failures—for example, the development of the disease in a vaccinated person," says Dr. Louis Greenberg, head of the Canadian center's Biologics Control Laboratories. "It would not be so easy to determine the successes, since there may be many reasons why a person doesn't acquire the disease." We will have to wait a long time for a conclusive report.

We shall have to wait a long time (perhaps ten years or so) for a gonorrhea vaccine. To combat other venereal diseases now beginning to appear, we'll need something like the development of laboratory-accelerated evolution (see page 55) of new viral strains.

Belt Gives Long-Distance Electrocardiogram

Simplified equipment is now available that can monitor a patient's heartbeat and body temperature at great distances. What's more, it doesn't require the usual technician or nurse to hook it up—the patient can do the job himself.

Taking an electrocardiogram isn't particularly difficult, but it does require special training. The proper amount of conducting paste must be applied to the patient's skin before electrodes are strapped in place, and recording equipment must be switched to the proper electrodes.

With recently developed equipment, dry electrodes can be attached to the patient by simply pressing them in place, and all necessary switching is done by microcircuit electronics installed

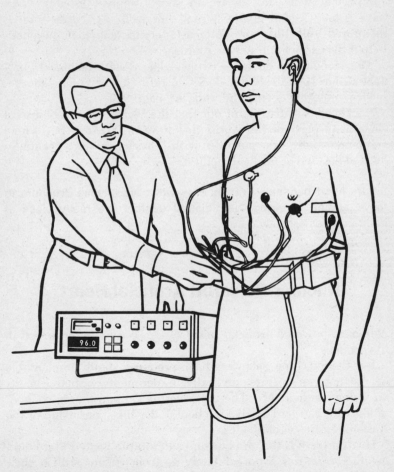

The biobelt worn with sensing elements is connected to a monitoring unit.

in a belt which the patient wears. The lightweight *biobelt* also controls a body-temperature sensor. A single cable runs from the belt to a display unit, where the patient's condition is monitored and recorded. Signals may be sent to computerized monitoring equipment as well, or they may be transmitted to a distant location for observation and analysis.

A patient wearing the belt removes it while he takes a shower, for example, and hooks himself up again without assistance. (Important when nurses are in short supply.) Even a heart patient may lead a nearly normal life while his cardiogram is monitored—full time—by automatic equipment that summons help if the cardiogram shows trouble.

The biobelt was developed by Lockheed with technical guidance from NASA's Manned Spacecraft Center. (For another heart-monitoring device, the Vida, see page 27.)

Lockheed scientists point out that the biobelt should be useful "in remote parts of the world that have no doctors, but where communications are possible with physicians at a centrally located hospital or medical facility."

Future heart patients—and others—will have unusual freedom to move around, knowing their distant doctors are really close at hand in an emergency.

Nuclear-Powered Artificial Heart

A nuclear-powered artificial heart system is now being tested in live animals.

For the first time, scientists have produced totally implantable hearts that can operate internally. Experiments with the hearts are being conducted by Thermo Electron Corporation in collaboration with Harvard Medical School under the sponsorship of the National Institutes of Health.

Heart disease is the number one killer in the United States and in other countries. Approximately 200,000 persons still in their productive years succumb to diseases of the heart annually.

PROJECTED TOTAL ARTIFICIAL HEART
WITH SELF-CONTAINED NUCLEAR DRIVE SYSTEM

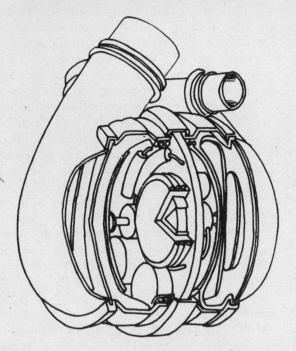

Implantable total artificial heart.

Heart disease also severely restricts the activities of a large number of persons and shortens their life-span. Obviously, millions could benefit from the development of a good artificial heart.

Artificial heart research is relatively new, but already it's come a long way. The first milestone was passed in 1967, when a blood pump was implanted in an animal and performed successfully. The heart, in its function, is fundamentally a pump—or, rather, two pumps. The right ventricle pumps blood under low pressure to the lungs, where carbon dioxide is released and oxygen is picked up. The left ventricle pumps oxygenated blood to the arteries at high pressure. Most heart failure takes place in the left side of the heart because it works about four times as hard as the right side of the heart.

Much early artificial heart development was concerned with the left heart. The typical system consisted of a booster pump connected between the left heart and the descending aorta. Later, booster pumps were connected with both the right and left hearts. A current system is powered by an engine fueled with a capsule containing plutonium-238, which has a half-life of 92 years. Various animals have survived for one or more years with a nuclear implant, suggesting that human beings will be able to tolerate the required exposure to radiation.

The next step is to design a totally implantable artificial heart suitable for human beings. Tests are under way with such hearts in animals. The artificial hearts are similar to the human heart in structure: they have two atriums and two ventricles with valves to control the blood flow. Included with the artificial heart are an energy storage pack, an energy converter, and a heart control computer to regulate the action of the heart so it will meet the body's changing needs. The computer, presently six inches long, may be reduced to the size of a dime with the help of present-day technology.

Much work remains to be done before scientists will have a total heart implant that can safely be used in the human body. Meanwhile, animal experiments are providing invaluable information about the effect of the artificial heart's pumping upon other body organs, the circulation and the nervous system. Investigators are using this information to improve the structure of the artificial heart system.

"The development of a totally implantable assist and artificial heart," declares Lowell T. Harmison of the National Heart and Lung Institute, "is a goal no less challenging than that of placing a man on the moon. The technological basis for these achievements exists now. The challenge posed by these developments can be met within this decade."

By the next century artificial hearts may be as common as artificial limbs are today. The lives of millions may be prolonged for decades, first with artificial parts, and then, later, by growing a replica of our original heart.

Heartbeat Transmission by Telephone

A new pocket-size device gives heart patients early warning of an attack and enables them to transmit their heart rhythms over the phone for a doctor's immediate analysis and diagnosis.

In most cases, abnormal heartbeats called ventricular premature contractions precede a major heart attack and warn that it is imminent. If the condition is diagnosed in time, medication can usually stabilize the heart rhythms and prevent a serious attack. To detect abnormal heartbeats, however, constant monitoring would be necessary, which until now has meant confining the patient to the hospital.

Several portable monitors are now available; one is called Vida—ventricular impulse detector and alarm. In the Vida unit three small sensors are pasted to the patient's chest and linked to a six-ounce battery-powered monitor that can be worn in a pocket or attached to a belt.

The monitor itself contains more active components than a color television. Each monitor is adjusted by the physician to respond to the specific danger signs of the individual patient. When the device recognizes abnormal rhythms, it alerts the wearer with a soft tone. He can then telephone his doctor and, simply by holding the phone against the monitor, transmit a clear electrocardiogram to a special receiving unit in the doctor's office. The doctor examines a printed readout of the electrocardiogram and decides what preventive steps to take.

Recently doctors at Saint Vincent's Hospital in Portland, Oregon, reported checking the ECG of an overexcited fisherman. The 56-year-old angler, feeling the effects of landing a big fish, transmitted his ECG to the hospital via shortwave radio from a boat five miles out at sea.

Other groups have developed similar early warning systems; for example, the Southwest Research Institute of San Antonio, Texas, has assembled a wristwatch ECG transmitter. Researchers

27

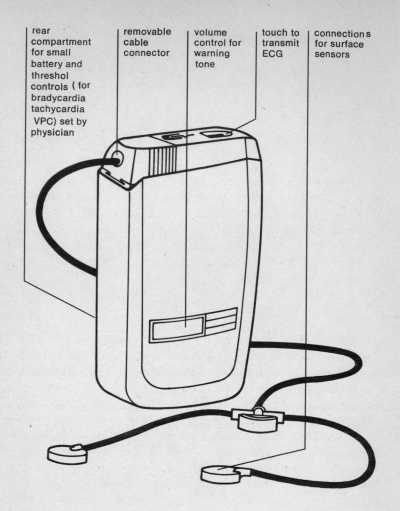

rear compartment for small battery and threshol controls (for bradycardia tachycardia VPC) set by physician

removable cable connector

volume control for warning tone

touch to transmit ECG

connections for surface sensors

A pocket-size monitor warns of heart attacks and provides an instant electrocardiogram anywhere, anytime.

at the Stanford Medical Center have estimated that a minimum of 100,000 lives could be saved each year if all high-risk heart patients were outfitted with portable heart monitors.

"The Vida system successfully accomplished the longest telephone circuit transmission of an electrocardiogram—a distance of

51,000 miles—with excellent data clarity," reports Cardiodynamics, Inc., the manufacturer.

This is another of many developments that will increase personal safety—and personal privacy. The automobile, television, electricity and the telephone, all help to keep out the intrusions of the outside world at the same time we benefit from society's experience and expertise. The new heart monitors make it possible to obtain an instant diagnosis of heartbeat irregularity if you can reach a telephone. Once they are in general use many lives will be saved.

Artificial Pancreas for Diabetics

Some four million Americans suffer from diabetes. Constantly at the mercy of malfunctioning pancreases, they run the risk of blindness, convulsions or coma as a result of too-high or too-low blood sugar levels. Now an artificial pancreas holds promise of removing these dangers.

The new device consists of two parts: one to measure the level of blood sugar in the body, and the other to provide a dose of insulin if the level becomes too high. These are functions normally performed by the pancreas. The glucose (sugar) monitoring device—a metallic disk no larger than a quarter—was announced late in 1972 as a joint project of the Joslin Diabetes Foundation of Boston and the Whittaker Corporation Space Sciences Division. A micropump and insulin storage device are under development for the second function.

Researchers believe the glucose sensor disk may have immediate value in diabetic relief. Essentially a fuel cell, it produces a small electric current which varies in intensity with the amount of glucose in the body tissue fluids surrounding it. Implanted under the skin or in the abdominal cavity, the sensor could be linked to a metering device the patient could periodically consult for a glucose reading; if the reading was too low, he would eat some sugar-rich food; if too high, he might require a dose of insulin. The micropump, small enough to be implanted in the body, would automatically dispense insulin when the sensor indicated a high reading.

The glucose sensor disk has been successfully tested with laboratory monkeys, but it still remains to be tested in humans. All indications are positive, however. The disk can operate indefinitely without recharging (since it is not a battery), and it produces no toxic materials, no corrosive activity, and no galvanic cell effects. All indications are for a relatively rapid development of this much-needed medical aid. Because of the large numbers of diabetes sufferers, the finished unit could be produced at a relatively low cost.

According to the manufacturer, "The glucose sensor has been under test in laboratory monkeys for nearly a year with excellent results. And plans are now under way . . . involving implantation of the sensor into diabetic patients."

Implantable artificial organs are useful engineering achievements. But they are also awkward technological solutions to physical ailments.

Future artificial organs will probably be more "natural." That is, a second heart will be grown in place—or in donor animals specially cultivated for the purpose. Not for many years, though.

 ## Diagnosis by Computer

Medical diagnosis is moving from the days of the homey housecall toward a time when we may go to the doctor's office and not even see the doctor—at least until we've poured out our troubles to his computer.

Physicians at the University of Wisconsin have found their computer to be as efficient as they are in taking health histories and preparing diagnostic reports. The machine can afford the time to make a comprehensive review of a patient's health. In

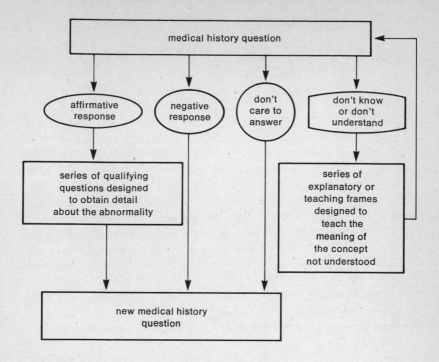

Logic of the interview.

addition, computer printouts are far more legible than physicians' handwriting.

During a computer-based interview, questions about the patient's health appear on a cathode-ray screen. The patient answers them by pressing keys to indicate "YES," "NO," "DON'T KNOW," or "DON'T UNDERSTAND." In areas where the patient appears to have health problems the computer asks additional questions.

The Wisconsin doctors claim their computerized general history compares favorably with general practitioners' records, but it's usually less complete than the work-ups of such specialists as gynecologists and allergists. A computer questionnaire can broaden a family doctor's understanding and scope, but it doesn't yet replace the close human scrutiny that we expect for our acute medical problems.

Apparently people don't feel slighted when they're asked to tell

31

their problems to a computer instead of a doctor. Some men and women actually report feeling more comfortable recording deeply personal problems on punch cards than discussing them face-to-face.

Dr. Warner Slack and Dr. Lawrence Van Cura describe the computer interview: "The words of encouragement have been found humorous by patients and have added to their enjoyment of computer-based history taking. At one point during the general medical history, the computer displays, 'YOU HAVE DONE WELL SO FAR: ARE YOU GETTING TIRED?' If the patient answers 'YES' the computer replies, 'WELL, ARE YOU WILLING TO CONTINUE FOR A WHILE LONGER?' If the patient replies 'NO,' the computer responds with a 'PLEASE.' If the patient persists with his unwillingness to continue, the computer gives in and replies, 'O.K. TAKE A BREAK.'"

Patient interviews and diagnostic reports by computer will help alleviate the growing shortage of physicians. Computers can also be programmed to furnish medical advice—and even prescriptions.

"Pill" Transmits Deep Body Temperature

A temperature transmitter the size of a vitamin capsule can be swallowed to transmit deep body temperature.

Measuring deep body temperature using a swallowable temperature transmitter is important. An internal transmitter gives a precise measurement of body temperature fluctuation—useful in studies of biological cycles and critically ill hospital patients. Hard-wired probes attached to the subject's ear have been used in past studies, but this method has several disadvantages: prolonged insertion produces discomfort for the subject and the hard wires are subject to breakage. Other problems are signal loss, large transmitter size, and low battery life.

The pill transmitter can easily be swallowed because it's contained in a very small gelatin capsule, which is treated to prevent

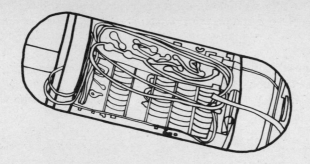

The pill transmitter, the battery, gelatin capsule, and the assembled unit.

dissolving. It's retained in the body for about three days. The battery inside lasts an average of 600 hours and provides a greater transmitting distance than other systems. The new device also provides great accuracy, recording temperatures to within 0.1 degree Celsius. It's economical because it uses readily available commercial FM receivers.

NASA researchers who developed it say the "use of the swal-

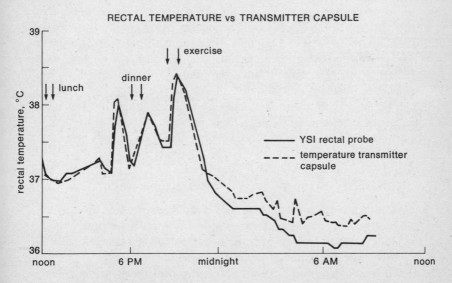

Internal body temperature of subject over a period of almost 24 hours.

lowable temperature transmitter permits accurate, long-term recording of core temperature without the discomfort of attached cables."

We'll see widespread use of the pill if the transmission distance is increased. A pocket re-transmitter module the size of a cigarette pack, being developed for this purpose, would relay signals from the pill to distant receivers.

 The Hoverbed

Dr. John T. Scales, a British orthopedist, has designed a bed for use in the treatment of large-area burn patients. His "hoverbed" utilizes a concept usually associated with aeronautical engineering, seances and levitation.

The patient is placed on the hoverbed when it is inflated with air at maximum pressure. The air pressure is slowly reduced until the patient's torso depresses the pockets along the midline of the bed. Air then escapes between the patient's body and the upper surface of the bed, and the patient's body floats, or "hovers," on a pillow of air that is constantly circulated, filtered and temperature-controlled by a mobile unit next to the bed.

The hoverbed's uniform support relieves pain by removing pressure from the burn area, and prevents the development of bedsores. Wounds dry and heal more rapidly than with any other patient-support system. Since the patient doesn't have to be lifted to be moved, nursing is simplified.

Hoverbeds are superior to waterbeds in three ways:

1. They provide a more uniform body support, due to the fact that gases are readily compressible and liquids are not.
2. The contour and attitude of a patient on a hoverbed can be mechanically adjusted, as on a regular hospital bed.
3. In terms of materials and mechanics, hoverbeds present fewer problems of construction than waterbeds.

Dr. Scales has also designed a variant of the hoverbed, the LAL (low air loss) bed, for patients who are bedridden for reasons other than burn injury, and who do not have to be supported directly on air. The LAL bed is a sophisticated version of the air mattress available in army-surplus and camping-supply stores. Interposing a flexible vapor-permeable film between the skin of the patient and the air permits a substantial reduction in the volume of air necessary for uniform support, and therefore in the size of the pump unit.

Dr. Scales says, "The introduction of this equipment into hospitals, although increasing capital expenditure, will bring about far greater savings in recurrent expenditure."

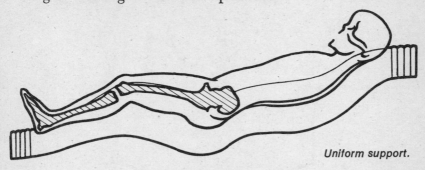

Uniform support.

Widespread adoption would undoubtedly lead to the mass production of hoverbeds. At that point the hoverbed is likely to follow its predecessor, the waterbed, out of the hospital and into the healthy and workaday consumer's world, there to be billed as the newest source of previously undreamed-of pleasures.

Medical Magnetism

Physicians are now measuring the magnetic fields around the heart, brain, muscles and lungs. With the information they gain, they hope to devise diagnostic tests to supplement present ones

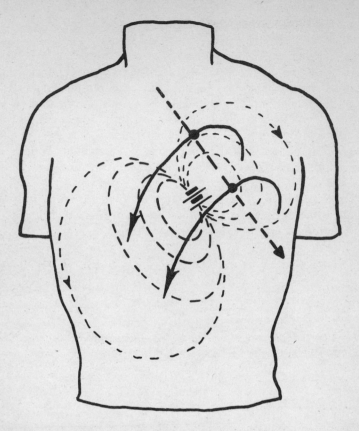

Electrical and magnetic activity of the heart. Broken-line ovals indicate the electrical current produced, and solid curves the corresponding magnetic field. It is as if the heart were a very small battery, as the schematic indicates.

like the electrocardiogram and electroencephalogram.

The magnetic field of the earth is thousands of times stronger than that of the human heart, and a thousand more times stronger than that of the human brain. To screen out background magnetism for his studies, Dr. David Cohen of MIT built a special room with five shielding layers and a special geometric shape. The subject must remove all clothing that contains magnetic material, such as shoes, pants and shirt. Then he sits down in a chair, and a special machine capable of detecting extremely

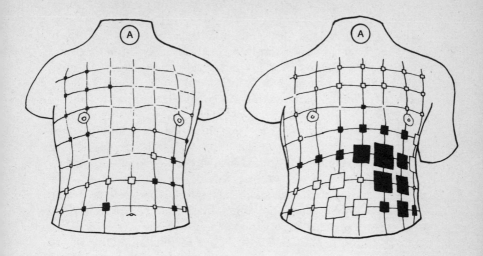

Tests for ferromagnetic contamination in lungs and other organs. Above is a magnetic map of a man before (left) and after (right) eating a can of green beans. Below is a map before (left) and after (right) drinking a glass of cold water. Dr. Cohen does not yet know why this effect occurs.

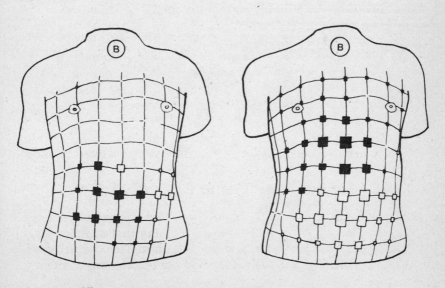

weak magnetic fields is moved close to the body area to be tested.

The test results look very much like those of tests presently in use. They aren't quite as sensitive, but they may be more useful in many cases. For instance, no matter how many leads are used, what happens inside a three-dimensional body cannot be completely determined by detecting electrical changes on the surface of the body. But because every electrical current produces a magnetic field, by measuring that field you can obtain more reliable information about the electrical activity inside the body—information that is critical to an accurate diagnosis.

In the process of performing this research, Dr. Cohen discovered another weak magnetic field of the body. It is due to what he calls ferromagnetic contamination and is produced by small metal particles from canned food and the like, which are magnetized by the earth's field. His test for contamination of the lungs is much more sensitive than x-rays.

Dr. Cohen doesn't expect his tests will replace the electrocardiogram, encephalogram or myogram (muscle test). But he thinks they can complement these tests and lead to an extremely accurate diagnosis. In some cases these new tests should yield information that the present tests cannot—say, on certain rhythmic disorders of the heart, and on the source of alpha waves in the brain.

The combination of an electrocardiogram and a magnetocardiogram and an x-ray could make some exploratory surgery unnecessary. The more different perspectives a physician has on a medical problem, the more likely his diagnosis is to be correct.

Skinlike Membrane Protects Burns and Wounds

A drug company has developed a new dressing for severe burns that functions like synthetic skin. The man-made epidermis accelerates the growth of new skin and reduces the duration of burn therapy by as much as several weeks.

Like man's own skin, this Parke-Davis product breathes; air is allowed in to promote healing, while foreign bodies are excluded. The self-adhering dressing keeps the patient more comfortable than conventional bandages and wrappings.

The outside layer is a microporous film so fine that it prevents liquids and even bacteria from passing through. This considerably decreases the chances of infection. Moreover, the dressing *keeps in* vital body fluids and plasma, reducing the need for fluid replacement as a part of burn treatment.

Beneath the film is a spongy material that soaks up the debris and liquid wastes produced by the injury. If allowed to stay in the wound, these wastes could provide a fertile growth medium for bacteria. When needed, the spongy material can be infused with antibiotics and other medicines.

The dressing can be used in skin grafting, too—both to prepare burned areas to receive the graft and to protect the area from which it has been grafted. Because it can be sterilized and used again for other patients, the product, named Epigard, is relatively inexpensive to use.

According to the inventor, Larry Wheeler, the "synthetic skin" is "applicable to many types of injury but is of particular use in the active therapy and dressing of the thermal, chemical, electrical and similar wounds conventionally classified as burns."

Future emergency aids, like synthetic skin, will be used to treat casualties from airplane accidents, building fires, and kitchen burns. Even plastic surgery (once available mainly to the wealthy) may adopt this dressing for routine, low-cost use.

Time-Release Drugs on Target

The Food and Drug Administration will soon permit doctors to dispense medicines in revolutionary time-release capsules.

One such capsule, which is expected to receive FDA approval, is the "Ocusert" system for treating glaucoma. Glaucoma is a disease characterized by pressure in the eyeball and progressive loss of vision. The Ocusert, developed by the ALZA Corporation of Palo Alto, California, is a membrane smaller than a contact lens, containing a reservoir of the drug pilocarpine. The tiny capsule is inserted in the corner of the eye. Contact with tears causes it to release minute amounts of pilocarpine, which effectively reduces the pressure in the eye.

Ordinarily, people suffering from glaucoma must squirt a drop or two of pilocarpine in each eye several times a day. The Ocusert eliminates this inconvenience and does not irritate the eye. Further, it ensures that the patient receives constant medication for as long as a week, even while he is sleeping. There can be no forgetting and no mistakes in dosage.

Unlike drops, which momentarily flood the eye with medication, the Ocusert releases a small, steady flow of the drug. This slow-release capability may make it possible to use more powerful medicines than pilocarpine in the treatment of glaucoma. Slow release could prevent the undesirable side effects caused by flooding the eye with highly potent agents.

Time-release drugs have still another advantage: They can be placed very near the trouble spot, on target, bathing it in medication without affecting the other organs of the body.

ALZA is currently working on a "uterine contraceptive system." Basically it is a time-release birth control pill containing progesterone that can be inserted into the uterus. It may avoid the side effects of the oral contraceptive.

A great many other time-release capsules are also under study.

According to ALZA, "Every time a patient takes a drug in a conventional form, the immediate result is a spike of pharmacological activity—far more than the treatment requires. And the initial surge of drug is followed by a tapering off—most often to a point far below efficacious treatment."

Rather than taking four tablets of an antibiotic per day, a patient might receive a ten-day pill. This would ensure that he receives the correct dosage, and also make certain that he continues to be medicated even after he begins to feel better. People who quit

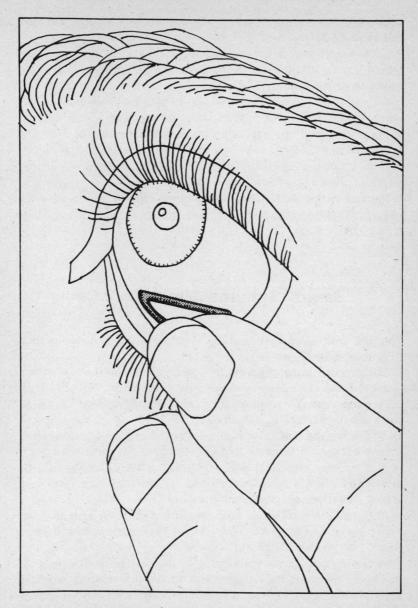

An antiglaucoma drug is released slowly from the tiny unit inserted in the eye.

taking their medicines too early—before all the infectious bacteria are destroyed—risk a relapse.

Someday we may see food capsules or hunger suppressants that would enable a person to go for weeks at a time without taking anything except water.

People with chronic diseases might receive time-release capsules lasting years at a time to keep the diseases under control.

Psychoactive drugs implanted in mental patients would enable them to lead normal lives. The small continuous dosage would eliminate many of the "ups" and "downs" of orally administered psychoactives.

Instead of cardiac pacemakers, slow-release drugs may be implanted next to the heart.

"Smart" Spheres Attack Sick Cells

Spheres with a special coating seek out and destroy certain tumorous cells.

Microscopic latex spheres are coated with antibodies which instruct them to destroy specific cells, such as tumor cells. They are called "smart" because their coating of antibodies makes them act specifically on certain cells.

At present the "smart" spheres are being used in the laboratory to act on the surfaces of red blood cells. An antibody-coated "smart sphere" attacks specific antigens. A tumor cell would be attacked by a smart sphere coated by an antibody geared to attack an antigen specific to the tumor cell.

Antigens are markers of biological individuality. Foreign ones evoke a reaction from the body, but it's not correct to call them toxic. The production of antibody is one response, but antibody does not actually destroy antigens. In the first place, it's the cells or viruses to which the antigens are attached that must be eliminated; in the second place, it's not antibody that does this job.

Dr. Alan Rembaum of Caltech hopes that the spheres can be developed into highly discriminating vehicles that can carry lethal drugs or radioactive elements to attack cancer or other unwanted cells.

This new method may eventually lead to combating cancer and other diseases.

New Teeth with Carbon-Root Implants

Artificial teeth can now be permanently implanted. Early artificial teeth often failed because the roots weren't strong enough—teeth are subject to fantastic stresses. A new material, vitreous (or glassy) carbon, is proposed as a solution. It's compatible with human tissue and completely nontoxic. In the new tooth, an artificial root of carbon supports a metal shaft on which a conventional artificial crown can be mounted. The complete tooth, after gum tissue grows around the root, remains permanently in place.

One special merit of the new technique is that no surgical procedure is necessary. The new tooth is not implanted in the bony structure of the jaw. Instead, it fits into the existing socket in the same way as a natural tooth, and the installation can be made by a dentist.

A disadvantage of the new implant is that it can't be used unless the tooth socket is in reasonably good condition. Gum infection frequently leads to bone depletion, and healthy teeth become useless because they aren't properly supported. Individual artificial teeth can't be used in this situation, and more complicated dental devices are required.

The inventor says, "The cone-shaped root section is easy to put in place. For example, the patient can put it in place himself simply by biting down."

The transistorized replacement for an old black and white television set—a color set—is far better.

Man can often, more and more, make some replacements better

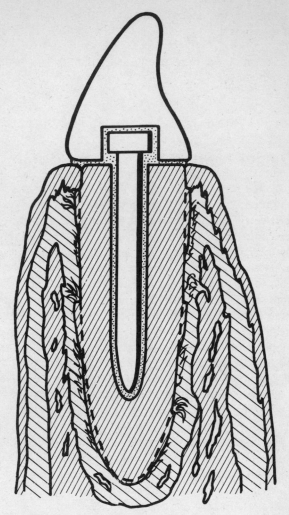

An artificial tooth in position.

than *nature's* originals. The new carbon-root teeth can last a life-time—and they won't give you a toothache.

Lasers Fight Tooth Decay

Lasers may "cap" teeth in a way that makes them permanently decay-resistant.

Capping molars with plastic is a common preventive procedure today, but the plastic chips or cracks, and the tooth usually has to be recapped at least once a year. The laser, which can accurately direct a tremendous amount of energy to a particular spot, would fuse a cap of toothlike material on the molar.

The problem is that the ceramic material expected to be used for this process will fuse at a temperature of 600 degrees Fahrenheit—but if the temperature of the whole tooth is raised by only 10 degrees the tooth will die.

The developer, Dr. R. F. Boehm, professor of mechanical engineering at the University of Utah, plans to direct a laser pulse of 1,000,000 watts at a tooth for less than a millionth of a second. In experiments on extracted molars, he has raised the surface temperature of a tooth to 270 degrees Fahrenheit, while the temperature near the root area was only raised by 1 degree. Soon he expects to be able to reach the desired surface temperature while keeping the root area of the tooth well within the safety zone of 10 degrees.

Dr. Boehm, an expert in thermal processes, says of this procedure, "It's actually safer than the high-speed drills in use today."

Dr. Boehm envisions special clinics staffed by dentists trained in the use of lasers. Soon we may be able to go all through life with our own teeth.

 ## Lightweight Cast for Broken Bones

Merck, Sharp and Dohme Orthopedics Company has developed a new system for making casts which could replace plaster of

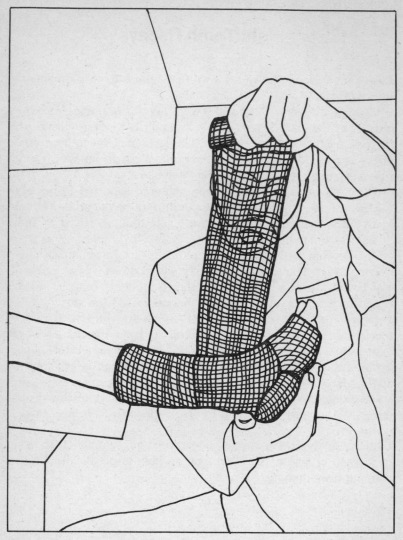

The webbed tape is impregnated with a photosensitive plastic resin.

paris. These casts are about half as heavy as traditional casts and three times as strong.

The casting system, called "Lightcast II," is composed of a flexible plastic stockinet, over which an open-weave fiber-glass

Just three minutes and the cast is cured by ultraviolet light.

tape is wrapped. This tape, which looks something like a net, is applied in several layers, and it molds like a conventional cast. The tape is also impregnated with a photosensitive plastic resin which dries under exposure to ultraviolet light in three minutes. This means that after the cast is molded it sets in minutes. Plaster casts, by contrast, reach full strength only after a full day.

Lightcast II has many more advantages over plaster casts. It can be immersed in water without damage, while plaster casts are destroyed by water. Not only does it permit normal hygiene, including baths and showers, but it's possible to wash the cast itself. The new cast is porous, and allows more circulation of air to the skin than plaster casts, which often cause great irritation. Since it's lighter, it gives the patient more mobility, which in turn makes it easier for him to adjust after the cast has been removed. Because it's stronger, it won't chip, crack or peel as plaster casts do.

This system might replace plaster of paris completely. Daily activity may not be severely curtailed by a broken bone.

New Materials for Bone Repair

Bone grows into the pores of two new materials to make a strong permanent bond.

A good orthopedic surgeon can go a long way in rebuilding broken or badly formed bones. A new hip joint, for example, is no longer a rarity. Attaching metal to bone, though, is still something of a problem—usually solved by bolting things together. A new *metallic* material called VMC (void metallic composite), now being tested on animals, avoids this difficulty because it's porous. New bone actually grows into the pores of the VMC so that the metal piece is firmly anchored to existing bone.

A new porous *ceramic* material (aluminium oxide) impregnated with plastic acts as a bone substitute. It is biologically inert and can be made with stiffness matching that of bone. The impregnated plastic can be partially removed to provide a porous structure into which new bone will grow and to which muscle will attach itself. With large enough pore size, tissue grows into the pores and bonds firmly to the ceramic material. The inventor, Allan Auskern, says that his bone substitute "is useful as a bone gap bridge, a skull plate, and in a system for pinning fractures."

Ordinarily a bolted metal-to-bone structure leaves something to be desired. The metal is stiffer than the bone, and light loads are carried by the bone alone. In effect, the combined structure of bone and metal is just that—a bone supported by pieces of metal. With a porous composite bone-to-metal joint, however, the result is a single, unified load-bearing member—possibly even stronger than the original bone.

The new metal has uses in dentistry, too. Artificial teeth, even a complete set of false teeth, can be fastened to VMC anchors implanted in a jawbone. This technique is useful when tooth sockets are damaged by destruction of the surrounding bony material—something that often happens in connection with gum infection.

VMC can be made of a variety of pure metals or alloys, and both the size and the shape of the pores can be varied for different purposes. According to the developer, Battelle Pacific Northwest Laboratories, "The VMC structure is readily fabricated into complex shapes either by machining or by use of a shaped mold. . . . Cell culture screening of the titanium alloy of VMC has shown good cell compatibility with no evidence of toxic reaction."

A strong bone-to-metal bond may also lead to permanently attached artificial limbs—possibly even with living skin and muscles.

Tissue grows into ceramic pores, and science marries an inert material to a living substance. More of these marriages are coming.

Electropharmacology and Obesity Control

Eating can be controlled by stimulation of certain areas of the brain with electrodes.

The hypothalamus in the brain plays an important role in affecting hunger. Stimulation of the lateral section induces eating, and stimulation of the center causes it to stop. Many studies with rats have been performed to determine the most effective form of obesity control using this information. A hungry rat, when stimulated with electrodes in the center of the hypothalamus, would not eat at all, and one who had just finished a heavy meal would start to eat again when stimulated in the lateral section.

Amphetamines, drugs now used by many dieters, are found to increase the current needed to stimulate the lateral section to induce eating. In other words, people must be made hungrier under the influence of these drugs to feel like eating.

The scientists working on this project wished to find out which sections of the hypothalamus, when stimulated, would yield optimum effect on hunger control. The form of amphetamines now in popular use decreases the electrical activity in the lateral hunger-stimulating section, causing no change in the center section.

A newly discovered drug, similar to amphetamines, has been found to work the other way around. It stimulates the center section which inhibits the hunger impulse, not affecting the lateral section.

Experimenters are not yet sure which sections of the brain would be most effective in controlling obesity, but through their experiments in pharmacology they are hoping to find out.

Almost-routine electrical brain stimulation will appear in brain-implanted devices (similar to heart pacemakers) for periodic control of our appetites with few side effects.

Electric Pain Relief

In the year A.D. 46 Scribonius Largus, a Roman physician, reportedly cured headaches and gout with the current from an electric fish. Throughout the intervening centuries doctors have been fascinated by the possibilities of electric therapy, but only in the 1900s have the practical medical applications of electricity been established: Thousands of heart patients now depend on electric pacemakers; shock therapy, though controversial, is still used to treat manic-depressive disease.

But what about Scribonius and his electric fish? Can electricity be used to treat pain? A number of physicians, including Dr. Norman Shealy of the Pain Rehabilitation Center in La Crosse, Wisconsin, say yes. These doctors are using low-voltage direct current to short-circuit pain.

The physicians apply electrodes directly to the patient's skin in the painful area. The patient feels a "tingling, buzzing, vibrating sensation." In cases of acute (severe but relatively brief) pain, Dr. Shealy reports major relief 80 percent of the time. For chronic (long-duration) pain, only 25 percent of patients experience major relief, but another 50 percent find partial relief.

Candidates for electric therapy are carefully screened to discover if the physiological cause of their pain has been correctly diagnosed. The main value of the treatment, after all, is in relieving the symptom; electrotherapy can occasionally reduce the pain of arthritis, but it cannot cure the disease itself.

Dr. Shealy and his assistants have treated more than 1600 patients. Their best results have been in the relief of nerve trauma, phantom limb pain (a throbbing experienced by amputees), and the pain of patients who have undergone unsuccessful spinal disc operations. In about 5 percent of his cases, Dr. Shealy recommends the implantation of electrodes near the spinal column. With this group adequate pain control is achieved in 56 percent of cases.

In the past three years at least nine patients have received electrode implants in the brain to control intractable pain—with excellent results in three cases. There have been few complications thus far, either with electrode implants or with electric stimulation through the skin. In comparison, surgery or ongoing drug treatment has a high rate of unforeseen side effects.

"Electroanesthesia," Dr. Shealy reports, "is advancing at a rapid pace and may be the next major breakthrough in electrotherapy." In other research, it's been shown that chemically induced epileptic seizures have been controlled with electric stimulation of the brain. And in test animals, such diverse disorders as impotence and spasticity have been modified by electrotherapy.

Dr. Shealy believes doctors will find many other applications for electrotherapy in the near future: "Dorsal column stimulation has already passed the magic 'five year' mark and its results are far superior to destructive surgery or to drugs . . . Perhaps the most exciting use of electricity is that of producing anesthesia. Local anesthesia for small wounds is feasible and has been accomplished. Generalized analgesia is possible. . . . Impotence is largely a psychological disorder. As such it may respond to stimulation of appropriate brain areas. We have demonstrated the possibility in monkeys and rats."

While conclusive results are not yet in, electrical anesthesia may prove safer than some drugs. . . . An epileptic might someday wear a kind of brain "pacemaker" to control seizures. And even more far out, low-level electric currents may promote the regeneration of amputated limbs.

Electrotherapy is part of a trend toward medical diagnosis that pinpoints a disorder, and then treats the localized disorder directly. As the body's electric system becomes understood, physicians will use electronics for more and more ailments.

 ## "Electric Aspirin"

Russian and Israeli scientists have performed experiments suggesting that electrically induced sleep has therapeutic possibilities. Positive results include the relief of migraine and post-traumatic and tension headaches.

To induce sleep electrically, three electrodes are used. One is placed on the back of the head, the other two on the eyes or nearby bones. A small current is applied which passes through the brain. In most people this produces sleep indistinguishable from normal sleep. The apparatus can easily be used at home; in fact, in the Israeli experiment a few patients received the instrument for home use for about a month.

The therapeutic value of this procedure, although still unknown, appears promising. It has been used to treat asthma, neurosis, schizophrenia, Parkinson's disease, peptic ulcers, paraplegia and hypertension.

The results are inconclusive because there is so much individual variation in reaction to the treatment, but it does not seem to produce complications. In more than half of the headache sufferers treated, headaches either disappeared or subsided.

Dr. Florella Magora, who developed the sleep stimulator, says, "Electrosleep is a state of mental relaxation. . . . The purpose of the treatment is to achieve long-term results . . . after discontinuation of the current."

Electrical stimulation will induce sleep and relieve headache. Like aspirin, it also reduces pain. And, as aspirin is now, it could be widely used soon.

Common Cold "Cure"

Don't look for anything dramatic yet, but there's progress toward a cure for the common cold.

The common cold is probably as old as man, and each generation comes up with its own "cures." Most of these remedies have little firm scientific basis—but some of them seem to work on *some* colds, for *some* people, *some* of the time.

There's a large body of current medical opinion which asserts that with treatment a cold lasts two weeks, and without treatment it lasts—fourteen days. Not too helpful if you're suffering.

Last year's "magic" cure was massive doses of vitamin C. Some evidence suggested it was worthless; other studies made it look like an infallible remedy. However, recent work in progress at the University of Dublin sheds more light on the question. Apparently, there are two varieties of colds: C-colds (catarrhal colds), the usual cold-in-the-head or nasal obstruction and discharge; and T-colds (toxic colds), the kind that make one feel generally awful, with headache, sore throat and fever. Both types can occur separately; in combination they're called W-colds (whole colds). Boys tend to get W-colds and girls tend to get T- or C-colds.

Large doses of vitamin C evidently tend to reduce the severity of C-colds in girls, but not in boys. They seem to have no effect on either the *severity* or the *duration* of T-colds. Large doses of vitamin C, taken as a preventive measure, do reduce the *frequency* of infection by C-colds and T-colds in girls.

The overall effect of vitamin C on colds is not yet understood completely, but it's obviously complex enough to explain the early confusion.

On another "cold" front, scientists at Du Pont de Nemours and

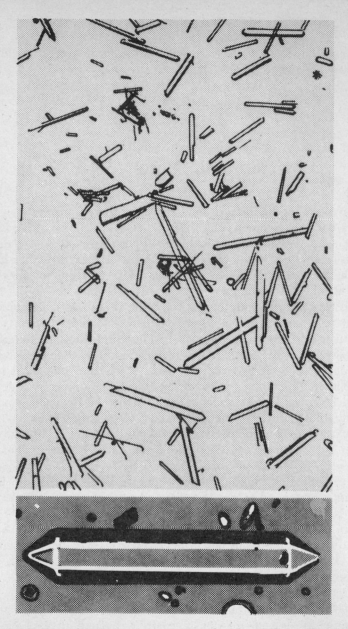

Electron microscopic photograph of human rhinovirus magnified 54,900 times. Crystal has hexagonal profile densely packed with virions, constituents of viruses. Agents may be found to inactivate human rhinoviruses.

Company are investigating the nature of *rhinoviruses*. These are a group of more than a hundred different strains of virus which are generally considered responsible for some 60 percent of all colds. The work at Du Pont includes studies of how the rhinoviruses are related to each other, how they attack host cells, how they reproduce, and other fundamental questions. One type of the human rhinovirus can be crystallized and seen under an electron microscope. In time, these studies should lead to the development of a chemical agent that can inactivate most of the rhinoviruses. The common cold could then be on its way out.

There are two approaches that may help us to avoid colds. One is to resist infection—that's the vitamin C way. The other, the goal of the work on rhinoviruses, is to inactivate the invading virus. Until one of these proves reliable, probably the best we can do is to treat the symptoms.

Vaccines for Future Viruses

It may be possible to anticipate Mother Nature and have vaccines ready for a future strain of influenza virus *before* it causes an epidemic.

Influenza is a well-understood disease. In spite of that, we have widespread influenza epidemics. A new approach to the problem may change matters.

Influenza is caused by a virus, and a mild infection of it confers lasting immunity on a person. A serious infection can be successfully prevented by an appropriate vaccine. Epidemics occur because the virus changes slightly—a normal process of evolution. Existing immunity does not protect against the new strain. Nor are existing vaccines effective against future strains.

Instead of waiting for the next epidemic, workers at the Pasteur Institute in Paris have developed a method of *forcing* the evolution of new strains of influenza virus. They select and breed those new strains which are both hardy and lethal. Consequently there's a high probability they'll have the right vaccine ready for the next epidemic when it occurs.

New strains of virus arise naturally, but until a new strain widely establishes itself it can't cause an epidemic. The institute's technique is to culture existing strains of virus, treat the culture with appropriate vaccine, and then look for evidence of a surviving vaccine-resistant strain. When such a strain appears, it is cultured and tested for virulence and stability. If it changes or mutates again to another (possibly nonvirulent) new strain, it is considered unstable and therefore incapable of causing a long-lasting epidemic.

The institute reports the virus associated with the 1972 influenza epidemic was isolated in the laboratory in 1971, a one-year lead-time. They believe their vaccines are now some five years in advance of the "natural" mutation-and-selection process.

Professor Claude Hannoun, who developed the new approach, says the institute has a new vaccine which will probably offer protection "not only against the strains prevalent today . . . but against all variants . . . for the next five years."

Forced evolution by artificial selection of plants to increase food production is an old story, but artificial selection of viruses to get the jump on nature is something new. The next epidemic, expected around 1978, may not amount to very much.

Our Immune System

For a long time the thymus, a gland in the chest beneath the breastbone, was thought to be a vestigial organ of no particular importance. The gland decreases in size as an animal grows older, and in many cases removal of the thymus after puberty appeared to produce no deleterious effects.

Research shows the thymus gland is involved in our immuno-

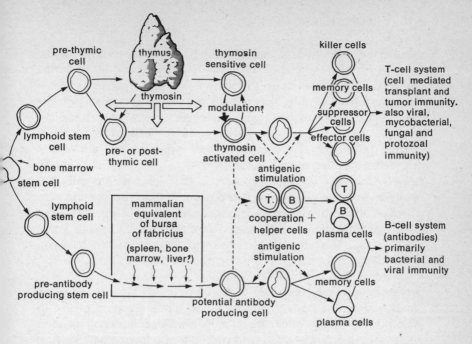

One working theory of maturation of our immune system. Thymosin may act upon cells outside the thymus gland which mature into T-cells, helper cells bearing special antigens.

logical response—that mechanism which causes our scavenger cells and antibodies to attack "foreign" cells but not our normal body cells. By this response our body rejects foreign skin grafts and transplanted organs. The success of modern transplant techniques depends, in part, on suppression of the immunological response.

The immunological response also serves as a protective mechanism, by attacking invading viruses and bacteria.

Some types of scavenger cells are long-lived, and mature in early childhood under the influence of a hormone secreted by the thymus, called thymosin. If the thymus is removed early enough, scavenger cells do not mature and the immunological response is impaired. Later removal of the thymus, after scavenger cells have matured, has no gross effects on the organism.

With this new understanding, the role of the thymus in adults has been reexamined. It now appears that malfunctioning of the thymus may be associated with a host of problems, all of which are related in some way to the immunological response. It's been suggested, for example, that the thymus has a "surveillance function"—that it screens out those scavenger cells which attack the body in which they exist. Other work indicates that thymus-related failure of the immunological response may prevent a protective reaction to malignant growths.

Dr. Allan Goldstein, a worker in the field, points out that "studies in mice . . . have demonstrated that the presence or absence of the thymus gland influences markedly the incidence of tumor formation following a viral challenge. Thymosin levels are very high in young people but decrease dramatically between 20 and 40 years of age."

A cancer cell may resemble a "foreign" cell which ought to be destroyed by the body's defenses. New understanding of immunological response could be a step toward conquering cancer, organ transplant rejection—and even old age (page 454).

Vaccine for Meningitis

Rapid advances are taking place in the field of disease prevention. Doctors and researchers, after relying heavily on antibiotics to *treat* disease, are turning back to vaccines to *avoid* it.

The idea of vaccination is 180 years old. Ever since, medicine has been trying to perfect new and better vaccines. The discovery of penicillin slowed down this drive for a while. Both antibiotics and sulfa drugs worked so well against bacterial diseases that vaccines against them were considered a waste of time.

Today this attitude is changing. Scientists are working doggedly to find vaccines for such diseases as influenza, pneumonia, meningitis, cholera and gonorrhea. Two reasons explain this shift of emphasis. One is the well-known fact that the germs that cause

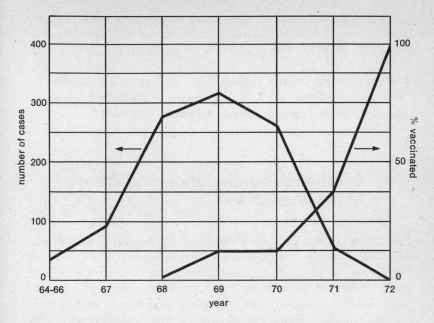

Chart indicates how cases of one type of meningitis declined when the U.S. Army began to administer vaccine in 1968 to increasing percentages (shown on right) of new recruits.

these diseases always seem to get one step ahead of the anti-biotics. Most strains of meningitis, for instance, have acquired resistance to penicillin. The other reason is that large numbers of people still die from pneumonia and influenza; in fact, these are the only infectious diseases among the ten most fatal human disorders.

The task confronting medical science is a tough one. A vaccine not only must work for all the strains of a given germ (there are 82 different strains of the one that causes pneumonia!)—it must also take into account possible future types. Even so, a whole battery of vaccines may soon be available for just about every serious bacterial and viral disease that plagues mankind.

Dr. Malcolm S. Artenstein of the Walter Reed Army Institute of Research, who is experimenting with a vaccine for meningitis, comments on the extensive work being done to develop new vaccines and improve old ones: "Behind all this activity is the concept, ages old, that it is far better to prevent disease than to treat it. The advances in bacterial vaccines may radically alter the impact of infectious diseases on mankind in the future."

The implications of this research are staggering—a virtually infectious-disease-free earth. Some people in the field hope to attack virus-related cancer in time. A cancer vaccine?

Synthetic Prostaglandins to Treat Many Illnesses

Forty years of worldwide scientific research involving prostaglandins, a remarkable group of hormones, are coming to a head. A tidal wave of pharmaceutical products may follow for use in areas as diverse as birth control, ulcer prevention and therapy, nasal decongestion and even, possibly, heart disease and cancer.

Prostaglandins, found in all mammalian tissue, produce an astonishing variety of physiological effects. Of the fourteen known prostaglandins—and there may be others—thirteen occur in man. These thirteen play basic roles in the stimulation of smooth muscle, the dilation and contraction of blood vessels, blood clotting, gastric secretion, seminal ejaculation, and the fertilization of ova. Prostaglandins also function as "second messengers"; they relay chemical signals for hormones secreted by glands, like the pituitary and thyroid.

Prostaglandins were first detected in the 1930s, in the United States and Europe, and named in 1935 by Dr. Ulf von Euler of Sweden, who thought they were secreted only by the prostate gland. After World War II a brilliant young associate of von Euler's, Dr. Sune Bergstrom, began his own pioneering work. In 1957 the Upjohn Company came into the picture, subsidizing this operation and conducting its own research program.

So far, most of the research has centered on the fourteen known compounds that occur naturally. But scientists have also begun to synthesize prostaglandin "analogues," some of which may turn out to be more useful than the original compounds.

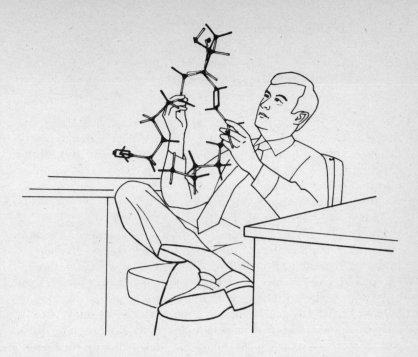

Structural model of a prostaglandin examined by Upjohn scientist.

Some old enigmas are evidently on their way to resolution, too. For instance, it now seems likely that part of the therapeutic effect of aspirin occurs because the drug inhibits a prostaglandin associated with inflammation.

Recently the world's first commercial prostaglandin products were introduced in the United Kingdom by Upjohn Limited. The two drugs were offered to physicians in selected hospitals for use in inducing labor in pregnant women and in abortions.

Dr. William F. Hubbard, Jr., of Upjohn's pharmaceutical division, says, "We are now dealing literally with the molecular basis of the elementary control of cellular metabolism, and that's where the action is."

Prostaglandins bring closer the day when complex diseases like heart disease, arthritis and cancer may at last be brought under control. An oral prostaglandin drug may prove to be the ideal contraceptive scientists have been seeking so long.

61

Blocking Viral Cancer

Dr. Martin Apple, a biochemist at the University of California Medical Center in San Francisco, has discovered two types of drugs, anthracyclines and cystomicines, that prevent and inhibit cancer in mice and chickens. These drugs may have a similar effect on cancer in human beings.

"Mr. Jones died after a long illness."

That's what the obituary says.

You can bet he died of cancer. Why the euphemism? Because cancer is a scare word for millions of people because cancer is presently incurable. But Dr. Apple's experiments with anthracyclines and cystomicines, and their effect on cancerous cells in mice and chickens, indicate that this may not be true for long.

In normal cells, genetic information is stored as deoxyribonucleic acid and transferred as ribonucleic acid. But when an RNA cancer virus, or onco-RNA (short for oncogenic, or tumor-producing, RNA) virus, invades a cell, it uses a maverick enzyme named reverse transcriptase to make a DNA copy of itself—what Dr. Apple calls a provirus. The cell mistakenly "thinks" of this provirus as an extra piece of DNA chromosome that has gotten loose, and incorporates the virus-controlled DNA into the cell's genetic material. At some future time, perhaps years later, this viral DNA is activated, and transforms the cell it inhabits into a cancer cell.

Anthracyclines and cystomicines block this enzymatic process, which is known as reverse transcription. In cells that are already virally infected when the anthracycline or cystomicine is administered, the viral DNA is never activated. In cells that are infected after one of the drugs has been administered, the onco-RNA virus is unable to reproduce in the first place.

Besides being 10,000 times more potent than any of the other inhibitors of reverse transcriptase that have been tested, anthracyclines and cystomicines have the added advantage of being nontoxic. All of the drugs presently used in cancer chemotherapy have toxic side effects.

Several studies are under way to determine whether the mere

presence of reverse transcriptase in a human cell, even if the cell is not virally infected, indicates a precancerous condition. Some of the women in a selected group of 200, ranging in age from 18 to 75, were found to have reverse transcriptase in ductal fluid extracted from their nipples, although they showed no clinical evidence of breast cancer. These women are being carefully observed, and a few have already developed detectable breast cancer. If these results prove to be conclusive, physicians will have a valuable new tool for the early diagnosis of cancer. The earlier the diagnosis, the more effective the treatment—which may consist of a dosage of anthracycline or cystomicine, or both.

Dr. Apple says, "We are designing new drugs that block the RNA to DNA reverse transcription, and now have drugs 10,000 times more potent than those available two years ago. These drugs, given once to an onco-RNA-virus-infected animal, now appear to delay or prevent cancer almost invariably. The ideas are all established by this work; the remaining steps are developmental and extrapolative."

Someday cancer may well be as clinically explicable, curable and avoidable as typhoid fever, bubonic plague and all the other once-mysterious diseases that terrified our ancestors.

Cancer Cure on Your Breakfast Table?

Scientists at the Cleveland Clinic attribute the pronounced decline of stomach cancer in the United States to the preservatives, or antioxidants, in breakfast cereals and margarine. They cite laboratory experiments showing a reduction in tumors among mice injected with antioxidants. And they point to a recent study showing lower cancer mortality in areas where selenium, a potent antioxidant, is present in the diet.

In 1930, cancer of the stomach was the leading cause of male cancer deaths and the second leading cause of female cancer deaths in the United States. Today, while other forms of cancer have shown alarming increases, the death rate from male stomach cancer is less than one third (the female rate less than one fourth) what it was forty-five years ago.

Statistics from twenty-four countries show that the United States has the lowest national death rate for stomach cancer. Australia, Canada and New Zealand (countries that share our taste for dry cereals) also have low rates. Higher rates are found in Europe, where cereals and food preservatives have never caught on. The typical Continental breakfast remains coffee, rolls, butter and jams.

All this could be dismissed as coincidence except for the confirmation of laboratory findings. Over twenty-five years ago it was discovered that animals injected with wheat-germ oil developed fewer tumors than those fed a control diet. Now it has been established that the antioxidants in the wheat germ were reducing the cancer rate. One theory is that antioxidants (BHA and BHT are the most familiar) prevent the cancer-causing agent from attaching itself to the DNA molecules in the cells.

The Cleveland Clinic researchers cite further evidence of the

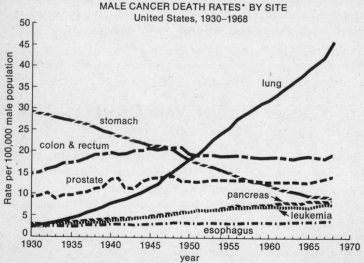

MALE CANCER DEATH RATES* BY SITE
United States, 1930–1968

*rate for the male population standardized for age on the 1940 U.S. population
Sources of data: National Vital Statistics Division and
Bureau of the Census, United States
Research Department American Cancer Society 7-71

cancer-fighting power of antioxidants: A 1971 study showed that in areas where persons were exposed to the antioxidant selenium in their food, the incidence of deaths from cancer of the pharynx, esophagus, stomach, intestines and bladder was lower than in low-selenium areas. Interestingly, there was no difference in cancer rates for parts of the body (lungs, pancreas and prostate) which would not ordinarily come in contact with the selenium.

Cancer cells need oxygen to grow. Deny it to them and they die. Negative side effects attract our attention. But some food additives and drugs have benign side effects. We should find others.

Blood Test for Cancer

A Swedish scientist, Dr. Bertil Bjorklund, has devised a simple blood test for cancer.

The TPA diagnostic kit is based on the same principle as existing tests for measles, mumps and smallpox. A small sample of blood is taken and analyzed for a telltale substance—a polypeptide antigen. Dr. Bjorklund, who isolated the antigen, is director of the Cancer Immunology Section of the National Bacteriological Laboratory of Sweden. He found that this chemical marker is often present at the site of malignant tumors.

People suffering from cancer have high levels of the antigen in their blood, while healthy individuals show only a trace. Tests performed on 5000 people indicate that flu and hepatitis can also produce high antigen values, but the readings return to normal when the noncancerous disease disappears.

If the test proves reliable, it will aid in early diagnosis of malignancy. Further, it will be used to monitor the progress of the disease and the effectiveness of treatment.

The Damon Corporation has acquired the North American rights to the TPA kit and is currently conducting the widespread clinical investigations required for U.S. Food and Drug Administration certification.

According to the Damon Corporation, "The test utilizes the hemagglutination inhibition technique, an efficient and reliable procedure commonly employed in the clinical laboratory."

The prognosis for cancer patients is much improved if the disease is detected early. So this blood test might save countless lives. And it might suggest mechanisms for a cancer cure.

The Thymus Gland and Aging

Nobody knows why we age—we just do. Now it seems that the thymus, an endocrine gland in the chest, may play a part in the prevention of aging.

Although once thought unimportant, the thymus gland apparently helps to develop our "immunological response" (page 56). It may also be implicated in the aging process.

A strain of mice used in the laboratory for experimental purposes has a high incidence of dwarfs. These dwarf mice suffer from pituitary deficiency. They're also deficient in immunological response, and don't live as long as normal mice of the same strain.

However, the immunological response of dwarf mice can be restored if lymph node cells from normal litter-mates or growth hormones are injected while the mice are still young. An unexpected effect of this treatment is to increase the life-span of the dwarfs. The same effects are obtained by administering hormones which stimulate activity of the thymus. Neither effect occurs, though, if treatment is delayed until the mice are mature.

Reasons for the effect aren't well understood. It's possible, however, that aging is a result of some failure of the immunological response. If malfunctioning cells are not attacked by the body's scavenging system of lymphocytes, *replacement* of old or weak cells by new ones may be impaired. The thymus plays a role in the development and maintenance of the immunological

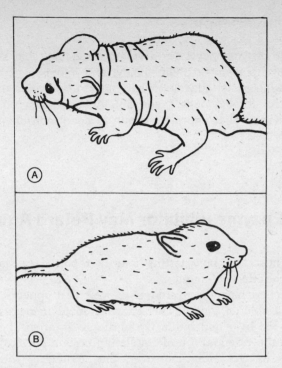

Untreated dwarf mouse at four months (A). *Treated dwarf mouse at seven months* (B). *All signs of aging are absent.*

response—the mechanism by which our body attacks invading bacteria and viruses. Evidently the thymus, by way of that response, also plays a role in preventing aging.

Dr. N. Fabris of the University of Pavia (Italy), who carried out much of the work on dwarf mice, with Professor E. Sorkin, of the Schweizerisches Forschungsinstitut (Switzerland), says, "The life-span of an organism might be decided within a critical segment of its life. Such a critical period could also be linked to sexual maturation, because castration before puberty in humans is known to prolong life-expectancy, while castration in adult life has little or no effect." He also speculates that "Caloric undernutrition in many mammals prolongs significantly their life-span, but only if treatment starts early."

In two or three years we'll have the results of another experiment:

Collection of lymphocytes in a young individual, cold storage of these cells to maintain their vitality, and injection of the same cells into the same individual when older. This avoids the body's rejection of foreign cells (page 56). Although it's too early to predict, it may offer improved health to aged individuals or prolong their life-span.

Enzyme Inhibitor May Retard Aging

U.S. scientists are now testing a drug reported to slow down some of the effects of aging.

Researchers have discovered an enzyme that appears to play a significant role in aging. This enzyme, monoamine oxidase, is found in the liver and brain. Up until age 45 or so, the enzyme performs the essential job of regulating certain chemicals in the body. As we get older, however, the amount of the enzyme increases. So does its effect on the chemicals, which may be reduced so much that the body's normal functioning may be disturbed. This reduction appears to be associated with some of the typical physical and psychological symptoms of aging.

About twenty years ago a Romanian scientist, Professor Ana Aslan, director of the Bucharest Institute for Geriatrics, developed a substance called Gerovital H3. This drug is based on procaine, the familiar pain-killer used by dentists. Dr. Aslan's preparation has been administered to thousands of elderly Europeans with reportedly beneficial effects on many of the disabilities of aging.

Gerovital H3 is not yet available in the United States, but it may be before long. Dr. Joseph P. Hrachovec and Dr. David McFarlane of the University of Southern California are testing the drug to satisfy the requirements of the U.S. Food and Drug Administration. So far their study shows that the preparation lowers the level of the enzyme without producing any of the undesirable side effects associated with other chemicals used for the same purpose. This work is, however, unconfirmed.

"It has been reported consistently that one of the drug's major actions in geriatric patients is to lessen frequently observed mental depression and to replace it with increased mental vigor and a brighter outlook on life," declared Drs. Hrachovec and McFarlane in a joint statement. Their initial work is aimed at verifying this one claim.

Gerovital H3 or other substances now being tested could bring added years within reach. For just pennies a day we might buy pills to prolong mental and physical vigor—as well as life itself—beyond age one hundred. An older population may change the character (and politics) of an entire country (see page 231).

A Step Toward Suspended Animation?

An Air Force doctor has successfully used a technique called "total body washout" to treat a patient who had lapsed into a deep coma brought on by infectious hepatitis.

A diseased liver was filling the patient's blood with toxins. The blood, in turn, was poisoning the liver, frustrating its natural efforts to regenerate. To break the dangerous cycle, Dr. Gerald Klebanhoff of the Lackland Air Force Base Medical Center connected the patient's circulatory system to a complex apparatus.

The machine siphoned off all of the patient's infected blood and replaced it with a cold, oxygen-carrying solution. For a few minutes, his life was sustained by this artificial blood alone. It coursed through his veins, preventing the brain and other vital organs from dying of oxygen starvation. Then gradually the solution was drained, as the patient was given a complete transfusion.

In the recovery room a few hours later, the patient dramatically came out of his coma. The new blood had given the liver a chance to get ahead of the disease, and the patient experienced no ill effects from having his circulatory system totally washed out.

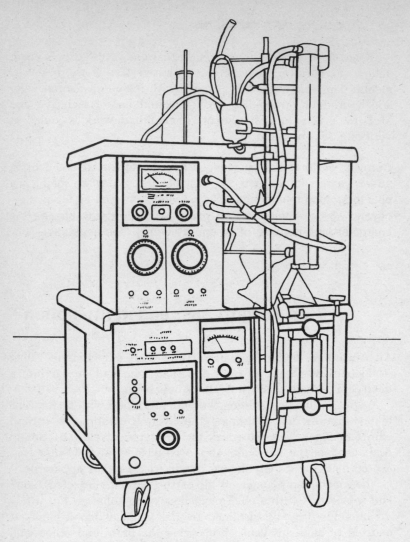

Apparatus for total body washout.

In the past, individual organs have been kept alive during surgery or prior to transplant by oxygen-carrying fluids. Dr. Klebanhoff extended that approach, asking himself, "Why not preserve the whole organism?" Now in still more far-reaching experiments Dr. Klebanhoff has taken a few tentative steps toward a technique of suspended animation.

His machine and artificial blood have sustained a mongrel dog for six hours. The animal's body temperature was lowered to less than 15 degrees centigrade. The lungs stopped breathing; the heart stopped beating; all other bodily functions were drastically slowed down. Only a few faint signs of metabolic activity were detectable. When the circulatory system was refilled with blood and the dog's temperature restored to normal, there was what Dr. Klebanhoff describes as "a full neurological recovery." The dog had been reduced to a state resembling death, then brought back to life without physiological damage.

Dr. Klebanhoff says, "As of this writing, I can say unequivocally that I can preserve a mongrel dog (adult) at zero hematocrit and at 10–20° C, core temperature, for six hours and expect *full* neurological recovery. In other words, the model, as designed, can preserve the brain, cord, and all of the remaining organs entirely safely for at least six hours. In my own mind I am certain that 24 and possibly 48 hours of preservation is possible using the same model.

"Where am I going?

a. "I am certain that 'suspended animation' of the human patient is a distinct possibility as a therapeutic modality for (1) interval care in trauma and transplantation; (2) adjunctive care for medical problems in which a radically altered environment may be selectively deleterious to a disease-causing agent while the organism is generally protected.

b. "Prolonged 'storage' of the human certainly is one alternative in prolonged interplanetary travel. My ultimate experimental design incorporates principles of hypercooling in addition to those of organ preservation already alluded to.

c. "In a more practical vein—I could preserve the brain-dead cadaver donor for one or two days while I collect appropriate recipients for the organs contained 'in situ, in vivo' [in place, alive] until needed."

Imagine astronauts placed in suspended animation for flights to the distant planets—flights that would take years.

When a patient has an incurable disease, suspended animation may be able to stall death until a cure is found.

71

Measuring Prolonged Life

Eternal life, long a cherished human dream, is beyond our reach. Lives 20 to 40 percent longer than we're living now, though, may soon be within our grasp.

Experiments with rats performed thirty years ago, and now controversial, indicated that caloric restriction can double their life-span. When rats were limited to 60 percent of their normal caloric intake (fasting one day in three) their life-span was greatly increased. This increase was achieved in some unknown way, perhaps by suppressing those causes of death (like tumors) which multiply with age. The animals on this restricted diet were active, underweight—and still young in a biological sense—when their counterparts on a normal diet had already died.

Such experiments have not been applicable in man up to now since mortality was our only sure measure of aging. New advances in biochemistry now make it critical to measure short-term aging rates, using standardized tests which make human study possible for the first time. These tests assess biological aging, as opposed to merely chronological age. Such tests were used in a study of Hiroshima survivors, in which the researchers looked for possible accelerated aging. The test results showed a fairly high correlation between biological and chronological age—a necessary condition to study agents which may prolong life-spans.

Available tests fall into three categories: straightforward tests such as human body measurement (or anthropometry), clinical examination, and sensory tests; those requiring a postmortem examination; and those involving biopsy. In the Hiroshima study, measurements of skin elasticity and hair graying showed biological age in terms of chronological age.

While rodent studies have also included the use of drugs for increasing longevity, dietary restriction is a good choice for human study, according to Dr. Alex Comfort, director of gerontological research at University College, London. Unlike the case with drugs, few ethical questions or government controls intervene.

Antiaging drugs may succeed because they cut down food intake or simulate such a process biochemically. Aside from actual dietary restriction, which may prove difficult for some people even if it's good for them, there is also the possibility of blocking the enzymes called amylases. Amylases convert starch to sugar. An amylase-blocking agent would leave our diet unchanged, but simply not allow the body to utilize all food; it's also a possible cure for obesity.

Comfort suggests that the test age in human study should be 50, and that males should be the subjects. Testing men avoids the complication of menopause and its relation to aging. The experimental strategy is to select those variables that change reliably over a period of three to five years, a reasonable amount of time for a study. The variables should correlate well with age, and measure as many underlying processes as possible.

Traditional medical practice aimed at eliminating individual causes of death. But antiaging agents aim at dealing with all causes; their purpose is to postpone processes that increase our susceptibility to death and disease. While medical research helps more people live to old age, it has not succeeded in prolonging our life-span much beyond the Biblical "three score and ten."

Comfort predicts direct experiments on the delaying of aging in humans will be well under way by 1975. "Given some decent human experimentation," he says, "we shall know by 1990 of at least one way of extending vigorous life by about 20 percent."

Our "longevity quotient" (see page 454) apparently increases if we are useful to society and maintain a positive attitude toward life, if we stay physically fit and avoid smoking. Perhaps we will add to the list: restrict food intake.

Eating from the "tree of life," a *Biblical* injunction, is not what the *doctor* ordered. Future research will give us the choice to enjoy food and life—or to enjoy *less* food and *more* life.

2
Power
and
Energy

Solar Power from Satellites

The National Aeronautics and Space Administration intends to orbit solar power stations someday. Huge satellites would collect sunshine and transmit the energy to earth on microwave beams.

Of course, it would be easier and less expensive to build solar energy plants on earth. At night, however, these plants would have to shut down. The solution may be to place the solar collectors in fixed orbit 22,300 miles above the earth's surface. There they would be bathed in 23-hour-a-day sunshine, spending only one hour in the earth's shadow.

Each satellite would have two enormous "wings," about 12 square miles in area, covered with solar cells. The cells would convert the sun's radiation into electricity, which would then be fed into a microwave generator. The microwaves beamed to an earth-bound receiving station would reconvert them into DC electricity.

One satellite of this size could generate 10,000 megawatts of electrical energy—enough to meet the estimated needs of New York City in the year 2000. The process would be virtually pollution-free. For comparison, a modern nuclear generating plant yields about 1000 megawatts.

The satellites would have to be launched piece by piece and assembled in space. Currently, the target date for the first orbiting power plant is the late 1980s, but this kind of large-scale extraterrestrial construction depends on the availability of the controversial space shuttle.

The process of transmitting a significant amount of power over a microwave beam has been demonstrated with a four-foot electrically driven helicopter. A microwave beam aimed at an antenna carried by the helicopter furnished all of the power required for flight.

We don't yet have a space shuttle that can repeatedly lift heavy loads into orbit, nor the maneuverable space tugs needed for assembling the station—but we are starting to build them.

The principal objection to this appears to be the small amount of power finally available after the massive effort of getting the station going—only about what we get from a dozen or so present-day nuclear plants.

NASA has awarded a $197,000 research grant to Peter Glaser of Arthur D. Little, Inc., working with Grumman Aerospace, Raytheon, and Spectrolab-Textron, to develop the technology for a system of power satellites.

The advantages of orbiting power plants, according to Grumman, are that they:

1. Consume no valuable earth-energy resources
2. Produce no chemical pollutants
3. Produce only a fraction of the thermal pollution that conventional power plants do
4. Are economical and safe
5. Will stimulate development of advanced technology to satisfy world power and environmental needs.

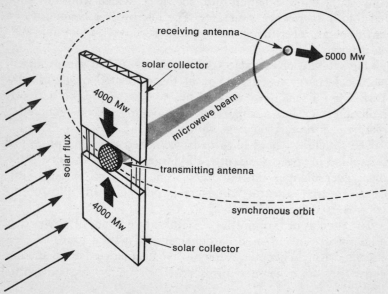

Satellite station beams solar power to earth.

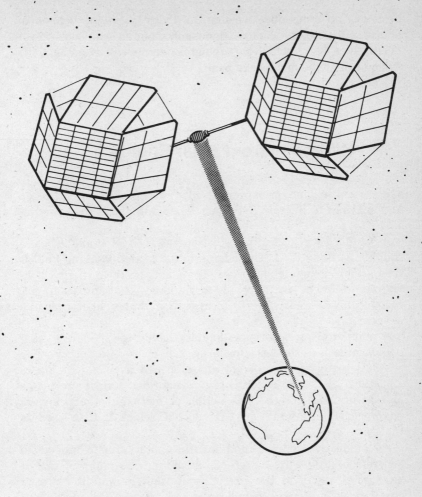

Artist's conception of the satellite seen from space.

According to legend, Archimedes used huge mirrors to set fire to the Roman fleet in 212 B.C. The Archimedes of tomorrow might use microwave beams as a weapon. And satellite mirrors could light up an entire city at night.

This system uses sunlight, something we won't run out of, and produces no radioactive wastes. But there is a large volume of space in the beam which is constantly flooded with high-power microwaves, harmful to living creatures nearby—for example, birds flying through the microwave beam.

Hydrogen from Solar Energy

An unusual scheme for capturing solar energy makes use of algae and enzymes to liberate hydrogen. The hydrogen is then used as fuel.

A standard way to capture solar energy is to let sunlight heat a suitable working fluid. The energy in the heated working fluid is then used to generate electricity. But plants produce energy in an entirely different way by photosynthesis. They use sunlight, carbon dioxide and water to form carbohydrates, liberating free oxygen.

A number of proposals, incidentally, have been made for using photosynthesis as the basis for large-scale energy production. The simplest merely grows plants to be burned as fuel (see pages 163 and 165)—the so-called energy plantations. Others use plants as raw material for the production of methane (the principal component of "natural" gas) or alcohol, which is then used as fuel.

An innovative scheme modifies the photosynthetic process to generate hydrogen from water and sunlight. Several varieties of blue-green algae, in the presence of sunlight and the proper enzymes, split water into hydrogen and oxygen. The algae then consume the oxygen, leaving free hydrogen as one of the by-products of their special photosynthetic process. So far this has all been on a test tube basis.

Recent work by Dr. John Benemann at the University of California indicates it may be possible to carry out the process on a large scale. The hydrogen could be used as fuel, in place of coal or oil. The algae could also be harvested periodically and converted to a food that is rich in proteins. However, this will require genetic engineering of a strain of algae capable of producing hydrogen and oxygen.

Dr. Benemann says, "Although the rates of hydrogen evolution obtained in the laboratory to date are low, there appears to be no basic reason why hydrogen output could not eventually reach that expected from known photosynthetic efficiencies."

This "future fact" is far from realization. But genetic engineering will hasten the arrival of the strain of algae required before cheap hydrogen is plentiful. Then, our cars and homes (perhaps even cities and airplanes?) may be powered by hydrogen manufactured by algae and sunlight.

Chemical Light

When the lights go out there's a new option: Rather than burning a candle, you can snap a lightstick.

The lightstick is a dependable, self-contained chemical light source that can illuminate an average room for three hours. The principle is simple: Two liquids are sealed inside a plastic tube somewhat larger than a fountain pen. One component is carried in a glass capsule floating in the second fluid. When you need light, you bend the lightstick slightly, which shatters the inner capsule and allows the fluids to mix; the stick glows immediately.

Cyalume, as it's called by the American Cyanamid Company, gives off a distinctive yellow-green light. On a moonless night it can be seen for distances up to one mile. For the first hour it shines as brightly as a flashlight, providing enough light to dial a telephone or even to read. During the second two hours the luminosity gradually fades, but the total volume of light produced is still ten times that of an electroluminescent night lamp.

Since Cyalume glows without heat or flame, it can be used safely near concentrations of flammable fumes or explosives. And, unlike candles or flares, the lightstick is weatherproof—it even works under water.

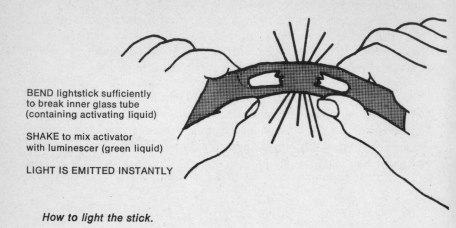

BEND lightstick sufficiently
to break inner glass tube
(containing activating liquid)

SHAKE to mix activator
with luminescer (green liquid)

LIGHT IS EMITTED INSTANTLY

How to light the stick.

American Cyanamid says, "Inexpensive and reliable, the lightstick has a shelf-life of at least two years when stored at ordinary temperatures. . . . The mixture of the two components, which is what you would get if the package ruptured, is nontoxic by swallowing or by contact with skin."

The lightstick has already been approved for use in underground coal mining and in some naval operations, but chemical lighting has never been tried on a large scale. It might be possible to light whole buildings temporarily with continuously recycled chemicals. Someday, when miniature television routinely probes our internal organs, this may be a source of light.

Cooking by Sunlight

A stove powered by solar energy has been designed by a Johns Hopkins engineer for use in emerging countries. It is mass-

Artist's conception of solar kitchen.

producible, easy to install, maintenance-free, and costs nothing to operate. Projected price per unit—about $100.

Called a "solar kitchen," this apparatus collects sunlight and transports this energy to a cooking unit containing a hot plate.

Collection is done by a parabolic cylindrical reflector that, thanks to a clever device, tracks the sun from dawn to dusk. The device is a spiral bimetallic element whose two metals expand at different rates.

The reflector focuses sunlight on a tube filled with Dowtherm A, a man-made substance. When the Dowtherm A heats, it changes from a liquid to a vapor. The vapor rises up the angled tube until it reaches the cooking unit. There, the Dowtherm A condenses back to a liquid. The energy given up in this condensation heats the hot plate. The Dowtherm A returns as a liquid to the reflector, ready for another cycle.

Low-cost materials are available in which heat could be accumulated and stored for evening use.

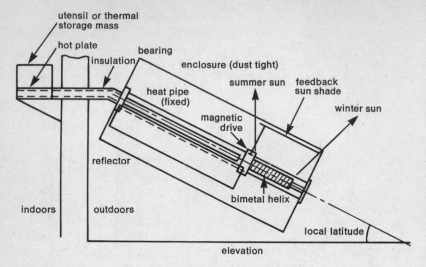

Cross section showing heat pipe, sun tracker, and hot plate.

"Many of the elements," according to Charles Swet, who developed it, "could be made and assembled with semiskilled labor in the country of intended use, and might cost less than $100 in some third-world areas."

Here is a stove for which the sun provides the fuel free of charge. It could prove a blessing not only in the third world but in every advanced country that is hungry for energy and blighted by pollution.

Solar House

The Institute of Energy Conversion at the University of Delaware has built a unique model home. Called "Solar One," it is the first house to convert sunlight into both electricity and heat.

The four-bedroom house was constructed to gather data on the feasibility of harvesting solar power for domestic use, and the early findings are promising: Sunshine provides up to about 80 percent of Solar One's heat and electricity. Conventional utilities supply the remaining 20 percent, mostly during the night hours, when demand for power is lighter.

The house has a high continuous roofline sloping at a 45-degree angle. This slanting roof, designed for maximum exposure to the sun, contains a large skylight protecting the solar-cell panels and heat collectors. Thin-film solar cells generate direct-current electricity that can be used immediately or stored in a series of batteries to provide power long after sunset.

Storing heat is more complex. The solar cells and black heat-gathering panels become very hot. Forced air picks up this heat and carries it over containers of eutectic "salts." These salts melt at low temperatures ($70°$ and $120°F.$) and efficiently absorb and retain much of the heat. When the air in the house becomes too cool, it's circulated through the salts and warmed.

During the summer, another eutectic salt "stores the coolness" of the night and is used for air conditioning in the daytime. On cloudy winter days, a conventional heat pump supplements the solar heating system.

While it's possible to build a 100 percent solar house, the object of the Delaware project is to prove that solar power can be practical. Dr. Carl Boer, director of the Institute of Energy Conversion, believes that public acceptance of solar power hinges on reducing the costs to less than 10 percent of the total pricetag on the house and on ensuring cheap, reliable and comfortable service after initial installation: "These conditions can only be fulfilled if solar energy is used as supplemental rather than substitutional energy."

In Solar One the total cost of the heating and power plants is only $3000 more than conventional utilities, or about 12 percent of the total cost of the house. Dr. Boer estimates that by the late 1970s the cost of electricity may rise to high enough levels to make the Solar One system attractive to consumers.

Dr. Boer explains the potential of solar power: "Solar energy impinging at high noon on an area of 35 km by 35 km equals the total peak capacity of all existing power plants [in the United

Dr. Boer standing in front of Solar One.

States] combined. Obviously there is enough solar energy to satisfy our demands. Even if we continue to increase our demand to the ultimate saturation level estimated at 45 kw per capita (22 times the current level), and even if the U.S. population increases to 500 million people, only 0.3 percent of the solar energy impinging on the United States would be needed to fill the resulting gigantic demand."

In Massachusetts the Audubon Society has a prototype solar-heated building for its headquarters. In England a largely solar-heated elementary school has been in operation for nearly ten years. Simple architectural changes in the placement of buildings and the location and type of windows can save energy up to 15 percent over the enclosed glass and steel skyscrapers of today. The sun will supplement regular heating systems. However, improved efficiencies for large-scale energy storage and solar cells must come before a total solar house is within the price range of the public.

Solar Heat Pump

NASA has a way to heat and cool houses with power from the sun. This could ultimately control the environment of manned or unmanned space stations.

Called a solar-powered heat pump, the new system gathers the sun's energy in a "solar collector" and then converts it to heat energy. The heat is used through a relatively complicated system either to heat or to cool a house, depending on the time of year. Moreover, the system contains what is known as a phase-change material (PCM), which is capable of storing enough heat energy for use during the night or on cloudy days. On the other hand, if the system has a surplus of energy it can heat swimming pools or hothouses as well.

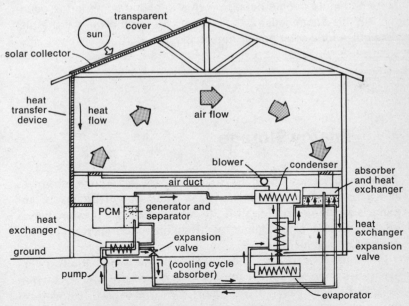

SCHEMATIC OF SOLAR HOME HEAT PUMP SYSTEM

Current methods of cooling or heating use fossil fuels (coal and oil), electricity, or some sort of combination of the two. Air conditioners, electric heaters, gas or oil heaters and furnaces are all widely used. However, the massive proliferation of these devices is creating a serious pollution and energy problem. NASA predicts serious consequences if these methods continue to be used.

But the solar heat pump is pollution free, and potentially much cheaper than current devices. Each of the component parts of the pump has been used separately for various purposes, but Robert L. Middleton, chief of the environmental control section at NASA and the inventor of the pump, says that this is the first time a heat pump has been successfully combined with a solar energy system.

NASA's technical estimates for the system are: "A heating capacity of 71,640 BTU/hr; a cooling capacity of 30,500 BTU/hr; the power required is 34 watts; the roof area required is 2460 square feet; and the amount of heat storage material required is 326 cubic feet."

More and more people hope to own a weekend home in the country. But this dreamhouse can freeze up during the week if the fuel runs out—not if solar power runs it, though.

Energy Storage

Two new batteries may help to solve a very large power problem and a very small but important one. The General Electric Company is working on electrical storage systems to prevent urban brownouts and to operate tiny lifesaving pacemakers for years without replacement.

For bulk energy, the sodium-sulfur battery potentially offers five times more storage capacity per pound than conventional lead-acid power packs. Researchers conceive of vast installations of sodium-sulfur cells that could provide extra power at times of

A sodium-bromine battery designed for heart pacemakers is the size of five stacked half-dollars. Its life expectancy of ten years exceeds the conventional mercury-zinc batteries (background) that have to be replaced every two to three years.

peak demand. During the early morning hours and over weekends, when full generating capacity is not required, excess electricity could be stored in the heavy-duty batteries. Then, during business hours, when the drain of machinery, air conditioners and office lights pushes demand beyond the capacity of the generators, the batteries could be tapped to meet immediate needs. The acres of batteries may be located underground to reduce their environmental impact.

Sodium-sulfur batteries use liquid reactants and must be operated at temperatures over 300 degrees centigrade. The major problem is to improve the ceramic material that separates the hot sulfur and sodium liquids.

Sodium-sulfur units might someday be used to power smogless electric vehicles. With the long-lasting cells, a car could travel as far on a single charge as today's automobiles on a tankful of gas.

A much smaller power unit, using sodium and bromine reactants, once tested will power miniature heart pacemakers. The new chemical unit, with a life expectancy of one decade, will be as durable as the nuclear pacemakers now in experimental use. Moreover, the price will be only a fraction of the $4800 the nuclear pacemakers are expected to cost.

Most of the 60,000 Americans presently dependent on pacemakers use models powered by mercury-zinc cells. The new GE battery is half the size and one quarter the weight of these units, and it can produce nearly three times the energy per pound.

Dr. Arthur M. Bueche, GE vice president for research and development, referring to the energy shortage, explains, "Such a bulk energy storage system would make more efficient use of available generating capacity."

Bulk energy storage batteries are a step toward solar power plants. One handicap of earth-based solar energy is that there is no input at night and only reduced input on cloudy days. Large-capacity batteries, charged on sunny days, would produce a continuous, reliable power supply.

Low-Temperature Heat Engine

A heat engine, using an organic working fluid instead of steam, recovers energy from the hot exhaust gases of a conventional power plant.

Today's steam-powered generating plant efficiently converts the energy delivered to it from hot steam. The boiler that heats the steam, however, wastes a good deal of energy in hot gases that go up the chimney. Like a boiler, a gas turbine also wastes energy in hot exhaust gas.

The hot exhaust gas can be used for heating, which is one way of recovering the energy that would otherwise be wasted. This isn't ordinarily done, though. In a small installation it's cheaper to

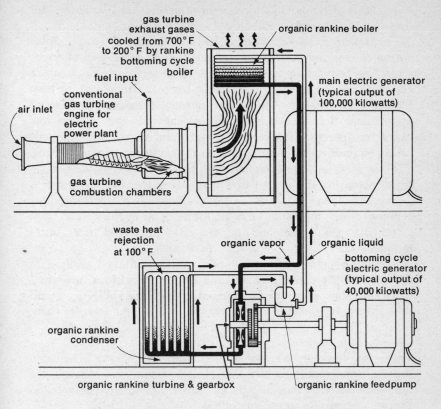

Energy at low temperature is extracted from the chimney above, to feed the organic heat engine below.

use conventional heating equipment. In a large one there's so much waste heat that only a fraction of it can be used for space heating.

One solution is to adopt some sort of a heat engine to recover energy from hot exhaust gas. But a conventional steam engine is inefficient when its heat source is at a relatively low temperature—as are the exhaust gases.

Various organic working fluids are attractive, instead of the steam-water fluid that is normally used, but they can be troublesome. Most of them will leak out through seals and bearings, and they have an annoying tendency to react with lubricants.

Thermo Electron Corporation has found a satisfactory combination of working fluid and lubricant that maintains an effective seal. The result is a new family of heat engines which make efficient use of the energy available from low-temperature heat sources. The new engines deliver outputs ranging from several up to more than 10,000 horsepower. They can be built as turbines, for operation at more or less constant speed, or as reciprocating engines for efficient operation over a wide range of speeds.

These engines were designed with the idea of recovering waste heat, increasing the output of a generating plant by as much as 40 percent. They also work well with other low-temperature heat sources—which are usually nonpolluting. The engines have been installed in small vehicles, and one is being tested in an automobile.

Thermo Electron, the developer, sums up the advantages of the new family of engines as "low exhaust emissions, multifuel capability, low noise levels, inherently high reliability . . . and the ability to operate efficiently with low temperature heat sources."

These engines can use waste heat from any source. They can make a significant reduction in our total consumption of fossil and nuclear fuels. They may also be one answer to efficient conversion of solar energy into electrical energy.

 ## Superflywheel for Electric Automobiles

A professional engineer at Johns Hopkins, David W. Rabenhorst, has designed an energy-storage system that can make all-electric automobiles competitive in performance and range with today's air-polluting "muscle" cars. His "superflywheel" can store and deliver three times the power per pound of the lead-acid batteries currently used in prototypes of electric cars. A powerful, nonpolluting electric car is not far away.

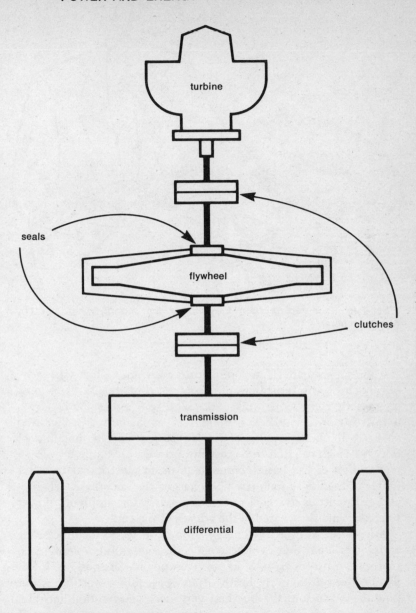

Flywheel installed in hybrid vehicle.

Fiber-glass rods radiate from the hub of the superflywheel, held by Mr. Rabenhorst.

The "superflywheel," a sophisticated version of the 5000-year-old flywheel, is a brushlike rotor composed of thousands of glass or graphite rods, looking like uncooked spaghetti radiating from a hub to form a wheel. Mounted in a vacuum chamber and charged by being spun, it quickly stores sizable amounts of energy, which can in turn be readily and variably tapped.

A design of the basic components in an electric car calls for batteries feeding a motor which charges the superflywheel. Discharge from this flywheel operates a generator supplying power to electric motors located in the wheels of the car.

A flywheel was the sole energy-storage device in the all-electric Swiss Oerlikon Bus, which went into successful operation in many countries in 1953. Made of 3300 pounds of solid steel, this flywheel could store (in terms of energy) only 3 watt-hours per pound. As a result, the bus had very poor acceleration and also had to be recharged from an external power source every half mile.

With new technology and materials, the superflywheel has a test-proven energy capacity of 30 watt-hours per pound, which is ten times greater than the flywheel used in the bus and three times greater than the capacity of lead-acid batteries. Operated in tandem with 100 pounds of batteries, a superflywheel weighing only 3.3 pounds could provide sufficient power for acceleration and range to make a 1300-pound electric car competitive with today's internal-combustion polluters.

Mr. Rabenhorst says, "The net result may be that the flywheel will be the single most important contributor to the reduction of automobile pollution . . .

"Ultimately the all-electric vehicle will predominate, particularly in the urban area. The list of potential applications appears to be endless. . . . A superflywheel rotor weighing slightly more than 2100 pounds can deliver 100,000 horsepower for 3 seconds. . . . And at the other extreme, a small superflywheel energy-storage system could provide many hours of silent, emission-free trolling for the fisherman."

Item: The earth itself is a massive superflywheel turning silently and efficiently; it stores massive amounts of rotational energy.

The superflywheel may be the energy-storage system of tomorrow, powering not only automobiles but tools, boats, airplanes and spacecraft.

Liquid Hydrogen—Fuel of the Future

New techniques for storing hydrogen make it attractive as a fuel for automobiles and aircraft.

Hydrogen may be the perfect fuel. It delivers more energy per pound than coal or oil. Environmentalists will love it. When it's burned with oxygen the residue is pure water, and even when it's burned with air the combustion temperature is low enough to minimize formation of polluting gases. Finally, it's easy to transport by pipeline.

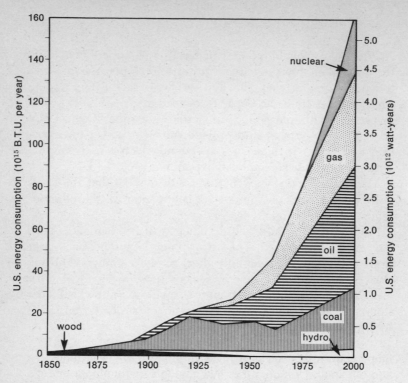

U.S. energy consumption, 1850–2000. The energy sources are also given.

The difficulty is that hydrogen is hard to store. Even at high pressure, you can't store enough to run a car very far in a tank of reasonable size—one that will fit into the car.

Liquefying the hydrogen is one answer; large rockets burn liquid hydrogen and liquid oxygen, but large amounts must be stored. For small amounts, the thermal insulation required to keep the hydrogen liquid takes up more space than the stored hydrogen. A new approach is based on storing hydrogen as a compound, a metallic hydride. The hydride, stable at room temperature, decomposes on heating, to yield free hydrogen. This may solve the problem of a small "hydrogen tank" for lawnmowers, automobiles and aircraft.

Hydrogen, now made from natural gas, is obtainable by the electrolysis of water, but only economically if electricity is very inexpensive. Electricity is used at the generating plant to produce hydrogen, which is then liquefied and transported by pipeline.

At the point of use, the hydrogen is converted back to electricity in fuel cells, which are highly efficient, or into metallic hydride for use in vehicles. Surprisingly, it is often cheaper to transport hydrogen by pipeline than it is to send electricity over long-distance power lines.

A point of special interest: We don't have to develop any new techniques in order to convert hydrogen into mechanical power. Any internal-combustion engine will run on hydrogen instead of petroleum-based fuel. And we can use existing power plants (which now burn coal, oil or gas) by converting to hydrogen burners—until large enough fuel cells are available to replace them.

Dr. Lawrence W. Jones, a scientist at the University of Michigan, has studied the possibilities of a hydrogen-based energy economy. "Conventional gas turbines and aircraft jet engines have operated on hydrogen," he points out. "Surprisingly, every serious effort to run an engine or an automobile on hydrogen fuel has, apparently, been successful."

In the very distant future, with solar power for electricity and hydrogen as fuel for vehicles, we may declare our independence of polluting fossil fuels and nuclear power. Sooner, with coal and its derivatives, we may declare our energy independence from imported oil.

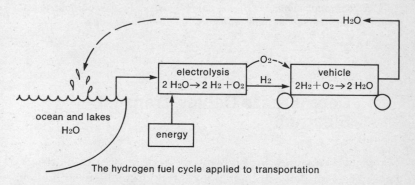

The hydrogen fuel cycle applied to transportation

Hydrogen is completely cyclic as a fuel. Drawn from oceans, water is electrolyzed. The resulting hydrogen, after burning, is returned to the biosphere as water.

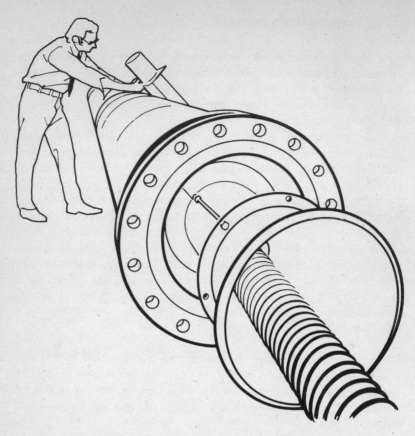

This 40-foot-long aluminum power cable—chilled to a supercold 320°F. below zero—has successfully withstood up to 435,000 volts.

Deep-Freeze Cables Transmit Electricity

For many years lines for high-voltage transmission of electricity have been suspended high above the ground—seven million acres are now set aside for high-voltage towers and rights of way. Very few transmission lines are underground, and when they are, the cost is six to twenty times more than overhead cables.

Now a new type of underground cable has been developed by General Electric as the climax of a three-year, $1.05-million-dollar project. It carries much more power than conventional underground lines. The new lines are cooled to liquid nitrogen temperatures (320°F. below zero). Scientists successfully passed 435,000 volts through an aluminum power cable cooled to cryogenic (very low) temperatures, and they predict full-fledged cryogenic systems at first would supply power to our ten largest cities.

Potential low cost and high power-carrying capability make cryogenic cables extremely appealing. Now the problem before the scientists is to find a material to insulate them. General Electric's choice for its test cable was spun-bonded, polyethylene-fiber paper, but many other materials are likely candidates, too.

Even with cryogenic transmission on the horizon, other means are being constantly explored, among them photovoltaic cells powered by light energy, piped hydrogen, and decentralized

Above-ground high-voltage lines from distant generating plants may merge with the underground cryogenic-cables transmission system at the outer edge of a city's suburbs. Refrigeration stations, similar to this artist's conception, would be spaced about every ten miles to rechill the liquid nitrogen coolant.

production of power to ease distribution costs. And there is still a lot of work to do on two items that may present problems for the cryogenic system: the massive job of installing the necessary refrigeration stations every ten miles or so, and the new and easier means of sabotage the system suggests. But with the nation's power needs expected to double by 1980, cryogenic cables will figure prominently in the search for more effective and economical ways to transmit electricity.

Dr. Arthur M. Bueche, General Electric vice president for research, says, "While the nation's cities are demanding increasing amounts of electric power with each passing year, the amount of above-ground space available for high-voltage transmission lines is becoming almost nonexistent. The ability of supercooled cable systems to transmit extremely large amounts of power—underground—through a restricted space may be the solution to this increasingly serious problem."

Future high-tension wires will go underground. With the soaring demand for power, cryogenic cable systems may eventually feed energy into most American cities with populations over 50,000.

High-Temperature Gas Generates Electricity

Magnetohydrodynamic (MHD) generators employ a charged-particle gas, called plasma, as a conductor instead of copper bars. For a given amount of fuel, they can produce half again more electricity than the best conventional power plants.

Most power generation schemes start by burning fossil fuel to produce heat; heat energy is converted to mechanical motion. Typical heat engines drive an electric generator, and the rotating generator produces electricity. Nuclear plants use almost the same process: heat is supplied by a nuclear reaction instead of by burning coal or gas (page 114). But the conversion of heat energy to electricity is quite conventional.

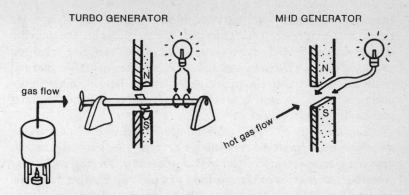

TURBO GENERATOR   MHD GENERATOR

gas flow

hot gas flow

In a conventional generator, electricity is derived by rotating a solid coil of wire, or armature, through a magnetic field. The MHD generator substitutes a high-temperature ionized gas for the armature, passes this gas through a magnetic field, and generates electricity.

Fuel cells "burn" fuel (combine with oxygen) at relatively low temperatures. They produce electricity directly as a product of the fuel-burning reaction. With no rotating generators and no heat engines, fuel cells (page 108) are significantly more efficient than all but the largest plants of conventional design.

Much higher efficiencies can be reached with MHD generators

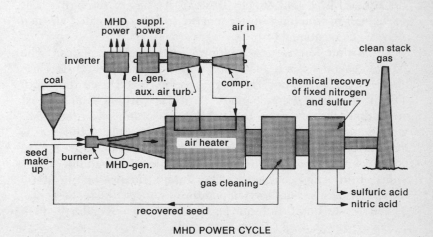

MHD POWER CYCLE

because they yield electricity by blowing a stream of hot gas through a magnetic field. Charged gas particles in the moving stream are deflected by the magnetic field: positive charged particles give up their energy to one electrode; negative charged particles, deflected in the opposite direction, deposit their energy on the other. The result is an electric generator in which nothing moves—but the stream of gas.

Small amounts of "seed" material are added to the hot working gas. The seed material becomes charged (or ionized) at the operating temperature of the MHD generator. During molecular collisions, molecules of the working gas pick up charges from the seed material. This ensures that a large fraction of the particles in the working gas carry charges. The seed material recovered from the exhaust gases of the generator is reused.

Instead of hot gas to strike turbine blades which rotate a conductor in a magnetic field, the MHD generator simply blows the hot gas through a magnetic field, substituting the hot gas for a metallic conductor. In both cases the heat energy of the gas is converted to electricity. Because the gas in an MHD generator moves through a simple tube instead of a complex gas turbine, high operating temperatures are possible. This means high efficiencies for energy conversion are possible.

Additional energy can be recovered from the hot exhaust gas of the MHD generator. But because it contains seed material, the hot exhaust isn't used directly. Instead, it's passed through a heat exchanger in which it transfers energy to air. The heated air then drives a conventional turbine.

Dr. Arthur Kantrowitz, a pioneer in the field, explains: "The MHD generator is a fundamental step along the path of development of prime movers. This path may be traced from the windmill through the piston engine . . . to the turbine, which is just a windmill inside a pipe. In the MHD generator, even the windmill is absent, the pipe alone remaining; the blade function is performed by lines of magnetic force. . . . The last step to MHD, with its profound increase in temperature handling capability, brings high efficiency. The static structure of the MHD generator easily handles temperatures above the highest projected for turbines and can handle even the exceedingly high temperature that a successful nuclear fusion reactor will produce."

Most gains in efficiency come at a steep cost—increased complexity. Other improvements appear when a complex process is replaced by a simple one. Fuel cells are an example of process replacement. So is the MHD generator. The combination of nuclear fusion and an MHD generating plant promises high-efficiency sources of future electric power.

Laser Triggers Thermonuclear Fusion

Laser-induced nuclear fusion may become a feasible energy source within a matter of years, but perhaps as long as decades.

Fossil fuels—oil and coal—aren't exhausted yet, but they won't last forever. And although nuclear fission is a good source of energy, disposing of radioactive by-products is something of a problem. Fusion, a more promising solution to the power crisis, not only is a clean energy source, but uses deuterium abundantly available in sea water. The only question is: How do we bring fusion about?

The fusion reaction keeps the sun going. Two atoms of deuterium, "heavy" hydrogen, fuse to form a single atom of helium. In the process they liberate energy, *much* more than is consumed in extracting the deuterium from sea water. The trouble is that the reaction doesn't take place—the deuterium atoms don't stick together or "fuse"—except at very high temperatures, something like 100 million degrees.

A good deal of work has gone into devising methods to contain hot gas at the required temperatures. Metal containers obviously won't work. Various arrangements of magnetic fields have been successful in confining the gas, but not for very long.

At the University of Rochester, scientists carry out the fusion reaction in a pool of molten lithium. Frozen pellets of deuterium

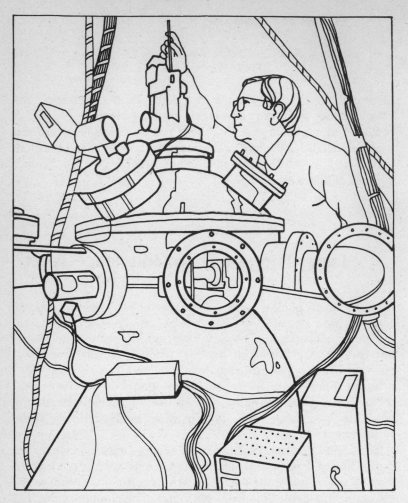

Inside this fusion vessel, target fuel pellets of deuterium are vaporized by bursts of light from high-power laser beam.

or lithium deuteride are fired into the lithium and hit by a high-power laser beam just before they submerge. Heat liberated by the fusion reaction is captured by the lithium. Next the hot lithium is pumped to a steam boiler and then returned to the fusion vessel. The steam powers a conventional electric generating plant with the usual turbines.

These high-power modulators are networks that shape the energy pulses.

Another approach to fusion confines the fuel by elaborate magnetic fields. Here a technician inside such a "magnetic bottle" adjusts the magnetic field coils.

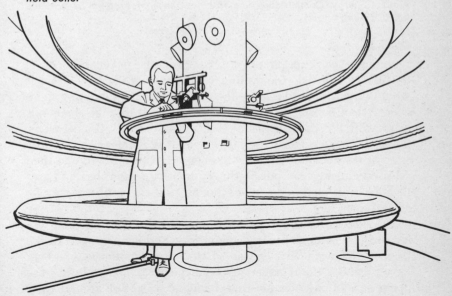

FUTURE FACTS

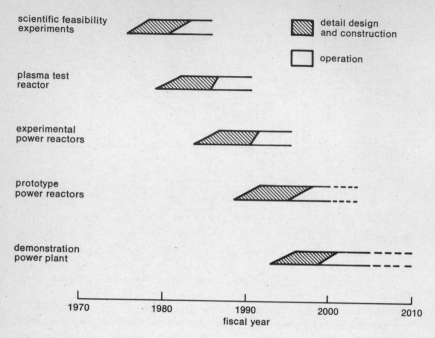

Atomic Energy Commission timetable for the major steps to produce fusion power.

Now a laser beam promises to compress the pellets and consequently to raise the deuterium to fusion temperature. Thus it would be a trigger to initiate the fusion reaction, liberating more energy than consumed. Laser beams can drill through diamonds or punch holes in razor-blade steel. But lasers with the necessary power to trigger fusion are just beyond the reach of the present state of the art. Vast amounts of energy must be stored and then released quickly to "pulse" the high-energy laser beam. Laser technology is well understood, though, and this problem may be solved soon.

The director of controlled thermonuclear research at what was formerly the Atomic Energy Commission and is now a part of the Energy Research and Development Administration, Robert L. Hirsch, says, "Both magnetic confinement and laser-fusion are being developed to demonstrate scientific feasibility around 1980.

Commercialization of fusion power should occur around the turn of the century."

And workers at the University of Rochester, where a three-year university/industry program is aimed at developing more powerful lasers, are convinced that "high-power laser technology is the key" to fusion.

The laser, which began as a scientific curiosity, may trigger the solution to our energy problems.

Nuclear-Powered Refrigerator

A nuclear-powered refrigerator has been demonstrated by the Atomic Energy Commission along with the Hughes Aircraft Company. This ultimate ice box can provide spot cooling to temperatures as low as minus 320° F.—colder than the surface of the planet Pluto.

The refrigerator, which weighs nine pounds and is usually powered by electricity, was adapted to accommodate a nuclear power package. Like home gas refrigerators, the atomic deep freeze relies on a heat source to produce cooling. The heat comes from decaying radioisotopes in three small capsules containing plutonium-238.

Since the half life of plutonium is 92 years, the unit can maintain the frosty temperatures for long periods of time without refueling. It also takes up a minimum amount of space. These features will make it ideal for supercooling aboard the spacecraft of the future.

Currently, supercooling is used in infrared, microwave, laser and radiation detection systems. It's expected that nuclear refrigeration will continue to be limited to space applications and highly specialized instrumentation.

According to the AEC, "Electrically powered models of this Vuillemier-cycle cryogenic refrigerator have been used by the Air

Force and Army for space, air and ground systems, including an Army ground-mobile night vision device."

Consumers shouldn't anticipate chilling their beer with nuclear energy in the near future. But remote settlements—on safari or on the moon—may.

Water and Sodium Make Power

Sodium combines with water for a power source that generates electricity or direct mechanical output.

Sodium, an alkali metal, reacts violently with water to form sodium hydroxide, free hydrogen, and a great deal of heat.

This fuel cell uses the same reaction, controlling it so that the liberated energy appears as electricity instead of heat. The result is a compact nonpolluting power source capable of delivering 100 times as much power as a conventional storage battery of the same weight. In another version, the fuel cell functions as a motor. It delivers mechanical power *and* electricity.

Hydrogen, generated by the fuel cell as a by-product, can be burned without pollution to provide additional energy. The spent fuel, sodium hydroxide, can be regenerated electrically in somewhat the same way that a storage battery can be recharged, but the fuel cell is much lighter than an equivalent battery.

The sodium-power fuel cell provides a new way of transporting energy from an electric generating plant to the point of use. Instead of sending electricity over power lines, sodium is shipped by truck or by rail. At the same time a flow of sodium hydroxide is shipped in the opposite direction, to be used again. In principle, no sodium is used up and the two-way flow (of sodium and sodium hydroxide) replaces the one-way flow of electric power over conventional transmission lines. The sodium-power fuel cell could supply energy to remote places, like isolated campsites or vacation homes.

According to Lockheed, the developer, "As long as the cell is fed with its two fuels—water and metal—it will continue to produce electrical energy. No electrical battery charging is needed, no catalysts are added, no special membranes are used. . . . Cells capable of using sea water are under development."

Sodium and water are both cheap. If the price of the fuel cell comes down far enough in mass production, it could be used to power a nonpolluting electric car, a house or a ship.

 ## Bettering the Battery

Bell Laboratories has developed a lead-acid battery with a life-span twice that of any previous power pack. The new battery not only lasts more than thirty years, its performance actually *improves* with age.

The traditional lead-acid workhorse has remained essentially unchanged since it was invented by Plante in 1859. Gradually each battery deteriorates and fails because of corrosion.

Now a new cylindrical design and a new energy-producing paste turn corrosion into an advantage. Up to a point, corrosion in the new Bell battery produces more paste and more power. An improved case and sealing compound add to its durability.

Telephone companies will use the long-lived battery to ensure uninterrupted communications service when regular power supplies fail. The present design is not intended for automobiles, but the principles involved could ultimately find applications under the hood.

According to Bell Labs, "In the new battery, the computer-designed grids are conical, cupped to a 10-degree angle, and are stacked, pancake fashion, one upon the other. These conical grids, which contain the new energy-producing material, consist of a series of concentric rings connected by radial spokes. The growth of these rings is controlled so that each increases in

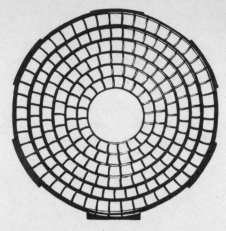

The circular structure of the positive grid has been designed so that, as growth occurs, the space between the hoops remains constant. Thus, contact with the lead-dioxide paste is always maintained, and the battery's electrical capacity increases with age as corrosion produces additional lead-dioxide material.

diameter at exactly the same rate (from corrosion), keeping the distance between the rings constant. Since the distance between the rings remains constant, the rings don't separate from the energy-producing paste. Thus, the battery's original capacity— that derived from the paste—is retained. As time goes on, however, some corrosion occurs, thereby effectively increasing the amount of paste. . . . Eventually the battery will fail, but only after a lifetime of what has been conservatively estimated to be thirty years or more."

Although presently planned to serve only as a standby in telephone plants, the new battery could provide rugged, long-lasting power for many other uses—including cars and boats, and even pacemakers.

Large-Scale Fuel Cells

Fuel cells are clean, quiet and highly efficient. And large-scale fuel cells will provide power for a household, a factory or even a whole community.

Fuel cells aren't new. The first one was demonstrated more than a hundred years ago. Until the space program, though, fuel cells weren't used as practical real-world equipment. Modern fuel cells developed from the need for lightweight power sources in space vehicles. On any extended mission, batteries are much too heavy.

The fuel cells for the Apollo program combine hydrogen and oxygen to generate electricity. More sophisticated versions, now being proved in extended operation, are able to use natural or artificial gas. Instead of pure oxygen, they use ordinary air (which is rich in oxygen). The modern fuel cell is a quiet, nonpolluting generating plant in which fuel is combined with atmospheric oxygen to produce electricity. The waste product is water and (if gas is used as a fuel instead of hydrogen) carbon dioxide. The output of a fuel cell is direct current, easily converted to conventional household alternating current by a solid-state inverter which has no moving parts.

Fuel cells are as efficient as large generating plants, those with capacities of 100,000 kilowatts or more. They are from two to four times more efficient than smaller plants. More important, perhaps, a fuel cell can be operated at a fraction of its maximum output capability without much loss in efficiency, which is not the case for conventional generating systems.

A group of companies have joined Pratt and Whitney, who developed the Apollo fuel cells, to create a major program for the development of large-scale units. Maintenance-free installations have already been successfully demonstrated. Connected to public-utility gas mains, which supply household gas to kitchen stoves, they have provided all of the electric power used at the test sites. Work goes forward on a 25,000 kilowatt fuel cell to meet the power requirements of a moderate-size community.

According to Pratt and Whitney, the fuel cell has "excellent

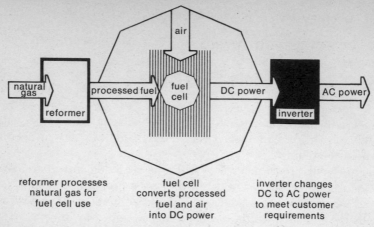

reformer processes
natural gas for
fuel cell use

fuel cell
converts processed
fuel and air
into DC power

inverter changes
DC to AC power
to meet customer
requirements

Elements of the fuel-cell power plant.

efficiency over the full range of electrical loads, delivers more electricity per cubic foot of natural gas than any present system." In field test units, "operation is fully automatic, safe, efficient, clean and quiet."

The fuel cell, using artificial gas produced by coal gasification, looks like a good medium-term solution to the problem of efficient nonpolluting power generation. The long-term solution may be a combination of solar-powered hydrogen plants (see page 80) and fuel cells.

Power system efficiencies.

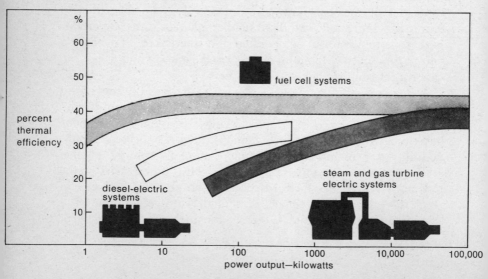

Power from Garbage

Efficient burning of garbage could supply the energy equivalent of 400 million barrels of oil each year—almost 10 percent of present oil production—in the United States.

Annual production of household waste—garbage—in the United States is something over 300 million tons. Much of this is used as landfill, some is thrown into the ocean, and the rest is casually discarded on local garbage dumps.

An efficient garbage incinerator can recover the energy equivalent of 60 gallons of fuel oil for each ton of household waste it processes. In addition, it can reclaim most of the discarded metal. What's left is a sterile residue—ash—that can be compacted and used for road building or nonpolluting landfill. Effective scrubbers clean the gas that's released and prevent atmospheric pollution.

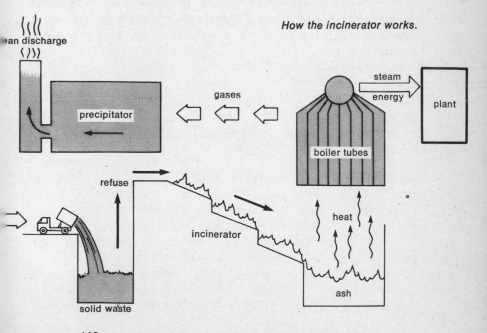

How the incinerator works.

A plant now under construction at Lynn, Massachusetts, will handle the household waste from sixteen nearby communities: about 1200 tons per day. The garbage will move down a stairlike set of grates, being shaken as it goes to ensure complete combustion. The hot gases provide heat to a steam boiler and are then released after scrubbing. The steam will be piped to a nearby power-generating plant, which would otherwise have to burn some 78,000 gallons of fuel oil every day.

The new incinerator is privately financed as a profit-making venture. Sale of the steam will more than cover the cost of operation. There are already sixty plants in Europe and Japan that produce clean energy by burning garbage.

Wheelabrator-Frye, the company that is building the new plant, estimates, "A capital outlay of some $11 billion would be required to process the currently collected domestic refuse," but the recovered energy would be the equivalent of some "6 percent of the entire U.S. oil production or about 270 million barrels a year."

A fine "shotgun wedding" of demand (for more energy) to surplus (of household waste). More of these marriages (and perhaps more divorces) will be features of our society—courtesy of technological innovation.

Improved Coal Gasification

New techniques yield clean high-energy gas from even low-grade coal.

Normal gas is a convenient fuel: it's easy to store and to deliver, it burns cleanly, and it leaves almost no polluting residue. Lately, though, the supply of natural gas hasn't kept pace with the growing demands of households and industry.

Gas can be made from coal. The process is well known—coal gas was used for street lighting early in the nineteenth century—but it worked efficiently only with high-grade coal. If the coal

COAL GASIFICATION TECHNOLOGY

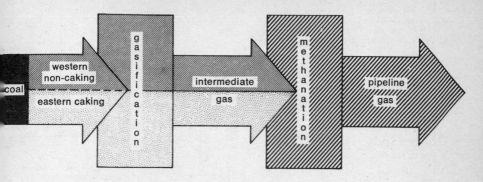

commercial

Steps in coal gasification. Eastern coals are caking and western coals are not. Methanation is the process that will convert intermediate gas into the equivalent of natural gas. This is one of the stages still to be demonstrated on a commercial scale.

contains sulfur it appears in the gas, which then generates pollutants when burned.

Low-grade coal "cakes" and interferes with its smooth flow through a gasification plant. However, a new technique developed at General Electric adds inert material to the coal. This mixture doesn't cake, even with low-grade coal. It does complicate the gasification process, though. Premixing is a required extra processing step, and the added material increases the tonnage of raw material that must be handled.

High-sulfur coal yields sulfur compounds along with the desired gas. A General Electric process uses semipermeable membranes to clean up the recovered gas. These membranes are well understood—they're used in drug manufacture, in artificial kidney machines and in uranium enrichment—but a high-volume filter of semipermeable membranes takes up quite a lot of space.

A new approach to the gasification problem carries out the reaction in a pool of molten iron. Sulfur dissolves in the iron and ends up as slag floating on the surface of the pool. The recovered gas is then sulfur-free. Low-grade coal produces more slag than

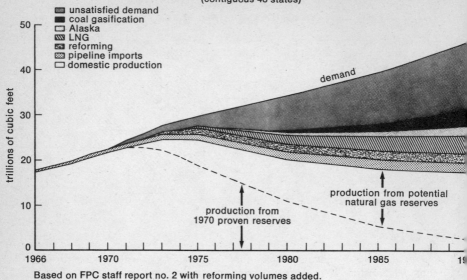

UNITED STATES GAS SUPPLY—DEMAND BALANCE
(contiguous 48 states)

The demand for gas. (LNG is liquefied natural gas.)

high-grade coal, but not enough to interfere with continuous-flow processing.

Coal is particularly abundant in the United States, and with new gasification techniques coal gas may take the place of oil, not only as an energy source but as the raw material for synthetic oil, lubricants and petrochemicals. Together, the developments point the way toward plants that can operate efficiently to produce clean gas at an acceptable cost. Underground gasification, while the coal is still in the mine, is also a possibility.

George Bolton, an engineer with Columbia Gas System, says, "Coal gasification will become commercially significant around 1985 and will have a major impact on the man in the street. It converts our most abundant domestic fossil fuel (coal) into a cheap convenient fuel (natural gas) that's cheap to transport and it's likely to be the 1990 solution to the energy supply crisis now under way."

"Coal gasification," according to Dr. Arthur Bueche of GE, "is one of the greatest challenges now confronting American technology."

The unsettling threat to our world position that importing more and more oil represents. The urgent requirement to use our precious natural gas supply for the best possible purposes. The intense demands for cleaner fuels. The common sense to utilize fully one of the nation's great industrial resources—our invaluable network of gas pipelines. All of these factors underscore why coal gasification is a crucial source of future energy.

Pollution-Free Energy from Offshore Winds

For centuries windmills have been used to grind grain and pump water. During World War II the Germans actually used windmills to supplement the energy of their dwindling coal and petroleum supplies. In recent decades, several nations have seriously considered harnessing wind power to generate electricity on a large scale. Now more will turn their thoughts to it as they face the reality of an energy crisis.

Professor William E. Heronemus, a civil engineer at the University of Massachusetts, and others believe the time has come to take a second look at giant electricity-producing windmills as a possible energy source to supplement oil, coal and gas. Professor Heronemus envisions windmills of every size and description. Some would generate electricity directly. Others would produce hydrogen gas electrolytically, which could be stored or piped like natural gas and then reconverted to electricity by fuel cells. There could be windmills for individual houses; small-scale windmills are already available commercially in France (called the Aerowatt) and in Australia (called the Dunlite). Acres of large units would supply most of the electricity needed to power a town. And, most ambitiously, there could be tremendous offshore arrays of windmills to take advantage of the strong, reliable ocean winds.

Professor Heronemus has drawn up a tentative plan for a wind-power system located off the northeast coast of the United States.

Thousands of windmills would float like huge buoys in the coastal waters; larger windmills would be anchored to the ocean floor. A complete system could generate an estimated 49 billion kilowatt-hours per year of electricity, and there would be no air, water or thermal pollution. As a by-product of electrolysis, the windmills would deliver 5 billion gallons of pure drinking water and 35.6 billion pounds of pure gaseous oxygen—at no extra cost.

The major drawback of wind-produced electricity has always been the high construction costs. But Professor Heronemus believes that the cost of conventional power per kilowatt-hour has

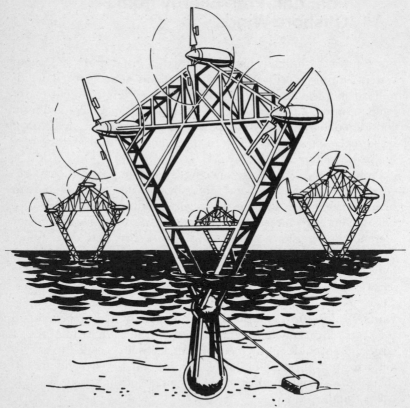

Windmill buoys could harness the prevailing westerlies and generate billions of kilowatt-hours of electricity.

This top-of-the-world view indicates the prevailing winds over the oceans in the months of January and February. The width of the arrow shows the strength of the wind, the length of the arrow its steadiness. Professor Heronemus says, "The imaginative viewer will immediately center his eyes over the Flemish Cap and wonder how we might create wind-stations riding on icebergs!"

risen now to a level where windmills could compete with nuclear and oil power plants. After an initial investment of 43 million dollars, he says the northeastern windmills could begin producing revenue. The total production and transmission cost per kilowatt-hour he estimates at 17.5 mills, which compares favorably with the current costs of nuclear-produced electricity—20 mills per kilowatt-hour.

So-called breeder reactors might bring down the price of nuclear energy, but Professor Heronemus believes thermal pollution will be an increasing problem as more nuclear power plants are constructed; it takes countless gallons of cooling water to run

119

an atomic installation. A balance of nuclear, solar, geothermal, tidal, wind and fossil energy production, he asserts, might avoid the environmental dangers inherent in relying too heavily on any one resource.

In Professor Heronemus's words, "Those who insist that there is only one way toward solution of our energy problems—the route of very large breeder reactors or even larger fusion reactors —should at least stop and pay some attention to the possibility that they have long since entered that economic purgatory called the region of diminishing return. And while they are stopping to think, they will be well advised to remain carefully concealed behind their radiation shielding, or their gray matter may change color."

Professor Heronemus also believes that Alaska has a valuable, untapped resource—in addition to its oil fields: "There is also a vast and powerful wind field along the Aleutian chain and the south coast of Alaska. Those winds are strong enough to bring out an energy product to the lower forty-eight states without spoiling the economics."

Wind power is a by-product of solar power. By linking the two— mounting a windmill on the roof of a solar home (see Solar House, page 84)—we might make households capable of producing almost their entire energy needs. Stormy weather would obscure the sun, but the winds could offer enough energy to get by on. A home windmill and storage battery (see page 117) could provide electricity for about 50 mills per kilowatt-hour. By the 1980s this cost and system might also be competitive with fossil fuel electricity. The giant windmills at sea would then supply energy for industry.

Air Reservoirs

Large amounts of energy can be stored by pumping compressed air into underground airtight caverns.

A power distribution system, to be useful, must meet the

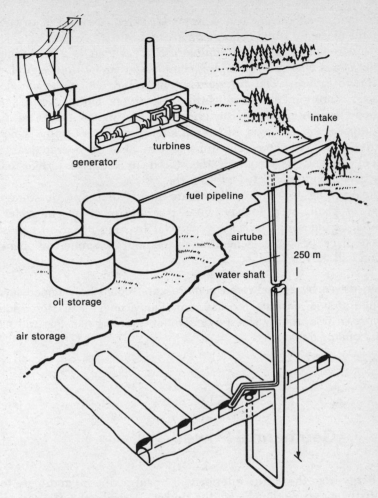

Complete air storage plant.

demands imposed on it. Either local generating plants deliver power at the level demanded by the consumer, or power must be brought in from outside to meet peak demands. Those systems of the future that depend on solar energy have the same problem. Sunlight is available only in the daytime, and any after-dark

121

demand is effectively a peak demand. What's needed is an economical way of storing energy on a large scale.

One scheme, already in limited use in Sweden, is a pilot plant that stores energy by pumping compressed air into underground storage caverns. The caverns contain water, which the air elevates, storing its energy much like a reservoir. During periods of excess capacity a generator, operating as a motor, drives an air compressor. The stored air is used later to power a turbine which drives the generator. The turbine can also be operated as a conventional gas turbine if the stored air supply is exhausted, which provides a safety factor for the system.

According to the Swedish State Power Board, "Air storage power plants seem to have good possibilities of becoming features in the supply of power. Special blasting of caverns must take place for storage generation of ten hours. Commercial operation will start in 1979."

Air, driven by sun-powered compressors, could be pumped into underground caverns for use on cloudy days. . . . More and more, hybrid energy storage-generation systems like this will fill our energy demands.

Geothermal Power

Energy from the earth's interior will be tapped more and more to satisfy our expanding need for power. Already the Geysers, a geothermal power station 80 miles north of San Francisco, is producing enough electrical energy to supply about 10 percent of the growth in power needs of the surrounding areas.

The Geysers is the world's largest geothermal plant. The installation draws upon high-pressure steam escaping near an extinct volcano and uses it to spin turbine generators. The first turbine generator was built at the Geysers in 1960, and expansion has continued steadily. An innovation is the recycling of condensed water to cool the spent steam. The conventional cooling method is to borrow cold water from a nearby stream and return warm water, sometimes endangering aquatic life.

Plans for other geothermal sites are beginning to multiply. While present technology uses mostly dry steam sources, scientists are working up proposals to utilize sites producing hot water, which are far more common. A plant is already operating on such a site in the Soviet Union.

Ultimately, planners hope to tap the immense heat of the earth's molten core. Heated rock relatively near the surface offers a potent source of energy, but the question is how to harness it. Experts now envision two approaches. One is to blast away land above a heat source, using nuclear explosives; water would then be circulated past the heated rock. An alternative plan calls for injecting water into cracks over heat sources, with deep wells pumping out the heated water. Because many heat sources are within five miles of the earth's surface, some researchers are confident that energy from the earth's interior is within reach.

Geothermal power, it should be pointed out, has one major advantage over fossil fuel and natural gas generators. The steam comes ready-made; there is nothing to burn. Even so, environmental precautions are called for. Trace amounts of ammonia and hydrogen sulfide must be cleaned from the steam before it is used.

The use of naturally produced steam to drive electric generators dates from the turn of the century at Larderello, Italy, south of Florence. With its steaming, boiling pools, Larderello was long considered an unwholesome place, and some say its fuming waters inspired Dante's vision of hell. Until the Geysers overtook it, Larderello was the world's largest geothermal power plant.

About the time of the California gold rush, explorer-surveyor William Elliott was tracking a wounded bear when he stumbled onto a canyon erupting with steam vents. Terrified, he too believed he had discovered the gates of hell. The area, now known as the Geysers, attracted interest among travelers, but until recently, it was little more than a curiosity.

"Geothermal power is not likely to replace either fossil fuels or nuclear fission as major sources of electricity," Allen Ham-

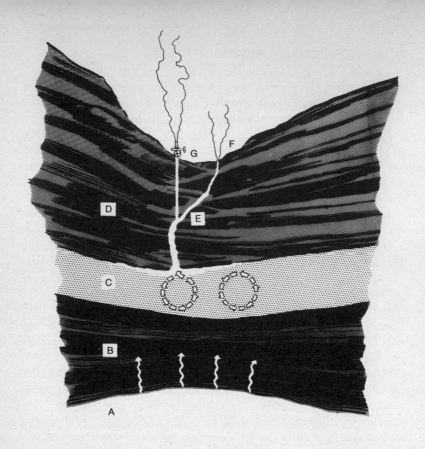

A geothermal field. (A) Magma or molten mass, still in the process of cooling. (B) Solid rock conducts heat upward. (C) Porous rock contains water that is boiled by heat from below. (D) Solid rock prevents steam from escaping. (E) Fissure allows steam to escape. (F) Geyser, fumarole, hot spring. (G) Well taps steam in fissure.

mond writes in *Science*, "at least in the near future. But conservative estimates are that 100,000 megawatts of generating capacity, a not inconsiderable resource, could with vigorous efforts be developed by the end of the century."

Geothermal steam is *not* the answer to man's energy needs, nor is it free of pollution.

But geothermal plants exist in New Zealand, Italy, Japan, Russia, Mexico, Iceland and the United States. Geothermal energy—and even volcanoes—will supply a growing portion of our future power.

Light Conveys Power

A beam of visible light may carry electric power to a remote site.

If laser beams of sufficient power are projected over large distances, they can then be converted directly into electric power. This tranfers electric power to remote receivers, such as space probes and mountaintop installations. The technology for such laser beams is derived from the United States space program.

Electromagnetic radiation impinging upon a laser is changed from a band of many frequencies into highly amplified radiation consisting of only one or two frequencies. Laser beams contain coherent or synchronized waves. Locked together, such waves don't spread out as much as normal light; hence they carry a lot of energy. An experimental apparatus developed by the United States National Aeronautics and Space Administration (NASA) verifies the conversion of laser energy directly into electrical energy.

Here's how it works. Laser radiation, directed into a laser plasmadynamic converter (LPDC), is responsible for the actual conversion to electric power. The LPDC is made up of two sections (see diagram). The upper section is lined with the metal molybdenum and the lower section contains a reservoir of cesium. Cesium carries the most positive electric charge of all the elements. The two sections are electrically insulated from each other, and serve as the opposite electrodes of an electric power generator.

Positively charged cesium molecules (or ions) are the source of electric current in an LPDC. After the laser energy passes through the condensing lens and the window in the upper section, it hits the surface of the cesium, which is liquid at room temperature. The laser energy strikes the cesium obliquely, so that no energy is reflected back along the incoming beam. Since the impinging energy is very dense, it vaporizes and then electrically charges some of the cesium. Like a pot of boiling water, when the density of resulting cesium gas becomes sufficiently large, it absorbs all incoming energy and becomes almost com-

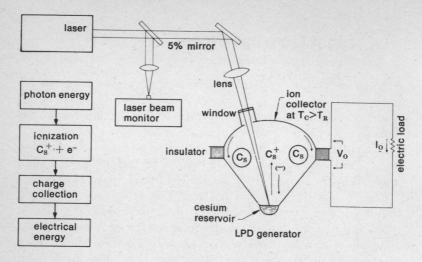

Conversion of laser beam energy into electric power (see page 103).

pletely vaporized and charged. The charged atoms flow upward to the metal collector in the upper section, and power can be extracted by an electric load attached to the LPDC electrodes.

The output of the electric current depends on the size of the LPDC and on the intensity of the laser beam. NASA says such a device "has a theoretical efficiency of 40 percent."

Suppose a distant spacecraft or moon colony were to run out of energy. (It can happen.)

With this system we could aim a laser beam from earth and transmit enough energy to help or save its inhabitants.

Hidden Energy

They are invisible. At the size of a tennis ball, they're as heavy as our planet Earth. They may make up half of the universe. And someday they will beam power back to us from outer space. What are they?

Black holes in the universe.

Astrophysicists think that stars exist in many species—like the fauna of the animal kingdom, the flora of jungles or forests, or the races of mankind. And they also change and evolve from one stage to another. They are born and they die. Red giants, white dwarfs, x-ray sources, BOIb stars, binaries, OB supergiants, neutron stars, pulsars. These are only a few of their names.

Astrophysicists also believe that after stars consume their nuclear fuel, gravitational forces tightly pull their burned-out remnants together into a superdense object. This process is called gravitational collapse. And the object may be a black hole. Its nuclear constituents—protons and neutrons—are so tightly compressed the compact mass prevents light from leaving its surface. So they are invisible. Space near them is "warped" à la Einstein's relativity theories. A nearby object falling into a black hole is never heard from again.

These properties make it difficult—almost impossible—to detect them by normal means. And so black holes are a controversy among specialists, though more and more indirect evidence seems to pile up for their existence. "I was uncertain that the discovery of a black hole was sufficiently well established," says astronomer Dr. Tom Bolton of the David Dunlop Observatory in Ontario. "Recent events have removed my last doubts."

Dr. Lowell Wood and colleagues at Livermore Laboratories think it may be possible to tap black holes for useful power. Suppose a tiny black hole—a "holelet"—were found in earth orbit. A satellite station power plant sent up could track it from a safe distance. Employing the same principles for terrestrial fusion power—forcing hydrogen atoms together to release energy—it would shoot fusion fuel at the hole. The enormous gravitational force would squeeze the fuel together and release vast amounts of energy, something scientists have not yet accomplished on earth. The energy, radiating away from the hole, could be captured by the power-plant satellite, reflected to earth, or converted to a form suitable for reflection to earth (see page 77).

There's no such thing as a free lunch. And it would be an expensive feat of planetary engineering to pull this one off. But the payoffs might exceed the immense costs.

Black holes may also tell us something about the future of the universe. Dr. John A. Wheeler of Princeton sees no evidence from relativity that a star will eventually emerge from the black hole. "Nor is there any indication that the matter will emerge somewhere else in space. But may it emerge somewhere in another universe?" Perhaps a black hole—the collapse of a star—is an early warning of a black *universe*. The gravitational collapse of the entire universe. The ultimate future?

3
Foods
and
Crops

Quick-Ripening Produce

High-yield crops and improved fertilizers have created the Green Revolution. Food production, by keeping pace with the population explosion, may forestall the famines some doomsayers have predicted. But if a worldwide food shortage is to be prevented and not merely postponed, agricultural researchers must continue to find new ways to make plants, and the land itself, more productive.

One promising area of investigation is "plant regulators"—chemicals that are found naturally in plants and control all phases of their growth and development. Scientists are attempting to isolate the regulators that influence germination, root and shoot growth, flowering and fruiting.

Ethrel, a nontoxic chemical produced by Amchem Products, is a regulator that helps farmers control the ripening of their crops. Applied by spraying, Ethrel liberates a plant hormone (ethylene), which is the natural ripening agent. In practical terms, this means that farmers can apply Ethrel as their fruits and vegetables approach maturity and precisely schedule their harvests. Some produce, tomatoes for instance, can be picked as much as two weeks ahead of normal ripening. The regulator also makes cherries, apples, walnuts, grapes, melons, berries, citrus fruit and other crops easier to pick; harvesting is speeded up and there is less risk of bruising or tearing the fruit.

Hothouse farming has put tomatoes and other seasonal vegetables on dinner tables all year around. Many greenhouse crops require artificial lighting to supplement the brief winter daylight, and until recently a combination of white fluorescent lamps and incandescent bulbs was recognized as the best source of imitation sunshine. However, plants don't need light from all portions of the spectrum, so much of the light and electricity was going to waste.

To make indoor farming more efficient, Westinghouse and

Gloxinias grown under Agro-Lite (B) and those grown under best conventional light source (A).

North Carolina State University worked together to develop Agro-Lite fluorescent lamps. The tubes give off an eerie purple-red glow, a mixture of the wavelengths necessary for optimum plant growth. Under Agro-Lite, plants bloom earlier and fruit better: the U.S. Department of Agriculture research center in Beltsville, Maryland, reports that lettuce and tomatoes have shown a 50 percent increase in growth.

The work of Israel Zelitch of the Connecticut Agricultural Experiment Station is in a more theoretical stage. He hopes eventually to be able to increase plant productivity by slowing the rate at which they breathe. Plants take in carbon dioxide, and photosynthesis converts much of it into food; the rest is "exhaled." Respiration can't be entirely eliminated because it's vital for many plant processes. But Dr. Zelitch has noticed that, in some plants, fixed carbon dioxide (CO_2 that is already partially converted to food) breaks down during periods of especially bright sunlight and is exhaled into the air. This, he believes, is wasteful.

"We are just beginning to find compounds that inhibit the [wasteful] reaction," says Dr. Zelitch. Other scientists at the agricultural station are selecting and breeding individual plants that exhale slowly, hoping to produce new varieties of food crops that can "hold their breath" longer. The outcome may be bigger, faster-growing fruits and vegetables.

By artificial selection, agricultural scientists are creating higher-yield food crops. Just imagine putting these three developments to work on the same tomato plant. New hybrids that use carbon dioxide more efficiently might be expected to yield 25 percent bigger tomatoes. Lighting could increase growth rate by 50 percent. Ripening regulators would permit harvesting up to two weeks earlier to make room for a new crop. All these effects may not be additive, but one thing is for sure—the Green Revolution is growing ever more verdant.

 ## Making Crops Fertile Year-Round

Dr. Robert J. Schramm, Jr., associate professor of ornamental horticulture at the University of Connecticut, has developed a method for improving plant growth and quality of stock over shorter periods of time than are standard at the present. With some species, plants achieved three years of normal growth in just two seasons and improved their leaf and flower color and density considerably.

Dr. Schramm's year-round fertility program has two basic features:

1. The buildup of all plant nutrients in the soil to optimum levels based on soil analysis. These levels are below the toxic level, but high enough to overcome what is known as "the law of the minimum"—the law that the low level of just one nutrient in the soil can keep a plant from reaching its maximum potential. ("A chain is no stronger than its weakest link.")
2. The year-round maintenance of these optimum levels through regular soil sampling and periodic application of the required nutrients, especially nitrogen, phosphorus and potassium.

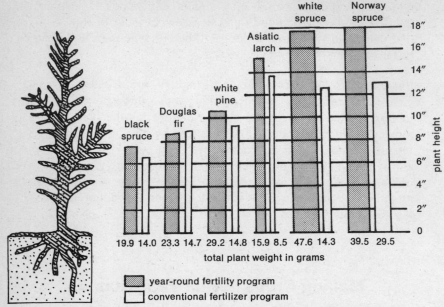

Growth of three-year-old forest tree seedlings under year-round and conventional fertilizer programs.

In conventional programs, fertilizer is applied during a plant's active growing period only, in the spring and summer. But even though the tops of plants are dormant in the late fall and winter, the roots continue to grow, taking up nutrients and moisture from the soil. These elements are distributed through the plant: when spring comes, plants fertilized year-round grow better and are healthier than plants fertilized only in spring and summer.

Weeds, Trees, and Turf, a leading magazine in the ornamental horticulture field, notes wryly: "One small problem that has been observed is the increase in the number of weeds in the nursery. Dr. Schramm's fertility concept really makes everything grow. Growers must plan to take care of this problem when they decide to adopt the year-round fertility concept."

A year-round fertility program could be used to great advantage in our national forests, especially as a means of speeding up the replacement of foliage, trees and other plants destroyed by fire or disease. Not only is wood for paper and fuel renewed, but the ecological balance is restored.

A year-round fertility program would be beneficial in any land-reclamation program in which trees or other plants are used.

Dr. Schramm's findings also suggest that future plants may be increasingly resistant to disease, insects and air pollution. Food plants will benefit from year-round fertilization, eventually.

Sugarcane Ripener

Worldwide demand for sugar will increase by 25 percent over the next ten years. Welcome: a chemical, called Polaris, increases the yield of raw sugar by up to 25 percent.

Sugarcane plants contain a variety of natural sugars from which commercial sugars are derived. While a cane plant is growing, it manufactures sugars it uses as its own energy source. When the plant stops growing, it begins to stockpile sugar in its

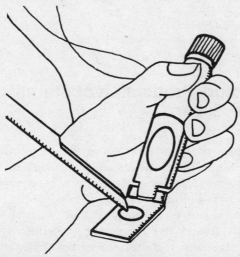

Sugar bends light. This device, a hand refractometer, indicates sugarcane maturity by the amount of bending.

stalk. Sugar content is at its height during this period, making it the best time to harvest. But if the weather changes and rainfall occurs, the cane will begin to grow again and use up its sugar reserves.

Polaris provides a means to overcome this problem. When the chemical is spread on sugarcane from the air four to thirteen weeks before harvest, the plant matures early. It has a long period when its sugar content is at a peak, giving the planter wide leeway to schedule harvesting. Also, cane treated with Polaris produces more refined sugar than a comparable amount of untreated cane. The sugar processed from the treated cane has fewer impurities and a larger proportion is usable.

According to Monsanto, "Polaris will be the first of a family of plant-growth regulators . . . it is within reason to believe that other plant-growth regulators can be developed for corn, soybeans, cotton, rice and more."

In addition to sweetening your favorite dessert, sugar is human fuel. Some years from now, sugar may replace petroleum, providing the raw material for detergents, solvents, plastics and paints. Gasoline is so expensive, alcohol from sugar may even fuel automobiles.

Factory Production of Starch and Sugar

Starches and sugar are the main energy foods used by the human body. Farmers provide them for us by growing corn, rice, potatoes and sugarcane. However, it may soon be possible to convert cellulose to starch and sugar in "factories."

The proposed system for making basic energy foods in factories is built around the processing of cellulose by enzymes. Enzymes are the "supercatalysts" used by plants and animals to speed up chemical reactions in their life cycles by millions of times. Here's how the system works:

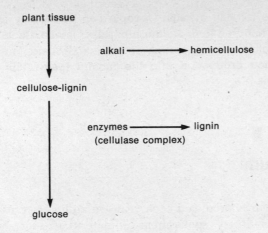

Enzymes convert plant tissue to glucose.

The source of the cellulose is sugarcane waste. The enzymes are obtained from common fungi (*Trichoderma viride*) and green plants grown in huge volumes for the purpose. After the sugarcane waste is chopped and milled, it's treated with alkalis to loosen up the structure sufficiently to allow attack by the enzymes. The alkalis also dissolve impurities contained in the raw material, like hemicellulose and lignin.

The pretreated material is then sent to a reactor along with the enzymes. After water-assisted decomposition (hydrolysis) in the reactor, which produces a 10 to 15 percent sugar (glucose) solution, the contents are filtered. The glucose passes out, and the enzymes and unused cellulose are retained for recycling and reuse.

An additional three-step process is necessary for the conversion of glucose to starch. Two enzymes are used to add a phosphate to the glucose, and in the third step this phosphorylated glucose is transformed to starch.

Spokesmen for the National Aeronautics and Space Administration say that the factory production of starch and sugar from cellulose is "immediately economic and feasible."

Almost all of bread flour is starch. One half of normal daily carbohydrate requirements for half a million people can be met by a plant producing one hundred tons of starch per day; it would cost about four million dollars plus operating and material costs. The trend is to move food production into the factory (page 156), making "factory farms."

 ## Sugar Suds

A vast amount of sugar is produced each year—70 million tons of sucrose alone—and industry spokesmen estimate that sucrose production could be doubled if the demand existed. But sugar faces growing competition on the world menu from artificial sweeteners and new natural sweeteners derived from corn and other cereals. So sugar scientists are looking for new ways to use the cane crop.

With some complicated chemical tinkering, sugar molecules can be converted into detergents. In carefully controlled experiments with dirty towels, sugar suds compared favorably with commercial laundry detergents in soil removal and "anti-redeposition performance." In other words, they got the dirt out of the towels and kept it from getting back in. But the discovery that sugar substances are more readily biodegradable than many of the active ingredients now used in detergents is the main argument for sugaring the soap.

Already sugar has been used as a cleanser in Cambodia: The famous temples at Angkor, having grown somewhat dingy over the centuries, needed a thorough yet delicate cleaning. A product containing crystallized sucrose was selected for the job. Sucrose absorbed the strong mineral acids on the buildings, simultaneously cleaning and hardening the limestone.

Scientists have also experimented with pouring molasses on troubled waters. When the shipwreck of the *Torrey Canyon* fouled the coast of Brittany with a gigantic oil slick, there was fear that nondegradable petroleum wastes would accumulate on the ocean floor, upsetting the ecosystem for years to come. Molasses and phosphoric acid were spread on the area, and as they settled to the bottom they mixed with the oily mess. As hoped, the resulting goo proved a rich medium for microorganisms, which soon broke down most of the heavy petroleum products.

Molasses may also become a regular additive in animal feed. As every dieter knows, eating sugar will put on the pounds, and that's exactly what a farmer wants his livestock to do. Piglets in particular have a sweet tooth. Like chocolate in milk, up to 10 percent molasses in feed encourages piglets to eat a lot of what is good for them.

Yeast also likes sweets. Diluted molasses or the waste waters of sugar refineries could feed a bumper crop of high-protein yeast. The yeast could be dried and used to supplement our diets or those of undernourished populations. At least 60 million tons of high-quality protein per year will be needed to adequately feed the world in the year 2000—about two and a half times the current production level.

Beyond these uses, sugar is also finding its way into a wide variety of consumer products, including paints and varnishes, textiles, plastics, pesticides, herbicides and cosmetics.

Professor Leslie Hough, head of the chemistry department at Queen Elizabeth College, London, believes, "A considerable quantity of sugar could be used (in these many ways) thereby improving the economy in underdeveloped countries by high production of sugar and the creation of new industries based on sucrose chemicals."

The uses for such natural products as peanuts, soybeans and sugar seem to be nearly limitless. Someday the sugar industry may distill molasses into alcohol to fuel internal combustion engines and replace gasoline.

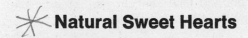 **Natural Sweet Hearts**

Water tastes sweet after eating an artichoke appetizer. The extract from one quarter of an artichoke heart has the sweetening power of two teaspoons of sucrose. The effect lasts a full four minutes.

Artichokes don't sweeten like sugar or saccharine. What the artichoke does is temporarily alter the chemical environment of the tongue—not the substance to be sweetened.

The potassium salts of chlorogenic acid and cynarin, both present in the artichoke, have been tested separately. Each has been found to produce a sweetening effect independently. Twenty-nine percent of the effect can be directly traced to chlorogenic acid. As cynarin doesn't account for all the rest, it appears that these two acids aren't the sole sweetening agents.

The effect doesn't seem to work for everyone. Six male subjects of a mixed test group of 40 didn't notice any sweetening effect on their water. The reason for this insensitivity, though possibly genetic, still remains to be established.

Dr. Linda Bartoshuk has graphed the measurement of taste according to subject reactions. Her technique, called "direct magnitude estimation," involves the plotting of the quantity of a substance against the intensity of the taste perceived. Subjects, incidentally, have been found to agree on their estimates of a food's sweetness, sourness, etc. This kind of taste judgment is not, apparently, as subjective as we might think.

"The artichoke, known to man since 700 B.C.," reports *Science,* "was originally popular partly because of the belief that it could be used as a diuretic and as an aphrodisiac. . . . The earliest published report of a taste-modifying property of the artichoke was Blakeslee's account of the 1934 AAAS biologists' dinner. After eating globe artichokes as the salad course, 60 percent of the nearly 250 people present reported that water tasted different—in most cases, it tasted sweet."

Many future protein substitutes—like those derived from petroleum, algae, fish or peanuts—may have unpleasant tastes. One remedy: Natural sweeteners and flavor enhancers, like artichoke hearts. They are nonnutritive and calorie-free.

Food Additives Just Passing Through

In 1969 the Food and Drug Administration banned the use of cyclamates to sweeten foods, focusing public attention on the potential health hazards of the more than 2500 food additives in use. Now a California company is working on a variety of jumbo additives that will enable processors to preserve, sweeten and color foods safely.

Unfortunately present-day additives are absorbed by the digestive system right along with the nutrients in the foods we eat. The fear is that when ingested in large quantities or over a long period of time, these ordinarily harmless chemicals can have toxic effects on the liver, kidneys and other internal organs. Unusually large doses of cyclamates, for instance, produced cancerous growths in test animals.

One can think of the walls of the intestines as a kind of tubular sieve that permits small, nutritive molecules to pass through and enter the circulatory system while larger molecules (such as cellulose) are excluded. Dr. Alejandro Zaffaroni, of the Dynapol Corporation, hopes to "leash" the small molecules of the additives to much larger polymer molecules, which cannot pass through the intestinal lining. The chemical engineering involved is very complex, but the advantage can be stated quite simply: If the additives cannot be absorbed into the body, they just pass through and are eliminated without doing any harm.

The preservatives and artificial coloring in a jar of artificial fruit are only important on the shelf and on the plate. But what about the artificial sweeteners? Don't they have to be absorbed by the cells of the taste buds for the fruit to taste sweet? The researchers at Dynapol don't think so.

They believe that, contrary to general scientific opinion, the chemical reactions necessary to the perception of taste take place on the surface of the receptor cells rather than inside them. The discovery of a natural polymer called Monellin, which is 300 times sweeter than sugar, lends support to their theory. If a natural polymer can be perceived as sweet, they reason, an artifi-

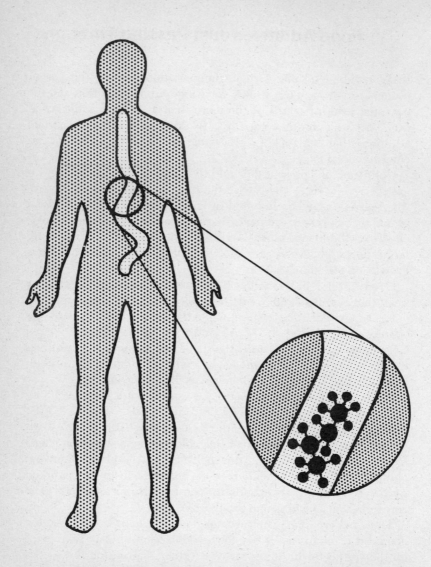

Food additives that are small molecules can be absorbed into the body but polymer-leashed food additives are not absorbable through the lining of the digestive tract.

cial substance attached to a polymer could also function as a sweetener.

Polymer leashing could also have useful applications in cosmetics and pharmaceuticals. Alluring eyeshadow that cannot be absorbed into the skin or eyes is one possibility.

Dr. Zaffaroni says, "Most additives are put into processed foods to do their job before we eat the food—to aid in manufacture, to preserve, to stabilize, to color. Others are there merely to make contact with the taste buds. There is no need for additives to act inside the body beyond that of being detected by the receptor cells of the tongue, in the case of flavorings, sweeteners or thickening agents."

Food additives may play a vital role in ending the food supply crisis in the developing nations of the world. Additives can make alternative sources of protein, such as fish meal, palatable and acceptable to people who have strong cultural biases against particular kinds of food.

Radiation Preserves and Sterilizes Food

Astronauts on Apollo flights 12, 13, 14 and 15 ate irradiated bread. Irradiated potatoes have been cleared for sprout inhibition by eight countries, irradiated onions by four countries, and irradiated wheat for insect disinfestation by three countries. And an optimistic report on the possibilities of using radiation to preserve certain foods has emerged from a study sponsored by the Department of Commerce.

The study, made by the U.S. Army Laboratories at Natick, Massachusetts, stresses that tens of millions of dollars could have been saved in Vietnam if five food items (canned chilled ham, six-way frozen beef, and frozen chicken, pork and bacon) had been processed by irradiation. The savings would have resulted from the reduction in refrigerated storage and transport facilities required and the lower distribution costs for nonperishables—factors that affect local supermarket prices as much as they do overseas Army mess budgets.

Using irradiated meats would cut the number of cases of salmonellosis, botulism and trichinosis, since radiation at the prescribed doses kills the germs that cause these food-carried diseases.

And taste is no problem. Tests at military establishments all over the United States show that irradiated meat, poultry and seafood are generally as acceptable as the same items in fresh or frozen form.

The Food and Drug Administration wants certain proof that irradiated foods remain wholesome and safe for human consumption before it gives the process its final approval. Wholesomeness studies are being conducted by the Army and the Energy Research and Development Administration (formerly the Atomic Energy Commission).

A spokesman for the Department of Commerce describes irradiated foods as offering "a wide variety of advantages as a *supplement* to refrigeration in food preservation."

The preservation of certain foods by irradiation instead of refrigeration could cut their net cost to the consumer, because storage would be built into the food at the factory.

Families might use smaller, and therefore less expensive, refrigerators and freezers. These smaller units would reduce electric bills. Camping and picnicking would be simplified.

Irradiated foods could be helpful in underdeveloped countries with scarce refrigeration facilities.

Deep-Sea Food Storage

Foods (protein, starches and fruit) recovered from a sunken vessel after ten months at a depth of almost one mile turned out to be well preserved.

Scientists at Woods Hole Oceanographic Institute believe that the combination of low temperature and high pressure slows down organic decay. They concluded that the extreme pressure of tons of seawater, in addition to the chill of the water, kept the food fresh. At one mile below the surface, the temperature was 38° F. and the pressure was 150 times the normal pressure at sea level.

Researchers ran tests on the food items that had been recovered from the *Alvin,* which went down southeast of Woods Hole, Massachusetts, in October, 1968. They found that the rate of decay was 10 to 100 times slower than on the land at the same temperature. At 38° F. on land, the recovered bread decayed further in 6 weeks, the bologna in 4 weeks, and the beef bouillon in 22 days. All the foods had been thoroughly soaked with seawater, which acted as a pickling agent.

The researchers said, "From general appearance, taste, smell . . . these food materials (sandwiches and apples) were strikingly well preserved."

These findings have produced more questions. Scientists are now questioning the use of the oceans for disposal of solid organic wastes. Because of the slow rate of decomposition deep at sea, huge deposits of human wastes could accumulate. The plan to fertilize the sea with man-made wastes would in itself be wasteful. Immense amounts of nutrients might end up trapped in solid form, unable to decompose and return to the life cycle.

Future refrigerators may also be pressurizers. And doctors may preserve human blood and tissue cells at low temperature and high pressure.

Food from Oil

The synthesis of protein—the idea is promising, but it's also complicated and expensive. Another approach to enriching the world diet is further along: British Petroleum is now constructing a plant in Sardinia which will produce 100,000 pounds of "natu-

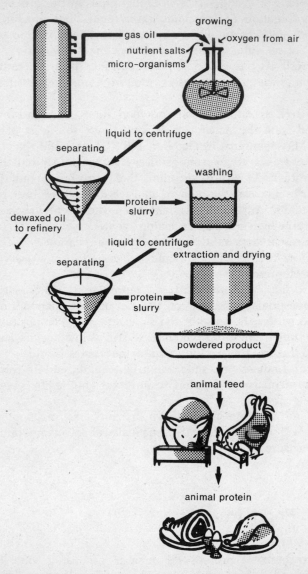

The hydrocarbons in oil become food for yeast in an industrialized farming process developed by British Petroleum. The yeast, in turn, becomes food for animals and soon perhaps people will be dining on yeast, too.

ral" protein each year from a seemingly unpalatable source—oil.

There is, of course, an intermediate step. Animals and people cannot feed on the hydrocarbons in petroleum, but yeast can. A special high-protein yeast, called Toprina, grows and reproduces luxuriantly in a bath of hydrocarbons, water, minerals and salts. All stages of sowing, tending and harvesting take place in the huge vats of sanitary factories, safe from the ravages of droughts and monsoons. When the unorthodox crop is mature, the yeast is separated, concentrated and dried into a fine beige powder.

More conventionally grown yeasts are already in use as supplemental animal feed, and Toprina has recently been approved as a fodder booster in six Common Market countries. Usually it's on a high-class menu—served to animals like chickens and pigs, who seem to find it very tasty. The British Petroleum scientists think high-protein yeast would be wasted on cows, sheep and other multistomached animals who have the valuable ability to convert "poor-quality proteins and even simple nitrogenous compounds to meat and milk" (page 149).

Originally British Petroleum intended Toprina as a supplement to animal foods only, even though it would be more efficient to serve protein directly to people. Researchers felt it would be difficult to convince people to sit down to a yeast dinner. But the limited success of protein concentrates derived from fish (page 154), peanuts (page 152) and soybeans (page 151) has changed their minds. They are now working on ways to further concentrate the protein content of Toprina—up to 90 percent, perhaps—and convert it into flour.

Alfred Champagnat, the founding father of the BP protein project, writes, "Toprina's novelty is that it is the first food—a food of high nutritional value—to be produced industrially using only mineral basic raw materials. The process is not synthesis, it is a biosynthesis—a synthesis carried out by life. . . . Human beings are very conservative in their eating habits, and there are well-authenticated cases of people dying of malnutrition because they would not accept food to which they were unaccustomed, even though this would have saved their lives. We do not, at this stage, know how or to what extent people will accept Toprina as an addition to, or as a substitute for, their more traditional foods."

These fat porkers are eagerly awaiting a dinner including yeast grown in petroleum baths.

Oil to food, a fantastic idea. But the energy crisis has triggered research converting food crops to energy sources. A general trend in the future, already in evidence today, will be interchangeable conversions of different forms of energy to different forms of matter.

Total world protein production runs over 80 million tons annually, against a deficit of nearly 25 million tons. The classic source of protein, livestock, may not be able to supply the enormous quantities necessary for the future. If and when the petroleum shortage is over, we may have a petroleum surplus. The reason is simple: boosted by the shortage, alternate energy sources will free oil-using countries from their heavy dependency on oil. Then the surplus *oil,* converted to protein, may alleviate the shortage of *food.*

 # Protein from Wastes

Many new protein sources are being investigated to forestall a worldwide food crisis. Researchers are working on techniques of changing wastes such as cow manure, garbage, sewage sludge, and old rubber tires into edible protein. Other materials that may find themselves recycled into foods are wood pulp (see page 136), whey, petroleum (see page 145), newspaper, green leaves, and seaweed.

The worldwide protein shortage is more immediate than the energy crisis. Five sixths of the world's population can't afford meat, fish, or dairy products. These people must rely upon plants for protein, but they're not an adequate source. According to the United Nations 25 to 30 percent of all children in developing nations die before their fifth birthday from kwashiorkor, a disease caused by extreme protein deficiency.

The protein shortage has made itself felt in the United States and other affluent nations in rising prices for meat, fish, and dairy products. These price rises only reflect the increase in the cost of soybeans, the main source of protein for animal feed. Scientists declare it's wasteful to feed such valuable food protein to animals because it takes 100 pounds of plant protein to produce 5 pounds of edible meat protein.

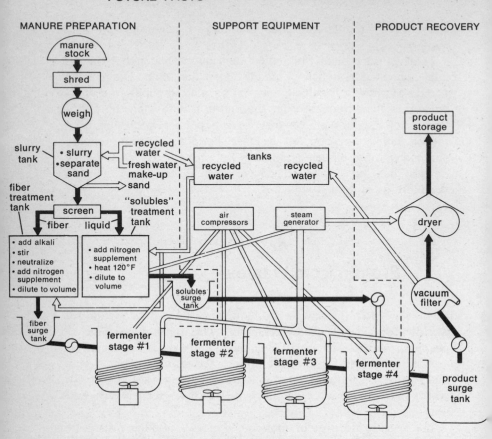

MANURE PREPARATION   SUPPORT EQUIPMENT   PRODUCT RECOVERY

How the nutrient reclamation process works.

At General Electric they're doing something about the problem. They've developed a process in which a heat-loving bacterium eats cellulose and lignin—the main components of cow manure. This occurs at temperatures of 130° F. From the feeding comes a microbial cell mass which is dried into a colorless powder with a protein content up to 60 percent. Chickens, horses, sheep and mice have dined on it, and the results are promising.

The new protein-rich foodstuffs produced from wastes are being developed for animals only. Reports from the Office of

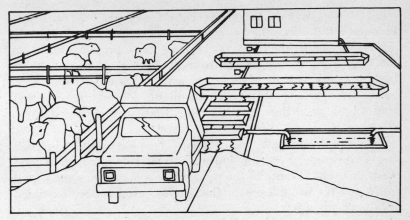

Artist's conception of a feedlot manure recycling system applying the principles developed by GE.

Nutrition of the U.S. Agency of International Development indicate it will be years before these materials can be turned into foods suitable for humans.

Chickens must have a high-protein diet, so unless a substitute for soybeans is found, "our grandchildren may not even know what fried chicken tastes like," according to GE researcher James Shull.

Someday bacteria may spin our household wastes into food for livestock or pets.

Soluble Protein for Liquids

An American manufacturer has developed a soy-based nutritive product. It can be used in powdered citrus- and tomato-flavored breakfast drinks, liquid and frozen concentrated juice drinks,

151

clear desserts, dietary beverages, baby foods, gelatins, beer, carbonated soft drinks, jellies, jams and hard candies.

Soy is currently the most common vegetable protein additive in the United States, but its use in products that contain relatively high amounts of acid, and foods in which opacity is undesirable, has posed special problems. The available soy additives weren't acid-soluble, and they clouded foods that were supposed to be clear.

Those problems have been solved. The new nutritive ingredient, developed by Ralston Purina, can withstand common food acids and retain clarity of the product. It comes in dry and liquid form, and doesn't thicken products when used at recommended levels, usually 2 percent.

At 2 percent, a seven-fluid-ounce bottle of orange soda will supply 20 percent of a young child's recommended daily allowance of protein, or 10 percent of an adult's needs. A four-ounce serving of gelatin will supply a significant amount of protein, in digestible form, to patients on soft or liquid diets.

The protein is bland in flavor. It's not totally flavorless, but the flavor isn't objectionable and is easily masked by flavoring. In another experiment in making protein concentrate palatable, Yoohoo chocolate soda was fortified with soybean protein. The chocolate drink is much more popular with South American Indian children than previous diet innovations.

K. P. Steffens of Ralston Purina says, "This product is presently in the experimental stage."

Our taste buds may suffer at first, but the critical state of the earth's food supply indicates the absolute necessity of exploring and adopting new sources and means of nourishment. Fast.

Peanuts Fortify Foods

Peanut flakes promise to be a versatile, protein-rich food supplement. Low in cholesterol and well balanced with fats and carbohydrates, the flakes may be used to enrich meats, cheese preparations, candy and many other foods. And they don't taste like peanuts.

The product was developed by Dr. J. H. Mitchell, a professor of biochemistry and food science at Clemson University in South Carolina. Assisted by home economist Rosalind Malphrus, he has combined peanut flakes with chicken, turkey and other meats to make inexpensive boneless meat rolls. A mixture of peanut and coconut flakes becomes a nutritious candy when coated with chocolate. Taste testers find the products highly acceptable; many tasters are unable to distinguish peanut preparations from the food they're added to. Peanuts contain 33 percent protein.

Dr. Mitchell originally attempted to prepare a potable peanut milk. He blanched and shelled the goobers, then removed their skins and hearts. Dehydration and grinding resulted in a milklike substance, but once it was sterilized the milk turned to a custard consistency that was too thick to drink.

Thinking of ways to use the custard, Dr. Mitchell came up with the idea for the peanut flake. By adding water to the custard, he forms an emulsion of oil droplets and a suspension of solids. This is preheated to release all flavorful compounds, leaving a bland substance. Heat also inactivates the enzymes, so the flakes can be stored at room temperature for up to six months without spoilage. Finally, the suspension is dried on a double drum. The finished flakes are 30 percent protein and up to 45 percent oil. If all oil is extracted, the protein content reaches 60 percent.

To help people on low-cholesterol diets, Dr. Mitchell states that the peanut flakes may substitute for some high-cholesterol foods. He scrambled eggs with rehydrated flakes, doubling the volume to make a serving of scrambled eggs with half the cholesterol content of an equal serving of eggs without peanut flakes, but protein and energy values were not reduced.

Peanut-flake foods—cheap, storable proteins—will supplement meats and other expensive foods in tomorrow's diet.

Fish Crackers

Crackers can be fortified with fish protein and made to taste good, too. These were the findings of Commerce Department researchers who tested Nabisco-formula crackers supplemented with fish protein concentrate. The crackers got high marks for nutrition, texture, taste and shelf-life.

The fortified crackers were made by replacing 4, 8, 10, 12 and 16 percent of the wheat flour with protein extracted from red hake. A panel of 50 lab workers taste-tested the fishy biscuits.

The nutritive value of crackers containing just 4 percent fish protein was three times that of the unfortified crackers. At 8 percent, the supercrackers were four times more nutritious. And until the crackers were loaded with 16 percent fish protein, the test munchers detected no difference in flavor.

Although they are somewhat darker, the experimental crackers compare favorably with the conventional kind in texture and firmness. Except at the highest concentrate levels and at temperatures over 100° F. there was no problem with spoilage.

"To be effective in providing protein for people," the researchers observe, "protein supplements must be in a form they will accept. Obviously, people eat 'foods' and not 'nutrients'; thus it is important that the nutrients be supplied in foods they enjoy eating. Snacks are popular and provide an excellent vehicle for supplying required nutrients."

Millions of people eat salty crackers as snacks. With protein added, their diet can be enriched.

Future astronauts, campers—and bachelors—can thrive on nutritious salty fish crackers.

Larger Lobsters Sooner

A team of scientists at the Massachusetts Lobster Hatchery on Martha's Vineyard have found that lobsters raised in captivity, in warm seawater, grow up to four times as fast as they do in nature.

A group of lobsters was raised in warm water a few degrees below room temperature. These lobsters ate better and converted their food into energy almost three times faster than their brothers in the wild. They also molted, or shed their shells, more often in the same time period. (A lobster molts when it outgrows its shell.) Lobster eggs in the warm water were ready to hatch 33 percent sooner. When the offspring of very fast-growing lobsters were mated with each other, *their* young tended to be fast growers too.

Scientists studied the offspring of about 300 lobsters raised over a 20-year period at the lobster hatchery. They compared their growth rates with those of another group living in typical seawater.

A lobster is adult (mature sexually) and of legal size—that is, it may be caught and sold for food—when it weighs a pound and measures about 3 inches. The lobster may molt 20 times before it reaches maturity. In the waters off Canada's Prince Edward Island, it takes a lobster 8 *years* to attain legal size; in southern Cape Cod waters, 5½ years. The warm-water lobsters in this study matured in 2 *years*.

"Our initial success in accelerating growth and in mating selected parents suggests that lobster farming may be possible," say the researchers. "Precise experiments to measure actual food conversion with a variety of inexpensive or synthetic diets are needed. The results of these studies indicate that *there may be a lobster farm in the future*."

Trout farming in the west; catfish farming in the south; oyster farming in France. Why not New England lobster farming?

Hurried-up growth for wheat, corn, beef—and now lobsters. Next candidate—people?

Embryo Transplants in Cattle

Scientists are perfecting a technique of embryo transplants in beef cattle, to enable a cow to produce five to six times the normal number of offspring.

Dr. Duane C. Kraemer, of the Southwest Foundation for Research and Education, and James E. Dula, of Livestock Breeders International, Inc., have been working together for several years on embryo transfers in cattle, with very good results.

Although the method itself is not new, its application to commercial purposes is. Kraemer and Dula emphasize that the procedure is still very much in the experimental stage, and will not be commercially feasible for some time.

The technique itself involves superovulation (stepping up the "donor" cow's production of ova), natural or artificial insemination, collection of the embryos from the uterus (during the fourth to sixth day of development), storage of the embryos, synchronization of the recipient cows, and deposit of the embryos into the recipient uterus.

The first calf to be produced by this method was born in 1950. Livestock Breeders International was the first commercial company to produce a calf using embryo transfer, in 1971. Their aim is to increase the number of offspring of especially valuable cows.

Three types of cows are considered eligible for the embryo transfer process: heifers who are cycling regularly but are too young for natural breeding, aged cows who have previously produced valuable offspring but who can have few remaining natural pregnancies, and mature cows who have exceptional genetic value but either cannot conceive or cannot bring the pregnancy to term.

By increasing the number of eggs produced by the donor cow, scientists have been able to collect an average of four embryos from each cow for transfer. The process can be repeated successfully without harming the cow, if there's no buildup of scar tissue. Although there is some risk to the animal involved, Kraemer and Dula reported in 1972 that they had neither lost a donor cow nor found any cases of uterine infection in their research.

In order to realize the benefits of commercial embryo transfer when it becomes practical, management practices on cattle farms must be improved, they add. More effort must be put into the identification and selection of genetically outstanding cows, and they and the recipient cows must be kept in top condition.

According to Dr. Kraemer, "Embryo transfer is not the answer to every cattle producing situation. Due to the complexity and expense of the procedures, embryo transfer is limited in its application to the most valuable animals. We've done nothing original, really. What we have done is put it all together in a commercial package."

An increasing population means more food has to be produced from fewer acres of land. Embryo transplants will increase meat production by "factory farming," helping along natural reproduction.

The Cool-Heat Countertop Range

Engineers at Westinghouse have developed a cool surface range that heats by induction. During cooking the entire surface of the range remains cool—only the pans get hot.

The principle of induction heating is this: When alternating current is passed through a coil, a magnetic field is produced. If a metallic object is held above the coil while the electricity is on, the current will flow into the object. In an object made of a metal having a relatively high resistance to electric current, such as iron or steel, the current will cause the object to heat up.

The new Westinghouse range has four such coils covered by a ceramic countertop. The counter can't be induced to produce heat, but iron and steel pans can.

If by mistake a copper or aluminum pan is used, the range automatically shuts off to prevent damage to the coils.

Because the surface is flat, clean-up on the cool-top range is simplified. Spilled food can't seep in or bake on.

157

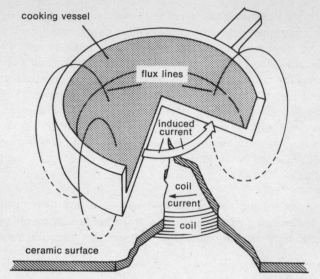

cooking vessel

flux lines

induced current

coil current

coil

ceramic surface

The coil current produces an induced current in the pot.

And the pot got hot—through a towel!

And since each coil is self-contained and employs solid-state circuitry, defective units are easily unplugged, and new ones put in their place.

"In many respects, the induction countertop range is a quantum jump in kitchen appliance technology and user convenience," says the manufacturer. "The solid-state design of its induction heating circuitry constitutes an important advance in circuit design engineering. And the application of the induction heating principle to cooking brings a variety of new conveniences and capabilities to the home environment."

Heat, delivered *efficiently* to food, will use less energy than a conventional gas or electric range. Less energy for cooking means more energy for other uses. Future kitchens may have more labor-saving (and energy-conserving) devices than we can imagine now.

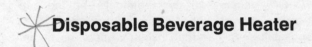

Disposable Beverage Heater

A chemical reaction heats coffee or soup instantly in a disposable cup. The chemical reaction providing the heat is triggered by a handle on the side of the cup.

This little invention is portable. You can hold the cup, which has a cover, in your hand while soup, coffee or food is heating inside it, and you can eat right out of it. (The cup is well insulated, so you don't burn yourself.)

The chemical reaction that heats your food takes place in a space between the inner and outer walls of the cup. The chemicals don't touch the food or you—they only provide the heat.

Underneath the cup, in a space inside the walls, are a solid chemical and a small capsule holding a liquid. When you pull the handle on the outside, the capsule bursts and the two chemicals mix. The resulting reaction produces heat that will boil water for coffee, heat soup, or warm a can of beef stew. When you finish eating, you just throw the cup away!

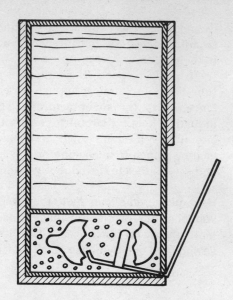

*Handle breaking the capsule
inside cup.*

For picnics, ball games, car trips, space voyages.

Cost is low—only pennies for the chemicals—so the cup is disposable. It seems safe enough. No forest fires likely.

Next: A disposable soda can that instantly cools the contents.

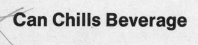

Can Chills Beverage

A self-chilling beverage container cools warm liquids instantly to near-freezing temperatures when the top is flipped.

A normal twelve-ounce aluminum can, containing a tiny "freezing unit," leaves room for eight ounces of beverage. The freezing unit contains a small amount of liquid under pressure, which evaporates when the can is opened. No chemicals touch the drink during the evaporative process, which reduces the drink's temperature 40° F. in 90 seconds. Its taste remains unchanged and, a minute or two after opening, the drink can be consumed directly from the can. The flip-top on this new can remains attached,

160

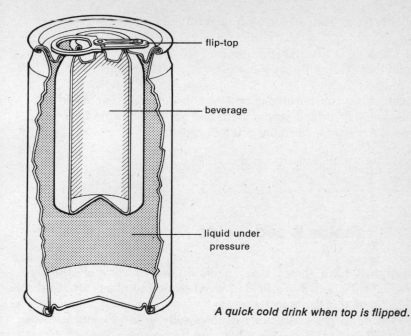

— flip-top

— beverage

— liquid under
pressure

A quick cold drink when top is flipped.

which helps to fight litter and is an aid to recycling. The container may be reclaimed and reused.

Testing has proved that the Chill Can, as named by its inventor, is sturdy and endures normal handling and abuse. Even when forcibly dropped, shaken and exposed to extremes of temperature, it still functions normally.

To produce the Chill Can, existing canning machines with special added attachments can be used to keep the costs low. The price range of the beverages will be 30 to 35 cents per can. This is well within the current cost of ice and cold drinks in portable coolers now used by picnickers.

The new can obviously lends itself to the canning of such beverages as soft drinks, beer and juices. But it can also be applied to premixed cocktails, consomme, canned puddings and other desserts. A special advantage is that the products can be stored in uncooled cabinets; expensive refrigeration won't be needed.

"It will work on practically anything that's canned," says John

R. Wray, Jr., the inventor, a former oil explorer. "Being out in the oil fields, I got so thirsty sometimes I thought I was going to die. I would have paid anything for a cold drink." Now his problem and that of other thirsty folk can be solved at minimum cost.

Instant heat for beverages and now instant cold. Part of a trend toward instant food preparation. And yet at the same time, more people delight in leisurely gourmet cooking.

Fields Weed Fields

Scientists have shown that an ultrahigh-frequency electromagnetic field is lethal to a field of weed seeds and plants after just a brief period of exposure.

Chemical pesticides, almost universally used to control weeds and other farm pests, have been under continuous attack for at least two decades. Although they destroy their targets, they persist in the soil and may harm useful plants, animals, insects and people. Many researchers are looking intensively for pest-control methods that don't require chemicals.

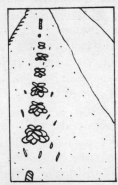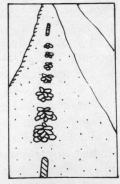

Nonchemical weed control for cantaloupes three weeks after one-day irradiation by UHF waves (increased power of electromagnetic fields, left to right) before planting.

Some years ago a Texas A & M scientist, Dr. M. G. Merkle, was watching a television commercial on the use of microwaves. The idea occurred to him that the microwave principle might provide a powerful weapon against weeds. After extensive laboratory and greenhouse study, he and his associates designed an apparatus incorporating a magnetron tube that produced an ultrahigh-frequency field of 2450 megahertz; a stainless steel radiator was connected to the tube, and from this the field was transferred to the soil.

Experiments were conducted in Florida and Texas under a range of soil and environmental conditions. Treatment of the soil gave good control of weed plants and seeds of a number of different species. Young plants and seeds in soil with a high moisture content were especially susceptible. Now plans are afoot to produce the device (baptized the Zapper) for commercial use.

According to Dr. Frank S. Davis, one of the developers of the Zapper, "The initial area of interest is in vegetable and row crops. As more machines are manufactured, we will move into other areas: aquatics, nurseries, lawns, rights-of-way, orchards."

After weeds and their seeds, nematodes and fungi. Finally, carefully calibrated, electromagnetic fields may be the "death ray" for harmful insects.

Trees from the Air

Light planes or helicopters can plant tree seedlings by air drop. The soil doesn't have to be prepared, and the cost of reforestation comes down like the seedlings.

The usual method of reforestation is to plant seedlings either by hand or with mechanized planting machinery. Seeds, suitably packaged, can be dropped from light airplanes but relatively few survive to become mature trees. A new technique makes it pos-

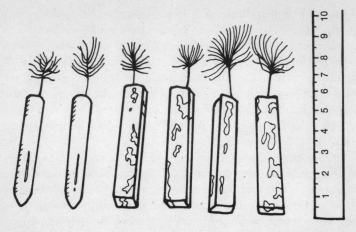

Pine seedlings, eight weeks old, are projectiles in plastic container (left), paper (center) and Japanese paper pots (right).

Direct seeding of trees from the air has helped reforestation in the South.

sible to air-drop well-developed seedlings with a high probability of survival.

One method involves packing each seedling and encasing it in a small bomb-shaped container of ice. Fins ensure that the "bomb" falls properly, digging itself into the ground. As the ice melts, the biodegradable packing expands to fill the bomb hole and the seedling is planted.

The air-drop technique makes it easy to reforest remote areas for the purpose of controlling erosion and maintaining the supply of ground water.

W. F. Mann, Jr., of the U.S. Department of Agriculture, says, "Labor will become more critical in the future, boosting costs even higher on sites that are already economically marginal for planting. Techniques must be perfected to regenerate these difficult sites by natural seeding, by direct seeding, or by planting seedlings from aircraft."

Not only ordinary seedlings but "supertree" seedlings (see next) can be planted from the air so they'll spring up faster and grow taller. With the proper "bombing" technique it should even be possible to plant them in perfect rows!

 ## Supertrees

Genetically superior supertrees have cut the growth cycle for Pacific Northwest timber from 80 years to 40—and further improvements may cut that to 30 years.

Intensive research in tree genetics and reforestation methods conducted by Georgia-Pacific Corporation of Portland, Oregon, has reduced by at least 50 percent the growth time of softwood timber compared with what it was only five years ago.

The secret is superseeds, which the company's foresters use to produce trees in the "super" category. So rapidly are the supertrees growing that in some of the company's plantations the increase in timber already outstrips the annual harvest.

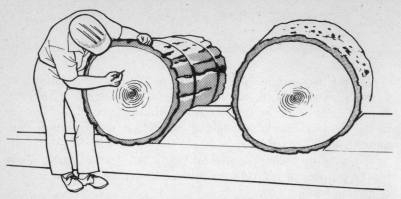

The results of nature's whim and man's managed forestry. Both of these Douglas firs are 30 inches in diameter. But the one at left is 460 years old, the one at right 60 years old. New superseedlings will do considerably better.

The company began its program in 1958. Foresters scoured over 100,000 acres of timberland in search of superior trees. Finally, out of millions of Douglas firs they selected just 15. Taking scions, or branch tips, from these trees, they grafted them to healthy smaller trees in a seed orchard.

Pollen was collected from other choice grafted stock, and the cone buds on the scions were artificially pollinated with hypodermic needles. To prevent pollination from other, less superior trees and to provide research control, the foresters protected the cones with strong paper bags.

Two ounces of seeds—worth more than their weight in gold—were collected the first year and planted in a greenhouse. When defective seedlings appeared, they were eliminated. The process was repeated again and again and methods refined in the foresters' effort to produce trees that would grow faster, have fewer defects, and be more resistant to disease.

"We are a long way down the road," says Vernor Schenck of Georgia-Pacific, "but it takes years to see the results of development of superior tree families. Now we are able to supply nearly all our planting needs in the Southeast with superseedlings."

So far the foresters have concentrated on softwoods—Douglas fir and loblolly pine—but the same techniques can be applied to hardwoods. Most trees of the future will be bigger than those few produced by nature at her best.

4
Transportation

New York to Los Angeles in 21 Minutes by Subway

Researchers at the Rand Corporation envision a "tubecraft" system capable of carrying passengers between New York City and Los Angeles in 21 minutes. The VHST (Very High Speed Transit) vehicles would shoot through airless tunnels deep underground at nearly 14,000 miles per hour.

A tubecraft would look like a streamlined subway car without wheels or a subterranean airplane without wings. According to Dr. Robert M. Salter, Rand's head of physical sciences, the vehicle would ride on, and be driven by, electromagnetic waves, "much

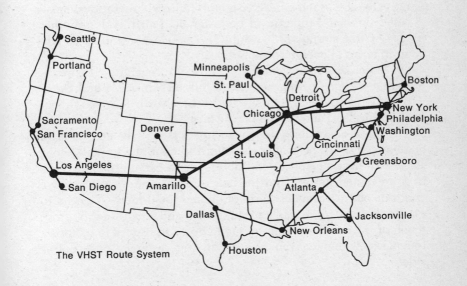

The VHST Route System

Rand Corporation's proposed system of airless tunnels linking major cities.

as a surfboard rides the ocean's waves." Superconducting cables would produce powerful opposing magnetic fields so the 100-passenger craft would float in the middle of the tube, and air would be pumped from the tunnels to reduce friction.

A proposed route would connect New York City with Los Angeles with brief stopovers in Chicago and Amarillo, Texas. Even with these stops, the total transcontinental time would be only 37 minutes. There would also be a network of connecting tunnels to Boston, Denver, San Francisco and other major cities.

Dr. Salter believes a coast-to-coast tunnel could pay for itself in about thirty years. He estimates that the central corridor of the system would cost about $90 billion, although the price could come down with such advances in tunnel building as nuclear or laser drills.

The fare for a transcontinental trip would be kept to a minimum to encourage heavy travel; a ticket might cost as little as $50. The tunnel would service other industries to help defray building and operational costs. It could include pipelines, power lines, laser and microwave communications channels, and a comparatively slow (100-miles-per-hour) railroad freight system.

Not only would tube travel be faster than air travel and other modes of transportation, it would also be cleaner and more efficient in terms of energy consumption.

Dr. Salter speculates about a world with tubecraft: "It is probable that we might even be able to link up American and Euro-Afro-Asian systems by tunnels under the North Sea via Greenland and Iceland and via the Bering Strait. . . .

"Are there compelling reasons for the VHST? The answer is an emphatic yes! We no longer can afford to continue to pollute our skies with heat, chemicals and noise, nor to carve up our wilderness areas and arable land for new surface routes. Nor can we continue our extravagant waste of limited fossil fuels. We need to get the bulk of truck traffic off highways and free these routes of much of the commuter auto traffic in order to restore to motorists the pleasure and convenience of driving through the countryside."

Around the world in three hours by subway? It may not be all that far-fetched. The technology for a tubecraft system is in the offing.

England may someday be linked to France by a tunnel. Magnetically levitated vehicles are being developed in Japan, Germany and the United States (see page 178). A special drill called the Subterrene, which melts through rock, is being developed at Los Alamos (see page 269). Put it all together, add $90 billion, jump on—and you are the commuter of the future.

Moving Sidewalks

Sidewalks move pedestrians between stores, offices, apartments and stations at a cost of one cent per ride.

A passenger conveyor belt may improve getting around in congested urban areas, at airports and bus terminals. At Expo 70 in Japan, one already carried over a million people each day at a speed of 2 mph.

To accelerate passengers safely they step onto a slowly moving (2 mph) belt. This gains speed slowly and smoothly as it moves in a curve until alongside a faster moving belt. Both belts are

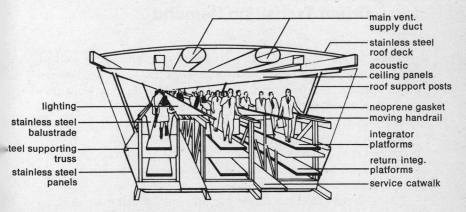

main vent. supply duct
stainless steel roof deck
acoustic ceiling panels
roof support posts
lighting
stainless steel balustrade
steel supporting truss
stainless steel panels
neoprene gasket
moving handrail
integrator platforms
return integ. platforms
service catwalk

When completed in 1976, a new business center in Paris may contain this moving sidewalk, serving up to 19,000 people per hour.

then going 10 mph and are locked together to prevent sliding or separating. Passengers can make an easy transfer to the fast platform. When people want to disembark, the process is reversed.

This system is designed for quick, short-distance (one-quarter to one mile) trips in downtown areas where buses and subways are normally used. Because it's continuous there's no waiting or congestion of people. It's also free of noise and fumes. The platforms may be underground or elevated to afford a view of shops and businesses. They can even "pass through" certain buildings such as bus and train terminals, hotels and department stores.

Dunlop Limited, the British firm whose "Speedaway" system is installed at London's airport, says it "can create a traffic-free pedestrian street or can form part of a deck development with direct access to important buildings. Similar layouts can link new airport complexes, railway stations, large shopping precincts, multistory car parks and large office blocks."

The bottleneck in any public transportation system is the transfer point—the transition from air to ground, from bus to train. Moving sidewalks open the bottlenecks.

Urban Transit on Demand

Personal Rapid Transit (PRT) is intended as an individualized, fully automatic, and inexpensive way to get around. A new concept in public transportation, it's quieter and safer than your own car and more private and convenient than a bus.

Personal Rapid Transit is a research-demonstration project in Morgantown, West Virginia. The driverless vehicles are electrically powered from a third rail along the guideway on which they travel. When the cars are filled to capacity, they carry eight people sitting and thirteen standing.

Two different kinds of travel are provided. During commuting hours, the cars run on a computer-timed schedule, stopping at predetermined stations to load and unload. At all other times the

PRT interchange over highway.

cars are ready upon demand. To summon one, you push a button at the station's computer, selecting your destination. The information reaches a vehicle, which heads for the station. Lightup display boards direct you to the proper platform and give destination and boarding instructions.

The Personal Rapid Transit system was designed to allow unlimited travel for less than ten cents per day. Fares are paid automatically by presenting a yearly pass. This model system has 90 cars and 6 stations serving a city of 29,000 people. It runs 24 hours a day, 7 days a week.

PRT, being electric, produces no direct air pollution. The cars ride on four hard rubber tires: no noise pollution. Elevated guideways are built adjacent to already existing roads and railways, leaving valuable property and land untouched. Guideways and stations are designed to blend into the architecture of the surrounding neighborhood.

The computer monitor avoids collisions since it regulates the spacing of the vehicles on the guideways, controls speed, switching, stopping, doors, and vehicle dispatching. Each car has a two-way radio so passengers can talk directly to the central operator in case of emergency.

"The PRT will be a strong competitor with the automobile,"

173

says Dr. Samy E. G. Elias, one of its developers. "The PRT is small, quiet, comfortable, quick and attractive, and won't be slowed by traffic or weather conditions."

Despite setbacks for this system, in a few years similar ones could operate in suburbs and new cities.

Quiet Short-Haul Aircraft

At the moment only the wealthiest of the suburban rich can commute to work by helicopter. But Dr. Rene H. Miller, head of MIT's department of aeronautics and astronautics, foresees a fleet of "copter-planes" that would provide a very quick ride to work at a price average commuters could afford.

Dr. Miller's plan is based on the continued development of an aircraft capable of vertical take-off and landing (VTOL). This cross between the helicopter and the conventional propeller plane could be operational within the next decade.

Hub V-port showing protected access to aircraft landing pad and details of V-port access and egress.

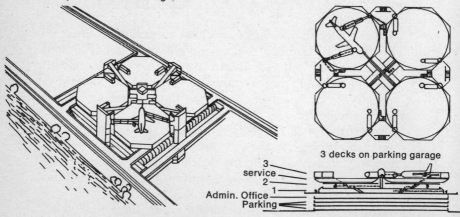

3 decks on parking garage

3
service
2
Admin. Office 1
Parking

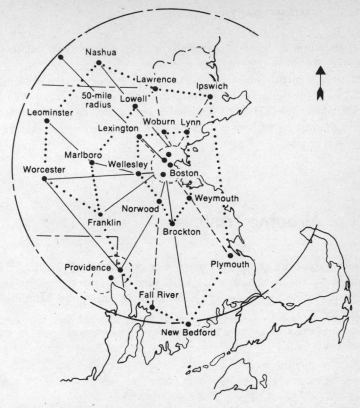

Possible locations of V-ports and air-transport network around Greater Boston.

A curious hybrid, the VTOL has propellers on the ends of its wings. Tilted straight up, the craft could take off vertically; tilted forward, it could cruise along at prop-plane speeds. It would run on a quiet, virtually pollution-free gas turbine. An automobile emits about 300 times as much pollutants per passenger mile as the new aircraft would; and according to Dr. Miller's studies as few as ten planes could service the Greater Boston area.

Terminals in the business district would be centrally located parking lots or rooftops, like the former heliport on the roof of the Pan Am building in New York. The suburban "V-ports" would be distributed according to demand, and could be virtually any large parking lot. A commuter living thirty miles from his office could go door-to-door in about a half-hour to an hour—

half the time it takes him right now. The actual flying time for this trip would be a speedy six minutes.

The cost of this service would be only ten cents per passenger mile, or three dollars for the thirty-mile ride.

Dr. Miller predicts that commuter trains will become obsolete, and commuting by car will be almost nonexistent for distances over ten miles.

Airborne Trolleys

Like a miniature trolley car, each Personal Rapid Transit (PRT) vehicle in the Morgantown, West Virginia, system has its own electric engine (see page 172). But near Minneapolis, Minnesota,

The levitation valve provides support for the lightweight cars with a continuous cushion of air, and the linear air turbine blows them to their destination.

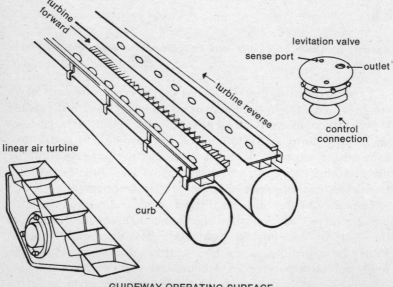

GUIDEWAY OPERATING SURFACE

The light passenger car on its track.

the U.S. Department of Transportation is sponsoring a test of PRT vehicles with no motors at all.

In the experimental Uniflo system, the compact six-to-ten-passenger cabs are passively blown along a computer-controlled guideway. A continuous series of hidden valves supplies a cushion of low-pressure air that levitates and propels the vehicles.

As in other PRT systems, a computer dispatches the cars and controls their speed and spacing. A single guideway would deliver two or three times more passengers than a freeway lane in rush hour.

The principal advantage of the Uniflo system is reliability. Since the vehicles themselves are extremely simple, they would rarely malfunction. And if one of the air jets failed, another one would automatically take over. A two-man repair car could cruise the guideway at low-traffic hours, checking for breathless valves and quickly make needed replacements.

Cost will ultimately determine which of the similar competing PRT systems (if any) cities will adopt. Developers estimate that the cost of the Uniflo guideway will be high: about six million dollars per mile. But the cost of the vehicles is low: possibly below $6000. And while public buses cost $1.80 per mile or more to operate, PRT systems are expected to cost less than 20 cents per vehicle mile.

Vernon H. Heath of Rosemont, Inc., which developed Uniflo, explains its appeals: "There are no motors, controls or other complex mechanisms to fail in the Uniflo vehicles. These and other functions, on-board on other PRT vehicles, are provided repetitively in the Uniflo guideway."

These small vehicles could be the prototype for full-scale hovertrains. By putting the propulsion mechanism in the track, the weight of the cars is greatly reduced, and little power is required to support the vehicles on their cushion of air. Blowers are not, however, sufficient to propel a full-size train at high speeds. Perhaps a hybrid vehicle will come, using jets of air to support the train and a linear induction engine (see below) for locomotion.

Flying Trains

The Stanford Research Institute has successfully tested a vehicle levitated by supercooled electromagnets. The process, called MAGLEV (magnetic levitation), would enable trains to travel up to 300 mph, revolutionizing mass transit.

If MAGLEV proves practicable, trains will fly several inches above their aluminum guiderails. With less friction and no problems with uneven roadbeds, levitated trains not only will outpace earthbound trains, they will run more quietly and smoothly, too.

In its first U.S. test, an experimental MAGLEV vehicle—3 feet wide, 14 feet long, 600 pounds in weight—traveled 250 feet along a 500-foot test track. A similar system has also been tested in Japan.

In a future full-scale model, four wheels will propel the train out of the station. Powerful electromagnets are mounted on its lower surface and sides; the motion of the magnets causes a current to flow in the U-shaped guiderails, momentarily magnetizing them. Since the magnetic poles of the car are similar (and likes repel each other) the car is levitated. When the vehicle drifts to one side on a curve, the magnetic forces on that side are strengthened, shifting it back to the center of the guideway. (In

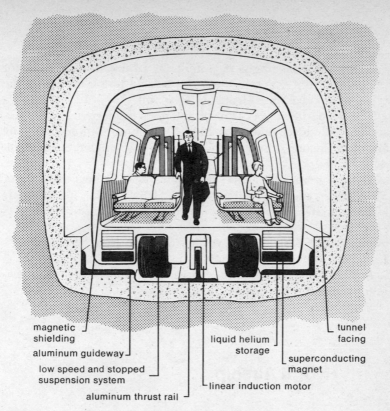

magnetic shielding

aluminum guideway

low speed and stopped suspension system

aluminum thrust rail

liquid helium storage

linear induction motor

tunnel facing

superconducting magnet

Artist's conception of a magnetic levitating train.

the Stanford test, the vehicle was towed until it was moving fast enough to "lift off.")

The magnets and coils are supercooled to −450° F. by a bath of liquid helium carried in the belly of the vehicle. At this extremely low temperature, the coils have practically no resistance to electric current. Current induced in the coils persists indefinitely, maintaining the magnetic field without requiring additional power. Power is needed to keep the helium supercooled, but the amount is minimal compared with the consumption of a conventional electromagnet of equal strength.

Levitated trains would probably be powered by linear induction motors. The linear induction motor can be thought of as a regular rotary electric motor opened up and laid out flat. Thus instead of torque (rotating power), thrust (straight-line power) is produced. In conventional motors, there are a fixed part (stator) and a moving part (rotor). In a linear induction motor the part corresponding to the stator is fixed to the bottom of the train, while the rotor is located in a live rail.

The Department of Transportation is underwriting the research and development of MAGLEV. Ford Motor Company and MIT, among others, are also developing "guided electromagnetic flight."

"This is a real milestone," said Howard T. Coffey, manager of SRI's Cryogenic Applications Group. "It is the first magnetically levitated system using superconducting magnets in this country."

When MAGLEV becomes a reality: Midtown New York to downtown Washington in half an hour.

And someday, sealed in partial vacuum tunnels, magnetic levitating trains at the speed of sound.

Hybrid Airship

Dirigibles can take off and land in short distances and at slow speeds; airplanes cannot. Airplanes are easy to jockey around at low altitudes; dirigibles are not. Each type of craft has its own special qualities—and the hybrid airship is an innovative compromise that blends the best ones of both.

Aereon Corporation developed a hybrid craft filled with a safe, inert gas. From the side the airship looks like a watermelon; from above its form is triangular.

This strange configuration gives the craft two means of lift. *Aerostatic lift* (the principle behind dirigibles) is provided by the lighter-than-air gas within the body. *Aerodynamic* lift (the principle behind airplane wings) is provided by unequal air pressures across the triangular wings. In the air the hybrid airship is propelled by smallish propellers.

Because of its dual lift, the airship can fly at extremely slow speeds. Thus, it can land virtually in a parking lot. It's as easy to load and unload as a cargo plane. But it can carry tremendous

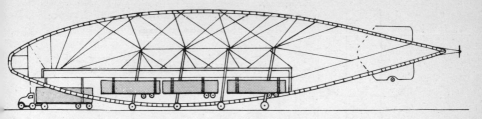

Cross section and perspective of the airship.

payloads at rock-bottom cost. And on paper the airship's size is limitless.

The developer, William Miller of the Aereon Corporation, says the hybrid airship concept is "an idea whose time is returning . . . a solution looking for a problem."

Dirigible passengers of the 1930s still mourn the ending of that silent, leisurely, graceful way of transatlantic passage. The hybrid airship may yet revive it for them.

Several giant airships could replace an entire transcontinental truck fleet.

Airship "ports" can be created in downtown areas of land-locked cities. Imagine Denver a port! A majority of the world's population live within fifty miles of an ocean coast—and major cities like NY and LA owe their existence and size to their convenient harbors. Inland cities and population centers will boom if they become large harbors.

Giant Flying Freighter

A giant 56-wheel plane, longer and wider than a football field, could haul—in one load—millions of pounds of crude oil, liquid natural gas or various ores from remote locations to processing plants. It could succeed in reducing transportation costs substantially.

181

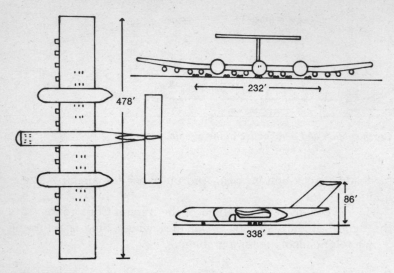

General arrangement of resources transport.

Now on the drawing boards at Boeing, the air freighter will weigh 3.5 million pounds gross and carry a staggering payload of 2.3 million pounds. Twelve engines, each with 50,000 pounds thrust, will propel it. The fuselage (358 feet) and the wing span (478 feet) exceed the length of a football field.

The payload, on two streamlined "pods," one under each wing, consists of four 8-by-8-foot standard cargo containers. The pods provide a rapid and economical way to change cargoes. The loaded aircraft, landing on a special three-runway airfield, would land into the wind on the outer runways, stop at a station to leave its containers, and then accelerate immediately for a downwind takeoff on the center runway. At the other terminal, the empty plane would land downwind and take off upwind. This arrangement would save fuel and time.

At present the giant freighter is being projected as part of an extensive transportation network in Canada. It could be used to exploit the great mineral resources of the country's Arctic islands and its northwestern region.

Marvin D. Taylor, product development supervisor at Boeing's

Commercial Airplane Group, says, "Capital investment could match capacity and revenue better than in the case of a pipeline. A pipeline requires almost total investment before the first drop of oil flows; an aircraft fleet and most ground facilities can be expanded gradually as needed.

"Terminals could be shifted more easily than railroads and pipelines, increasing flexibility in serving markets or tapping new resource reservoirs. Right-of-way costs are also avoided.

"Environmental questions need more study, particularly those relating to spills due to accidents. The 12-engine craft, even without further improvements, would be able to meet federal noise and emission standards."

Perhaps the flying freighter will carry oil or liquefied natural gas from the Middle East someday. And minerals from far off. Or domestic coal to foreign users.

Now imagine it filled with *water*. Fly it to a drought. Spray the parched land. Save the crops from disaster. Keep the farmers— and the consumer—from famine.

Satellites Control Air Traffic

"Space," someone once said, "is what prevents everything from being in the same place." And our air lanes are crowded with airplanes during peak traffic hours. A new traffic control system using two satellites, called Aerostat, will double the capacity of North Atlantic air lanes.

Navigational aids for transoceanic flying get an airplane to its destination. But they aren't good enough for precise traffic control. At present, collisions are avoided by keeping each plane well separated from its neighbors—current practice allows a "block" of air space about 120 miles long for each aircraft.

In the Aerostat system, two satellites in synchronous orbits (orbits in which they remain fixed with respect to the earth's surface) will provide precise data on the position of each air-

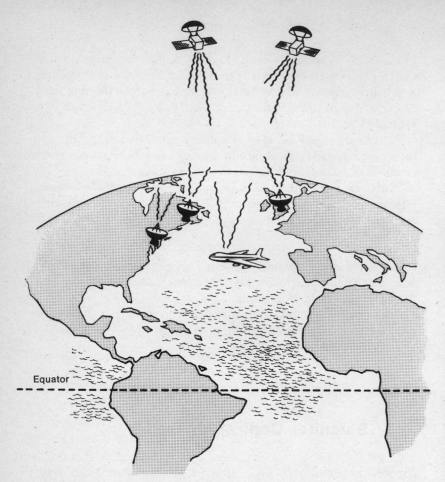

Two satellites and ground stations help pinpoint aircraft.

plane. This information, plus improved communication between aircraft and ground-based traffic control centers, will "chop" reserved transoceanic air space into smaller blocks. The system will be able to handle traffic at twice the present peak density, which is the expected traffic level for 1980.

Present communication facilities aren't yet overloaded—they have some reserve capacity even during peak traffic hours. By 1980, though, they won't be adequate. The satellites in the new system will also provide high-capacity communication channels.

Aircraft positions will be determined by ground-based equipment analyzing signals transmitted by aircraft and relayed by the satellites. No special equipment will be required on the planes.

The first installation of the new system will handle traffic over the Atlantic. Additional systems will cover the Pacific and the Indian Ocean. Aside from its use for traffic control and related communication, each new system offers extensive voice-band and digital communication facilities. It will also serve as a navigational aid for operation outside the high-density regular air lanes. These services will be available to both aircraft and ships.

RCA, the leader of the Aerostat project, says, "In-flight processing for customs, public health and immigration purposes could be facilitated using satellite digital data transmission. It will even be possible to offer passengers telephone service. You could transact business in-flight; in essence, you will be able to travel in real time."

"Invisible" Planes

The next generation of military aircraft will be hard to detect because of a new structural material that absorbs most of the energy from incoming radar beams.

Antireflection paints have been in use for some years to reduce the radar detectability of airplanes. A new radar-absorbing material with special electrical properties has recently been developed by North American Rockwell under Air Force sponsorship. Strong enough to be used for load-bearing structures, it eliminates the need of periodic repainting and reduces overall weight. The material is composed of advanced structural plastics: panels have survived high-temperature tests for long periods without losing their strength or radar absorptivity. The material is "non-parasitic" because it does not add weight without carrying loads.

By increasing the survivability and performance characteristics of aircraft, the new material may enable them to pass through enemy radar surveillance. However, the material does not make aircraft or missiles undetectable by radar, only more difficult to see.

The Air Force says, "A prototype engine inlet cowl has undergone more than 200 hours of flight testing without encountering operational problems. Compared to a standard production cowl, the prototype weighs significantly less, is superior electrically, and could be mass-produced at competitive cost."

Penetration of the radar "fence" around a country can tip the balance of deterrence among major powers. So it's likely that others are at work to develop similar defense penetrators—or better.

The Vapor Turbine Car

The Lear Motors Corporation has successfully tested the world's first steam-turbine-powered car. A Lear steam bus has already logged over 6000 highway miles with exhaust emissions levels markedly below the federal emission standards.

Water vapor powered the old Stanley Steamer, but it was allowed to escape into the atmosphere, so the harried driver had to make frequent stops to take on more water. This inconvenience led to the extinction of the Stanley and discouraged research on steam automobiles for about forty years. Now the closed modern steam turbine has solved that problem: After spinning the turbine, the vapor is cooled and condensed into a liquid that can be reused. And to prevent freeze-ups and wear on parts, water has been replaced by a more adaptable working fluid, Learium, specially developed for the turbine.

The steam turbine isn't totally pollution-free. It still uses gasoline or diesel oil to boil the fluid, but the emissions levels are only a fraction of those produced by present internal-combustion engines. Moreover, the results of Lear's road tests suggest that the steam turbine can be practical as well as clean.

In 1972 Lear installed a 240 brake horsepower steam-turbine engine in a GM bus. It was tested on actual passenger routes in Reno, Los Angeles and San Francisco. From these tests Lear

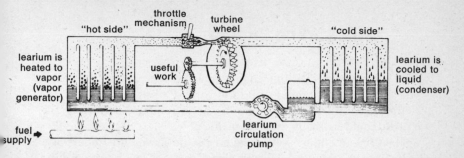

Simplified diagram of the Lear vapor turbine system. The system cools the vapor after it goes through the turbine, condensing it to a liquid that can be reused. A pump circulates the fluid, Learium.

concluded the turbine bus "can compete with diesel power for public transportation propulsion in terms of road performance and system weight." Noise levels are one third those of conventional buses.

Early in 1973 Lear began testing the steam turbine in a Chevrolet Monte Carlo. From a dead stop, the Chevy Steamer can accelerate to 60 mph in 16 seconds—not enough pickup to make her a drag-strip contender, but fully adequate for actual traffic conditions.

The Environmental Protection Agency has awarded Lear a contract to further develop the steam car to the point where it can generate over 100 horsepower, deliver at least 8.5 miles to a gallon of gas, and achieve 65 percent of full power within 45 seconds after start-up.

William Powell Lear is the founder and president of Lear Motors. He is best known for the Lear jet—the most popular small jet aircraft—but he also has an impressive string of firsts to his credit: the first radio in an automobile, the first navigational radio for light planes, the first effective radio-direction finder for aircraft, the first lightweight automatic pilot, the first eight-track stereo tapeplayer and cartridges. He says, "The time of the clean air automotive technology is here."

Future steam engines could burn a wide variety of alternate fuels —alcohol from sugarcane, wood and even coal.

The Stirling Engine

The low-emission Stirling engine may power cars of the 1980s. The Ford Motor Company and the N. V. Philips Company of the Netherlands are jointly developing an experimental Stirling car, which should be ready in a few years.

The Stirling engine was invented by the Reverend Robert Stirling over 150 years ago. The Philips Company has been simplifying the design since 1938—reducing its size, weight and cost.

The Stirling engine is an alternative to the conventional internal-combustion engine. Continuous combustion of fuel *outside* the cylinders heats a working gas *inside* the cylinders through the walls. After heating, the working gas, initially compressed at low temperature, expands at high temperature to move the pistons.

Cross section of a Stirling engine.

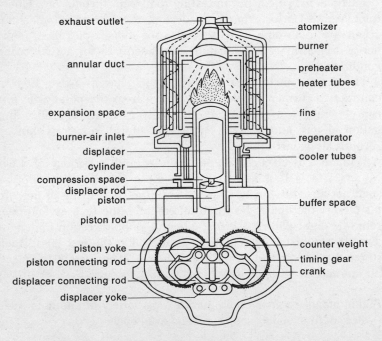

The engine, reportedly, should be able to run on almost any fuel.

Tests indicate that a Stirling car would be very clean and quiet, operating well within federal emissions standards. Moreover, it would require less fuel while offering performance comparable with current power packages.

The prototype car will be a modified Torino with a 170-hp engine. Ford has also entered into a separate agreement with United Stirling of Sweden to build a second experimental Stirling car.

Spokesmen say much remains to be done to establish durability, reliability and manufacturability while keeping the price low enough to interest the car-buying public. Ford doesn't foresee using the Stirling engine in production vehicles before 1980.

The agreement between Philips and Ford requires Philips to design, build and develop a 170-hp engine. It requires Ford to perform vehicle package work, modify a Torino vehicle to accept the engine, develop a cooling system, develop a combustion air blower and design the preheater, and develop and furnish the accessory system.

The future of the Stirling engine depends on its ability to burn virtually any fuel quietly and cleanly. This promise, now under intensive study, is considerable.

Automobiles Run on Hydrogen

Automobile engines produce almost no pollution when they're operated on hydrogen instead of gasoline.

Two University of Miami engineers have modified the engine of a Toyota station wagon to use a hydrogen-air mixture as fuel. Polluting exhaust emissions were significantly lower than in the original engine. They also modified a four-cylinder Pontiac engine with the same results.

Hydrogen would make a good automotive fuel since it burns

cleanly, but carrying a supply of hydrogen poses a problem. A new technique uses a catalyst to generate hydrogen from gasoline or kerosene, and makes the hydrogen-powered car a practical possibility.

A modified engine, together with a catalytic hydrogen generator, costs no more than the original engine plus required anti-pollution equipment. As an unexpected bonus, the modified engine without antipollution gear has a cleaner exhaust than the original engine *with* such equipment.

Overall efficiency of the modified engine with its hydrogen generator is about the same as that of the original engine. They both deliver about the same number of miles per gallon of gasoline. Improvements in the catalytic generator, though, should soon increase efficiency by more than 30 percent.

The modified engine uses the original ignition system. The carburetor is discarded, the cylinder head is slightly altered, and the intake manifold is replaced by new equipment. Like a conventional engine, the modified engine sucks the fuel-air mixture into its cylinders. The problem of handling high-pressure hydrogen is completely avoided. And engine speed is controlled by a throttling valve in the hydrogen line.

Michael R. Swain and Robert R. Adt, Jr., who modified the engines, point out that, for gasoline engines, "even if all of the hydrocarbons and the carbon monoxide and nitric oxides could be eliminated, carbon dioxide would still be produced." By contrast, with a hydrogen-burning engine, "the products of combustion are mainly water vapor and free nitrogen" and "the engine is [almost] pollution-free."

These engines don't free us from dependence on gasoline as a fuel, but they could be one way of handling the automotive pollution problem.

Light "Pipes" Replace Auto Wires

Small optical fibers may control many electrical functions of to-morrow's cars, replacing the complex wiring systems in present models. One bundle of fibers no thicker than a pencil could honk the horn, turn on the lights, run the wipers, and perform all the operations now requiring many pounds of copper wire.

Nearly one hundred copper wires connect a driver's controls with lights, horn, buzzers, pumps and motors, and new accessories and safety devices will require even more wires. But copper is bulky, heavy and expensive. It must be insulated to protect against electrical fires, and in time it becomes brittle and breaks.

Du Pont has demonstrated a system with no wires linking the dashboard, headlights and horn—all functions are performed by a single fiberoptic cable. When the horn button is depressed, an infrared light of a predetermined frequency is sent through the clear plastic fibers. A receiver at the other end of the cable is activated by that frequency and honks the horn. When the light switch is pulled, a different light frequency is emitted, which turns on the headlights.

"By varying the wavelength of the signal, one cable of optical fibers can control every electrical operation in the auto, either

Optical light guides which are rustproof and require no additional electric power will pipe the light from any bulb to a monitoring jewel on the dashboard.

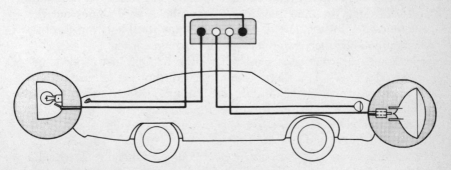

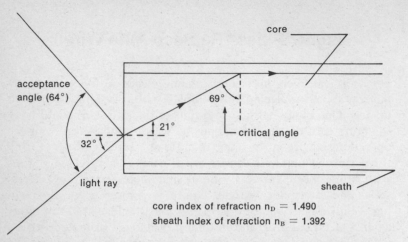

core index of refraction $n_D = 1.490$
sheath index of refraction $n_B = 1.392$

A basic principle of fiberoptics is that light travels in a zigzag path through the transparent core of each fiber by internal reflections from the sheathing medium.

consecutively or simultaneously," according to Du Pont scientist Aaron Brennesholtz. A cable with sixty-four filaments which could control sixty-four different electrical functions would only measure an eighth of an inch in diameter, about the size of two insulated wires. The plastic fibers are more durable and much cheaper than copper. Theoretically two pounds of glass could be spun into a fiber that would reach from New York to San Francisco and back.

Optical fibers are made of clear plastic covered with a protective sheath. They transmit light from one point to another as pipes carry water. Light focused on one end is reflected back and forth along the inner surfaces of the plastic and shines out the other end; little is lost or absorbed. Since the fibers are flexible, light can be piped through loops and around corners.

Some 1974 model cars use fiberoptics to illuminate speedometers, dials, switches, ashtrays and other dashboard features. Light fibers also monitor headlights and taillights so the driver knows at all times whether each bulb is functioning. Other applications of piped light include airport runway signs, table lamps, computer displays and animated signs.

Says Aaron Brennesholtz of Du Pont, "With new electrically

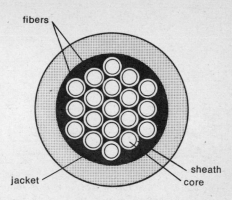

Cross section of light fibers in a light guide.

FIBER OPTIC LIGHT GUIDE

operated safety devices and comfort features being added constantly to the American automobile, a control device of this sort can simplify the car's complicated electrical harness by substituting a single fiberoptic cable for dozens of electrical wires. From the standpoint of both auto assembly and servicing, it seems apparent that such a system must be developed."

Lightweight light pipes mean lighter cars. And lightweight cars will save us fuel and energy.

Car Radar and Sonar

RCA has developed radar for cars that can help prevent rear-end collisions, the most common kind of auto accident. The radar tracks the car ahead and sounds a warning when the distance between cars is dangerous.

The radar, slightly bigger than a shoebox, fits on the front end of a car. Its signal bounces off a special reflector, about the size of a license plate, mounted on the rear end of the car ahead. The reflector doubles the frequency of the original signal, which avoids confusion with rocks, bridges and other natural and man-

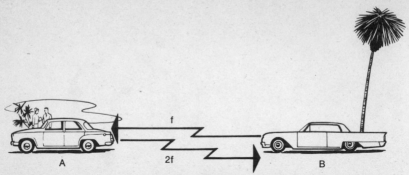

The radar frequency (f) from car B is reflected back from the car A ahead at twice the frequency (2f). This eliminates false targets like bridges or cars traveling in the opposite direction.

made objects on the road. It also prevents two cars equipped with radar and passing in opposite directions from "blinding" each other's radars. It can easily be modified to apply the brake as well.

The cost of this radar mass-produced is estimated at $50 to $100, about the same price as a car radio. But before it becomes a standard feature, it's expected to be used by the army to keep convoys moving steadily with all vehicles evenly spaced. A convoy can travel at high speeds at night without lights to avoid detection.

A different device, employing sonar, would also warn the driver when he's tailgating, or when it's unsafe to merge into a crowded freeway.

Sonar units emit ultrasound (pitched higher than humans can hear) and would be mounted on the front and rear of all vehicles. Utilizing the Doppler effect (or change in the echo frequency) and the strength of those echoes, the sonar device would display the distance and speed of cars both ahead and behind.

According to RCA, "The radar ranks among the most promising electronic developments yet achieved in the area of highway safety. We envision the day when a wide variety of automotive systems, ranging from anti-skid devices to collision avoidance systems, will be automatically controlled in a truck, bus or automobile by solid-state electronic systems."

Distance and speed are shown on dashboard dials. A buzzer, flashing light or automatic braking occurs when the separation distance is unsafe.

Some form of radar (or sonar) will be among the optional equipment found on future automobiles. Statistics show that a major cause of traffic accidents is "tailgaiting," or the inability of one vehicle to stop in time to avoid collision with another.

And radar or sonar can penetrate bad weather to provide extra visibility and safety. Someday, cars may drive themselves with only an occasional assist from the driver.

Deceleration Warning Lights

A new slow-down light supplements conventional stoplights.

A normal stoplight serves the very useful purpose of warning a driver when the car ahead is about to slow down. It supplies relatively little information, though. It lights up when the brake pedal is depressed, but it doesn't distinguish between a panic

195

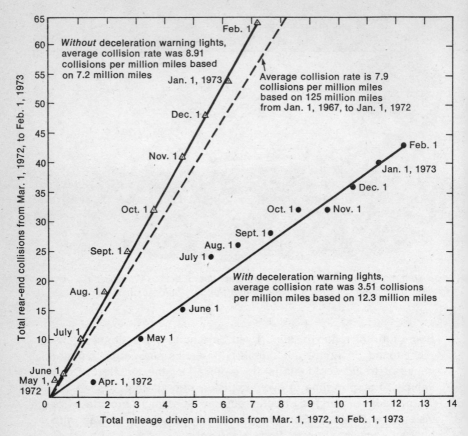

Rear-end collisions and total mileage.

stop and a gentle decrease in speed. It can even give a false warning if a driver "rides" the brake—and many do.

A new scheme adds a rear-mounted amber light to the set of existing stoplights, taillights and turn signals. The amber light flashes when the car slows down. The greater the deceleraton, the more rapidly the lamp flashes. The system, called CYBERLITE, is easily installed.

The new warning lights were tried out on several hundred taxis in the San Francisco area. A year of test operation in taxis shows that the probability of rear-end collision (in which another car runs into the back of a vehicle carrying the new warning light) is cut by over 60 percent. Moreover, the damage caused by those collisions that *do* happen is less for CYBERLITE-equipped cabs.

Dr. John Voevodsky, who developed the new warning-light system, says the "value of cab damage is $424 per million miles for equipped cabs compared with $1350" for cabs not equipped.

More information isn't always a good thing. Human sensory circuits, like other communication channels, can be overloaded. But in this case, flickering lights are very effective early warnings of disaster. We need the same sort of thing to give us advance warning of possibly irreversible damage to society and to the environment.

Computer-Controlled Traffic

A computerized scheme for handling traffic uses computer-controlled lights and sensors at each intersection, speeding the flow of cars.

Most traffic lights operate on a fixed program, so many seconds north-south and so many seconds east-west. On two-way streets, all lights change color at the same time. On one-way streets, the lights are "staggered" to accommodate traffic at, say, thirty miles per hour. The results aren't bad, yet they don't approach the traffic-handling capability of a group of well-trained traffic officers.

Demand traffic lights are a step toward adaptive traffic control. On a major north-south artery, for example, the light at a minor intersection stays green (for north-south travel) as long as there is no east-west traffic. When an east-bound or west-bound car appears at the intersection, the light changes for perhaps twenty seconds and then reverts to its normal state—green for north-south traffic. A timer ensures that north-south traffic flows without excessive interruption. East-west demands aren't honored more often than about every ninety seconds.

With a more sophisticated control scheme, the period of east-west flow is lengthened when the frequency of east-west demands rises above some specified level. The demand traffic light, in this way, automatically matches its behavior to the traffic pattern during peaks of east-west flow.

A demand traffic light can do a good job at an isolated intersection. For a network of intersections something more complex is needed. Each traffic light must adjust its control sequence in response to traffic demands *and* in response to the network's ability to handle the flow. If a neighboring intersection is blocked, traffic headed for that intersection must be diverted to an alternate route.

A new traffic control system called SAFER (systematic aid to flow on existing roads) collects information from standard sensors at each intersection and transmits all of the data to a central computer. The computer, on the basis of conditions throughout the whole traffic network, sends appropriate orders to the control devices that operate individual traffic lights. The system is fail-safe. If the computer drops out, each controller goes into a preprogrammed fall-back operating mode: the traffic lights continue to function in a conventional way.

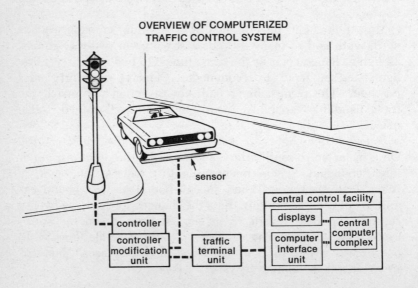

OVERVIEW OF COMPUTERIZED
TRAFFIC CONTROL SYSTEM

In a typical case the new system can reduce the number of stops by 75 percent and the length of the average stop by as much as 90 percent. The system also gathers detailed information about traffic patterns and identifies bottlenecks.

As TRW, the developers of SAFER, explain, "The system does not select from a set of precomputed plans, but continually calculates the best solutions for existing conditions." It adjusts traffic signals "to keep cars moving through the network with minimum delay. Automobiles emit less pollutants, and rear-end collisions are minimized with fewer stops and starts."

New technology can improve the usage of our existing resources. We won't need to build so many more roads—if we make better use of those we already have! The demand traffic signals avoid the stop-and-start traffic that gobbles up fuel.

Impact Absorbers for Highway Safety

NASA engineers have patented an energy-absorbing system to minimize the impact of a spacecraft or an air-drop landing on the surface of a planet. The same system could cushion the impact of automobiles against the pillars and abutments that line our highways.

NASA's energy-absorbing system calls for surrounding a payload with crushable hollow spheres bonded together in layers of progressively smaller diameter. The outer spheres with the largest diameter receive the initial impact. Because they're bigger, they absorb greater amounts of impact force, when they are crushed, than the adjacent inner layer of smaller spheres. This second layer in turn absorbs more of the remaining impact force than the third layer of still smaller spheres, and so on, until the impact is totally absorbed.

The chief advantage of this system is that the arrangement of ever-smaller crushable spheres eliminates the "rebound" normally associated with crushable structures like springs.

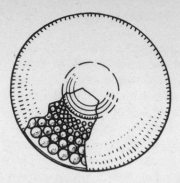

Spheres of diminishing size surround the payload.

Apart from spacecraft landings and air drops, the system could also be used to form a protective, crushable barrier around the pillars, abutments, walls and other objects on highway shoulders. The system has a "one-shot" capacity, of course, and would require replacement after each substantial impact. But the cost would be offset by the savings in lives and damage to vehicles.

According to NASA, "The material chosen for fabrication of the spheres characteristically must be brittle and hence readily fracturable, but it also must be capable of suffering minimum deformation prior to sudden fracture, so that impact force may first be strongly resisted and then absorbed by cave-in of the sphere . . ."

Another future *cushion* for a future *shock*. But not only for use on pillars and abutments for highway safety. Crushable spheres could be mounted on the front and rear ends of cars and trains. Perhaps even entire fields might be constructed of crushable spheres for aircraft emergency landings.

Vibratory Locomotion

Every once in a while a startled housewife witnesses vibratory locomotion in action: During the spin cycle, a washing machine with an unbalanced load will chatter and walk a few inches across the laundry floor. One well-known device, the pogo stick, puts vibratory locomotion to work.

Navy engineers are currently investigating more serious applications for "jiggle motion." They envision a new breed of tractors, forklifts and military landing craft that would move without wheels or caterpillar treads.

Basically a vibratory vehicle would be a giant jiggler mounted on a simple flat base called a skid. How a jiggler operates is rather difficult to describe: A gasoline engine powers a crankrocker, which in turn vibrates a heavy mass in a regular cycle—upward and forward, then downward and backward. The upward cycle lifts the skid and slides it slightly forward; the downward cycle pushes the skid into the ground, preventing it from slipping backward. Navy computers have analyzed how best to balance the vibrator and angle the skid to achieve the most motion per jiggle.

A vibratory vehicle will never win any races. At best it will shuffle along at speeds of about four or five feet per second. For dislodging heavy objects, though, it might have up to twice the pulling power of a conventional tractor. And since the undersurface is flat, with no moving parts, vibratory vehicles could operate efficiently on soft terrain such as sand or mud.

Cyclic vibration of the heavy cylinder (top) jitters and shuffles the device along without tires or caterpillar treads.

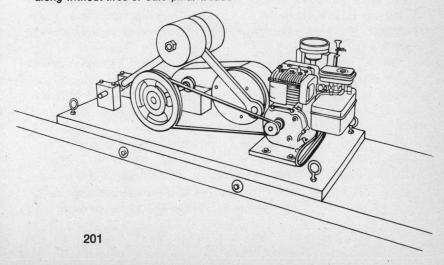

Naval engineers H. A. Gaberson and P. L. Stone describe their expectations for vibratory locomotion: "We do not predict the demise of the tracked bulldozer. But the simplicity of the device, its unusually large footprint, and its high drawbar pull capability lead us to believe that the device will become practical for a portion of the specialized land locomotion requirements of the Navy." But Dr. Gaberson cautions, "The project is still in an early stage of development; it has yet to be proven a cost-effective locomotion means. No commercial applications of vibratory loco-motion have been undertaken as yet."

Cross-country skiers of the future would welcome a tiny unit, attached to their skis to boost them uphill.

With its few moving parts and simple maintenance, this vehicle could give the tractor serious competition in a few decades.

Man-Powered Aircraft

The "birdmen" were the earliest pioneers of aviation. Outfitted with homemade wings, they stood on windy hilltops flapping their arms frantically, aspiring to fly under their own power. Contemporary birdmen, with the help of computers and wind tunnels, may yet realize the ancient dream of man-powered flight.

British industrialist Henry Kremer has offered a $24,000 prize for the first man-powered aircraft to fly a one-mile figure-eight course without losing altitude. With planes constructed of balsa wood, paper, aluminum, fiber glass and a few dabs of glue, several groups have made valiant runs at the prize.

One plane, christened the *Puffin,* flew nearly one hundred times before it was retired to Liverpool University in England. Another plane, the *Jupiter,* has made the longest flight so far, 1172 yards, less than 600 yards short of Kremer's requirements. Other teams, including the Man-Powered Aircraft Group of the

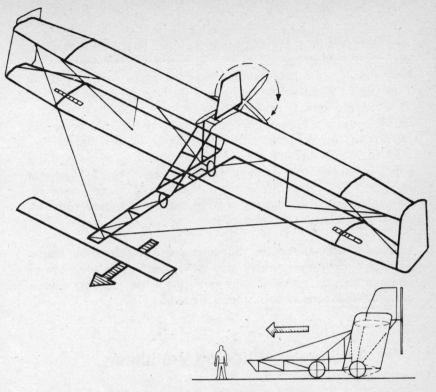

A group of scientists at MIT have designed a man-powered aircraft. Two pedalers of better-than-average stamina can cruise along at 18 mph. The record flight for such a craft is nearly three-quarters of a mile.

Massachusetts Institute of Technology, are planning assaults on the Kremer course.

The MIT group worked for two years designing a model, analyzing its structure with computers, running tests in a wind tunnel, then redesigning. Finally they settled on a two-man, biplane design, with a pushing propeller in the rear.

At every point in construction, considerations of strength had to be balanced against weight. The wings, elevating rudder, and propeller are all made of balsa. The fuselage is thin-wall aluminum tubing. Spirited pedaling of the two-man crew will provide an estimated cruise power of 1.1 horsepower, enough to propel the delicate contraption at speeds of up to 18 miles per hour.

The plane, without crew, weighs only 126 pounds. The fuselage is 27 feet long, but the wingspan is 62 feet. This makes the plane look something like a hybrid between a tremendous sea bird and a bicycle. In the air, however, it only appears to fly backward; the canard design uses a pushing propeller with the elevating rudder in *front* of the wings.

While the plane undergoes preliminary testing, the crew will attempt to work themselves into shape for the maiden flight.

"After going through several different configurations, we decided on a two-man, biplane canard design," the MIT group explains. "We chose this configuration for its lower power requirement, structural rigidity and lightness, and maneuverability. Construction began in February 1972."

Perhaps a two-man crew will succeed where Daedalus and Icarus failed. It's not likely, however, that the day will come when everyone has his own wings. Man-powered flight will probably always be a rather expensive and precarious hobby.

Triangular-Wheeled Vehicles

NASA engineers have invented a unique triangular wheel. The new wheel will enable a vehicle to span crevices, negotiate steep and rugged slopes, and even climb over obstacles higher than the vehicle's own length.

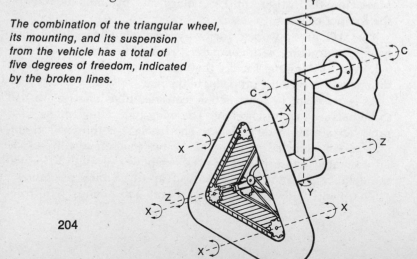

The combination of the triangular wheel, its mounting, and its suspension from the vehicle has a total of five degrees of freedom, indicated by the broken lines.

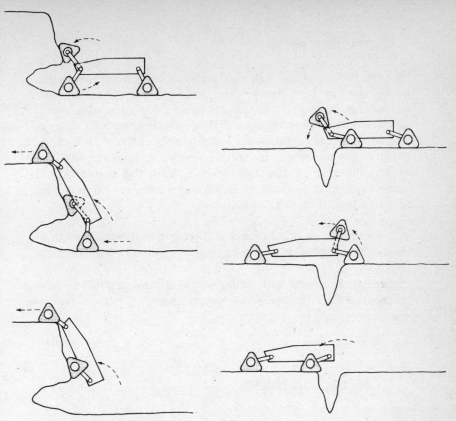

The triangular wheel can negotiate slopes (left) and cross crevasses (right).

These highly mobile and flexible vehicles are designed to meet the needs of lunar and planetary exploration—but they may also find applications on earth in such hostile places as arctic regions, deserts, mountains and terrain marred by warfare.

A triangular-wheeled vehicle is a modification of familiar track-laying vehicles like the tank and bulldozer. It would have four relatively small wheels, each consisting of a wire-mesh tire and belt circulating around a triangular-shaped hub. Each wheel could be operated independently. By means of double-elbow suspensions, it could be rotated about five axes (see diagram), giving it freedom of movement comparable with that of the arm assembly of a mechanical man. The driver could lift the wheels off the ground and position them wherever he could obtain maximum traction or pulling power.

205

Where the terrain is flat, the vehicle would track along the surface like any other track-laying vehicle. Where crevices and boulders lay in its path, its wheels could "step" over them, as if the vehicle itself were "walking." When confronted with a larger but surmountable obstacle, the front wheels of the vehicle could be placed on top of the obstacle and used as leverage to allow the repositioning of the rear wheels; thus the vehicle could "climb" onto the obstacle in much the same way as a young puppy pulls itself up onto a sofa.

Such a vehicle has great mobility in rugged and hostile environments—it can find wide use in exploration, rescue efforts, military actions.

Someday a vehicle with square wheels may negotiate curbs and steps: A boon for the wheelchair traveler.

Hydrofoil Boats

Boeing Aerospace Company has developed a boat named Jetfoil which will cruise comfortably at 50 miles per hour in 12-foot waves.

Boeing calls it the most advanced hydrofoil vessel ever built, and they have already been bought by Hawaii for interisland transport. The hydrofoil boat comes in two models—one designed for 250 commuters, the other for 190 passengers with baggage. Boeing developed the Jetfoil from the Tucumcari Patrol Gunboat, an earlier model hydrofoil they created for the U.S. Navy which has logged many hours including combat time in Vietnam.

Hydrofoil is the general name for a particular type of boat with structures called foils; at high enough speeds they will support the weight of the boat and "plane" across the water. Once the craft is "foilborne" it can reach extremely high speeds with little effort, because very little of the boat is actually in the water. Although few such boats operate in the United States, in Europe

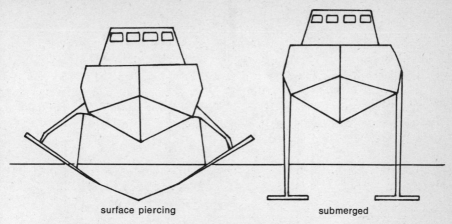

surface piercing   submerged

Surface-piercing foils cut through waves and give a rough ride; submerged foils give a smooth ride.

and Russia they are commonly used as passenger boats for short trips—for instance, across the English Channel.

Hydrofoils were invented in 1861 in England when Thomas Moy decided to study the aerodynamics of wings by observing the swirls they created under water. He attached wings to his boat and discovered, much to his surprise, that it rose above the water. In 1918 Alexander Graham Bell designed a hydrofoil powered by two airplane engines. His boat reached 81.5 miles per hour—a speed record that lasted until 1962. Even the Wright brothers investigated hydrofoils before they invented the airplane.

Clearly, hydrofoil and aircraft technology are closely related, a fact that Boeing, a leader of aircraft technology, stresses with some pride. The foil itself is actually a kind of wing and lifts the boat out of the water the same way an airplane wing lifts an airplane off the runway. They both are shaped so that when air or water flows over the wing or foil, a low pressure area results on the top surface—thus providing "lift."

Most designs are "surface-piercing" foils; they follow the surface action of the water and the boat has a rough ride. But the Tucumcari and Jetfoil have a completely submerged foil, which ensures a smooth ride. An automatic control system minimizes the normal pitch and roll by controlling small flaps on the foil.

207

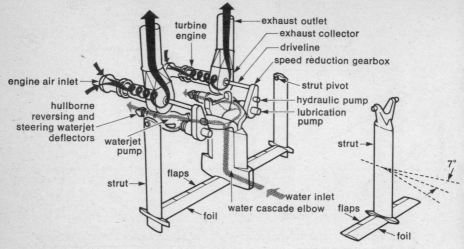

Details of foils and waterjet propulsion.

Turns are automatically banked, so that they are even and smooth. Boeing has studied the comfort characteristics of the Jetfoil's ride compared with conventional boats, other hydrofoils and airplanes, and has found that it resembles more an airplane ride than anything else.

Other features of this craft may make it likely to flourish. The cost per passenger mile is expected to be competitive with existing mass-transit systems. Boeing says the Jetfoil does not pollute air or water, is remarkably quiet, and produces no wake even at high speed. The foils and struts are retractable, after which the Jetfoil draws only six feet of water, so any current docking facility can be used.

Boeing says, "the introduction of the Boeing 707 jet, back in 1958, created a revolution in commercial air transportation. The Jetfoil should do likewise for commercial water transportation. For the first time it will be possible for people to travel at high speeds in comfort over water on a safe and dependable means of transportation."

Perhaps, after these are publicly accepted for mass transit in and around our large harbor-cities, we'll travel across oceans at high speeds and in comfort on hydrofoils.

Artist's conception of Jetfoil in operation.

5
Behavior
and
Society

Learning and Unlearning Illnesses

Baffled Western scientists have witnessed remarkable exhibitions by yoga adepts, who purportedly can stop their breathing, bleeding and even their hearts by deep concentration. The accuracy of these reports aside, current research into biofeedback shows a person *can* actively influence many bodily functions that were previously thought to be beyond his bodily control.

Sensationalized by the press, biofeedback, like yoga, has become something of a national fad. Responsible researchers urge caution and warn that many results of biofeedback experiments are not reproducible and that the miraculous claims of enthusiasts have little or no basis in fact. Preliminary research indicates humans are capable of a kind of "visceral learning" that may have profound implications for the diagnosis and treatment of physical and mental illnesses.

Biofeedback research points to two related applications in the health field. First, experiments suggest some symptoms of physical and mental illness are learned; the hopeful corollary is they can also be "unlearned," or "extinguished." Second, and perhaps more dramatic, these experiments offer hope that patients will learn to control certain symptoms of organic origin. Dr. Neil Miller, a pioneer in biofeedback, speculates that people might be taught (in some cases) to recognize and fight off such problems as high blood pressure, heart arrhythmia, insomnia, spastic colitis, and even epilepsy and asthma.

As an example of how a person learns a symptom, consider the case of a child faced with a difficult test at school. The youngster is afraid and tense. Fear of a test might produce genuine stomach cramps. If his mother responds by allowing the youngster to stay home from school, two factors combine to "reinforce" this symptom—the test is postponed, and the child receives a kind of reward in the form of buttered toast and chicken soup with rice. When another stressful situation occurs, the chances are increased that the child will again respond with cramps. The stress

213

is the underlying illness, but he has "learned" a physiological symptom.

Suppose laboratory test animals are presented with this stressful situation: Unless they exhibit a certain kind of behavior they will receive an electric shock. Under these conditions, rats learn an amazing variety of gut responses. Dr. Miller has shown that they speed up or slow down their heart rate, contract or relax their intestines, change their brain waves, and effect many other bodily changes. Once such functions were classed as "autonomic" —they were regarded as simple, automatic behavior that could not be willed or learned.

If you were offered ten dollars to speed up your heart rate, you might think for a moment, then run up and down the stairs and collect your sawbuck. But people also use their muscles and other "voluntary" systems to control their "involuntary" responses in subtler ways. In animal experiments, however, it's possible to eliminate the effect of skeletal muscles. By paralyzing the voluntary muscles and organs of rats with a drug, Dr. Miller has proved that visceral responses can be taught (and taught better) without the intervention of the voluntary systems.

How can these findings be applied to the case of the child with cramps? It's the learned symptom that is debilitating and there is hope it might be unlearned. Perhaps biofeedback could teach the child to relax his stomach and intestines in times of stress. But why stop there? Why not learn to fight symptoms that have their basis in organic disorders?

Research is now turning to this question. B. T. Engle and K. T. Melmom have had some encouraging results in training patients with cardiac arrhythmias to regularize their heartbeats. Miller and his associates see some promise in training epileptics to suppress the paroxysmal squiggles in their electroencephalograms.

Dr. Miller points out, "To the extent that functional neuroses are acquired during one's lifetime, they must be learned. . . . Perhaps we have evolved so that our mental health depends on an environment that forces us to perform coping responses."

In the seventeenth century, Sir Isaac Newton observed that a certain force accelerates a massive object slowly. But the same force makes a less massive object accelerate rapidly. This principle summarized and unified many different natural phenomena.

Yet there's nothing comparable to Newton's laws for social behavior and emotional phenomena. No single guiding principles like Newton's laws or "action and reaction" simplify behavioral "forces," mental processes, or learned illnesses.

But imagine biofeedback as the beginning of a simple social "law" that could explain how society teaches or "forces" us to learn acceptable behavior. Society itself encompasses a vast feedback loop we are all part of.

Eyes May Reveal Learning Ability

Two Canadians have designed a controversial intelligence-type test which measures what they call "the brain's physical ability to learn." They are Dr. John Ertl, a psychologist at the University of Ottawa, who invented the system, and Dr. Bernard Elliot, an electrical engineer, who built it. They call it a Neural Efficiency Analyser.

Conventional IQ tests are known to be somewhat unreliable. This is because a child's score can vary as much as twenty or thirty points on similar tests. Moreover, the tests are considered culturally biased in favor of white middle-class children whose native tongue is English. Dr. Ertl claims that this new test gives consistent results and is totally free of cultural and socioeconomic bias.

To take the test, the subject sits down in a comfortable chair and places on his head a helmet that contains electrodes to pick up his brain waves. These are amplified, and an oscilloscope makes them visible. The subject looks at a light that flashes each second for two minutes, and a computer analyzes how quickly his brain responds to it.

Dr. Ertl contends that the response is completely involuntary and is an objective test of learning ability. In a study of 1000

Canadian schoolchildren the test revealed a significant number of students who had been mistakenly placed in slow classes on the basis of low IQ scores.

Dr. Ertl, who once scored 77 on a conventional IQ test, but later discovered his IQ was really 140, says, "Intelligence is a concept equivalent to truth and beauty. I don't know what intelligence is, but I do know what it is not. It's not the score on an IQ test, and it is not what our equipment measures."

Those "windows on our soul"—our eyes—can foretell our interests and emotions (see page 229). When and if this development is perfected, our eyes may reveal our mental abilities and intellect.

Intelligence may someday be improved through eye training.

Expansion of Human Memory

Computer-aided techniques may improve your memory and make your mental images easy to recall, detailed and accurate.

The computer system monitors your brain waves while you look at something you wish to remember. Later, the same brainwave pattern is "played back" to you as an aid to recall. The computer feeds back those temporal and spatial cues that serve as keys to memory retrieval. (Remember how the smell of apple pie can trigger a flood of childhood memories.) It's too early to say whether or not the idea will work—but the concept is an intriguing one.

Another possibility that looks very promising is to stimulate your brain (using external electrodes) while you look at whatever it is that you want to remember. The idea, in this case, is to reinforce your mental image so it will be stronger and longer-lasting.

The program is still in its exploratory phase. As is the case with all basic research, it's almost impossible to say where it may lead. At present Dr. David Lai of Stanford University is examining the correlation between eye movements and brain-wave patterns. He's trying to isolate the patterns (or the pattern components) that are associated naturally with looking-and-remembering. He is also looking at the problem of *predicting* brain-wave patterns. A predictable pattern is likely to be nonrandom and therefore meaningful.

Dr. Lai, who is doing the work under a contract from ARPA (Advanced Research Projects Agency), describes the program as "investigating the possibility of devising new and unusual techniques that will permit the development of stronger imagery in men with normal memories. Since it is definitely an asset to absorb information rapidly and retain it intact for long periods of time, we seek to intensify the post-stimulus imagery as far as possible in the direction of photographic memory."

This program is pushing into very new territory, making a computer work *with* a man—not just *for* him. Drugs may enhance memory (see page 220), eye reflexes reveal learning ability (see page 215), and eye movements command machines (see page 367). But reinforcing mental retention is almost like imprinting messages on the brain. The danger? Perhaps it will be irreversible. The advantage? Every man his own photographic memory. Chemical or electronic instant recall, once the bugs are out, will be invaluably efficient for education, job training, and entertainment.

Dreamless Sleep Aids Memory

Sleeping directly after learning facilitates memory, according to research psychologists at the University of Colorado conducting a series of experiments on sleep patterns. Recall is better after the first four hours of an eight-hour sleep than after the last four hours; and in both cases memory is better than after four hours of wakefulness.

In one experiment the subjects were divided into three groups: A, B and C. Subjects in group A were given a list of fifteen paired words to learn. After that the group A subjects slept for four hours, and then were awakened and tested to see how much they remembered. The subjects in group B slept four hours, were awakened and given the list to learn; they slept another four hours, and then were awakened and tested. The subjects in group C learned the list, remained awake four hours, and then were tested for recall.

The results were that the subjects in group A had better recall than those in group B, and the subjects in both groups had better recall than those in group C. This indicates that while sleep facilitates memory, some types of sleep enhance memory better than others.

A full night's sleep is broken down into five stages: I, II, III, IV and REM (rapid eye movement). Each stage is characterized by a different type of mental activity. Stage IV is characterized by a very deep dreamless sleep, and REM sleep by many dreams from which the subject can be easily awakened. Experiments have shown that the first four hours of an eight-hour sleep consist of a high degree of Stage IV sleep, while the last four hours consist of a high degree of REM.

The subjects in group A experienced a high degree of Stage IV or dreamless sleep, while those in group B experienced a high degree of REM (dream sleep). The difference in recall suggests that deep, dreamless sleep (Stage IV sleep) enhances recall, and dream (REM) sleep inhibits it, though this has not been proven conclusively.

The difference in recall between groups A and B warrants caution, according to Dr. Bruce R. Ekstrand, one of the researchers: "The effects of prior sleep on subsequent memory consistently show that prior sleep produces an inhibitory effect on memory . . . and could interfere with memory for subsequently learned materials."

It's not only college students who have to remember a lot of detail. More and more jobs require more and more to remember, especially in our "knowledge industries." Memory is invaluable to the future. Indeed, the best memories are planned in advance.

Speech Compression for Speed Listening

Speed reading is a technique that has been used by millions to shorten reading time. Now a machine makes it possible to compress speech for faster listening and learning.

The speech-shortening device, called VOCOM, is small and compact—only 6½ inches high by 14 by 19 inches. It uses standard cassettes, compatible with any cassette player. The machine records directly from a microphone or from another source, such as a phonograph, radio, television or audiotape. Working on electromechanical principles, it cuts the speech material by shortening pauses, vowels, and nonessential sounds. At the same time it maintains the natural voice quality and intelligibility of the original. It was developed by PKM Corporation of St. Paul, Minnesota.

Ordinary speaking rates and rates of comprehension differ strikingly. The average person speaks from 100 to 180 words a minute. Yet the brain is reportedly able to process information at about 400 words per minute. The result is that when we listen to a slow speaker, our minds may wander and we may miss some of what's said. Compressing speech helps to bring the delivery rate up to the comprehension rate. Studies with compressed speech done with college students and others showed that compressed tape is a more efficient teaching method than the lecture method or normal-rate tapes. Researchers have found that elementary-school children learned best at a rate of about 250 words per minute.

VOCOM has many possible uses. If your time is worth five dollars an hour and you can save two hours a week by using compressed tapes, you'll save $520 per year. You'll also need much less tape for a library of recorded speech materials. In addition, a special playback on the device makes it possible to slow down recorded speech to an extremely slow rate. A typist, for example, can slow it down to her own typing speed. Foreign language material can be recorded at the normal rate, and the student can slow it down to study the articulation.

"The natural method of speech compression," says the developer of VOCOM, "is to drastically shorten the pauses, retain all the consonants, and shorten the vowel sounds. With this technique, compression to 30 to 40 percent of the original delivery time is possible without perceptual error."

With VOCOM we can absorb in forty minutes what might have taken up to two hours to listen to. This new tool saves time, money, space, materials. It's bound to catch on.

Chemical Transfer of Learning

In recent years researchers have made extraordinary advances in the study of memory, advances that may profoundly affect the future of the human mind. Their work suggests there is a chemical code for memory, just as there is a genetic code for life itself. Already, in lower species, it's possible to extract the memories from one animal and transfer them to another.

The story of this research is fascinating. In 1962 Professor McConnell of the University of Michigan patiently trained planarian worms to behave in a specified way when exposed to light. Then the trained worms were chopped up and fed to hungry, untrained planaria. After their cannibalistic meal, the untrained worms were taught the same response their ingested brothers had learned. They learned faster than the ordinary worms. It was as if they had fed on the knowledge of their fellow planaria.

By 1965 other scientists had demonstrated that memory transfer was possible in vertebrates, and the memories transferred were quite specific. For instance, Dr. Georges Ungar and his associates at the Baylor College of Medicine extracted chemicals from the brains of mice trained to run a maze and injected them into the brains of untrained mice. The mice receiving the injections learned to run the maze significantly sooner than mice receiving no "brain shots." If placed in a different maze, however, the injected mice performed no better than uninjected rodents.

From these experiments Dr. Ungar hypothesized that learning is encoded in chemical substances in the brain: "The nervous system can be compared to a computer programmed by the genetic code but capable of reprogramming itself continuously by the input of new information." Dr. Ungar believes that "the reprogramming code, like the genetic code, consists of the twenty amino acids that can combine to form sequences of a practically infinite variety."

To prove his theory, Dr. Ungar set out to isolate a "learning peptide." First he trained rats, which ordinarily are afraid of *light*, to be afraid of the *dark*. He then extracted fifteen amino acids from the brains of his night-fearing rats. By comparing these chemicals with the chemicals in light-fearing rats he managed to isolate a single peptide, called scotophobin—the first positively identified "memory chemical."

Scotophobin *is* fear of the dark. When artificially synthesized scotophobin is injected into normal rats, they too learn to fear the dark. The chemical even works on animals of a few other species. Researchers are now at work isolating other chemical correlates of memory.

How and why memory chemicals are formed remain a mystery. Peptide formation is probably only a small part of the complex process of memory—a process that is far more complex in humans than in lower animals. But Dr. Ungar insists, "The important fact is the first demonstration of a chemical correlate of memory, that is, the presence in the brain of trained animals of a substance that was not there before training."

Scientists are already speculating on the eventual outcome of this research—a memory pill that would alter the chemistry of the brain and promote more efficient learning. Senility and other defects of the mind might someday be "cured." The possibilities are limited only by the imagination; but with proper chemical treatment the imagination too might be improved and expanded. However, other research suggests that memory and other brain functions derive from the organization of cells in the brain.

Dr. Ungar anticipates some negative reaction to this far-reaching research: "As far as the methods derived from the molecular coding concept are concerned, there should be little apprehension of their leading to mind control. They deal with cognitive content of memory, not with attitudes and beliefs. Their

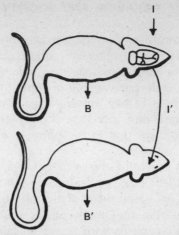

Donor animal (at top) received information (I) resulting in learned behavior (B). Extracts of its brain administered to recipient animal (bottom) produced a behavior (B′) similar to B. This can only have come from new information (I′) present in the brain extract.

applications could therefore be useful during the period of education, training for a profession, and especially in cases of memory defect or amnesia of traumatic, toxic or infectious origin. Knowledge of the mechanism by which information is acquired, stored and retrieved could enable us to devise means of dealing with its defects."

A slowdown for senility, knowledge pills, a new language by injection—these are just a few of the long-term possibilities raised by the work being done on the molecular code of memory.

Behavior Cycles

Scientists have found that human behavior seems to be affected by the combined influence of three internal biological "clocks" or rhythms. Their cycles may determine individual and team moods —high and low.

The three types of cycle are physical, emotional and intellec-

222

tual. They can be traced from a zero point, to a high point, to zero, to a low point, and back to zero again. The cycles run simultaneously, beginning at birth, and periodically crossing and recrossing throughout one's lifetime. The "physical" cycle determines strength and physical capabilities and takes 23 days to complete. The "emotional" cycle, found in both men and women, takes 28 days, and the "intellectual" or "mental" cycle lasts 33 days.

A study by behavior researcher Hans Schwing suggests that subjects are more prone to accidents and are low on good common sense when the physical and emotional cycles reach "zero" days or neutral points. Lows and highs are not dangerous but are days of stress and attentiveness, when a cycle is changing direction. Spurts of learning are charted as well, with those duller moments occurring on mental "zero" days. Particularly critical are "double zero" and "triple zero" days, which occur six times a year and once a year, respectively.

Michael Wallerstein and Nancy Lee Roberts charted the season's biorhythms for the offensive unit of the Los Angeles Rams. They discovered that when all the players were at or near a "high," the team had an overall low performance; but that when the players were at or near "lows," the team prevailed. They concluded that players *at* their peak play for more individual achievement, and that individuals *off* their peak play as a team and work better for collective success.

Wallerstein and Roberts say, "We hope to apply bio-curves towards the training of athletes and also to introduce it as a new form of sports statistics. Possibly there will come a day when lineup engineering becomes commonplace; where athletes can look to fewer injuries; where children can learn that losing comes from having had fewer capabilities on certain days than on others . . .

"In business, group productivities and teamwork also appear clockable, recognizing that individuals have different peak periods from those of the group in which they work."

These mood cycles of 23, 28, and 33 days are not the only ones. There are 80- to 120-minute cycles during sleep. There are 4- to 6-week mood cycles found in factory workers. There is an 8.3-

week cycle to the mood of *The New York Times* front-page news stories; and a 9-week cycle in the mood of their editorials. There are annual cycles for suicides and accidents. There are seasonal cycles of the common cold and sunspots. There's a 3-year cycle in the sports performance of men. There's a 17-year cycle in cotton prices and international wars. A 50-year cycle in pig iron production. A 90-year cycle in weather. One hundred and five years in women's fashions. Famines appear in 242-year cycles. And the growth of empires follows 667-year cycles.

Someday our knowledge of these cycles and why they appear may help us to predict or avoid unpleasant moods.

Change Hurts

Health disorders usually follow changes in life's routine. Everybody knows an unhappy experience can be painful. But many of life's changes and events also increase our susceptibility to disease. The greater the change, the more serious is the ailment.

Dr. Thomas Holmes and Dr. Minoru Masuda demonstrate there is a connection between changes and illness. Any change in life's routine seems to increase the chance of illness.

Forty-three events in our life were defined as *life changes*—changes that require some sort of social readjustment when they occur. Some examples of life changes are marriage, divorce, taking out a large bank loan, entering college, being fired or starting a new job. Marriage was given an arbitrary value of 50 on a scale of life change units (LCU). Several hundred people then ranked each of the life changes according to their importance. The group's average rating reflected the importance of a given life change.

Opposite

Life events may trigger future ailments. Add up the right-hand column for your life events that took place in the past 18 months. If your score is under 200, your risk is low and your chance of illness in the next 8 months is about 9 percent. This rises to 25 percent for a score above 200, and to 49 percent above 300.

Rank	Life Event	Mean Value
1	Death of spouse	100
2	Divorce	73
3	Marital separation	65
4	Jail term	63
5	Death of close family member	63
6	Personal injury or illness	53
7	Marriage	50
8	Fired at work	47
9	Marital reconciliation	45
10	Retirement	45
11	Change in health of family member	44
12	Pregnancy	40
13	Sex difficulties	39
14	Gain of new family member	39
15	Business readjustment	39
16	Change in financial state	38
17	Death of close friend	37
18	Change to different line of work	36
19	Change in number of arguments with spouse	35
20	Mortgage over $10,000	31
21	Foreclosure of mortgage or loan	30
22	Change in responsibilities at work	29
23	Son or daughter leaving home	29
24	Trouble with in-laws	29
25	Outstanding personal achievement	28
26	Wife begins or stops work	26
27	Begins or ends school	26
28	Change in living conditions	25
29	Revision of personal habits	24
30	Trouble with boss	23
31	Change in work hours or conditions	20
32	Change in residence	20
33	Change in schools	20
34	Change in recreation	19
35	Change in church activities	19
36	Change in social activities	18
37	Mortgage or loan less than $10,000	17
38	Change in sleeping habits	16
39	Change in number of family get-togethers	15
40	Change in eating habits	15
41	Vacation	13
42	Christmas	12
43	Minor violations of the law	11

The results are striking. The likelihood of a future illness depends on the number of life change units accumulated during the past two years. College football players were divided into three groups: low, medium and high life change units. At the end of the playing season, half of those with the highest total of LCU's had been injured. A quarter of those in the mid range were injured, and only 9 percent of those with the lowest total.

Similar results, involving illness instead of injury, were found in a group of 2500 Navy men on sea duty.

Drs. Holmes and Masuda explain why: "Life-change events, by evoking adaptive efforts by the human organism that are faulty in kind and duration, lower 'bodily resistance' and enhance the probability of disease occurrence."

The gap between behavior and medicine is closing. Life changes from the past haunt our future. And contemporary health care, recognizing this pattern, is moving toward *preventive* medicine. Within years we'll see routine tests for life change included in our annual health checkup.

Midlife Crisis

Many people apparently undergo a personal crisis in their thirties that's just as severe as the crises of adolescence and old age.

Dr. Kenn Rogers, a psychologist and professor of business administration at Cleveland State University, conducted four separate but interrelated studies of married couples in their thirties, of widely varying backgrounds and situations. The studies, embracing about 2000 people in London and New York, were spread over a period of 25 years. These studies all suggest that at some point between the ages of 30 and 39 most people undergo a real crisis, in the course of which profound changes occur in their feelings about themselves and their relation to their environment.

There are two major causes for this crisis, which is often accompanied by feelings of depression and frustration. The first cause is a reawakening of unresolved problems that occurred in the earlier stages of a person's life. In other words, it's at this point that the effects of an unhappy or traumatic childhood are felt, and most people react by trying to make changes in themselves or their surroundings to avoid repeating the pattern of their parents' lives.

The second, deeper cause is the conscious or unconscious awareness of approaching death. The aging process, which begins to accelerate in the thirties, is an unwelcome reminder to every individual that his life is already half over, and that many things he may have wanted to accomplish will never be done.

These two sources of stress and anxiety contribute to what Dr. Rogers calls the midlife crisis, a problem that has been discussed by other researchers, notably Carl Jung, Erik Erikson, Elliott Jaques and Alfred Kinsey. The crisis tends to be characterized by an increase in criminal behavior, depression, serious accidents, suicides, broken marriages, infidelity, and derailed careers.

There are two ways to combat the problem, however—"fight" and "flight." According to Dr. Rogers, "Flight is characterized by a feeling of helplessness, of withdrawal into oneself; 'life is too tough,' or 'there are no good professional prospects for people after 40.'

"Fight, on the other hand, means using this critical period to strengthen one's ability to face eventual death, to adjust to it. It involves giving up adolescent idealism and the accompanying radical desires and impatience in favor of a more reflective view of reality. . . . Individuals who have faced and successfully fought their fear of death tend toward changing conditions around them in the belief that the world can be improved.

"Indeed, the midpoint in life appears to represent a final, decisive period. . . . It seems that those who have chosen flight give up the effort to learn, and stagnate. Those who fight continue to learn and grow."

The postwar babies will be entering their thirties during the coming decade. If they dominate the country—in numbers or influence —one prognosis is a midlife crisis *nationwide.* Yet midlife *can* be intensely creative: Gauguin, Bach, Racine, Goethe, Moses, Buddha, William Shakespeare all achieved great things in their thirties.

Ripples of Friendship Circles

When two strangers find they have a common acquaintance, they often deliver the hackneyed exclamation, "Small world, isn't it?" And it's commonplace to observe that because of advances in transportation and communication "the world is getting smaller all the time." But exactly how small is it?

Social psychologist Stanley Milgram devised an experiment to find out. He chose a random sample of Americans and sent each an envelope containing the name and a brief description of a "target person," also selected at random. The odds were 1 in 200,000 that the person receiving the envelope would know the target individual personally, so he was asked to forward the envelope to a first-name acquaintance who might be more likely to know the target. If the second link in the chain did not know the target person either, he was asked to continue the chain. The object was to discover approximately how many intermediate circles of acquaintances separate any two people.

Most chains were surprisingly short. The range was from two to ten, but on the average *five* intermediates sufficed to link any two individuals, no matter where in the United States they lived. The first finding, then, is we do indeed live in a small world. As Dr. Milgram observes, "We are all bound together in a tightly knit social fabric"—more tightly knit than many of us might have suspected.

But Dr. Milgram's chain letter may tell us still more about communications within our society. The kinds of intermediaries between two people provide information about how both sender and receiver are laced into the social fabric. Often there was one key person, "a sociometric star," through whom the target person received most of his envelopes. Whether or not the target person realized it, the sociometric star was a vital link between him and the rest of the world.

Dr. Milgram also considered how many circles of acquaintances separate members of different subgroups—blue-collar and white-collar, whites and blacks. He says the study "reveals a potential communication structure whose sociological character-istics have yet to be exposed. When we understand the structure of this potential communication net, we shall understand a good deal more about the integration of society in general."

People who extend or change their circles of acquaintance change their position in society, as well as their outlook on life. These chains of friendships may tell us how rumors, gossip, jokes, ideas, new products, and propaganda are spread. Identifying one's cir-cles of acquaintances might someday prove a useful therapeutic tool.

Eyes Foretell

According to Dr. Eckhard Hess of the University of Chicago, "Anatomically the eye is an extension of the brain; it is almost as though a portion of the brain were in plain sight for the psychol-ogist to peer at." Novelists, magicians and Oriental traders have always insisted that the eyes reveal a great deal about what a person is thinking, and Dr. Hess has confirmed this intuition. He's found that light intensity alone isn't responsible for the dila-tion and constriction of the pupils. But change in pupil size is, in fact, a reliable measure of interest, attitudes and emotions.

In an early series of experiments, male volunteers were shown a series of photographs of rather commonplace landscapes. A special viewing apparatus permitted Dr. Hess and his associates to snap continuous close-up pictures of the subjects' eyes at half-second intervals. When an especially bright photo of a scantily clad pin-up girl was projected on the screen, one might have expected the pupils to contract, adjusting for the higher intensity light. Actually the opposite proved true: Male subjects' pupils dilated—as much as 30 percent. Similarly, subjects who were shown unpleasant pictures (one of a disabled child, for instance) reacted as if they were trying to shut out the image, constricting pupils markedly.

The eyes also reflect attitudes toward nonvisual stimuli: Subjects were asked to sip a variety of beverages and choose which flavor they preferred. In most cases, a person's pupils opened widest when he was sipping his favorite drink. Further, when music of any kind was played, from rock to Bach, the pupils generally dilated in appreciation.

Even more conclusive were experiments performed with hungry and satiated subjects. Two groups were shown a slide series including pictures of appetizing foods. The group who had eaten a large meal only an hour before the test showed only slight increases in pupil size when viewing the food slides. But the group who had been deprived of food for five hours showed significant dilations—11.3 percent on the average—when staring at a photo of a sizzling steak.

Dr. Hess has also studied the correlation between pupil size and more abstract attitudes. Looking at photos of political figures, pupil dilation or constriction tended to correlate with favorable or unfavorable attitudes toward political personalities. After subjects were asked to examine a photo of Lyndon Johnson, they read an article critical of his Presidency. When they again examined the photo of Johnson, their pupil size had decreased, reflecting a modified judgment of the man.

Finally, men react to a picture of a woman with dilated eyes—with corresponding dilations of their own. Although they could not say exactly why, they preferred the picture to one of the same woman with more constricted pupils; some said she seemed "softer" or "prettier." This would seem to explain the practice of women as far back as the Middle Ages who dilated their pupils with the drug belladonna (which means "beautiful woman" in Italian).

Dr. Hess speculates on one possible application of eye watching: "Suppose a patient seeking psychotherapy has a fear of people with beards. We ought to be able to get a pupillary measure of his attitude by showing him photographs of bearded men, among others, and then be able to check on the course of treatment by repeating the test later."

Psychologists aren't the only ones interested in watching eye pupils. The technique is used by Chinese jade dealers who watch a buyer's eyes to know when he's impressed by a specimen and is likely to pay a high price. Politicians, poker players and advertising men, among others, need an unequivocal measure of attitude change. Because it's under the control of the autonomic (involuntary) nervous system, the eye cannot lie.

Is Demography Destiny?

People who count their chickens *before* they're hatched act very wisely, said Oscar Wilde, because *afterward* chickens run about so absurdly that it's impossible to count them accurately.

Like those slippery hatchlings, personal beliefs and values are elusive quantities. But it's now possible to count some chickens before hatching.

Personal values of social groups are important indicators and propagators of change. Often responsible for our attitudes and actions, deeply held values reflect our priorities of likes and dislikes.

Reliable census estimates project the size of various groups by age, income and education. Since our personal priorities change as we get older—and as time marches on—the age bulge in our population provides valuable hints about the future.

What's missing, though, is a clear and simple way to measure these elusive personal values and priorities. Of the imperfect but useful measuring instruments created for this purpose, the "value scale" designed by Milton Rokeach is especially suitable.

Here's how it works: Given a list of words that mean the same to everyone and represent personal "values," individuals sort them; they rank the words in order according to their own personal preferences and priorities. Fortified by these priority lists, social scientists can clearly differentiate liberals from conservatives, men from women, fifth-graders from seventh-graders, and so on. Furthermore, statistical comparisons can be made across age, income and educational levels.

Men place "capable," "independent," "ambitious" and "sense of accomplishment" typically higher than women do, nationwide. And women give higher priority than men to "loving," "forgiving," "cheerful" and "true friendship." At equally high priorities both men and women rank the values "honest," "family security," "freedom" and "happiness."

As income rises from poverty to affluence, the following values *decline in priority*: "clean," "helpful" and "obedient." In fact, for 1968 annual incomes below $2000, "clean" is at the top, but above $15,000 it is at the bottom of the priority list. It may be that cleanliness is paramount precisely because it's so difficult to achieve amidst poverty. And the affluent downgrade "clean" because in their system of values it's taken for granted.

With rising incomes, the following values assume increasingly *higher* priorities: "a sense of accomplishment," "wisdom," "an exciting life," "intellectual," "mature love" and "independent." Often a precursor to financial rewards, a desire for accomplishment may nourish our appetite for independence and excitement.

Compared with 1965, the 25- to 34-year-old age group will have doubled by 1990. And between 1975 and 1990 approximate doubling will occur among 35- to 44-year-olds. Young adults, then, are the fastest-growing age groups, and soon to be the largest, in the United States. To the extent that they dominate the country numerically, they will also dominate the United States by their values, attitudes, feelings and activities. In this sense, *demography is destiny*. We should, therefore, look very closely at past trends and how value priorities evolve with age.

As they mature, young adults give consistently *declining* priorities to the following values: "equality," "wisdom," "sense of accomplishment" and "loving." Displacing and outranking these are *ascending* priorities for "national security," "salvation," "cheerful," "broadminded," "clean" and "a comfortable life." Extrapolation of these trends rests upon the substantial assumption that they are more intrinsic to an age group than to a social epoch.

But this caveat aside, the ascending trends among young adults imply that their priorities will characterize the country in the next decades. The most sharply rising of all these values is "national security."

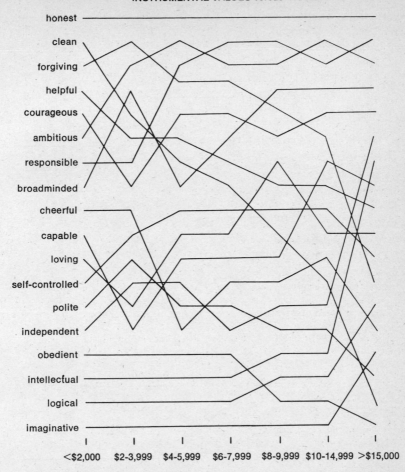

INSTRUMENTAL VALUES versus INCOME

Word lists of "values" are ranked by a nationwide sample of Americans in order of personal preference. They are analyzed according to income and other demographic characteristics. Here, across all income levels, "honest" is of paramount priority. The value "clean" drops dramatically as income rises.

The most precipitous drop is in the ranking of "equality." Those who demote "equality" and those who elevate "national security" are apparently in the mainstream—that looming wave of young adults on the horizon.

TERMINAL VALUES versus AGE

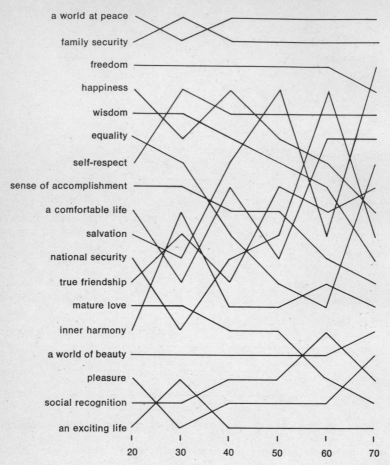

The ranking of values according to age. As adults mature, the values "equality," "wisdom" and "sense of accomplishment" decline in priority. But "national security" and "salvation" ascend in priority.

The bulging adult population has inclinations that will unfold over the next decades owing to three distinct phases that occur during the human maturation process. One phase corresponds roughly to the ages 30 to 49, in which most men tend to emphasize their strivings toward autonomy, competence, competition and control to achieve mastery over external systems; they are wary of others limiting their actions and choices. Their aura may dominate the eighties.

In the next phase, from about 50 to 59 years of age, men may tend to feel they can influence the powers-that-be only indirectly; they tend to reshape themselves to fit the expectations of powerful and ambitious providers; they may emphasize mildness (rather than challenge), accommodation or conformity to outer pressures; and they may suppress their aggressive tendencies that could lead to dangerous conflict. This age group could begin to dominate around the year 2000.

In the third phase, beyond age 60, men often see the world around them revised as if by fiat, and they may define dangerous or troubling external events as innocuous or benign; they may tend to hold others responsible for their own troublesome thoughts or actions. I would hope this aura does not permeate our society in the new century.

Altering the Past, Present and Future

How would you react if you could no longer conceive of the future—but live only in the present and past? It sounds like a philosopher's puzzle or a science fiction nightmare. But with the use of posthypnotic suggestion, Dr. Bernard Aaronson has explored this and other drastic alterations in our perceptions of space and time.

In experiments conducted at the Bureau of Research in Neurology and Psychiatry, Princeton, New Jersey, Dr. Aaronson and others gave this posthypnotic instruction to six volunteers: "Do you know how we divide time into the three categories of past, present and future? When I wake you, the future will be gone. There will be no future."

The researchers didn't know what to expect when one region of time was suddenly erased or ablated. The results were extraordinary. In some cases the subjects experienced behavior changes that one would anticipate only with the use of powerful psycho-active drugs. One subject "found himself in a boundless, imma-nent present." He became fascinated with colors and textures, and went so far as to describe his feelings as "mystical." Ordi-narily goals and deadlines are located in the psychological future; these plans, in turn, produce hopes and anxieties. But without a conception of tomorrow, the subjects generally lost all their moti-vation and all their anxieties.

Later, when the subjects were asked to experience "an *ex-panded* future," the effects were different but equally remark-able. The subjects felt they had been given all the time they needed to accomplish everything they ever intended. They were calm and happy, and any apparent fear of death vanished.

In other tests, Dr. Aaronson hypnotically expanded or eradi-cated his subjects' past and present. Eliminating the present was by far the most disturbing: subjects felt profoundly depressed and behaved almost schizophrenically. One volunteer described the sensation of "unbeing," a lonely, deathlike detachment. Eliminating the past also had a negative impact, characterized by drowsiness and impaired functioning; several people suffered memory losses and had difficulty speaking. Everything seemed meaningless.

In contrast, expanding the past and present produced good feelings. Widening the world of the present encouraged exuber-ance and enhanced both visual and auditory sensations. On a car ride one subject asked the experimenter to stop and let him out; for many minutes he stood by the side of the road watching a cow leisurely chewing its cud. Expanding the past brought on dreamy retrospection.

Dr. Aaronson can also alter the subjective passage of time by hypnosis. Telling someone to live three seconds for one second on the clock not surprisingly produces a manic state. Slowing people down makes them bored. Stopping time altogether is more seri-ous. As when the present is obliterated, there is a sensation of death: "The world moves on, but I don't." Spatial perception is disrupted. In still another set of experiments, Dr. Aaronson de-creased and increased the spatial dimensions of depth and size.

Dr. Aaronson says, "Time is particular and idiosyncratic. We perceive time as moving quickly when we are happy, slowly

EXPANDED and ABLATED AREAS OF TIME UNDER POST-HYPNOTIC SUGGESTION

no past	no present	no future
confused	immobile	euphoric
disoriented	responseless	semi-mystical
bored	death-like	anxiety-free
sleepy	lonely	less motivated
language	depth loss	identity loss
loss	withdrawn	discouraged
	depressed	stopped growing
	hostile	no ambitions

expanded past	expanded present	expanded future
happy	happy	happy
reminiscent	fascinated	no fear of death
relaxed	by colors	anticipation
slow	exuberant	fulfilled
movements	time slowed	calm
	enhanced senses	lots of time
	clarity of	more full and rich
	objects &	
	sounds	

Posthypnotic suggestions eliminate or expand the past, present and future. These words describe how hypnotized subjects see the world under altered states of time.

when we are sad. In experiences such as the panoramic death vision, a lifetime may pass by in only a few seconds."

According to J. T. Fraser, "A person's view of time is a way of discerning his personality. We may almost say: 'Tell me what you think of time and I shall know what to think of you.' "

A new vacation idea—hypnotically induced time travel. Perhaps an expanded future "time vacation" after exhausting work. For pleasure seekers an expanded present "time vacation." For the religious—a "dose" of increased depth. For cardiac cases with the "hurry-up" sickness, doctors may prescribe a changed rate of passage through time. These "trips" may be the only form of time travel man will experience.

Measurement of Romantic Love

A scale to measure romantic love is the result of recent social psychology research.

The varieties of love include filial, sexual and platonic. But this research was on love between unmarried opposite-sex peers—the sort that could lead to marriage. The first step in this study, done by Dr. Zic Rubin, now at Harvard, was to develop a "love" scale, which was then compared with a "liking" scale. A large pool of question items was assembled to tap the subjects' attitudes or feelings toward a target person of the opposite sex. The items probed aspects often associated with romantic love, such as physical attraction, idealization, and the desire to share emotions and experiences. On the "liking" scale items dealt with respect toward the other person as a human being—estimating their maturity, integrity and popularity.

Each item was answered on a scale ranging from 1 ("Not at all true") to 10 ("Definitely true"). The average couple, who had been dating for about one year, consisted of a college junior man and a sophomore or junior woman.

The "love" scale responses were virtually the same for men and women; the most popular items (those with highest scores) were "I would do anything for_____." "If I were lonely, I would seek_____out." "I would forgive_____for anything." And "It would be hard for me to get along without_____." This would indicate that dependent need and a predisposition to help are predominant among love partners. Apparently the concept of romantic love includes three components: affiliative and dependent need, a predisposition to help, and absorption or exclusiveness with one's partner.

Women responded to the liking scale with much lower scores

than they put on the love scale; but the men's responses were nearly the same on both. It was unexpected that men would correlate love and liking to a greater extent than women, but they did. A possible explanation is that women are more likely than men to discriminate between the two sentiments; it's also more socially acceptable for women to declare love for a person of the same sex.

Harlow wrote in 1958, "So far as love or attraction is concerned, psychologists have failed in that notion. The little we know about love does not transcend simple observation, and the little we write about it has been written better by poets and novelists."

Romantic love may be a link between the individual and society. For better or worse, perhaps social scientists could try to predict successful marriages even before couples become engaged.

Chemical Male Contraception

Almost all efforts in human contraception have been directed toward the female. Now a chemical sterilizing agent effective in rats may provide male contraception to humans.

The agent, U-5897, belongs to a class of antifertility compounds known as alpha-chlorohydrins. It produces reversible infertility in rats, as well as in guinea pigs, boars, rams and monkeys. Only in the rat, however, does U-5897 cause irreversible sterility when given in doses five times those of the minimum dose necessary to produce antifertility; the chemosterilant causes a lesion in the caput epididymis, part of the spermatic duct system. The epididymis transfers sperm from the testes to an inside reproductive organ for storage in male rats. Other species failed to develop lesions.

Dr. R. J. Ericsson and his associates at the Upjohn Company in Michigan did several studies in which U-5897 was presented in oral form to rats, either in their water or in dog food presented as bait. Although the chemical was accepted by many rats even in its uncoated form, encapsulation of it in a vinyl resin-based coating greatly increased its acceptance. The chemosterilant maintained good chemical stability over time and was effective in producing lesions, whether given in lower repeated doses or in one higher single dose.

The lesion blocked passage of sperm and prevented removal of fluid from the testes, which then swelled. This swelling placed extra pressure on the epithelium, or membraned covering of the sperm-producing cells, inhibiting the growth of sperm. Even after a year, cell examination of the epididymis still showed the presence of a lesion.

An important finding was that the sterilized rats showed the same level of libido—they had desire as well as ability to mate. Their general health continued to be good, and their growth was normal except for some loss in size of the testes.

Dr. Ericsson believes that the action of U-5897 can serve as a new tool for the study of sperm maturation in the epididymis.

Tests in both the laboratory and the rats' natural environment indicated that one dose of U-5897 was sufficient to produce sterility. An overdose, however, could cause death.

According to Dr. Ericsson, "The attributes of U-5897 make it one of the promising male chemosterilants known for rats . . . making possible the further testing of the concept of a mammalian chemosterilant."

Are male oral contraceptives the wave of the future? Probably medical—as well as social—needs will create some demand for these methods of human birth control.

Dietary Control of Aggression

Experiments performed by Dr. John Calhoun at the National Institute of Mental Health suggest that high doses of vitamin A reduce aggression in rats. Though no comparable experiments have been done on man, he cautions that the healthy aggressive instincts of Americans may already be jeopardized by the eggs, milk and liver we consume.

Three groups of rats were given powdered diets which differed only in the amount of vitamin A. Certain differences in behavior were noted, especially between the rats on the low vitamin A diet and those on the high vitamin A diet. For example, rats fed the high dosages of vitamin A were found to have fewer wounds when autopsies were performed. Rats sustain wounds when they engage in social "status" interactions—what's normally called "fighting." The rats on the high vitamin A diet were involved, on the average, in only 30 percent as many such interactions as those on the low vitamin A diet. Higher levels of vitamin A intake apparently reduced aggression in these rats.

Though the reduced aggression might be seen as a good thing, other effects of increased vitamin intake were less beneficial. The male rats displayed more homosexual behavior and mounted very young females who are likely to miscarry or neglect their young after birth. The female rats showed disturbances in maternal behavior. Calhoun attributes these effects to perceptual problems. The fourfold increase in vitamin A for the "high" rats apparently impaired their ability to integrate stimuli and carry out complex behaviors.

What are the implications for man? Dr. Calhoun points out that the average American consumes a lot of eggs, fortified milk, cheese and liver—foods naturally rich in vitamin A. Other foods, such as dry cereals, which don't normally contain vitamin A are now being vitamin-fortified. More and more people are taking vitamin pills with breakfast, sometimes of high dosages. Although recent federal legislation prohibits the sale without a prescription of very high dosages of vitamin A and D over-the-counter, the average American diet may already consist of doses of vitamin A as high as those fed the "high" rats. If so, this may well lead to reduced aggression.

As Dr. Calhoun says, "To the extent that vitamin A produces a comparable effect on the physiology and behavior of man that it does on rats, one must conclude that the current elevation of vitamin A intake by man will simultaneously reduce the likelihood of involvement in agonistic [competitive] relations . . ."

Dietary control of aggression seems like a simple cure for war, which for so long has eluded solution: a small vitamin pill served along with juice at the United Nations cafeteria might imaginably make the delegates (and their respective countries?) a lot less hostile to one another.

But healthy instincts of aggressiveness have led us to progress. Without them man can't conquer nature or disease, be inspired to invent machines or to create art.

We might consider limited use of dietary control, though, perhaps with young children prone to violence or even criminals who commit violent crimes (*Clockwork Orange* notwithstanding). Since it's probably reversible, this may be a more effective way of handling crime than years of imprisonment.

Mercy Killing

"To please no one will I prescribe a deadly drug, nor give advice which may cause his death," reads a section of the Hippocratic oath. Throughout history, of course, there have been occasional, sometimes famous cases of mercy killing: After countless operations for cancer, Sigmund Freud conspired with his physician to receive an overdose of morphine. But euthanasia as a public *policy* has remained anathema to doctors and to society as a whole.

Recent advances in medicine, however, have made the moral questions involved more complicated than ever. Heart and lung machines, repeated transfusions, and other treatments can often sustain vital signs for weeks and even months after the body has grown incapable of living on its own. When there is hope of eventual recovery no one would question the use of extraordinary lifesaving devices. But what if there is no *realistic* hope? Is it the doctor's duty to keep his patient alive—even when the patient himself prefers to die peacefully?

Increasingly patients, doctors and families are accepting the practice of "passive euthanasia." Instead of resorting to one medical "cure" after another, all persons involved agree that the physician will make the patient as comfortable as possible and let life come to its natural end. It remains a difficult ethical decision, yet Pope Pius XII, among many others, maintained that a doctor is not in conscience required to use "extraordinary means" to prolong life. Dr. Malcolm Todd, the president of the American Medical Association, has proposed a commission composed of lawyers, doctors, clergy and laymen to set forth guidelines for "death with dignity."

This leaves the question of "active euthanasia," where, as in Freud's case, the doctor is asked to administer a fatal injection to a terminal patient suffering great pain. Legally, in all fifty states this is still considered murder. But a few people have stepped forward to defend what has been termed "the right to die," and the state legislature of Oregon, for one, has considered fundamental changes in the law.

Oregon Senate Bill 179, proposed in 1973, would permit a person with an "irremediable" condition to subscribe to the following statement:

> *If I should at any time suffer from a serious physical illness or impairment reasonably thought in my case to be incurable and expected to cause me severe distress or render me incapable of rational existence, I request the administration of euthanasia at the time or in circumstances to be specified by me, or, if it is apparent that I have become incapable of giving directions, at the discretion of the physician in charge of my case.*

Elaborate precautions surround this provision to ensure that the declaration is not signed under duress or out of momentary despair, and it would only take effect thirty days after it is signed. The bill would, nonetheless, entail two highly controversial precedents: It would allow doctors to administer "active euthanasia," and under certain circumstances, it would delegate authority to the doctor to decide whether or not to give a lethal dose of drugs.

The bill received a great deal of opposition, and was eventually withdrawn by its sponsor. Still, it's a significant indication that euthanasia will be a subject of growing debate.

In withdrawing the euthanasia bill that he cosponsored, Oregon State Senator Ted Hallock said, "I have a son in his early twenties who has been retarded since birth. . . . He is virtually a vegetable. Though there is no hope for him, I have hope. I would certainly not ask for his death. But if Christopher were not retarded, if Christopher were mentally perfect, yet suffered from some terrible cancer, and he asked to be put out of his misery, I would want him to be allowed to make that decision."

There's no way to estimate the number. But doctors undoubtedly practice passive—and active—euthanasia in complicity with patients and families. Moreover, doctors often decide who receives needed kidney machines. So they're already making life and death decisions—tantamount to involuntary euthanasia. But legislating on euthanasia is a delicate matter. In approaching it, it's worthwhile to consider a fact that democratic societies may like to forget: Many systems work better when they're *not* discussed openly.

Confirmation of Electrocerebral Silence

The most common test for death was the "breath of life." A mirror held close to the lips of a live patient would collect foggy moisture. Or a pillow feather placed across the lips of a live patient would flutter from a trace of breath. For centuries the approach of death could be recognized in many ways—but the actual moment of death was not always easy to determine.

New criteria for the determination of death require unambiguous results: The irreversible absence of vital human functions. No spontaneous breathing or movements. Repeat of all these tests unchanged a day later would confirm the diagnosis.

As sophisticated life-support systems developed it became desirable to know, for moral as well as medical reasons, precisely when death occurred. Surgeons performing transplant operations had to know the exact moment of death for legal as well as ethical and medical reasons. If they wait too long, a transplantable organ is lost. And furthermore, a living body should turn into a corpse for biological reasons *only*—not by declaration or signing of a certificate.

The electroencephalograph, commonly called EEG, was developed to diagnose brain injuries and other malfunctions. Any activity of the brain is electrically sensed by electrodes placed on the patient's head and recorded by the EEG. When all other signs of self-sustaining life had failed, it was found the brain frequently continued to function. When the brain ceased to function for a given period of time (ten or twenty minutes) the patient was pronounced dead. Doctors had found a safe, reasonably sure measurement to determine the moment of death.

When the EEG records a reading of less than two microvolts from the brain's activities, the brain is said to be dead. But this is a negative determination of death open to the possibility of error. A malfunction of the EEG apparatus, particularly its amplification channels, could cause a recording of less than two microvolts from the brain of the patient. If the electrodes from the EEG are improperly placed upon the patient's head, the inadequate electrical contacts could result in higher resistance, which would in turn produce false readings of less than two microvolts.

Dr. Edward F. MacNichol of the Marine Biological Laboratory, Woods Hole, Massachusetts, has developed a method of double-checking an EEG reading that has indicated electrocerebral silence or death of the brain. His apparatus injects a small electric current into the patient's head in a location and in a fashion that will allow the signal to be monitored by the EEG in all its channels. The EEG will read this signal only if each of its electrodes is in proper contact with the patient's head. A second signal is then injected into the patient's head, which can be monitored by each channel of the EEG selectively. The second signal is of a predetermined strength and provides a reference measurement against which the strength of monitored brain activity can be measured. Dr. MacNichol states that his testing method and apparatus provide "positive criteria to assure that even small signals from the head and scalp of the patient would be monitored by the EEG apparatus if such signals existed."

The moment of death poses an urgent question for physicians and patients, especially in an era when the elderly population is large and rising, and when disasters strike. Biomedical advances of the seventies (see Chap. 1) raise ethical life-and-death questions. But raising these moral issues will probably not halt the advance of medical progress. Public support of research depends, in part, upon responsible researchers and their willingness to raise the issues.

The Metric System's Coming—
Sooner or "Liter"

The United States is going metric.

As this book goes to print, the Congress is considering a bill to promote the metric system as the "predominant, although not the exclusive measuring system" in the United States. After an initial planning year, the conversion will gradually take place over a period of ten years.

The yard, originally established as the waist size of a Saxon king (yard is derived from the Old English *gerd,* or girth), will give way to the meter (39.37 inches). And the mile may become as obsolete as the league.

Already Maryland requires the teaching of metrics in the schools, and California will follow suit by the fall of 1976. Many consumer products are now marked with both the metric and U.S. measures of their contents. Weather forecasters—even on TV —are beginning to announce the temperature in both Fahrenheit and Celsius (centigrade) degrees.

Other countries with the traditional weights, measures and monetary systems of the English-speaking nations are converting, too. England itself has forsaken the pound (weight) and the pound sterling (20 shillings or 240 pence) for decimal base-ten measures and currency. Australia and New Zealand began the changeover in 1970.

The impetus is economic. Industries want to market the same products at home and in countries using the metric system. But for industries to make so fundamental a change, employees must

246

learn the equivalents of meters, liters and grams, and this calls for national reeducation.

Once the conversion is completed, *time* will be the only dimension not commonly measured on a decimal scale.

As Dr. John L. Feirer, director of the Western Michigan University Center for Metric Education, notes, "We're becoming a have-not nation. If we fail to convert to metric standards, we're putting ourselves behind an extra eight ball. Metric conversion can simply mean more jobs for more people."

The calendar and the clock will soon be the only measures not based on the decimal system. Both retain the convention of allotting 360 degrees to a circle. But even the clock and calendar (see below) are not safe from change. In fact there may be a digital timepiece in our future.

Calendar Reform

On what date will Easter fall next year? On what day of the week is your birthday? For the answers you'll have to consult your calendar. As an alternative, however, several organizations recommend settling these questions of timing once and for all. They propose a variety of reforms—from regularizing the Gregorian calendar to scrapping it altogether.

The Western calendar is a hand-me-down from the ancient Egyptians, who adopted a solar calendar in 4236 B.C. The Romans had a ten-month system until 46 B.C., when Julius Caesar remodeled it after the Egyptian pattern. Pope Gregory XIII revised it again in A.D. 1582 to stabilize the date of the spring equinox. Still irregularities remain.

One inconsistency that peeves computers is the wide variation in the number of working days in each month. First, there's the problem of whether the month has 28, 29, 30 or 31 days. Then the machine must worry about how many weekends there are.

Finally, there are the holidays to consider. The total number of working days can vary as much as 19 percent.

As far back as 1849, the French philosopher Comte proposed what is now known as the International Fixed Calendar. He suggested a year divided into 13 months, each exactly 28 days long; the extra month, Sol, would be squeezed between June and July. To make a total of 365 days, an extracalendar holiday, with no designation as to month or day, would occur after December 28. In leap year there would be a second extracalendar feast. The first day of every month would always be a Sunday, and the last a Saturday. Unfortunately, Comte's year would not divide evenly into quarters, a major drawback from a business viewpoint.

The World Calendar, devised by the French astronomer Armelin in 1884, keeps the 12-month system and equalizes the quarters. Every quarter has 91 days: January, April, July and October have 31 days, and all other months have 30. The provisions for a 365th day and leap year resemble Comte's calendar. Although during the 1930s, 47 nations endorsed the concept of the World Calendar, no action was taken. Two recurring criticisms have been that each month spans parts of five different weeks, and each month of a given quarter begins on a different day.

An American industrial engineer, Wallace Barlow, has extended the idea of the extracalendar day into 29 extracalendar days. He conceives of a working month of 28 days; every month begins on Monday, and there are no holidays (except Saturdays and Sundays) in this period. All holidays are gathered together into a series of extracalendar festivals at the end of each month. The Christmas holiday, for instance, begins on Saturday, December 27, and runs through the 28th and five extracalendar feast days. The total work year is shortened by 14 days, but Barlow argues productivity will actually increase because there are no "broken weeks" (midweek holidays). This is the equivalent of reducing the workweek to 38 hours.

A first step to calendar reform in the United States was the passage of the Monday holiday bill. Polls show over 90 percent of the population support this change. The Calendar Reform Foundation, which endorses the Barlow Calendar, advocates setting a fixed date for Easter, and changing Christmas and Thanksgiving

THE BARLOW CALENDAR

M	T	W	T	F	S	S
1	2	3	4	5	6	7
8	9	10	11	12	13	14
15	16	17	18	19	20	21
22	23	24	25	26	27	28

every month is the same,
except that the 28th of April is Easter Sunday

The Extra-calendar Days

all are holidays
and follow weekends

January 29th . . . . Winter Festival

February 29th . . . . National Hero's Day

March 29th . . . . Spring Festival

April 29th, 30th, and 31st . . . . Easter Holiday

May 29th, 30th 31st, 32nd (and 33rd on Leap Year) . . . . Summer Festival

June 29th, 30th, 31st, and 32nd . . . . Festival of Peace

July 29th, 30th and 31st . . . . Festival of Independence

August 29th and 30th . . . . Festival of Friendship

September 29th and 30th . . . . Autumn Festival

October 29th . . . . Music Festival

November 29th and 30th . . . . Thanksgiving Holiday

December 29th, 30th, 31st, 32nd, and 33rd . . . . Christmas Holiday

The Barlow Calendar has 12 months of 28 days each and a series of extra-calendar holidays that would fall at the end of each month.

so they too are Monday holidays. The Vatican's ecumenical council has voted overwhelmingly not to oppose a fixed date for Easter or a perpetual calendar.

"The cost of accomplishing this calendar reform is substantially nil," the Calendar Reform Foundation reports. "The savings in the cost of accounting operations alone will approximate $1.5 billion; however, as Maurice Maeterlinck wrote, 'At every crossway on the road that leads to the future . . . each progressive spirit is opposed by a thousand men appointed to guard the past.' "

One group that's sure to oppose any kind of calendar reform is the calendar manufacturers. With each of these proposed changes, one calendar would be good for an entire lifetime.

Adolescent Homicidal Behavior

Homicide may not be as haphazard a phenomenon as we're usually led to believe. Studies by researchers at the University of Michigan point to certain specific personality patterns in adolescents that make them likely murderers.

Data were collected over an eight-year period on adolescents in the United States and Great Britain from clinical interviews, psychological tests, and physical and neurological examinations. Based on the data, Dr. Derek Miller and Dr. John Looney of the University of Michigan were able to make correct predictions of homicidal attempts for all but two of the teenagers. In one of these two cases, a prediction of homicide had been made years earlier by another psychiatrist.

Miller and Looney believe that what sets off a murderer from a merely violent person is his capacity to dehumanize, to see other people merely as objects who lose their individuality. The murderer can form only superficial attachments, if any.

Earlier tests on adolescents who eventually commit murder did not adequately distinguish homicidal individuals from violent but nonhomicidal individuals. Both groups had past histories of severe emotional deprivation and violent parents, low self-esteem and poor control over their own aggressive impulses. Miller and Looney's findings appear to distinguish between these two groups.

The researchers were also able to isolate three types of potential adolescent murderers, differing in the degree of risk that they'll commit homicide. The three types also came across differently during diagnostic interviews.

The very high-risk individual is capable of totally dehumanizing others. The violence in his personality is so pervasive that murder is a real possibility whenever his wishes are actually being thwarted or he thinks they are. He sees other people merely as frustrating objects that have to be eliminated. When interviewed, he appears cold, detached and brutal, and is unable to form an attachment to the doctor. A typical reaction in the physician, which also aids in diagnosis, is an anxious hostility toward the patient.

The high-risk individual partially dehumanizes others. He suffers from what is known clinically as "episodic dyscontrol"—occasional instances of loss of control over his impulses. When certain other people represent to him the unacceptable parts of his own personality, and stir up conflicts, he's tempted to commit murder. This type is easily distinguished during an interview because he acts out his murderous fantasy with a tremendous excitement that's almost sexual.

The low-risk person is the most difficult to diagnose. He also dehumanizes others occasionally, but only when he feels he has the agreement and permission of a peer group. It's possible this pattern of dehumanization is what leads to slaughter of innocent civilians during wartime. It's also the mechanism at work in gang slayings. Unlike the high-risk types, the low-risk type can and needs to form attachments to others.

According to Miller and Looney, "It is the hypothesis of this study that the capacity to dehumanize others, easily produced under stress . . . is the issue that differentiates the murderous from the violent."

Many adolescents who commit murder have previously been in contact with probation officers, court social workers and school therapists. If these agents knew how to predict homicidal behavior, they might prevent murders, instead of trying to treat delinquents.

Nonlethal Weapons

The police officer pursuing a fleeing suspect is confronted with a dilemma. Usually he has only a pistol and a nightstick. If he fires, he runs the split-second risk of inadvertently executing a man without a trial—for a crime that might bring only a short prison sentence. Yet it's his duty to apprehend the wrongdoer instantly.

Although research and development have been distressingly slow, a few new weapons may give the police nonlethal alternatives. Several companies are developing dart guns, like the Cap-Chur, produced by the Palmer Chemical Company in Douglasville, Georgia. The Cap-Chur fires a hypodermic syringe; on impact the dart injects a dose of a vomit-inducing chemical that acts within three to five minutes. The Rodana Research Corporation, Bethesda, Maryland, has developed a similar weapon built right into the end of the conventional billy club.

Of course, the hypodermic rifle has been used for years in capturing animals for zoos and circuses, where the consequences of administering a fatal dose are not so grave. Converting the weapon for use on people is a twofold problem: First, a dart must be developed that can administer the drug safely. Second, the drug itself must be fast-acting and safe—whether the target is a young boy or 280-pounder. So far, these problems haven't been ironed out.

The killings at Kent State and Orangeburg, South Carolina, focused attention on the need for nonlethal weapons for crowd control. In some parts of the world rifle-fired projectiles that stun but don't kill are already in use. The Hong Kong pellet gun, for instance, shoots a wooden cylinder that emits a piercing whistle and travels slowly enough to be seen. The cylinder deals a severe bruise, but rarely penetrates the skin. The rubber bullets made familiar in Northern Ireland have a similar effect. Both rubber and wooden bullets are primarily psychological weapons, causing crowds to panic and disperse.

The Stun Gun, produced by M. B. Associates, San Ramon, California, is designed to go one step farther and knock a man off his feet. A standard grenade launcher is converted to fire an eight-

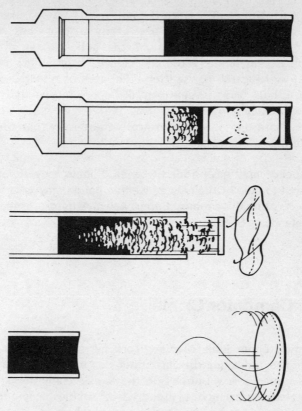

The "stun-bag" spins its way out of the rifled barrel, opening under cen-trifugal force to a flat pancake.

ounce "bean bag" filled with buckshot. Instead of penetrating the flesh, the bag expands to saucer size in flight and delivers a hard whack. Unfortunately, at least one independent evaluator warns that the Stun Gun could cause death or serious injury if fired within twenty feet.

Other new weapons sound like an inventory of Batman's arsenal. There's a foam machine that generates an ocean of bubbles, submerging whole crowds and causing them to lose their bearings. Another concept is a slicking agent, known as Instant Banana Peel, which makes streets so slippery that walking becomes nearly impossible. Even the net-casting gun of comic-book fame is now a reality. None of these zany weapons has yet been tested in the very serious setting of actual police action.

Joseph Coates of the National Science Foundation's Office of Exploratory Research has written, "The lack of research commitments will hold back development of benign incapacitation. . . . These approaches to weaponry involve effects which are more complex, more subtle, and intrinsically more risky than the application of topical irritants."

Future police may have added worries. Should they shoot to kill —or shoot to stun? Criminals as well as police may take to using the new nonlethal weapons. Either way the hard-pressed police officer stands to benefit.

Computer Crime

The Union Dime Bank of New York City was robbed of $1.5 million. The quiet, middle-class thief did not pack a pistol. He merely tapped a few buttons on the bank's computer keyboard and juggled the balances of hundreds of savings accounts, while carefully tending to his regular duties as chief teller.

This caper, the largest savings bank embezzlement in history, points to the prospect of a new kind of crime wave. As Michael Fooner, a writer and consultant on crime prevention, has observed, "There are some 80,000 computers in the United States, and 140,000 are expected to be operating by 1975. Based on the computer crimes that have come to light in the past few years, the potential is enormous."

A computer will tell you everything it knows, if you know how to ask the questions. Anyone can pull a heist on a computer bank by simply pushing the right numbers on a pushbutton phone. All one needs is access to the computer, an understanding of computer language, a confidential password that unlocks the computer's memory, and, for big-time operations, a teletype machine.

Although manufacturers are hastily devising more sophisticated security procedures for their machines, the likelihood of detection remains small.

A Los Angeles student scavenging in the trash cans of the Pacific Telephone and Telegraph office found a series of manuals that explained the company's system for buying equipment. He learned the code and began ordering equipment by pushbutton phone. To avoid arousing suspicion, he purchased, at an auction, an old telephone company van in which to pick up his orders. It all worked without a hitch.

Soon he opened a shop and began supplying companies with sophisticated electronic equipment. Business flourished. The young entrepreneur hired ten employees, rented a warehouse, and even placed an advertisement in the Yellow Pages. His mistake was to let one of his employees in on the secret of his success; the employee let Pacific Telephone in on the secret, too.

But that's small time. Using computers, a gang of technological pirates diverted 275 Penn Central boxcars worth up to $60,000 each to a remote railroad siding. The ownership markings were painted out and changed, and the computer records were "fixed" to indicate that the cars had been wrecked or scrapped. The culprits were never caught.

Money or equipment is often the target of the computer crook, but information can also be valuable. In several cases, companies have tapped competitors' computers for the details of their secret processes and financial dealings.

But the grandest computer swindle of all time was perpetrated by the Equity Funding Corporation of America. Listed on the New York Stock Exchange, the insurance conglomerate counted the Ford Foundation, Morgan Guaranty and other prominent financial institutions among its stockholders. In addition to its legitimate operations, the company kept a staff of clerks busy making up 60,000 phony life insurance policies, as well as falsifying medical reports and records of premium payments. Then, they subcontracted these policies to other insurance companies, a perfectly legal procedure, in return for quick cash. They even "killed off" some of their phantom policyholders and collected the benefit checks issued to their phantom beneficiaries. All in all, using computers to fool subcontractors, investors and auditors, the company credited itself with $3 billion in nonexistent assets. Again, a disgruntled employee tipped off authorities. Soon after, Equity Funding collapsed.

"The Equity scandal has been called the biggest fraud in the history of the United States and the worst corporate financial disaster of modern times," writes Michael Fooner. "It has also focused attention on the newest and potentially greatest criminal in the world—the computer. . . . With shock and fascination, people have come to realize that computer crime is often committed by respectable, middle-class folks—like themselves.

"Meanwhile, a new profession is coming into being—computer sleuths. New firms offer services ranging from security checkups to rebuilding a company's computer system."

A would-be computer criminal realizes that his is the white-collar crime with the whitest collar. Making computers foolproof may be the rehabilitation therapy for computer criminals of the future.

Computers and the Neighborhood Cop

In San Jose, California, a computer is bringing back the institution of the neighborhood cop.

From both an interpersonal and a law-enforcement perspective, it's desirable to have policemen answering calls whom the neighborhood knows and who know the neighborhood. But as San Jose Deputy Chief William H. MacKenzie explains, this hasn't always been possible: "Although we have emphasized neighborhood responsibility in the past, we found that 70 percent of the calls had to be answered by police officers from outside the neighborhoods because of the patterns in which the calls came in."

An innovative computer system, developed by IBM's San Jose Research Laboratories, enables the police to design a pattern of forty beats that help put the officers in the right places at the

Computer maps police beats and calls.

right times. Called the Geo-Data Analysis and Display System, the computer operates with a simplified language that nonprogrammers can use. Moreover, it can retrieve and display data such as maps, graphs and tables on a television screen to help the operator visualize his work.

For the police study, a broad collection of data was placed in the computer, including figures on crime by area, time spent per call, the number of calls requiring more than one police unit, and groupings of calls by various times of day. After checking the appropriate figures, the operator could "draw" a beat on a televised map and compare its efficiency with other possible patterns.

The Geo-Data system has also helped the police to equalize workloads among the more than three hundred patrolling officers; to establish beats that conform to natural boundaries and prevailing traffic patterns; and to ensure that the police districts supervising the beats are also efficiently designed and administered.

"With a different data base," reports IBM, "the Geo-Data system has also been used by the Planning Department of Santa Clara County, within which San Jose is situated, to study such factors as land use and economic growth."

The human advantages of this system are obvious: The neighborhood policeman, a familiar face on the street, is not an anonymous invader in blue. Familiar with the people and dynamics of the area, he might be expected to handle trouble more efficiently and more tactfully.

Look for hundreds of other computer applications to police work: computers in police labs, computer traffic control, computer forecasts of crime waves based on the temperature, the air quality, and even the phases of the moon.

There are also controversial applications on the horizon: the universal criminal data bank and computerized surveillance of convicts. Imagine: Instead of having to report to his parole officer once a week, a person might have a miniature transmitter attached or implanted for constant parole monitoring by computer.

Explosives Detector

A new device detects minute traces of explosives. Dynamite in an air traveler's luggage, or a gun that has been fired, even a long time ago, can be found without a physical search.

The system detects nitro groups (nitrogen bonded to a pair of oxygen atoms), which are constituents of many explosives. Small amounts of residue, containing nitro groups, cling to the hair, skin and clothes of anyone who has recently handled explosives or fired a gun. A vacuum hose samples the air around a person or a piece of luggage, and the air sample is automatically analyzed. Nitro groups are detected by "chemiluminescence"; combined with air they produce light, which, when amplified by a photomultiplier, sets off an alarm.

The device, invented by Dr. Sidney Benson of Stanford Research Institute, can detect one part of nitrogen in ten billion parts of air. It is not yet sensitive enough to detect explosives inside a new bullet, but with more development Dr. Benson says it should be able to.

To spot potential skyjackers easily and quickly, this system would have to be used in conjunction with a metal detector.

Dr. Benson, the inventor, says that "two or three detection devices could serve an average-sized airport," and that they could be mass-produced for around $2,000.

It might be useful in the post office, too—letter-bombs are easy to find, but the search ties up manpower.

Advanced technological marvels—like the computer and the jumbo jet—are very vulnerable to terrorist countertechnology. To combat "terror by technology," more of these protection devices will be needed, and developed, in the next decades.

Chemical Antagonists Treat Addicts

Chemical antagonists can block the action of narcotics on the nervous system and give an addict a fair chance of being cured.

The habit of using narcotics is partly learned behavior, and a long-term cure may require adequate psychiatric treatment. Narcotic addiction, however, is also a physical problem, and the very real pangs of withdrawal symptoms may keep the habit alive long after the emotional dependency is gone.

The psychiatrist who treats addicts faces a two-choice situation, with neither choice very attractive. If the addict continues to use narcotics during treatment, the euphoria produced by the narcotic (the everything-is-fine feeling) makes him decide treatment is unnecessary. If he stops taking narcotics, the withdrawal symptoms are so painful they make treatment (and almost everything else) seem unimportant. In either case, the addict isn't likely to take an active interest in the hard job of self-rehabilitation.

Methadone, a synthetic narcotic, is one way out. A heroin

addict is switched from heroin to methadone. Methadone blocks the effect of heroin, and it's less euphoric than heroin. An addict on a methadone maintenance program is in closer touch with reality than one taking heroin, making successful psychiatric treatment possible. In effect, an untreatable heroin addict is turned into a possibly treatable methadone addict.

Other chemical antagonists, which block the action of heroin but which are *not* narcotics, show more promise. Cyclazocine and naloxone are two antagonists now being used experimentally. A slow transition from heroin to the antagonist, over a period of several weeks, can be accomplished without any withdrawal symptoms. Termination of maintenance on the antagonist produces some withdrawal symptoms, but these differ markedly from the symptoms of heroin withdrawal and can be easily handled by a well-motivated patient.

Cyclazocine and naloxone are superior to methadone, from the standpoint of psychiatric treatment, because they produce no euphoria. A patient on antagonist maintenance lives in a drug-free real world. With no crutch, he's disposed to cooperate with the psychiatrist in resolving his problems and returning to a useful life.

According to Dr. Martin of the National Institute of Mental Health, "The cyclazone abstinence syndrome is quite mild and does not give rise to drug-seeking behavior."

The addict can't get rid of his habit unless he's cured—and he can't be cured until he gets rid of the habit. The nonnarcotic antagonists are a way of breaking the loop. They suppress the habit until a cure can be effected.

Drug May Reverse Intoxication

Dr. Cleamond D. Eskelson, a research chemist connected with the University of Arizona at Tucson, is investigating ways to combat the effects of too much drinking.

The United States has approximately nine million alcoholics, but only 5 percent of them are Bowery-type bums. Alcoholism and problem drinking are without doubt a major cause of many personal and social problems. Over one third of all suicides are alcoholics, and about one half of all highway deaths are due to drivers under the influence.

Dr. Eskelson, taking a hint from the widely accepted idea that a drink in an empty stomach affects us more, is looking for the precise nutrient that helps us metabolize alcohol or a substance that prevents its absorption when we have a full stomach. He has found that sodium acetate, given to animals, inhibits alcohol absorption.

This research is still in a very early stage. But the doctor is optimistic, and predicts that within five to ten years we will have a drug that will take us from drunk-as-a-lord to sober-as-a-judge in minutes.

Dr. Eskelson observes, "The philosophy of the research scientists working with me at the Veterans Administration Hospital in Tucson . . . is that most people who drink are responsible individuals. Thus those who occasionally drink in excess would, if they could, sober up rapidly. In this way they would maintain control of their mental faculties so as not to commit some irresponsible act. With this as a goal we are attempting to determine methods which would give mankind this privilege."

A sober-up pill is a useful treatment for the *symptoms* of alcoholism. More practical would be a pill to stop alcoholics from drinking. *That* would prevent future tragedies.

The Body's Own Sedative

Bubble baths or warm milk? Tranquilizers or alcoholic beverages? An endless array of favorite sleeping aids have come down to us from folklore. Now researchers believe an effective sedative may come from the body itself.

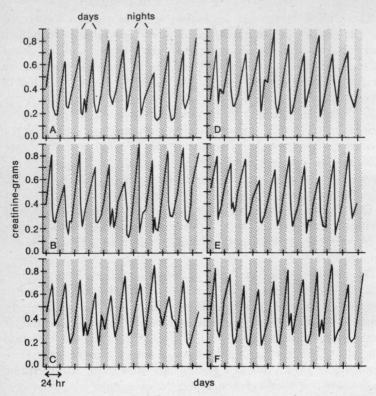

Ups and downs of creatinine excretion from adult males day and night. The peaks occur in the morning and evening.

The substance is known as creatinine. Up to now it's been considered merely a waste product of metabolism excreted in urine. Dr. Adam Lis, head of a research team at the University of Oregon Medical School investigating its effects, believes creatinine is responsible for the drowsiness that leads to sleep.

Creatine and its derivative, phosphocreatine, are produced in the muscles. After muscular activity, the creatine and phosphocreatine are changed into creatinine, and excreted from the body. Creatinine production is unusual because it doesn't require enzyme action. And lactic acid, also formed after muscular activity, speeds up its production. This process suggested creatinine might be more than just a waste product.

When they injected commercially available creatinine into mice, Lis and his associates found its effects resembled a weak tranquilizer. Unlike many tranquilizers, though, it didn't impair consciousness or the central nervous system (which consists of the brain and the spinal cord). The mice showed diminished arousal and body movement, or sedation of the motor nervous system, which controls impulses from the brain to the muscles.

A chemical similarity apparently exists between creatinine and certain anticonvulsant drugs used to treat epilepsy—those drugs that act on nerve endings. A slight change in some of these substances can enhance their sedative properties. Furthermore, drugs derived from creatinine resemble various psychoactive drugs—tranquilizers and antidepressants, histamine, hypnotics and sedatives.

Fluctuations in the quantity of creatinine excreted associate with a diurnal-nocturnal cycle: Early in the morning, and then again toward evening, are the peaks.

The actual mechanism of sleep onset is still unknown, and scientists cannot pinpoint the spot in the brain where sleep is triggered. Lis and his associates, however, arrived at the notion that creatinine is a chemical "messenger" that tells the nerve endings to stop stimulating muscles and let them rest. This message produces drowsiness that leads eventually to sleep. The diurnal-nocturnal variation in creatinine excretion is associated with muscle cell recovery.

Dr. Lis thinks drugs based on creatinine will have few side effects that characterize many current drugs, and may not be physically addictive. "On the basis of preliminary findings," he says, "it is evident that creatinine derivatives selectively sedate the motor nervous system without impairing consciousness. The sedative properties of creatinine may be responsible for sleep onset, drowsiness."

Freud once predicted that eventually a biochemical basis would be found for psychological disorders. Psychiatrists routinely prescribe (and perhaps overprescribe) psychoactive drugs to control depression and anxiety. These drugs have uncomfortable and sometimes serious side effects for the patients. Some are habit-forming or even addictive.

Since normal amounts of creatinine are safely handled by the body—they are, in fact, the body's own substance—it's possible that nonaddictive creatinine-based drugs will eliminate such side effects. Any drug with sedative properties is also extremely important in the treatment of high blood pressure, irregular heart rhythm, epilepsy, and even for routine anesthesia.

Creatinine research will also shed light on two age-old problems: the "mind-body relationship"—and how to get a good night's sleep.

New Rural Society

Long-distance medical diagnosis, "live" satellite theater performances, and "faxmail" are all part of the New Rural Society.

The New Rural Society is the title of a national pilot effort which aims to correct population imbalances, relieve urban problems and revitalize rural communities. It's being conducted in Windham County, an undeveloped highly rural area in Connecticut. The effort stems from the work of a panel on communications technology created in 1968 by President Johnson's Advisory Group on Telecommunications. Peter Goldmark, president of Goldmark Communications, Inc., is chairman of the panel.

Windham County (whose western border is 25 miles east of Hartford) consists of 10 townships with a population of 65,000, centered around the city of Willimantic. The goal of the Windham study is to expand their existing towns moderately by providing facilities to attract new people into the area and by stemming the tide of commuters from the area. The findings may be applied beyond these local goals, perhaps nationally.

Complete utilization of telecommunications (electronic transmission of impulses) will serve as the foundation of the New Rural Society. Phase I of the project, currently under way, looks at businesses, industries and government agencies to determine what office practices result in meetings, memorandums and other communications. This phase includes laboratory experiments to

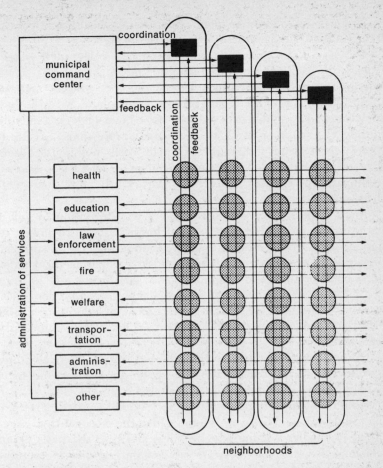

The coordination and feedback of New Rural Society services by electronic communications.

learn what electronic communications systems can most successfully substitute for face-to-face meetings between individuals and for conference situations. One assumption of these studies is that companies are reluctant to establish branches in rural areas because of anticipated communications problems.

Future phases of the project will create electronic links between the towns in Windham and Greater Hartford. They hope to bring increased employment opportunities, health and educational services, and cultural pursuits into the area.

One electronic link already functioning is a new mail system connecting Willimantic and Hartford. Known as "faxmail," it's a facsimile system which sends letters, pictures, graphs, medical records, invoices and purchase orders via telephone wires. It may slowly replace regular mail and the use of messengers. Available during the working week to businesses, professional organizations and private individuals, faxmail costs nothing to users beyond what they pay to bring the items to and from the two terminals. The effects of the service, particularly on business, will be assessed.

Another possibility is the use of two-way television to link a large urban medical center to local hospitals, in turn linked to mobile medical units. Since doctors reside in big cities disproportionately to the local population, nurses and paramedical aides who conduct tests and examinations in rural areas will consult with doctors in urban centers. Entire diagnoses can be done over two-way television. A similar arrangement in education would link local colleges via two-way television to large university campuses.

Cultural performances and sports events can be telecast by satellites hovering over towns (see page 357). Local antennas would pick up high-definition TV signals.

Goldmark hopes the New Rural Society will exist substantially by the year 2000. He says, "We must plan the reasonable enlargement of smaller communities in rural areas on the basis of an efficient, self-sufficient network of communications, transportation and services. With meticulous planning and follow-through, the New Rural Society will become reality. We have all the equipment necessary to solve the problem; we need only innovate, not invent."

Some 80 percent of Americans live in urban centers, on less than 10 percent of the land. This creates a concentrated drain on energy and natural resources. And social discomforts may arise from overcrowding and congestion. But building new towns is too slow. Planned expansion of existing towns, taking into account the services and communications networks that attract people into cities, is a practical future.

6
Construction and Materials

Melting Rock

While the very idea of melting rock may be a novelty for most people, a drill-like rig capable of melting a hole through rock has already been successfully field-tested by engineers at the Los Alamos Scientific Laboratory.

Equally novel is what this new excavating system, known as a Subterrene unit, does with the molten rock. Part of the melt is transformed into a glass lining, thereby sealing and supporting the walls of the hole. The remainder of the melt solidifies in the form of glass rods, pellets or glass-cased rods, which can be easily removed from the hole.

The self-contained rock-melting rig, deployed from a single trailer, consists of a number of relatively conventional modular elements. A generator provides electric power to a hydraulic pump and to an air compressor. The pump, connected to thrusting cylinders set up over the hole to be melted, forces an electrically heated penetrator downward into the rock. Mounted on the end of modified drill-stem sections, the penetrator exploits the resistance of the rock under pressure to elevate its temperature sufficiently to induce melting. Air from the compressor, circulating within the stem sections, cools and consolidates the molten rock into the glassy state.

Periodically, the mechancial chuck that clamps the thrusting cylinders to the stem sections is loosened, the cylinders are raised, and additional stem sections added, so as to permit further penetration. At the end of the operation this process is reversed, in order to extract the penetrator, stem sections and glassified debris.

This new rock-melting system constitutes a significant technological advance in that it accomplishes the three major tasks of a typical excavation process—making a hole, supporting the walls and extracting the debris—in one operation.

Commercial feasibility of the system is quite likely, for it uses

Modular rock-melting system shows the arrangement of thruster, hydraulic and power lines, and generator.

largely unsophisticated components which are readily available at modest cost (the entire field unit costs less than $40,000). Two men can easily transport, assemble, operate and repair these components.

According to R. E. Williams, one of the engineers working on the project, "This new technology, when perfected, will offer the possibility for desirable advancements in excavation and tunneling, and thus permit a more efficient utilization of the earth's resources."

Tunnel technology: melting rock with heat and shattering rock with electrons (see page 271). Future projects, like the coast-to-coast subway (see page 169), will need even more elegant tunnel technology.

Rock Shattering with Accelerated Electrons

An intense burst of electrons, invisible and moving almost as fast as light, pulverizes rock in laboratory tests. Someday electron blasts may be used in enormous excavation projects, such as digging hundred-mile tunnels for high-speed underground railways.

Engineers at the AEC's Lawrence Berkeley Laboratory in California have demonstrated that an advanced particle accelerator, until now used in investigations of subatomic components of matter, can lend itself to a more earthly application. Using a commercially available accelerator, they found that an intense electron burst produces a significant "cratering" effect in such rocks as granite, basalt and limestone. For example, a single highly focused burst, lasting only one twenty-millionth of a second, left a crater two inches in diameter and one twenty-fifth of an inch deep in a granite slab.

Operating like the "ray gun" of science fiction fame, an accelerator used in tunneling would fire machine-gunlike bursts of electrons, at a rate of several hundred times a second, at the rock to be removed. The shattering disintegration by impact, called "shock spalling," would turn the rock into sand and dust, which could then be easily vacuumed out of the tunnel.

While technical problems exist, like the need for a more powerful accelerator capable of firing hundreds of pulses a second, electronic tunneling may prove to be the rapid, economical means of excavation that engineers are searching for. It could make feasible such projects as a 300 mile-per-hour train, hurtling underground between Boston and Washington, D.C., between Los Angeles and San Francisco, or even New York and Los Angeles (see page 169). Other projects would benefit, such as urban mass transit and the underground placement of factories, power plants, utility lines and fuel depots.

According to Robert Avery of the Lawrence Berkeley Laboratory, "It has been demonstrated that *shock spalling* produces

Granite bombarded by electron blast.

effective rock removal by producing mini-explosions within the rock. This technique may produce the much-needed break-through in the speed and cost of tunneling and underground excavations through rock. It offers sufficient promise to merit further study."

High-speed electrons may someday blast a tunnel for high-speed trains running underground from coast to coast.

Bursting from a particle accelerator at almost the speed of light and pulverizing rock, electrons can make it possible for us to mine coal, our most abundant underground source of energy.

Enormous excavation projects may also be feasible by elec-tronic tunneling. Entire factories and power plants could be placed underground, preserving the environment above.

Space-Age Explosive

An explosive called Jetcord provides enormous detonative power, cutting through structures with greater precision and fewer blasting effects than conventional blasting charges.

The new explosive is a product of and for the space age. It was originally created in 1961 to separate the stages of the Gemini launch vehicle. As work on the explosive continued, its developers found other uses for it. It is so precise and powerful it cuts through—rather than simply blows up—massive steel structures like bridges, smokestacks and high-rise buildings. Yet it can also be used so delicately it can instantly cut through the fuselage or door of an aircraft to allow passengers to escape in an emergency.

Jetcord exploding. The detonation products and liner material are focused at high velocity from the shaped charge into the material to be cut.

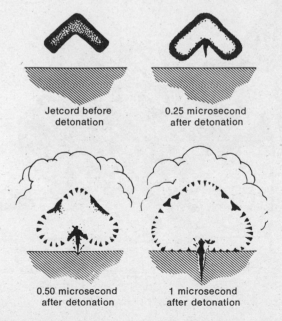

Jetcord before
detonation

0.25 microsecond
after detonation

0.50 microsecond
after detonation

1 microsecond
after detonation

Jetcord contains an explosive charge inside a metal column shaped like a V. The inside of the V faces the point to be cut. When the explosive is fired, the V shape causes the detonation products to emerge between the arms of the V, concentrating them into a thin cutting jet that pushes its way through the target material. The jet's velocity reaches 10,000 to 30,000 feet per second; pressures are in the millions of pounds per square inch. The explosive (usually only ounces per foot) varies and so does the metal, depending on the job.

In traditional demolition jobs, contractors have to use large quantities of blasting gelatin to bring down steel structures. The new explosive makes it possible to cut the steel with only a small

Demolition of the Covington-Cincinnati Bridge over the Ohio River with Jetcord.

quantity of explosive and at a safe distance from the structure.

According to the developer, Explosive Technology, "There are more than 5000 steel bridges in the United States that are either obsolete or in obsolescence, many in populated sections of large cities. With Jetcord, these bridges can be removed and cut into easily handled sections at one time, increasing safety and efficiency."

Noise Silencer

A thin sheet of steel-and-plastic laminate may be easily bonded to any surface for noise and vibration control. Applied to walls, panels or machine enclosures, the laminate traps noise at its source.

Silent sandwich. The energy-absorbing viscoelastic sheet turns the offending noise into a small amount of heat.

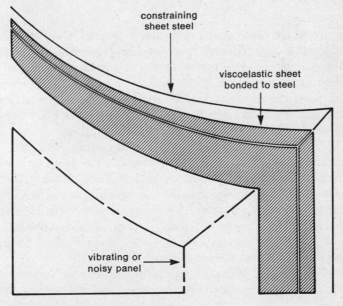

constraining
sheet steel

viscoelastic sheet
bonded to steel

vibrating or
noisy panel

Called NEXDAMP, the laminate is a sound and vibration absorber. Also available as a steel-and-plastic sandwich, NEXDAMP is a structural material as well. The plastic sandwich filling absorbs sound and vibration; the outer layers provide strength and rigidity. Simple mounting brackets of the new material can replace complex vibration-isolating supports. Automobiles, office machines, and household appliances can also be quieted by NEXDAMP housings.

The manufacturer, U.S. Steel, says, "Any flat surface that serves as a source of noise can be stilled by the application of USS NEXDAMP laminate."

A low-cost way of trapping noise at its source will lead to a more private, quiet world. Airplanes, cars, home appliances, office equipment—all contribute to noise pollution that will be silenced.

Heated Glass Sandwich

Scientists at the Sierracin Corporation in Sylmar, California, have developed a new concept for providing electrically heatable automotive safety glass for rapid, silent removal of ice and fog condensation from windshields and backlights. The concept is based upon the continuous deposition of a transparent, electrically conductive coating onto a flexible, transparent polyester film that's sandwiched between the layers of safety glass.

The ability to deposit this coating on a continuous plastic film substrate, called the carrier film, comes directly from technology developed for the application of similar electrically conductive, transparent coatings on aircraft windshield plastic substrates. Electrically heatable interlayers have been used in plastic aircraft windshields since 1959, but many technical and economic obstacles had to be overcome before the product could be introduced to the mass market for automobiles.

The electrically heatable interlayer consists of a section of carrier film placed between two sheets of polyvinal butyral. Metal-

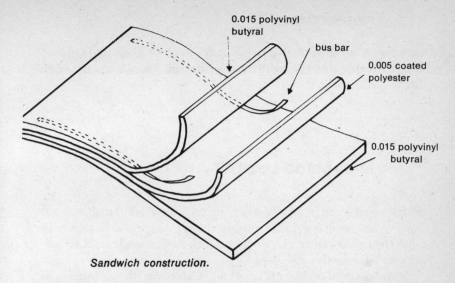

0.015 polyvinyl
butyral

bus bar

0.005 coated
polyester

0.015 polyvinyl
butyral

Sandwich construction.

lic foil strips are incorporated in this construction as "busbars," to
distribute the electric current to the coating. Current is provided
by a common 12-volt dry-cell battery wired to metal tabs that
extend from the interlayer after it has been laminated into the
safety glass.

The optical properties of the heatable laminate satisfy all industry and federal standards. The luminous transmission of the
heatable laminated glass, while slightly dependent upon the resistance of the conductive coating, is comparable with that of the
standard tinted windshield—except it exhibits significantly
greater transmission in the yellow-orange-red spectral region.
This is a distinct advantage in view of the prevalence of yellow,
orange and red highway and vehicle warning devices, instruction
markers, and driving aids.

By virtue of the reflective properties of the coating, the electrically heatable windshield exhibits a useful degree of solar shielding, and thereby contributes directly to another aspect of
occupant comfort.

The heated glass interlayer, says Sierracin's B. P. Levin, "now
forms the basis for a variety of transparent, electrically heatable
products, most notable among which is the 1974 Continental
Mark IV and Ford Thunderbird quick defrost system."

Autos may someday also have controlled transparency windshields or windows that darken at the flick of a switch. Or, like those special sunglasses, they may darken spontaneously when the sun is too bright.

Man-Made Leather

Strict vegetarians who object to using animal-source shoes, but live in climates too cold for rubber thongs, may be able to satisfy both their convictions and their comfort. A man-made leather substitute will be ready for them soon.

Manufactured by Scott/Chatham Company, the substance is called Tanera. Like leather, Tanera has an all-fibrous structure. This makes it unlike most other man-made materials, which consist of a polymer (or plastic) coating reinforced by backing. Tanera's fibers are fine and tightly packed near the grain surface, duplicating the dense entangled fibrous structure of leather itself.

Tanera's similarity to real leather is the reason for its leather-like appearance, durability and strength. Its fibers make possible a shoe that absorbs moisture and allows the foot to breathe, enhancing comfort for the wearer. It also conforms to the foot as comfortably as leather does.

Tanera has been used for uppers in men's, women's and children's shoes of all kinds—dress, casual and work. In the past, man-made leather substitutes have not been successfully applied to heavy-duty shoes. It is also applicable for other personal apparel—wallets, purses and belts—as well as for industrial uses such as power transmission belting.

Tanera duplicates leather's manufacturing advantages. Multi-layered cutting, a time- and money-saving technique, can be applied to it. Damage during manufacture, such as cuts, shield burns or surface breaks, can be repaired. It also displays good adhesion to soles.

Tests comparing shoes made from leather with those from the new leather substitute showed that Tanera is both resistant to abrasion and wear, and comfortable.

According to the Shoe and Allied Trade Research Association, which conducted the tests, "Tanera is a very promising shoe upper material that undoubtedly could fill an important need for leather replacement in the shoe industry today."

Here's an example of a material designed for man. The future will bring many other man-centered substances our way—to be time-tested by "survival of the fittest."

Plastic Paper

A menu that can withstand spilled glasses of water and pats of butter may soon be on restaurant tables.

Grease- and water-resistant menus are only one of the many possible applications of a new plastic paper called AcroArt. It's manufactured by the Acroline Company, an affiliate of Union Carbide, from the plastic polyethylene. Though virtually indistinguishable by sight from ordinary paper, it's superior to it in performance.

Regular paper is easy to tear. But plastic paper is very tough, almost impossible to tear and highly resistant to abrasion. These qualities make it a particularly suitable material for children's books, which are often subjected to rough handling, and for toy labels. Regular paper has to be folded along the line of the grain. AcroArt has no fibers and no grain, and is easy to fold into as many parts as are desired.

Plastic paper is relatively unaffected by changes in temperature and humidity, either indoors or out. It's also resistant to ultraviolet light. Outdoor signs and banners made of AcroArt are more durable than those made of ordinary paper.

AcroArt also has high "dimensional stability." A wall poster made from plastic will not stretch easily and lose its shape with hanging. Plastic paper can be easily bound and sewn and picks up print easily, so it creates no special problems for printers and book publishers.

The most unusual qualities of AcroArt are its impermeability to water and its resistance to grease and water stains.

According to the Acroline Company, "Because AcroArt is an all-plastic sheet it has qualities and characteristics impossible to obtain with conventional (cellulose base) printing paper."

A plastic-paged cookbook can shed food stains, and a tear-stained plastic piece of stationery will not smudge. Since the paper shortage is so severe, a substitute seems timely. But plastic is a synthetic derived from petroleum—also in short supply.

Hollow Fibers

Cattail floss. An artificial kidney. A fabric that adjusts itself to changes in temperature. What do these have in common? The answer is hollow fibers.

Hollow fibers are tubular filaments of exceptionally low density. They may be finer than human hair, the hollow interior visible only microscopically, or as large as standard plastic tubing. Their length can vary, and they can occur individually or in clumps of hundreds or thousands.

They are found naturally in such "floating fibers" as cattail floss, milkweed "silk," and Spanish moss. Attempts to commercially exploit these fibers have failed, although a fourth hollow fiber, kapok, has been widely used as the buoyant material in life jackets.

Synthetic hollow fibers can be readily formed out of such materials as nylon, polyester, acrylic, cellulose, rubber and glass. Of the numerous production processes available, the commonest consist of either draining or extruding a polymer solution through slotted orifices, as well as a process known as "wet spinning," which is used to form rayon and acrylics.

That technological advances are often accidental is well exemplified by hollow fibers. Their first appearance as voids or air pockets in synthetic textiles was quite a nuisance; they were regarded only as serious manufacturing defects to be avoided. In order to eliminate the voids engineers had to investigate them, and subsequent research furnished an understanding of how the hollow fibers were produced and a gradual appreciation of their unusual potential.

A major breakthrough occurred when imaginative engineers and designers recognized the capacity of hollow fibers to contain or transmit liquids and gases. The first application is a recently developed foamed polyester fiber containing a fire-extinguishing gas under pressure. Upon exposure to heat of sufficient intensity, the gas diffuses through the fiber walls. Mattresses, carpets and upholstery are likely to incorporate these fibers within the near future.

A second container concept is a thermally responsive fabric. Hollow elastic fibers can be filled with a gas dissolved in a low-melting solvent. As the temperature drops, the solvent freezes, thereby expelling the gas, which in turn causes the fibers to expand. The inverse process, contraction of the fibers, occurs as the temperature rises. These inflatable fibers, combined with regular fibers in a deep pile fabric, would produce a coat whose artificial fur would rise upon exposure to cold, warming the wearer, and settle back as it became warmer. You probably won't wear a thermostatic fabric like this for many years, though it's technically feasible.

It's as transmitters of liquids and gases that hollow fibers will probably have the greatest impact. Hollow fibers are ideally suited for use as dialysis membranes—as partially porous barriers permitting the separation of substances through unequal diffusion.

A prime example of such an application is the extremely successful artificial kidney. The unit consists of some 14,000 hollow cellulose fibers, shaped into a cell about the size of a large flashlight, and placed in an extracting solution. Blood from an artery flows into the fibers at one end of the cell and out the other end into a vein. In the process, metabolic wastes, such as urea, uric acid and creatinine, diffuse through the walls of the fibers and purify the blood.

Hollow fibers as filtering membranes have also been used in a new device for separating bacteria, some viruses and other pollutants from water.

Future developments along these lines, and now in progress, include an artificial lung, an encapsulated long-term contraceptive, and a new fuel cell.

According to Dr. A. Charles Tanquary of the Southern Research Institute, "We cannot say with certainty when the problem was first recognized as a potential advantage. Perhaps the idea of deliberately producing a hollow fiber arose first in one of those companies having a propensity to patent anything unusual, even an unusual nuisance, the distinction between nuisance and new product being hazy at best. . . . Hollow fibers fully deserve the widespread attention they have generated. . . . We can only guess where the technology may ultimately lead."

Pseudo-Silk

Silk and wool are proteins. Since it became possible to synthesize amino acids and chain them together into complex proteins, textile manufacturers have zealously sought to produce artificial fibers that chemically resemble natural silk and wool. Although many silklike and woollike fibers have been spun, they have all had shortcomings: Some would dissolve in liquids, others were weak, and still others were chemically unstable. In fact, the nearest scientists could come to replicating silk was a fiber spun from a natural protein—a protein now used as an artificial meat. Thus, until very recently, silkworms and sheep have retained control of the means of producing these popular fabrics.

Finally, in November 1973, two Japanese scientists, Seigo Oya and Juzo Takahashi, announced that they had synthesized a fiber which "very much resembles silk." The base for their pseudo-silk is glutamic acid, one of the twenty amino acids that make up all proteins and a chemical long used in the production of monosodium glutamate, the controversial seasoning found in many meals, ranging from baby food to egg rolls. With some extensive chemical rearrangement, glutamic acid can be spun and drawn into long fibers of approximately the same density as silk.

In its other properties, artificial silk is also very much like the mile-long strands in the silkworm's cocoon. In luster and moisture sorption, for instance, the resemblances between the real and the fake are unusually close. But the most important quality to silk fanciers is the feel, what textile people call the "hand." And from all reports, pseudo-silk is decidedly silky.

There is one drawback. Certain microorganisms can cause the artificial silk to deteriorate. While this may not be a problem over the few years that a garment is in fashion, it may decrease the chances of your artificial silk gowns surviving to become treasured heirlooms. On the plus side, glutamic acid is a readily available chemical raw material, and it is cheap—about a dollar per pound.

Drs. Oya and Takahashi say, "The application of this fiber is expected not only in textile use, but also in fundamental and applied fields utilizing the characteristics of protein."

Paper Honeycomb—A Metal Substitute?

Parents of schoolchildren may already be familiar with a heavy-duty cardboard that is widely used in art rooms to build sturdy tables and bookshelves. Now a far tougher reinforced paper product is being used in the construction of truck trailers, cargo containers and even modular homes.

The new building material, called Panelcomb, has a honeycomb made of resin-stiffened paper sandwiched between two layers of fiber glass. Pound for pound, the paper sandwich is stronger than steel and considerably cheaper. Moreover, fabrication and maintenance costs are also lower than for steel, aluminum, wood and other common construction materials.

The air cells formed by the honeycomb provide good thermal insulation, and by filling the spaces with urethane foam, sandwich panels can even be used for the bodies of refrigerated trailers. The material is sufficiently rigid to resist denting and scarring from shifting truck loads.

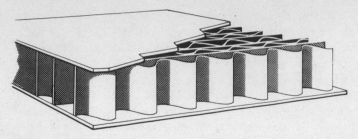

A cutaway of the paper honeycomb used for truck bodies, trailers and marine containers.

Panels come in a variety of different designs suitable not only for truck trailers but also for marine cargo containers and the interior walls of homes. The fiber-glass skin prevents deterioration or corrosion of the panels. Cosmetically, the panels come in many colors and can be cleaned with detergent and water.

According to Panel/Comb Industries, "The core is kraft paper in a honeycomb pattern which creates a myriad of 'I' beams. The paper is impregnated with phenolic resin which adds stiffness, prevents deterioration. . . . The standard panel is seven-eighths inch thick and weighs only 1.9 pounds per square foot."

"Paper trucks" will be lighter, causing less wear to highways and lower tare weight taxes for truckers. And paper walls, after all, have always been standard in Japanese homes.

Inexpensive paper homes may be on their way.

Ultrasonic Sewing

When Elias Howe invented the sewing machine in 1846, seamstresses and tailors of the era must have been dumfounded by how far advanced the new device seemed in comparison with painstaking hand stitchery. Now, a century and a quarter later, a sewing machine comes along that would dumfound Elias Howe —and may make needles and thread virtually unnecessary.

CONSTRUCTION AND MATERIALS

The Branson Sonic Power Company is marketing a machine that "sews" ultrasonically. High-frequency sound, beyond the range of human hearing, causes the sewing tool to vibrate. As the synthetic fabric is fed between the sewing tool and a specially designed "stitching wheel," one piece of material vibrates against another at a very high speed. The frictional heat melts or welds the two layers of fabric together.

The ultrasonic machine can seam, hem, tack, baste and pleat synthetic fabrics of most weights and gauges—and the seams are generally as strong or stronger than those produced by Mr. Howe's invention. A wide variety of welds or "stitches" can be obtained simply by changing the stitching wheel, an operation that takes only twenty seconds. Buttonholes are made with an attachment that slits and sews in one operation. The welds, of course, are colorless, so there is no problem matching thread and fabric colors; moreover, if desired, the welds can be embossed with contrasting colors.

An ultrasonic sewing machine uses no needle or thread. Instead it welds two pieces of fabric together with very high speed vibrations.

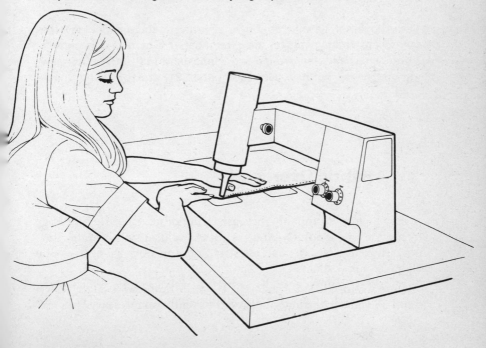

There is one drawback: natural fabrics such as cotton and wool cannot be welded. But most synthetics can, including polyesters, polypropylene, nylon, mod-acrylics, vinyls and even synthetics blended with up to 35 percent natural fibers. Because it cannot be used on natural fibers, the ultrasonic sewing machine isn't likely to be a feature in many homes, at least until fabric buying habits change. Increasingly, however, clothing manufacturers will be using the new machines, because with an automatic feeding attachment, it may be possible to sew up to 150 feet per minute. Many suits and dresses on store racks will soon have ultrasonic stitches.

According to Stephen Goldstein of Branson Sonic Power, "Conventional sewing machines have limited capabilities. For instance, because of the high rates of speed used in industrial sewing, heat is generated which melts or breaks thread. . . . Conventional sewing of woven synthetics requires special three-part folding of seams to prevent slippage and unravelling. Because ultrasonic sewing causes the fibers in the seam to melt into each other, a far more secure seam which cannot slip is achieved."

The altogether new invention is a rarity. Instead most developments are refinements or new applications of older inventions. Ultrasound has been around for a long time (not to mention sewing machines), but new uses (see page 391) are still being uncovered.

Fabric Overhead?

A new fiber will probably increase the number of fabric buildings in the very near future. And, as these buildings proliferate, they may radically change our construction concepts as well as the shape of our skylines.

Fabric structures actually consist of fabric roofs, which serve as membraned domes for the underlying structures. There are

A model of the fabric-coated roof to span the University of Minnesota's Memorial Sports Stadium.

two kinds. Tension structures drape the fabric roof over metal columns and cables kept under tension. Superficially these resemble a large tent. Air-supported structures, which are used most often as shelters for outdoor sports facilities, maintain the shape of the fabric by an air pressure system that keeps the internal pressure slightly higher than that of the atmosphere around it. An example of an early air-supported structure was the United States Pavilion at Expo '70 in Japan. A semipermanent structure, it covered an area of two and a half acres and was able to withstand typhoon winds of 150 miles per hour.

A new fiber, woven from fiber-glass yarn and coated with Teflon fluorocarbon resin, has advantages that thus enable architects and builders to construct *permanent* fabric structures. It's virtually nonflammable, needs little maintenance and is very strong. In fact, fiber-glass yarns are, under tension, even stronger than steel. The Teflon coating is resistant to chemical and weather changes; and its antistick quality, the reason it's commonly used in cookware, makes cleaning easy. The combination fiber withstands even hurricane winds, and since it's partially translucent, sunlight comes through for lighting and heating.

It's estimated fabric buildings can cost about half as much as present-day buildings made with traditional materials. Moreover, the fiber is now available in sizes big enough to cover vast areas, and fabric roofs have a life expectancy of at least twenty years.

The first large fabric structures in the United States are now nearing completion. They are an air-supported, cable-restrained fieldhouse at Milligan College in Tennessee, and two tension-structure buildings for student activities at LaVerne College in California.

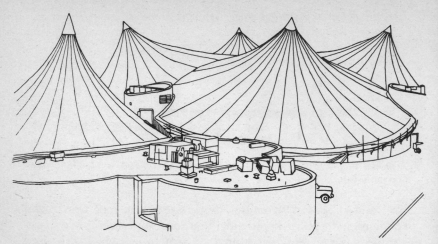

Tension structure at LaVerne College covered with fabric roofs, expected to last more than twenty years.

Dr. David Geiger of Geiger Berger Associates, structural engineers for the fabric buildings at both colleges, says, "Fabric structures allow full utilization of space. In a football stadium you can increase the number of seats. In a school's center you can include office space and recreational facilities for all types of sports. . . . And you can do it all at lower initial cost and lower operating cost than with traditional methods of construction."

Imagine 200 acres of wooded trails and golf greens—climate-controlled under a translucent dome. Or a temporary fabric warehouse erected in days to store a large shipment of food. Only 1500 fabric structures exist today. But soon, we'll see more of these around. To save energy, perhaps entire towns or cities will cover up for the winter.

Multiple Helicopter Lift System

Frank N. Piasecki and Donald N. Meyers have invented a system whereby two or more conventional helicopters are linked together by structural beams to form an integral unit. The rotor drive systems of the attached helicopters are interconnected so the engines and rotors spin at the same speed. The flight controls of all helicopters in the system are also interconnected so that one pilot controls the rotational path and pitch of the rotors from a single master station.

In conventional multiple helicopter lift systems, each helicopter is operated as an individual entity. This method has a severe drawback, however. If any of the helicopters has a partial power failure, the entire system's lift capacity is drastically reduced because of the necessity for keeping the helicopters in equilibrium.

Consider two 10-ton, two-engine helicopters. If each helicopter can lift 20 tons, including its own weight of 10 tons, the two

A Piasecki-Meyers three-helicopter lift system.

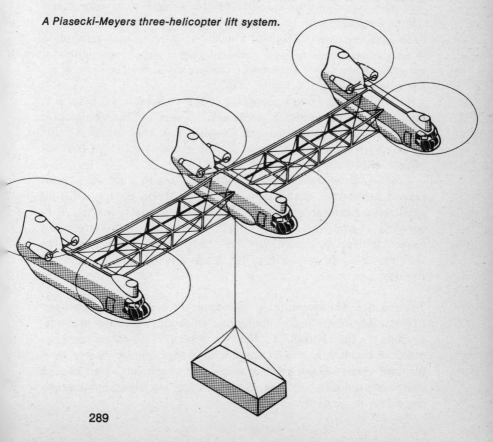

helicopters acting jointly can lift 40 tons, 20 tons of which is useful load. If one engine of one helicopter fails, however, that helicopter can only lift one-half its normal amount, or 10 tons. Its payload capability is now zero, instead of 10 tons. And the other helicopter in the autonomous system has to reduce to one-half power in order to maintain the equilibrium of the combination. A safe useful load for the entire system, then, if engine failure is considered, is zero.

Another disadvantage of individually operated helicopters is the difficulty of obtaining the necessary coordination between the pilots of the separate helicopters. This coordination requires an exceptional degree of pilot skill and flawless communications.

The Piasecki-Meyers system was developed with these problems in mind. The failure of one or more engines will not affect the maneuverability or stability of the assembly adversely, nor will it decrease its lifting capacity disproportionately. The altitude and vertical position of the entire assembly is controlled from a single station. And the helicopters are of conventional varieties: upon being detached from the assembly they can operate independently in a normal fashion.

To return to the two helicopters of the example used before: if they were rigidly joined in a Piasecki-Meyers multiple helicopter lift system, and one engine got knocked out, they could still lift three quarters of their original 40-ton capability, or 30 tons—of which 10 tons would be useful load.

The inventors state, "This invention relates to a system of connected helicopters that will provide a platform having a lifting capacity considerably exceeding that of a single helicopter. Regardless of what the lifting capacity produced by the latest and largest helicopter that comes off the production line may be, requirements always exist to lift loads beyond the capacity of that helicopter."

The Piasecki-Meyers multiple helicopter lift system could be used to great advantage in any number of emergency airlift operations, such as the transportation of heavy machinery into otherwise inaccessible country, or the evacuation of people and property from disaster areas—even sinking ships—in which all other escape routes are rendered useless. Imagine a floating island habitat (see page 292) in jeopardy.

Submarine Home

Protected from storms and waves, a submerged housing unit offers complete facilities for offshore living and recreation.

Living quarters and work space are contained in a submerged

The stabilizing mat is an undersea "pasture," attracting plants and fish.

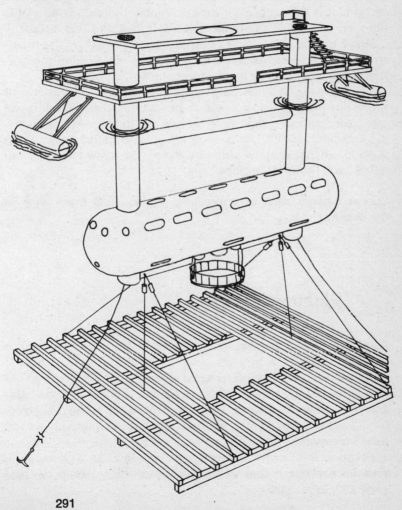

capsule equipped with observation ports. A superstructure carries a helicopter landing pad and docking facilities for surface craft. The unit is held in place by anchors and is stabilized by a concrete mat suspended beneath the capsule. Plants attach themselves to the mat and fish are attracted, making the entire unit an integral part of the undersea environment. An air lock and elevator offer easy access to the mat, to the ocean floor and to the surface.

In extremely bad weather the superstructure is sealed and the entire unit is submerged. In case of trouble the stabilizing mat is dropped and the living-quarters capsule floats to the surface.

Wave motion drives float-equipped arms carried by the superstructure. These are coupled to generators which supply a portion of the unit's energy requirement.

The inventor, William Barkley, points out that "The oceans of the world provide a vast territory of unused space and dormant resources," and says that many people are "interested in organizing communities . . . to live, work and raise their families in an oceanic environment in order to escape the crowded, contaminated, land-borne large cities."

Sooner or later we'll be harvesting, mining—and even living in the oceans.

Floating Island

Land values near large cities are skyrocketing. Public resistance to building massive projects, such as airports, near residential areas or on reclaimed lands is at an all-time high. So attention has turned to offshore areas of the continental shelf to provide valuable real estate. A floating island, consisting of a buoyant structure constructed by joining modules together, will provide a solid base to support a whole airport facility at sea.

Designed by Tancho D. Georgiev and Robert M. Scanzani, the modules are tetrahedral (with four plane faces) or octahedral

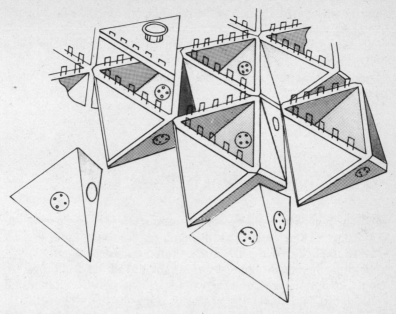

Cutaway of a buoyant structure composed of tetrahedral modules fastened together.

(with eight plane faces); they interlock like a massive jigsaw puzzle.

Aircraft carriers have been with us for many years. But a sea-drome constructed by fastening modules together would have virtually no limit to the length of its runway. It could accommodate the most modern aircraft, such as the jumbo Boeing 747, the huge military C-5A and the noisy supersonic Concorde. Linking a great number of modules would absorb the wave action of the ocean, and simultaneously absorb the stress of aircraft landings and takeoffs. The load from heavy planes would be shared among the many modular units. Furthermore, the modules could be hollow to accommodate offices, apartments and accessory or support systems.

Nuclear power plants or a major housing, commercial or recreational development could be built on top of a floating platform. Think of a high-rise suburb of New York City, a few miles off the

Hudson River estuary, cooled in the summer and warmed in the winter by winds from the Gulf Stream current.

A floating airport is already planned off the Thames River estuary to serve the congested city of London.

And what about another Coney Island—a real island playground!

Instant Modular Homes

Modular homes and offices, schools and stores are inexpensive to build and fast to erect. The durable, factory-built units can be stacked or clustered and are easily altered and rearranged.

Modular homes designed by Grumman Modular Buildings are groups of single, self-contained units. At the construction site, a crane hoists and stacks the units according to the architect's design. The steel frames that ring each module are then bolted together. Water and electrical connections are made and the job is completed. In less than one day, a home is ready for people to move in.

Doors and windows can be located for the best views and lighting, and according to interior traffic and use of the dwelling. Walls and room partitions are fixed or movable. Any fuel may be used for heating and cooling. Designers may also choose from a variety of exterior wall finishes and may pick the number and locations of such built-in features as shelves, bookcases, wood panels, cabinets and closets. Since the interiors are completed at the factory, the only thing needed at the site is furniture.

When erected, the modular frame is supported by four concrete pillars sunk deep in the ground. In some locations, natural rock outcroppings or wood piles might be used to anchor the units. Modules are shipped in half sections—12 feet wide and up to 50 feet long. There is no limit to building size, however, since extra units can be added whenever needed. This system may be adapted to one-family homes, apartments, motels, office complexes, stores, schools, laboratories and clinics.

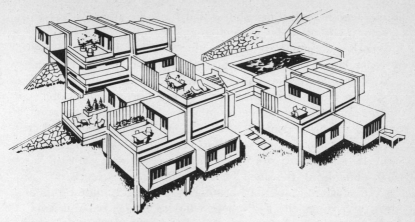

A resort development is a modular cluster.

"Structural steel stacking frames," says Grumman, "are a unique solution to speed, flexibility and economy in building. The frames are the link between modules and serve as an assembly fixture, transporting device, hoisting sling, and provide an attractive architectural detail to the finished structure as well."

More and more city dwellers seek second or country homes. But the necessary leisure and affluence don't seem to be as abundant as we'd like. Modular construction may bring a second home within reach for many of us.

Building with Lasers

The laser, no longer merely a specialized laboratory instrument, is becoming a practical tool for farmers, machinists, construction workers and many other tradesmen.

For example, a helium-neon laser is commonly used for the nitty-gritty job of aligning gravity-flow sewer pipelines. A low-intensity laser light casts a true and constant guideline to ensure that the pipes are laid straight and at the proper downward slope. One manufacturer claims that the laser aligner boosts contractor productivity by as much as 25 percent.

Another similar laser tool is the Rotolite, built by Spectra-Physics, Inc. The Rotolite emits a pencil-thin beam of harmless red light that rotates rapidly in either a horizontal or vertical plane. In effect, it draws a straight red line on every object it shines on. Builders use the beam as a constant reference point, a kind of visual carpenter's level: When installing acoustical ceilings, wall partitions, or precision flooring (needed in computer rooms), a workman simply lines up his materials with the laser line, eliminating the need for string lines, spirit levels, and the like. A constant downward beam acts as a steady plumb-bob and provides a quick check of whether the laser itself remains level.

A laser system originally designed to ensure that tunneling and dredging operations are straight and true has been adapted for agricultural applications; laser beams are now being used experi-

The Rotolite uses a rotating laser to "draw" a harmless red line of light. The line is used in place of levels and string lines on construction jobs, and contractors report productivity increases of between 20 and 50 percent.

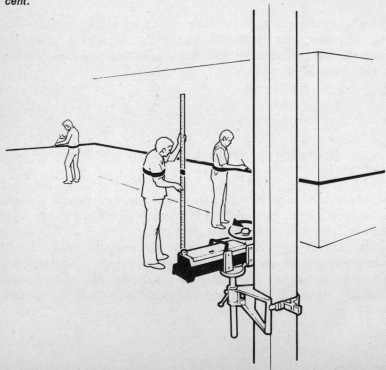

mentally to plant vineyards in straight rows and to aid in harvesting a number of crops. Laser measurement and alignment have also come to machine shops, particularly in the metalworking industry, for precision calibrations. Currently the sales of laser metrological products are growing at a rate of 30 percent per year.

Herbert M. Dwight, Jr., president of Spectra-Physics, Inc., says, "To date, fifteen possible applications (for lasers in the building trades) have been identified and will be tried. Ten of these have been certified as technically and economically sound using existing laser equipment. . . . Four of the nation's largest tunneling projects are currently using Spectra-Physics alignment lasers to control the advance in line and grade of the tunneling mole."

A Mobile Bridge

Road repairs, the bane of every expressway traveler's existence, may soon be accomplished with minimal delay and bottlenecks.

The Mobile Overpass Roadway Repair Vehicle, or MORV as it's called for short, is a new concept in highway repair. It's a mobile bridge placed over the repair area, allowing traffic of light vehicles to detour *over* it uninterrupted. Repair operations go on underneath. Inclined ramps lead cars up to and down from the bridge. Only heavy vehicles like trucks have to be rerouted into another lane.

The MORV reduces traffic capacity by about 22 percent, and this figure is much lower than conventional detours. The MORV is narrower than a normal highway lane and cars going up the on-ramp have to slow down somewhat. Traditional road repair, though, often involves closing two lanes even if only one has to be fixed. The repair equipment is hard to handle within one lane. With the MORV, the equipment is suspended above the work site and below the bridge of traffic. Only the lane being repaired is put out of service, and there's no need for traffic to slow to a standstill to merge two and possibly three lanes into one.

The MORV consists of two ramps and four individual modules, or repair units, under the flat part of the structure. It can move either forward or backward at slow speeds. Each module is brought into place one at a time over the defective road surface, and the repairs are done sequentially. All the units are linked electrically to a central control unit located outside the MORV, usually right off the highway. A crew controls the repair operations remotely from the central unit.

The on-ramp houses an environmental control system that keeps the interior temperature-controlled. This is necessary for proper mixing of new concrete. The system also drains off rainwater and melts accumulated snow with heat. The off-ramp, which is brought over the repair first as the MORV moves forward, contains highway fault-detection equipment. TV cameras bring information to the crew on what needs to be repaired and how. A material transport trailer located under the off-ramp brings defective concrete away from the MORV, and new materials to it. Only when the trailer is in operation does traffic in the MORV lane have to be rerouted elsewhere.

The first module removes old concrete if the cracking is too extensive to be simply refilled. A removal system then cleans the repair area. The second module holds utilities. The third module stores each of the ingredients for making fresh concrete in separate bins, and the fourth pours and levels the new concrete.

Cars ascending MORV at night.

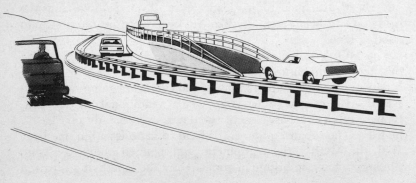

Roadside signs placed up to two miles ahead of the MORV give early warning to drivers of its existence. The road on top of the MORV is light-colored for improved night visibility, and light reflectors are mounted on the side rails. Flashing lights ahead of the MORV spell messages such as "resupply operations" or "stalled car" to keep drivers informed of changed conditions.

Professor Rollin Dix of the Illinois Institute of Technology, and father of the MORV concept, says, "The MORV is designed to permit smooth automobile traffic over the work site while providing ample work space beneath for repair operations."

Old Tires into Highways

A University of Wisconsin professor has demonstrated that rubber tires, after freezing, can be beaten into a powder and recycled.

Old tires, like old automobiles, are an ecologist's nightmare. Billions of discarded tires litter the American landscape, and 240 million more are being added to them every year. Only about 9 percent are being recycled at present. It's illegal to burn the rest because of the pollutants released, and landfill sites are becoming scarcer and scarcer.

The new process, developed by Norman R. Braton, a professor of mechanical engineering, may avoid the tire nightmare. Professor Braton has applied the science of cryogenics to the worn-out tires. He finds that when they are cooled to −80° F., they become brittle. He then uses a hammer mill to fragment them. After pulverizing, the components are separated. These include not only rubber but wire and fabric.

A mobile cryogenic recycling unit weighs 30,000 pounds and fits on a 30-foot truck. Liquid nitrogen is used to chill the tires, which are then passed through the hammer mill. The mill can process 30 tires a minute. Braton visualizes a fleet of these trucks traveling from tire lot to tire lot. The salvaged rubber can be used as a bonding material in asphalt highways and fabric in the manufacture of plastics.

"Cryogenics," says Professor Braton, "is today where the furnace was 100 years ago—in its infancy. This pollution-free cryogenic process is so versatile it can be used to fragment and separate any material that becomes brittle at reduced temperatures. . . . Freezing for recycling appears to be a natural."

The Goodyear Tire Company has set up a heating plant in Jackson, Michigan, that uses old tires as its fuel exclusively. (The plant is pollution free.) Firestone has shown that a ton of tires can yield 150 gallons of oil and 1500 cubic feet of heating gas. When all of these processes are put on a commercial basis there may even be a shortage of old tires.

Roadbeds Made of Discarded Glass

If a roadway looks shiny next winter, don't be surprised because it may be a new paving mixture called "glasphalt."

Conventional asphalt paving of roadbeds isn't possible under cold weather conditions, because asphalt mixtures cool too rapidly between the time of spreading and the time of compaction by rollers. Yet it's just these cold weather conditions—snow and ice, freezing temperatures and thaws—that are most damaging to roadways. Potholes, cracks and crevices are plentiful, but any restoration of a road surface beyond temporary patching must await warmer weather. For the same reason, the paving of new roads is a spring-to-fall enterprise.

The new paving mixture incorporating waste glass may change this. "Glasphalt," which is 60 to 85 percent glass and 15 to 40 percent stone aggregate, has a thermal conductivity much lower than that of asphalt mixtures. In other words, it retains heat considerably longer than asphalt does; this permits effective rolling of a new surface even in winter.

Anchor Hocking and the Glass Containers Corporation have

jointly produced and road-tested "glasphalt" samples. Additional analysis and testing is being performed under contract by Professor Philip Dickson of the Colorado School of Mines.

Discarded glass on a roadway takes a toll on tires. Yet the same glass, made into a paving mixture, may make smooth winter driving possible.

Plastic Cars

A new plastic has been developed by Monsanto which could replace metal parts in cars, kitchen appliances and industrial machines. It's cheaper than the metal parts, faster to produce and highly resistant to wear and tear.

Usually plastics are reinforced with glass or fiber. The new plastic, called Vydyne R, is a kind of nylon strengthened with mineral particles. Since the minerals distribute themselves more evenly than glass, the plastic has uniform strength in all directions.

Plastics have a tendency to lose their working characteristics as the temperature rises, so Vydyne R comes in two grades: a general engineering grade and a heat-stabilized grade. Monsanto is currently working on an even tougher fire-retardant grade. Both the current grades are comparatively inexpensive—less than sixty cents a pound before the oil shortage.

This superhard nylon can be molded on standard, commercially available equipment. In fact, it takes 15–50 percent less time to produce a molded piece of Vydyne than for other thermoplastics, and it can be easily machined. Vydyne resists scratching and marring, as well as the corrosive and dissolving effects of a wide variety of chemicals. Monsanto foresees automobiles with everything from plastic engine parts to plastic fenders.

"The gap between engineering thermoplastics and metals has narrowed considerably over the past few years," says Richard

Gnecco of Monsanto. "We're now closing it further with this major advancement in reinforcing technology."

Plastic engine parts and car exteriors—if petroleum shortages don't intervene—will reduce collision repair costs, weight and possibly fuel consumption.

Light Copies Sunlight

Artificial lighting resembling the color of sunlight will soon bathe our houses and offices. A fluorescent bulb invented by the Duro-Test Corporation and a light source developed by General Electric reproduce natural light indoors.

Known as "Vita-Lite," the Duro-Test bulb is the first fluorescent light to simulate the color and ultraviolet spectrum of natural sunlight. Although other ultraviolet lamps do exist, these don't serve as general-purpose lamps, whereas "Vita-Lite" does. After manufacture, a special system analyzes the light output of the bulbs, wavelength by wavelength, to compare it with the sun's ultraviolet rays.

General Electric's light source is a small, high-intensity discharge lamp whose spectrum matches the color of noonday sunlight. It's called a "molecular arc lamp" since it produces light by passing an electric arc through a vapor of tin chloride molecules. Unlike other high-intensity arcs that emit light in separate color bands, it emits light fairly evenly over all the colors in the continuous spectrum of visible light. This continuous emission of light produces superior color which requires no phosphor coating for improvement.

According to the General Electric Company, the molecular arc lamp is the first lamp to successfully include tin chloride, which plays an important part in producing light with a continuous spectrum. It has a life expectancy of nearly 5000 user hours, compared with about 750 for a conventional incandescent bulb.

Its light output is about four times that of a standard 100-watt household bulb, and it maintains 95 percent of its original intensity throughout life.

Duro-Test Corporation's "Vita-Lite" is already being manufactured in final form. General Electric perfected the molecular arc lamp in developmental form in late 1970 and is now working on a practical version for general marketing.

The Duro-Test Corporation states, "Until more is understood about the profound effects of light on life, the most logical approach to lighting the workday environment is to simulate as closely as possible the color and spectrum of natural light."

The immediate effect of sun-imitating light is to brighten sunless days and improve color and visibility indoors. But there may be long-range effects we can only guess at. Since life itself is impossible without the sun, future designs may change our moods in tune to our illumination.

7
Communication and Information

The Discovery of the Future

How can you "study" the future—it doesn't exist? One answer is, we already study history . . . even though the past has ceased to exist. Traditional education has been concerned largely with teaching us what's been done in the past. In recent years, however, educators have turned their attention to the future, and courses in "futuristics" are growing in number, variety and presumably quality.

Individual businesses, institutions and government have been making plans for the future for a long time. But it was only recently that Americans recognized they had to think about "the shape of things to come" on a systematic, society-wide basis. In 1969 Mr. Richard M. Nixon set up the National Goals Research Staff to forecast future developments and assess the longer-range consequences of social trends today. And in 1973 former Governor Nelson A. Rockefeller launched the Commission on Critical Choices for Americans to determine what "desirable and realistic objectives" the nation could achieve by 1985 or even 2000.

In the United States, college courses devoted to teaching about the future had already begun to appear earlier in the 1960s. Early teachers in the field were Richard L. Meier, now at the University of California, and Daniel Bell, the Harvard University sociologist. Within a few years, courses in the future were popping up all over the country. Eighty were reported in 1970; today they number in the hundreds, and they cover a broad spectrum of fields, from education to law and from theology to computers. High schools and even elementary schools now include the future in their curricula. In typical courses, field trips, films, guest lecturers, multimedia presentations, and computer models are used to help students visualize the world in which they're going to spend the rest of their lives.

A course called "Futures of Urbanism and the City," given by Professor Meier, offers one example of futurist studies. The course concentrates on Asia, where Meier says many important decisions about the organization of cities will be made in the next twenty years. Students look at such problems as how to house poor immigrants in the metropolis and how to design tropical urban communities that produce their own perishables.

"Formal education in futurism," says H. Wentworth Eldredge, professor of sociology at Dartmouth, "will continue to expand in American colleges and universities . . . the academicians, aided by research institutes, private corporations, and government laboratories/research teams, will play their dual role of developing new reliable information—as well as transmitting it to the young . . . to educate a rapidly growing network of men throughout the world who peer ever further and ever more clearly into the future."

In a society that grows more complicated every day, the need for predicting the future and planning ahead is becoming increasingly urgent. (Remember Pearl Harbor—and the petroleum shortage?) When even conservative leaders of our times formally incorporate elements of long-range planning into our national programs, we can hope the future might be at least better than the past—and the present.

Encyclopedia of the Future

Traditional encyclopedias deal in hard-and-fast facts and provide answers to questions. But now experts in Europe and America are working on a provocative encyclopedia of forecasts—one likely to raise more questions than it answers.

The Encyclopedia of the Future, as it will be called, is being developed under the editorial supervision of the Hudson Institute in Paris. This is the European office of the world-renowned "think tank." The encyclopedia is planned to cover every field of knowledge and will be made up of five volumes. Titles of the volumes are "Politics and Economics," "Science and Technology," "Society," "The Individual" and "The Arts and Leisure."

The editors have signed up over sixty internationally known authorities to prepare articles for the encyclopedia. Among the writers are the physicist Edward Teller, who helped develop the hydrogen bomb; Marshall McLuhan, the communications expert; Ashley Montagu, the anthropologist; Dr. Joshua Lederberg, the biologist who won the Nobel Prize for his studies of genetics; Arnold Toynbee, the historian; and Wernher von Braun, the space scientist. Dr. Bruno Bettelheim, the psychologist, will do a piece on the future of child rearing, and Dr. Margaret Mead, the anthropologist, one on the family.

Although the encyclopedia looks ahead, it won't look too far ahead. It will restrict its predictions to developments that may be expected in the next fifteen years or so. Peering far into the future is too risky, say the editors. The project is the brainchild of Philippe Daudy, a French writer, who will also publish it. He promises an annual supplement to keep the encyclopedia up to date.

"We want the encyclopedia to shake up readers, provoke them to think," says Edwin Stillman of the Hudson Institute. "Most of the readers we hope to attract really aren't abreast of reality. They're thinking ten to fifteen years in the past, laboring under the weight of outmoded ideas that don't correspond to the real present."

In the new encyclopedia the authors, who include eminent scientists, will don the robes of Nostradamus. Forecasting in such volatile fields as society or the arts is a venture into uncharted seas. But developments in technology, science and economics are predicted with a good expectation that many will come true—even if prophecy *is* the most gratuitous form of error.

New and Future Words

New words, or new meanings for old words, are constantly bobbing up in the English language. Many of them reflect new inventions, new developments in government or society, or
changing concepts in science and the arts.

Words we take for granted today were once novelties. Sociology was an up-and-coming science in 1907 when William
Graham Sumner of Yale introduced the word *folkways* as a term
meaning group habits or customs. George Eastman coined the
name *Kodak* for his picture-making invention even earlier. In an
age when people were looking critically at government, W. E.
Woodward created the word *debunking*.

It's the job of dictionary editors to keep tabs on new words and
new uses of old ones. At G. & C. Merriam Company, the country's biggest dictionary-makers, twenty full-time lexicographers
keep a constant lookout for verbal novelties. In their search, they
screen hundreds of publications and make citations or notes of
their findings. When they accumulate enough citations of a
word—meaning it has gained wide currency—they admit it into
the next edition of the dictionary.

Many words are gathered but few are chosen. Here are some
(courtesy of *Compton's Yearbook*) that are now being watched
as possible candidates for the dictionary. Some have virtually
made it already.

air bed: a hospital bed that consists of a sheet-covered tank filled
    with tiny glass beads through which warm air is pumped to
    provide support for the patient
agricorporation: a large company engaged in raising, processing
    and selling food products
alimony drone: a self-indulgent, indolent divorcee who lives on
    alimony
apocalyptician: one who predicts devastating calamities
automobilitis: the problems caused by the increasing use of auto-
    mobiles
carboholic: a compulsive eater
carnography: gory acts of violence in motion pictures

digital watch: a watch that shows the time with numerical digits, not hands

ecopsychiatry: psychiatry that deals with the effects of environmental pollution on mental health

ESV: an experimental safety vehicle

Flextime: a system that allows employees to choose their own starting and finishing times

futuriasis: a morbid fixation on or fear of the future

futurizing: giving a future dimension to

hovernaut: one who operates a hovercraft

letter bomb: an explosive device concealed in an envelope and mailed to the intended victim

macroreading: reading with the purpose of comprehending only the large ideas (as themes and plots) of a prose work

phonomontage: a sequence of sounds intended to create a particular mood

rotorbatics: spectacular flying feats perfomed with a helicopter

tanout: a deliberate reduction of electric power during a period of heavy demand to prevent overtaxing the generators

ultrasuede: a washable synthetic fabric that resembles suede

"The purpose of the dictionary is to provide a record of the language as it is used by educated people who have been speaking and writing it all their lives," says H. Bosley Woolf, editorial director of Merriam. "What we do here is all based on citations."

Editors make dictionaries but the people (including inventors) make the words that fill the pages of those dictionaries. The names of some of the new developments reported in this book—like the millimeter waveguide, the Jetcord and others—will find their way into the dictionaries of tomorrow.

Chimp Language

"Sarah insert apple pail banana dish."

These are not the words of a two-year-old child babbling with-

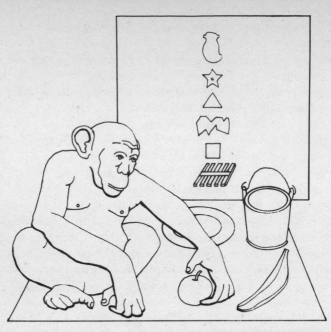

After reading the message, "Sarah insert apple pail banana dish," on magnetic board, the chimp placed the apple in the pail and the banana in the dish.

out grammar, or a Hollywood version of a native learning English from a missionary. They are written instructions to a chimpanzee named Sarah. Since 1966 she has been learning to read and write from Ann and David Premack in their University of California laboratory, and has a vocabulary of well over a hundred words.

The Premacks believe that trying to teach apes language can tell us more about the nature of language than about the nature of apes. They want to clarify the dividing line between the general system of language as used by all animal species, and the peculiarly human one. They chose a chimpanzee as a subject because chimps have an elaborate system of "calls" in their natural environment. Chimps have been taught by other researchers in the past to use sign language, sort pictures into classes, and even "speak."

Plastic symbols which varied in color, size and shape were the language units used by the Premacks. Each stood for a specific word or concept. The plastic pieces were backed with metal so they would adhere to a magnetic "language board." Sarah seemed to prefer reading and writing vertically so the researchers placed words vertically on the board.

In teaching Sarah, they took into account the concepts and social interactions already present in the chimpanzee mind and world. They began with the concept "giving," since it occurs among chimps both in the laboratory and in the wild. The first step was teaching Sarah which words the plastic symbols represented. A trainer placed a banana in front of Sarah, which she was allowed to eat. After repeating this procedure for a while, the trainer removed the banana and placed a plastic square in front of Sarah. She had to put the plastic word on the language board in order to receive the banana. The trainer later introduced various other fruits and the plastic symbol representing "give" in the same manner. Sarah learned the name of the trainers, the other chimpanzees and her own. She was able to read and follow instructions to give a fruit to a specific trainer, and write instructions asking for one herself.

The next step was to teach Sarah language with language. The trainer introduced an object together with the matching plastic symbol. Sarah placed a symbol for "name of" between the object and its symbol; and a symbol for "not name of" between the object and an inappropriate symbol. She was also able to learn the class concepts of color, shape and size.

Some evidence emerged that Sarah was able to think—store information and solve new problems—in the plastic word language. This implies understanding the meaning of words in the absence of their external representation. Sarah was taught the phrase "Brown color of chocolate," and later presented with four discs, one of which was brown. Upon instructions to "take brown," she removed the brown disc from the board. Since no chocolate was present, this suggests she was able to picture the property "brown."

According to the Premacks, "Linguists and others who study the development of language tend to exaggerate the child's understanding and to be extremely skeptical of the experimentally demonstrated abilities of the chimpanzee. It is our hope that our findings will dispel such prejudices and lead to new attempts to teach suitable languages to animals other than man."

Chimp language may help brain-damaged and autistic children

who have difficulty with learning. It may transform our notions of intelligence from performance on tests to the underlying brain mechanisms. Someday, animals will be bred for their abilities to comprehend language and to perform routine chores around the house.

College Degrees Offered by Corporations

The Rand Corporation, a private organization engaged in research work, has set up an institute that awards a doctoral degree in policy analysis.

Rand is an independent nonprofit organization established in 1948 to do research on problems that public leaders face in making policy decisions. The corporation has a faculty of highly qualified specialists and a unique bank of experience. In 1970 it decided to put these resources to a special use: it founded the Rand Graduate Institute for Policy Studies, to concentrate on the advanced training of a small number of policy analysts.

The graduate program couples formal academic training in techniques and concepts involved in policy research with actual on-the-job training. While taking academic courses, students work on projects that Rand has been commissioned to do. Among Rand's clients are government agencies, institutions, and units as diverse as the Air Force, the City of New York, the Agency for International Development, the Office of Economic Opportunity, and the California Committee on Regional Medical Programs. Rand also works on the problems of foreign countries. Students participate in current projects, first as graduate assistants and later as members of the research teams.

Requirements for admission to the institute resemble those of any other institution of higher learning. The candidate has to have a master's degree in some field of physical science, social science or mathematics, or equivalent training. He submits academic and professional references, transcripts and a recent research paper that reflects his best work. He pays tuition, but he

314

also gets compensation for his on-the-job work. The three-year curriculum includes seminar workshops based on completed Rand studies which are conducted by the people who made them. In his third year the student writes a dissertation, generally based on his on-the-job training.

Rand is seeking accreditation for its program from the Western Association of Schools and Colleges.

According to Rand, "The Institute expects to make a small but distinctive contribution to meeting the growing national need for trained analysts, and to satisfy the growing desire among some of the nation's best graduate students for innovative educational programs that combine academic rigor with relevance to issues of public policy."

Rand isn't the only private corporation offering degrees. We may be witnessing the beginning of a trend in which corporations with special needs and something unique to offer will enroll students to fill out their work teams and spread their know-how to the traditional universities.

Failure Teaches

At the Massachusetts Institute of Technology, students are taking a first-of-its-kind seminar that explores the causes and effects of failure and seeks ways to deal with them.

Although most Americans dedicate their lives to success, many of their institutions are set up to deal with failure. Millions are supported by the unemployment or welfare systems; hospitals, courts, prisons, bankruptcy referees, arbitration associations, the insurance industry, even the Army and Navy are essentially there to pick up the pieces when society fails. The purpose of the new course, says MIT, is "to examine the individual, organizational, societal and ethical implications and consequences of serious failure as an essential component of the normal everyday living, learning, coping and succeeding experience."

Called "Failure of Human Systems," the course began in 1973.

315

It's the creation of Frank P. Davidson, an attorney and systems engineer who has worked as a planner on the tunnel linking England and France under the channel.

Davidson is a member of the Systems Dynamics Group at MIT. This group takes complicated systems and analyzes them into their essential parts. Then mathematical models of them are built so they can be studied abstractly. Davidson is applying this technique to study why institutions fail. According to him, many failures that are viewed as personal are actually caused by the failure of institutions. The economy fails, the school fails, or the institution of marriage fails, but the individual views it as his own failure. In the course the students analyze the role of the larger systems in individual failure.

A variety of disciplines contribute to the course, as the students listen to talks by experts in medicine, architecture, theology, engineering, law and other areas. One lesson the students learn is that in any field it's a mark of maturity to accept the risk of failure. Another is that if they accept traditional standards of success uncritically, their careers can suffer for it.

Davidson, founder of the course, wants it to create a new kind of engineer at MIT. "I am hoping we will be graduating modern-day Lincoln Steffenses—to take institutions that are obviously not working and reform them."

So far we've been more concerned with success than with that frequent occurrence, failure. Early exposure to failure may teach students to avoid superficial labels—and to use what they learn to achieve a less monetary, though perhaps more important, kind of success.

College Degrees Through the Public Library

Public libraries have often been called "the people's university." Now they're purposefully living up to the name by helping members of the public pursue regular courses of study and obtain college credits.

The new library program is called "On Your Own" (OYO), a name that emphasizes the courses are self-directed. It was launched in 1972 under the aegis of the Denver Public Library and has been growing steadily. The program has the support of many institutions in the area, among them the University of Colorado, the University of Denver, local colleges, and the Colorado Commission of Higher Education. Four national agencies are also backing it: the Council on Library Resources, the National Endowment for the Humanities, the U.S. Office of Education, and the College Entrance Examination Board.

Here's how the program works. Suppose you're a high school graduate and you want to begin studying a subject that interests you or continue studying something you've already begun. You go to your library (if you live in the Denver area) and discuss your plan with a special librarian. The librarian provides you with the guidance you need to start your program of independent study, including a list of recommended readings. Not only does the library have the books on the list, which may be checked out, but it's also equipped with study areas, films and other resources. All of the library's services are free. If you have difficulty with your subject, the library will even help you find a tutor, but there may be a charge for the tuition.

Now suppose you want to receive credit for your course of study. Any of the colleges or universities participating in the program will give you credit if you obtain a satisfactory grade in an examination. Most of the schools administer tests supplied by the College Level Examination Program, which is affiliated with the College Entrance Examination Board. The credit enables you to shorten the time you have to spend in residence at the college to qualify for a degree. There is a modest charge for taking an examination.

"The proponents of the project," says the Denver Public Library, "believe that while the credit-by-examination route to a more personalized education must continue to be connected with institutions of higher education, programs oriented toward this concept can be based off the campus. . . . Libraries will continue to have a more important role as educators in the society of the future."

Perhaps libraries in other parts of the country need to take a les-

son from Denver. In the world of tomorrow a wide range of knowledge will be indispensable. Not everyone has the time to go to
college—but the public libraries, with their books, films and
courses, can help to bring college-level learning to all who want it.

Cooperative Computers

Students may soon find themselves acquiring a broad spectrum
of skills with the help of an audiovisual teaching machine developed by Borg-Warner.

System 80 looks like a television set, but it acts like a private
tutor. A console unit about two feet square, it contains a record
player, a viewing screen, a row of buttons, and a memory bank.

After typing his answer, boy awaits verdict of computer.

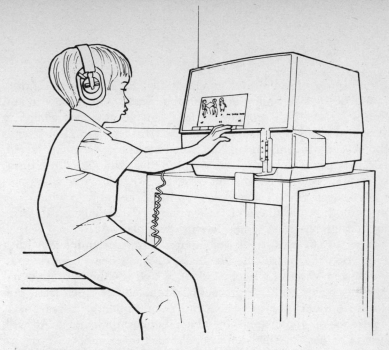

A child operating the System 80 learning machine.

With it comes a set of learning programs consisting of phonograph records and color filmstrips.

The student inserts a filmstrip and a record on a chosen subject into the machine. He hears a question and at the same time he sees illustrations that represent possible answers to the question. To show which answer he thinks is correct he presses a button. If his choice is right the machine automatically moves to the next frame. But if his choice is wrong the machine either continues to repeat the question until the child responds correctly, or changes to a remedial frame that explains the concept behind the question further.

At the end of each lesson there is a progress check, and review lessons are spaced throughout each series of lessons.

The machine has been tested in inner-city schools in Chicago and Washington, D.C. Students of any age can work it, and so can illiterate adults and physically or mentally handicapped students. The machine can be modified for children with severe motor disabilities, such as cerebral palsy. These students respond to questions by moving their head, breaking a photoelectric beam like that used in automatic doors.

319

Other emotionally and intellectually handicapped children now talk to "Mr. Computer" when they want to learn how to add and subtract. Mr. Computer is the language of a new computer system developed by General Electric. It's been tested in schools for special students in upstate New York and on Long Island, and may prove to be a useful teaching tool. Although other forms of computer-aided instruction exist, the GE computer offers personalized programs to children who need special help with learning. Another advantage of the system is that teachers can write and design programs themselves for students.

The system consists of a computer terminal equipped with a typewriter keyboard. Before class, the teacher prepares individualized lessons for each student, which are then programmed into the computer. The procedure doesn't differ much from preparing ordinary lesson plans. And each student's program concentrates on those areas in which he has difficulties. At will, programs may be further personalized. For example, a program may instruct the computer to ask the child about his hobbies or favorite color.

The children sit at the computer one at a time. First, the computer types out a question for the student. The student uses the keyboard to type out his or her answer. This ongoing interaction between the computer and the child keeps up interest, because the computer gives students instant feedback. If the child answers the question correctly, it compliments him and then moves on to more difficult problems. If he answers incorrectly, the computer gives him a hint based on simpler problems he had previously answered.

Dr. Philip Lewis, one of the creators of Mr. Computer, feels there are many reasons for its success. For one, "Mr. Computer is like a game. The student types on the keyboard, and Mr. Computer types back. It's give and take."

If it looks like a typewriter or television set, kids will love it. . . . Not only handy in any remedial situation, it will also be of special worth in outlying districts, where children get their instruction by radio. Or it can be loaned to children who are kept out of school by illness. When the next wave of young students overloads our public schools—perhaps in a few decades—we'll be ready for them.

320

Data Privacy Through Cryptology

Gluxlbzx Jontdwpf.

If this encoded information concerned your personal affairs, and was stored in a computerized "data bank" that fell into unauthorized hands, could it be decoded?

The answer is yes, provided sufficient quantities were available to an intruder.

The need to guard against unauthorized "withdrawals" is acute. Cryptology, the centuries-old discipline of making and breaking codes, has been enlisted by engineers at IBM to keep out busybodies. They've designed a system permitting the storage of private data encoded so it's not only unintelligible but also inaccessible to a would-be intruder.

Data banks are typically located in centralized computers reached through a network of remote, typewriterlike terminals. Given this arrangement, privacy of data can't be guaranteed simply by requiring processed information to be merely coded, for any user of the system would have access to such encoded data. Almost any code, however sophisticated, is theoretically breakable. So an unauthorized user would need only sufficient portions of the encoded data, plus the assistance of another computer, to decipher the data.

To ensure that encoded information be inaccessible to a user-intruder, the IBM system requires both a user and the central computer to "recognize" each other as authorized to proceed with the transmission and reception of the personal data in question.

One method of mutual recognition, reciprocal testing, serves as a kind of "electronic handshake." Here's how the elaborate system works. A user signs on by transmitting his own identity along with an arbitrary segment of data enciphered with his own code. Then the computer retrieves the user's code, deciphers his arbitrary sequence, and sends it back to the user, along with the computer's own arbitrary sequence enciphered with the same code. By virtue of the correct decipherment of his initial input, the user will know that he's dealing with "his" computer. Before continuing, however, he must satisfy the computer as to his

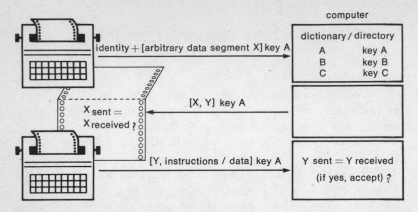

The "electronic handshake."

actual identity by deciphering and sending back the computer's arbitrary segment of data. After the user and the central computer are each satisfied through this trial run that the other is familiar with the code they alone share, normal interchange of encoded private data between them can proceed.

To overcome the cryptological burdens placed upon an authorized user of this secured-data system, IBM has designed a special console, nicknamed Lucifer, which can be attached to a remote terminal. Upon the insertion of a wallet-sized magnetic-stripe card bearing the code unique to that user, this device accomplishes the numerous coding and decoding operations required by the system.

The system isn't perfect, but according to M. B. Girsdansky of IBM, "The problems in traffic-security and cryptanalysis faced by a potential intruder would appear to be formidable to overcome when considered in realistic terms of time and expense. Taken together, the various features of the system . . . seem to furnish both a high degree of security and potentially wide flexibility in application."

Knowledge is power, Francis Bacon observed. In the wrong hands it can be abused. But the advances that present us with the security "problem" also provide us with the "solution."

Voice Scrambler for Privacy

For the post-Watergate Era, Charles K. Miller has come up with the perfect invention for high government officials and other people who want to keep a secret. His voice privacy device prevents eavesdropping on important telephone conversations by operators, secretaries, neighbors on the party line, or more sinister agents.

Basically Mr. Miller's gadget is a new kind of voice scrambler, not unlike those used by the Joint Chiefs of Staff and other VIPs. As you speak into the microphone, the complex circuitry rearranges your voice into an incoherent garble. A similar unit at the other end of the telephone line ungarbles your voice. Both parties to the conversation can hear each other plainly, but anyone cutting in would hear nothing but a droning, kazoolike sound.

Until now, good scramblers have required a very expensive oscillator—a luxury reserved for well-to-do secret-keepers. The simpler, cheaper scramblers use a harmonic system that can easily be decoded by a snooper with some electronics know-how.

A "scrambler" ensures private telephone (or radio) conversations. A person speaks in the microphone (left), and his voice goes round and round, and it comes out at the transmitter (right). A similar device at the other end of the line undoes the electronic jumble.

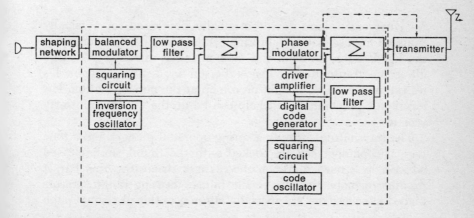

Mr. Miller's device, in contrast, scrambles without an oscillator, and it can mix up voices in a variety of different patterns, which makes unauthorized unscrambling difficult. The caller simply phones in a code word that informs the receiver which scrambling pattern is being used. And as the *pièce de resistance*, the code word is scrambled, too.

The electronics of how and why it works are confusing to the layman—after all, confusion is the whole idea. But the apparatus isn't much more difficult to operate than the telephone itself.

The Technical Communications Corporation of Lexington, Massachusetts is developing the voice privacy device.

The inventor tries to explain: "Still another object of the invention is to provide an improved voice privacy coder system in which a synchronizing signal for reconstruction of the code is buried within the coded communication itself and is transmitted with the coded communication in a common frequency band."

Many new developments (see page 321) exhibit new conflicts: technological defenders of privacy are a response to various technological invasions of privacy.

Sounding the Alarm

An emergency alarm device originally developed for a racially troubled high school in California is now being used in homes for the aged. Each resident and staff member carries a pen-sized ultrasonic transmitter. When a person in distress triggers his transmitter, it sparks a light on a map at the nursing station. His location is pinpointed, and help can be on the way within thirty seconds.

The transmitter is simply a spring-operated plunger and a tone bar. The plunger can be cocked with the thumb and released when help is needed. When the plunger strikes the tone bar, it produces a note high above the human hearing range. Sensors placed in each room are specially attuned to this ultrasonic pitch

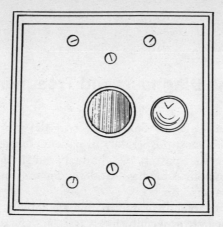

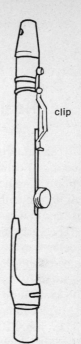

clip

The SCAN transmitter (on right) is operated by releasing the clip. A nearby SCAN receiver (on left) lights up indicating that the emergency signal has been relayed to the master control panel.

and carry the alarm to the central wall map, showing where the emergency is.

The system, known as SCAN (Silent Communication Alarm Network), was developed after the principal at John F. Kennedy High School in Sacramento, California, called on engineers at the National Aeronautics and Space Administration for help in combatting a plague of violence at the school. Parents and community leaders were invited to join in the $1,300,000 project that succeeded in creating SCAN. Installation of the system throughout the 44 acres of Kennedy High School cost only $21,000 and sharply reduced incidents of violence.

Several schools in New York City are experimenting with SCAN, and other potential applications have been noted: Miners might use the system in case of cave-ins, or prison guards might call for help when there is trouble in the cell block.

When these tiny units become commonplace within a few years, their cost will drop.

Hikers, skiers or children might carry these to signal for help when lost or in danger. Perhaps future kidnappings will be averted.

Real Time Diagnosis and Treatment

Fifteen hundred years ago in Babylon it was the custom for doctors to exhibit their most desperately ill patients in the public square. The hope was that passers-by who had seen similar cases might remember possible remedies. Modern doctors may soon use computers for the same purpose.

The vast amount of biomedical information available to today's doctor can be confusing, especially if he is relatively inexperienced. The doctor must accurately interpret symptoms in order to identify the illness and choose an appropriate treatment. At the same time he must keep his patient alive until his prescribed therapy can take its long-term effect.

Dr. John H. Siegel and scientists at IBM Research Institute have developed a computer system that helps a doctor make an accurate diagnosis and then suggests to the doctor the best minute-by-minute course of treatment for his patient's illness. At present the system is limited to coverage of a few critical illnesses that have required that patients be constantly monitored on special equipment. This provides the computer with highly specific physical measurements in addition to more common information such as laboratory test results.

A doctor treating a patient who has an illness "covered" by the computer secures information from the central computer via telephone lines. He scans samples from hundreds of other patients at a glance, either in a written print-out or on a televised image. He quickly notes different forms that the illness has previously taken. Then the doctor analyzes his patient's symptoms and predicts what direction the illness—and treatment—is likely to take.

Physician at Albert Einstein College of Medicine communicates via terminal with the Thomas J. Watson Research Center computer 35 miles away. The physician, from patient records, furnishes information through his terminal and requests a computer review of the data or complex calculations based on it. Similarities and differences are established between critical cases.

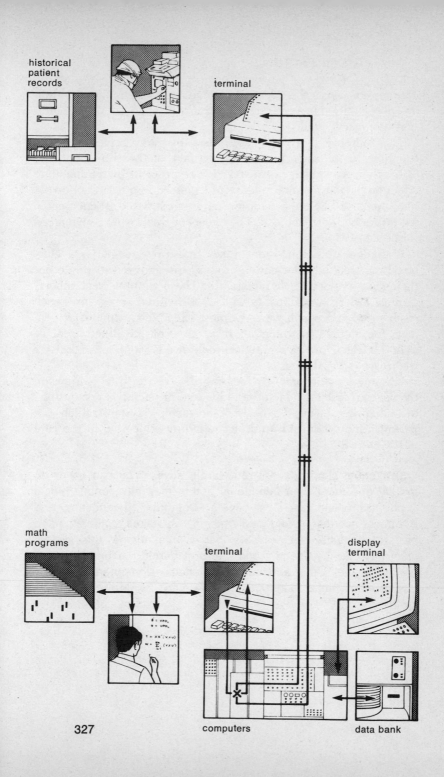

historical
patient
records

terminal

math
programs

terminal

display
terminal

327

computers

data bank

The system warns the doctor if changes in his patient's condition are potentially dangerous, and indicates where treatment should first be concentrated.

The computer not only keeps track of many separate bodily functions at the same time, it keeps track of them in relation to each other. Any change is analyzed in terms of its own immediate effect on the patient and in terms of its effect on other functions of his body. No change is considered as an isolated phenomenon. All information is balanced. The effects of treatment are balanced in the same way.

Physiological measurements taken from previous patients, clustered into related information groups, are analyzed to single out their most important characteristics. The computer "remembers" groups and relationships as well as individual cases, how each case varied and which were the most effective treatments; it projects the course, treatment or recurrence of the illness, real or hypothetical. Thus it's a practical tool for education as well as for the treatment of illness.

Dr. Siegel points out, "By focusing data retrieval techniques on the specific case for which the individual physician is responsible, the computer forms the basis of a teaching system which can permit a more relevant kind of continuing education in the care of the critically ill."

With elegant simplicity, Garrett Hardin says, "You can never do merely one thing." An intentional action may have unintentional —but overwhelming—side effects. Computer diagnostics and treatment may help avoid costly medical mistakes, epidemics and bad side effects. Not only applicable to medicine, this system also may classify, identify and interpret heroic amounts of information in the social and natural sciences. Computers may one day predict riots, bountiful crops—even fashion changes in clothes.

Rapid Image Transmission by "Laser Writing"

Newspaper pages and photographs are now transmitted from coast to coast by publishers who want to put out two different editions of a newspaper the same morning. But the facsimile process used is slow compared with a new laser-writing method invented by Dan Maydan and two colleagues at Bell Telephone Laboratories.

By using the laser technique and a high-capacity transmission line, a full newspaper page can be transmitted across thousands of miles in four seconds. If a regular-capacity telephone line is used, the page takes about four minutes to transmit. The page is recorded on microfilm, projected on a screen or printed on paper.

The laser-writing system is based on a scanner in which a pulsed laser beam picks up the text or image and "burns" it on a

This hole, one tenth the diameter of a human hair, was "machined" by a laser pulse on a thin metal coating over a transparent plastic film.

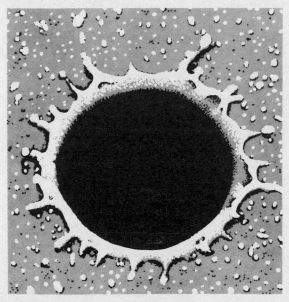

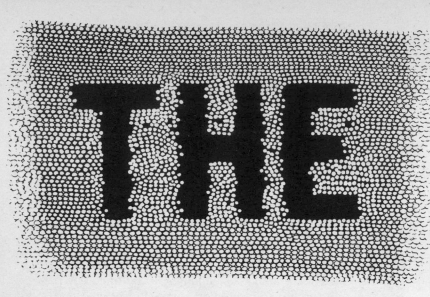

The word "the" is formed by machining many holes, with many laser bursts, in the thin metal-film coating.

distant 16-mm microfilm with a bismuth metal coating. The varying intensity of the laser beam makes millions of tiny holes or dots on the bismuth surface, giving it black, white or gray shades like newspaper photos. No film developing process is involved. In addition to newspaper pages, the device can be used to transmit documents and even x-ray photographs.

The three major components used in laser writing are a simple low-power helium-neon gas laser, which generates about 1,000,000 pulses per second; an acoustooptic modulator (located within the laser), which deflects and controls the high-energy pulses from the laser cavity, and varies according to the strength of the signal received; the Mylar microfilm, covered with bismuth, which is only two to three millionths of an inch thick.

A three-dimensional "stereo" picture can be produced by transmitting two frames and assembling them in a stereofilm viewer to give it depth. Color pictures are transmitted by sending three color-separated images by pulsed laser and then combining them at the receiving end. All images may be stored on microfilm for later copying.

According to Maydan, "The significant departure from previous work rests in the use of very short laser pulses to record the image in the form of an array of discrete holes in the metal film, and in the modulation of the intensity of the laser pulses so as to vary the size of the holes."

The laser-writing technique could speed the newspaper into your home daily. With the receiver at home, the publisher will "deliver" the paper by radio or telephone. And vast remote files, records and computer data are reachable instantly.

Portable Telephones

A hand-held, completely portable telephone will make it possible to place calls while riding in a bus, walking down the street or sitting in a restaurant. Developed by Motorola, Inc., the first "portaphone" system will be installed in New York City by 1976.

The portaphone looks like a fat Princess® phone or a high-fashion walkie-talkie. Weighing less than three pounds, the unit can dial and receive calls anywhere within FM signal range of the system's computer-controlled receivers.

As the caller talks over the portaphone, his voice is radiocd to the nearest receiver. The signal is relayed into a central computer, then fed into conventional telephone lines. The computer can track the speaker as he moves about the city, switching the conversation to different receivers to maintain a loud and clear connection.

A portable phone user can contact any conventional or portable phone. The initial cost will be $60 to $100 per month, but as the market demand increases, the costs are expected to go down.

The FCC has proposed 115 MHz of spectrum including channels 73 through 88 for two-way applications. Portaphone will probably operate in that frequency range.

Each telephone has a pushbutton keyboard; it's dialed like a conventional pushbutton phone.

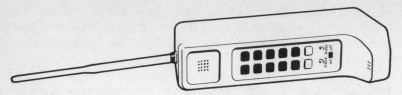

The portable electronic telephone fits into a briefcase or purse.

Motorola sees a bright future for the portaphone: "We expect there'll be heavy usage by a widely diverse group of people—businessmen, journalists, doctors, housewives, virtually anyone who needs or wants telephone communications in areas where conventional telephones are unavailable."

For a while at least, the portaphone will remain a business tool or luxury item. In time, however, portaphones will get smaller and cheaper, just as transistor radios have.

One day you'll call almost anyone, anywhere. You could have instantaneous contact with your doctor or the police. People might be brought closer together than ever before—with the potential to be in voice contact with others. Next step: two-way wrist radios?

Talking Beams of Light

Researchers are hard at work on a system of communications that may prove to be the biggest breakthrough since the invention of the telephone. It will enable thousands of people to talk simultaneously over a beam of light.

Up until now, most modern communications systems have transmitted electronic impulses through wires or the air. The upcoming optical communications system will use minute lasers and hair-thin glass fibers to send voices, data, and video signals—in the form of pulses of light—from one place to another.

The laser, which has the ability to produce an intense beam of light that can travel enormous distances, first appeared in 1960. Even well before, scientists recognized light had a vast capacity for transmitting information. Light beams can carry more information than radio signals because light has a much higher frequency than radio waves. But it took close to ten years to develop some of the apparatus needed to control the beam as an information-carrying medium.

Bell Laboratories, where much of the research has been conducted, has for months been operating a battery-powered semiconductor laser no bigger than a pinhead. It has announced it can send over one billion bits of information over the laser beam in one second. That's the same as transmitting the contents of 200 books of average size in that second.

Bell is also experimenting with glass fibers no thicker than a human hair. Theoretically it's possible for one of these fibers to carry 4000 telephone conversations at once. About 100 of the fibers can be packed together to fill a cable as thick as a pencil.

Much more needs to be done to make the system workable. Like ordinary electric signals, light pulses have to be boosted or regenerated, and Bell is working on an optical "repeater" for this purpose. It's also developing photodetectors—devices to pick up

This solid-state laser (small rectangle atop block) is much smaller than the grain of salt at its right.

salt
grain

the pulses of light and change them into electric signals that can be converted into sound for your telephone.

"Glass fibers, packed into a cable perhaps one-quarter inch in diameter," says Bell Laboratories, "may someday carry as many communication signals as thousands of ordinary telephone wires. Also, tiny fiber cables could be fed through structures that now contain underground telephone cables in major metropolitan areas. This would potentially reduce the need for major construction expenditures."

Like the millimeter waveguide system (see below), the optical fiber transmission system, expected to be perfected by the early 1980s, can't arrive soon enough. The growth of cable TV, computer data transmission, and telephone use in general has created such a demand for communications circuits that there aren't enough to go around.

A Quarter-Million Phone Conversations in a "Pipe"

A pipe no thicker than your wrist will be able to carry a quarter of a million telephone conversations at once. And that pipe will be hollow.

The copper-lined steel tube will be buried at a depth of four feet. It will be encased in a steel sheath and cushioned with spring supports to offset the effects of local earth movement.

The new system is known as the millimeter waveguide. Through the controlled atmosphere inside the tube, communications will be carried on electromagnetic waves just a few millimeters long. The waves are about one tenth the length of those used for microwave radio transmission.

The information carried on the millimeter waves is coded into pulses and transmitted through the waveguide tube. All types of information—voice, video and data—can be carried in the coded pulses. After traveling about twenty miles or so, the pulses are amplified and regenerated by repeaters. In today's coaxial cable systems the corresponding distance is only about two miles. The waveguide's quarter-million telephone circuits also contrast with the 36,000 circuits on typical cross-country coaxial cables.

The Bell System plans to use the millimeter waveguide on high-capacity routes. Every year the system's interstate business has been growing about 12 percent, so Bell will have to triple the capacity of its interstate communications network by 1981. Bell hopes to have its first commercial waveguide system in service between New York and Philadelphia several years before that date.

Research on the waveguide has been going on since the 1930s at Bell. The work, conducted on a small scale, began with short-waves, continued through microwaves, and then went into milli-meter waves. Increasing pressure for a high-capacity system finally propelled the millimeter waveguide into an operational reality.

Says John deButts, AT&T's board chairman: "Waveguide's capacity is more than twice that of our most advanced coaxial cable systems. What is more, we anticipate that with some modi-fications we can increase the capacity of a millimeter waveguide system to almost 500,000 circuits."

Waveguide pipes represent just as great an advance as the coaxial cable and the microwave radio relay system did in their time. The pipes—along with the projected laser communications (see page 332)—offer good hope that we'll be able to cope with the develop-ing communications crisis.

A Stop-Action Video Telephone

RCA Corporation has developed a way of "freezing" and storing a single video frame for later recall and viewing on demand. Among many applications is that popular feature of science fic-tion—a videophone that transmits a picture as well as a voice.

FUTURE FACTS

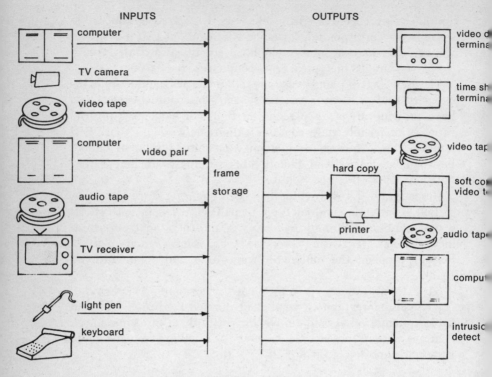

Inputs and outputs of the frame storage system.

RCA is already marketing a videophone they call Videovoice. It's a small desktop unit with a TV camera and monitor and a tiny computer. A telephone connected to the system houses the controls. The machine transmits a still frame in less than a minute to anyone anywhere in the world with another Videovoice unit. It also "freezes" subjects in motion and transmits the image within 30 seconds. During fuel and energy shortages, Videovoice may replace many business trips, since products can be demonstrated and documents examined immediately without the expense of travel or the delay of mail delivery.

In standard TV, 30 full pictures or frames are transmitted every second, creating the illusion of motion in the picture. However, it takes about 1000 voice-grade telephone circuits merely to transmit those 30 frames a second. One "motionless" frame every 55 seconds (or one "freeze" frame every 30 seconds) can be transmitted over a *single* voice-grade telephone circuit.

Stop-action service for cable TV owners means they could freeze any frame of a program and review it later. Of course, do-it-yourself stop-action for sports programs comes to mind; and the cable TV companies may offer all sorts of information services to the consumer—news, recipes, stock-market prices and the like—storable for future reference.

Furthermore computers that use digital information on tape can be married to TV that uses videotape or film. The videotape information that creates the picture can be stored in a computer as well as physically on the tape. Based on this interlocking information system, RCA employs stop-action TV more generally, in what it calls the FSS or frame storage system; possible uses range from image enhancement to anti-intrusion systems, to electronically generated text and graphics.

According to RCA, the heart of the frame storage system is a new silicon storage tube that stores an individual TV picture frame and displays it on command. "It offers many alternatives and RCA systems use this device in varied forms. . . . A home TV console is equipped with two TV screens, one for the continuing TV program, the other to display the single picture."

The video telephone could adopt your future two-screen home TV console to cut its costs. And someday when wall-size flat TV screens (see page 437) are commonplace, a telephone conversation will have most (if not all) of the "presence" of a face-to-face meeting.

Telecommunications by "Meson" Beams

A mu meson is one of several mysterious subatomic particles whose functions are only imperfectly understood. Technically, it has a mass 207 times that of an electron, with a positive or negative charge and a spin of one half, but this information is hardly demystifying for most of us. There is, however, one property that may make mu mesons (or "muons") more familiar to laymen: They can penetrate thick concentrations of matter—buildings, forests or even conducting substances such as steel plate—with little loss of energy.

As an example of their unique penetrating power, muons from cosmic rays were used to "x-ray" the Egyptian pyramids. The pattern of penetration provided a detailed picture of the inner structure and hidden chambers of the ancient tombs. Scientists are currently exploring other equally exotic applications.

Since muons can pass through obstructions with a minimum of interference, Dr. Richard Arnold of the Argonne National Laboratory reasons that they may be useful for some specialized needs in telecommunications. In his words, "They provide . . . an alternative to microwave communications for point-to-point systems if physical barriers intervene."

Dr. Arnold has already demonstrated that present-day atomic accelerators can provide the muons necessary for such systems at a price that could make them competitive with microwave and satellite communications systems. In April 1972, he sent the first muon messages. The mechanism was relatively simple: A beam of muons was aimed on a course that took it through one and a half yards of concrete and other massive obstacles to a measuring device (a scintillation counter) 160 yards away. To vary the intensity of the beam a few percent, a block of brass was alternately inserted and removed from the front of the muon "broadcaster," and the counter, in turn, registered these modulations. Thus by moving the brass in and out of the line of transmission, a Morse code message was communicated.

By increasing the intensity of the muon signals, this system could be used to send messages over distances of several miles—right now. Once methods for collimating the beams have been improved, Dr. Arnold believes the range could be extended to about 500 miles. Further refinements might make it possible to send voice and teletype signals.

Neutrinos are elementary particles that are even more penetrating than muons. They can pass through billions of miles of the dense lead used as nuclear shields. Dr. Arnold asserts that the development of muon communication systems might someday lead to neutrino communications.

Dr. Arnold says, "[Neutrino beams] could penetrate any amount of earth and provide direct line-of-sight communications between any two points. . . . Even with present technology, the reception of a few neutrino events per hour may be possible at global distances, for example, between the National Accelerator Laboratory [Batavia, Illinois] and Australia."

Just as muons can be used to "x-ray" the pyramids, muons might be used to look for mineral deposits in mountains or for miners trapped underground. Muon and, later, neutrino communications will prove useful in those situations where it's impractical to use microwaves or satellite communications systems.

Electronic Newsrooms and Video Typewriters

In tomorrow's newsrooms reporters will "bang out" their stories on video typewriters that use no paper and make no noise. They're already using them for some newspapers.

One video typewriter goes by the name of the Harris 1500 Editorial Input Terminal. Equipped with a standard typewriter keyboard, it's about as large as an ordinary electric typewriter. But there the resemblance ends. The writer sees his copy directly on a five-by-ten-inch cathode ray tube or TV screen as he writes. If he wants to erase an incorrect word or letter, he strikes over it and the correct one appears on the screen in its place.

When the writer finishes his piece he can store it in a computer memory connected to the keyboard by cables. An editor can retrieve the piece from the computer to evaluate it, cut it, add to it or update it. When he's satisfied with the piece, he presses the "Set It" button. This automatically dispatches the copy for composition by high-speed computerized phototypesetters. The copy completes the journey from the writer's brain to finished reproduction proofs without involving a single piece of typing paper or punched tape.

339

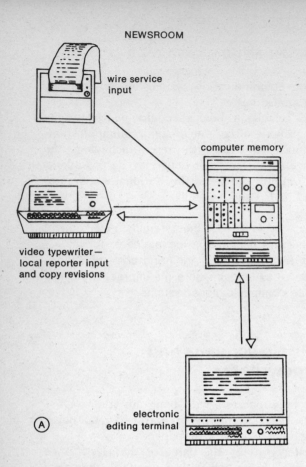

NEWSROOM

wire service input

computer memory

video typewriter— local reporter input and copy revisions

electronic editing terminal

(A)

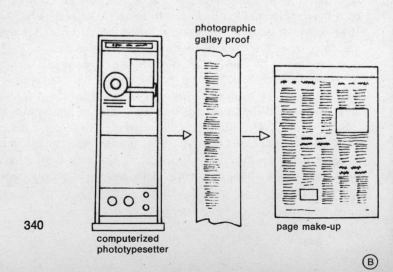

COMPOSING ROOM

photographic galley proof

340

computerized phototypesetter

page make-up

(B)

A useful feature of the system is an index of all local and wire service stories available, with the length of each. If the editor sees one that looks interesting he presses the "Get It" button and the complete text comes into view on the screen of his editing terminal.

According to Harris-Intertype, the manufacturer, "Prime initial prospects for the system are 300 to 400 of the nation's 1750 daily newspapers—those with circulations of from 40,000 to 250,000. The systems range in price from $200,000 to $600,000, depending upon size."

The new system should produce big savings in time and money for newspapers. And the reader will benefit someday when newspapers come into the home television set.

Superfast Printing

Thermal printers—machines that print by heat—are the last word in printing machines. They have an output of up to 6000 words per minute.

The new printers are all-solid-state, and range in size from a shoebox to a table television set. They have just one moving part, the paper-feeding mechanism. To do their printing, they combine logic, integrated circuitry, thin-film print heads, optical techniques and a special coated paper.

Here's how a thermal printer works. Input signals are fed into the printer, which decodes and processes them into digital signals. These signals are fed into a matrix font of thin-film print heads which are in direct contact with the coated paper. The signals generate slight amounts of heat in the print heads, and these activate chemicals in the paper. At the point of contact, blue-black characters instantly become visible.

With the printer is a keyboard the operator can use as a conventional teletypewriter or as a control system to feed in data stored in computers. He can also use it to edit outgoing information. The printer has only one consumable item, the thermal paper.

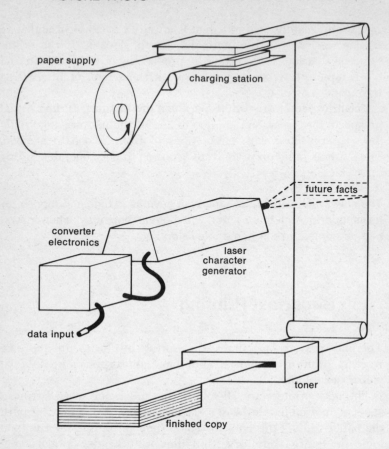

In the Zenith system the charged paper (top) is discharged by the laser beams (center) coated with ink (bottom), to produce finished copy.

"Size and design vary with application and environmental requirements," says the manufacturer, Electronic Communications, Inc., a division of National Cash Register. "The printers and keyboards have found applications on military land vehicles, ships, aircraft, submarines and spacecraft—a total of twenty space and military programs."

Another approach to superfast nonimpact printing, called the acoustooptic laser printer, is under development by Zenith Radio Corporation. Here's how it works. Special red-sensitive paper is uniformly charged with electricity in darkness. Laser light beams, containing the information to be printed, then "expose" the paper. Where light strikes the paper, charge is selectively removed. The charged image remains on the paper, passing through a unit in which fine ink powder (or toner) particles are deposited. The ink is affixed making the image permanent.

Zenith says applications include high-speed computer printout, microfilm and microfiche printing, high-speed hard-copy printing for stock-market quotations and facsimile transmission. "Computer data generated in Chicago," according to Zenith, "could be transmitted to New York where it would be automatically printed out at 5000 lines per minute."

Dial a Computer

General Electric Company has developed a liquid crystal unit that can "talk" to computers by telephone, and displays the "conversation" on its own viewing screen.

This machine comes out of the same technology as the display devices on some of the now ubiquitous pocket calculators—liquid crystals, the transparent fluids that become translucent when voltage is applied. Since they reflect light instead of generating it as other displays do, they need very little power to operate and can be seen easily in normal room light.

The unit looks like a push-button desk telephone. In order to talk to a computer (any computer anywhere in the world), you put the receiver of a telephone on the cradle designed for it and dial the computer's number. You can transmit messages by punching the appropriate keys on the unit, and the computer will respond. The liquid crystal screen will hold two lines of sixteen characters each, and for longer messages the lines can be rolled at will scroll-fashion, creating space for more information.

Although this is only a display model, and GE says they have no plans for commercial applications, the usefulness of this unit from a commercial standpoint is quite apparent. As GE describes

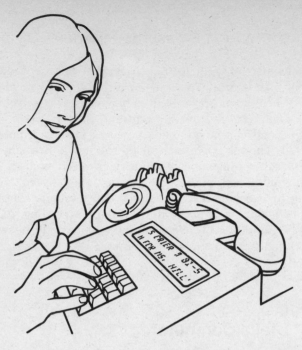

A telephone cradled in the liquid crystal data communications terminal.

it, this machine is "a major step toward a portable data communications terminal that could be used by salesmen, assembly line workers, stockbrokers, bank tellers, businessmen and almost anyone needing brief, on-the-spot communication with a central computer."

As the level of basic technology in this society becomes more and more sophisticated, perhaps "almost anyone" will need immediate access to a central computer.

Drawings by Computer

Computers now draw line sketches, diagrams and charts for engineering, architectural and space projects. This use of computers for illustration of technical data is called computer

344

graphics. By bringing together the research of several electronics engineers, Dr. Ivan E. Sutherland of the Evans and Sutherland Computer Corporation of Utah has programmed computers to draw three-dimensional, color or black-and-white solid pictures on the face of a two-dimensional TV screen. The flat images of solid objects move to show their hidden surfaces in accordance with programmed instructions; they're also enhanced by realistic light and dark tones, like movie or television pictures.

The computerized drawing system used for this purpose produces pictures of three-dimensional objects, shaded life photographs, with obscured parts removed, instantly. It projects electron beams on a televisionlike screen, but the picture comes from a computer—not a real object. The computer visually translates data in such a way that the observer thinks he is moving. Some of Dr. Sutherland's motion pictures are so realistic that it's hard to believe they are not transmitted by a TV station. This

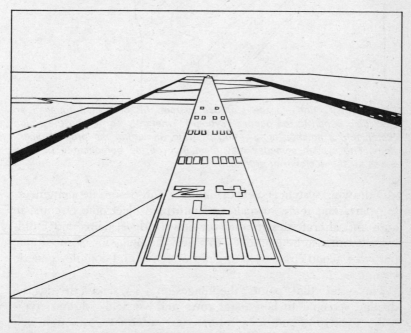

Reproduction by computer of the Los Angeles Airport runway as "seen" from an approaching aircraft ready to land.

To give instructions to the graphics system the draftsman touches an electronic pencil to the paper "keyboard," instantly converting the rough sketch into a finished engineering drawing, including the proper dimensions. The system someday may even incorporate complicated building codes for the designer or architect.

3-D drawing system is used to simulate and design new engineering parts and tools, to make miniaturized electronic circuits, in auto and aircraft design, and for new bridges, dams and buildings. It can also be employed to study the behavior of subatomic particles, blood circulation, organ functions, and complex genetic structures.

The system that "paints" the images on a TV screen divides the display screen into horizontal rows and vertical columns; typically, 1024 rows and 1024 columns are adequate, although Bell Labs engineers have built a high-resolution display with 32,000 horizontal and 26,000 vertical lines.

The computer then draws the image by translating its mathematical routines into picture-sorting information that guides the electron beam inside the TV screen. Electron beams appear on the screen as dots at intersections of specified rows and columns. Characters and lines are built on the screen from millions of dots, whose coordinates move in such a way as to give motion to the whole picture.

Dr. Sutherland says, "I tend to think of a computer display as a window on Alice's Wonderland in which a programmer can depict either objects that obey well-known natural laws, or partly imaginary objects that follow laws he has written into his program. . . . Through computer displays I have landed an airplane on the deck of a moving carrier, observed a nuclear particle, and flown in a rocket at nearly the speed of light . . . I believe that computer-generated motion pictures . . . not only will entertain but will also convey a message."

Another system, still in an experimental stage at IBM, rapidly converts rough sketches (no matter how out-of-scale) into final engineering drawings.

An aircraft or ship captain can bring his craft in "blind" using an on-board video computer to simulate the runway or navigation channel and the craft's motion. The "feel" of steering a new airplane, rocket or spacecraft can be simulated in great detail— before an expensive prototype is built.

Superspeed Computers

The Josephson logic gate can make a binary decision in ten trillionths of a second. This represents a hundredfold increase in speed over existing computer technology.

A trained operator using a desk calculator can carry out something like a million operations—additions, subtractions, multiplications, divisions—in a working year. This amount of work is

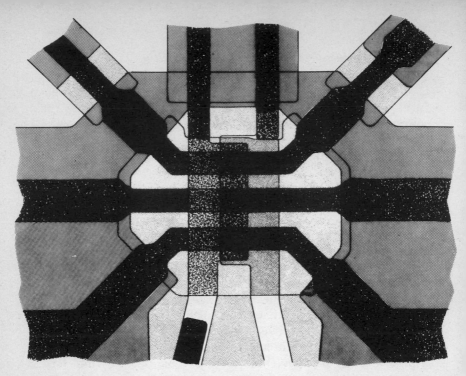

A highly magnified view of a Josephson logic gate in which three control lines pass over the tunnel junction.

sometimes called a Horner, possibly after Jack Horner who put his thumb in a pie and pulled out a plum. Modern large-scale computers process data at rates of about one Horner per second.

For some work this rate is too slow. A detailed look at almost any global problem may require several million Horners of processing—and there are only about a half-million seconds of working time in a week. Spacecraft problems, calculation of orbits and trajectories, are almost as large; and the work must be done on line or in "real time." Ten-Horner/second computers are used in jobs like these, but faster ones would be useful.

The Josephson logic gate is really an electronic switch that operates about 100 times as fast as the best switching transistors now used in data-processing equipment. The present version must be operated at liquid helium temperature (about −450° F.) because it is at these temperatures that superconductivity (no electrical resistance) takes place. All of the heat generated in the logic gate must be removed by refrigeration. This problem is eased, though, by the low-power level at which the Josephson gate operates—about one ten-thousandth that of the equivalent switching transistor. In the Josephson junction (named after the British scientist Brian Josephson) electron pairs in a superconducting state can "tunnel" through an electrical insulator if it's thin enough and placed between two superconductors. A weak magnetic field applied to the junction can "steer" the electron current from one superconducting branch to another, and thereby represent the basic "yes-no" language of a computer.

IBM believes that the Josephson logic gate will be required for computers capable of handling "the heavy demands of missions in space and long-range weather forecasting." Although it's in a very early stage of development, "It is now a real possibility that the world's fastest switch may become a part of computers in the years to come."

Unfortunately, superspeed computers will also make it possible for the government to audit *all* tax returns, monitor *all* financial (and other) activity, and generally behave like a superspeed big brother.

Magnetic Bubble Storage

A forthcoming method of storing data will lead to smaller and faster computers. Information in binary form—either a "zero" or a "one"—is stored on a thin film of magnetic material by magnetizing small regions in one direction or the other. The magnetized region (less than five ten-thousandths of an inch in diameter) is called a bubble, and the new storage devices are called bubble memories.

Bubbles can be moved from place to place in the magnetic film by changing the external magnetic fields. A bubble memory is organized as one or more strings of bubbles, with a bubble-injector at one end of each string and a bubble-detector at the other. Information is stored by injecting a bubble at the end of a string, moving the whole string one step, injecting another bubble, moving the string again, and so on. Information may be retrieved in similar fashion, one bubble at a time, from the other end of the string. The presence of a bubble signifies a binary "one," and its absence a binary "zero."

Bubble memories will be used in situations where large amounts of information must be stored in a well-organized way. A page of text—perhaps 500 words—can be represented by about 25,000 "bits," (or *bi*nary digi*ts*) and stored as 25,000 bubbles. Since information is always stored and retrieved in the same order, the fact that a particular bubble cannot be detected until it is brought to the end of its string poses no problem.

Relatively unorganized information is ordinarily stored in a random access memory (RAM), from which it's directly retrieved wherever it happens to be stored. RAM technology is highly developed and costs only about one cent per "bit." Bubble memories will offer significant cost and speed advantages over RAMs.

IBM, a pioneer in bubble memory technology, says that storage density of "a million bits per square inch is routinely achieved, a hundred million bits per square inch has been demonstrated, and higher densities are projected." By contrast, RAM technology offers only densities of the order of 10,000 bits per square inch. IBM expects to reach and surpass "data rates of ten million bits per second" for storage and retrieval, which is about the same as existing RAM technology.

The future impact of bubble memories depends on a constellation of useful characteristics. RAMs offer higher access rates, photographic film offers higher storage densities, and an ordinary long-playing record offers lower storage costs. But nothing else in sight offers the same attractive combination as magnetic bubble storage. We shall also see "bubble stretchers" and "bubble compressors" to amplify the information that bubbles contain.

Human- and Machine-Readable Information Retrieval System

"Microfiche," formerly readable only by humans, can now be read by computers.

Harris-Intertype Corporation is using holography—a three-dimensional laser-photographic technique—to squeeze 2.5 million bits of information onto a square inch of a microfilm card, called a "microfiche." They have developed an information retrieval system that both people and computers can use.

This effort represents one of the first uses of holography for information storage and retrieval. The system will record visual images—words, pictures, drawings and numbers—using conventional microfilm techniques for human use. The same data will be "digitized" and recorded holographically at rates of up to 250,000 bits per second using a laser scanner. Digital forms of information are readable by computers.

Sixty microfilmed pages can be recorded on a standard four-by-six-inch microfiche, which is compatible with commercially available filing and retrieval equipment. The holograms are recorded on the same card without altering the standard format. A hologram is placed horizontally at the upper corner of the microfilmed information, which uses up most of the card. Because of its readability by both humans and computers, the system is called "human readable/machine readable," or "HR/MR," and nicknamed "The Hummer."

Hummer cards are automatically retrieved from the master file and displayed on either local or remote video terminals in ten seconds; this can be done an unlimited number of times without reducing the quality of the record. The complete system links up with existing computer systems. It generates, stores, processes and retrieves microfilm images and holographic data—entirely under machine control.

According to Harris-Intertype, the present "packing density" of 2.5 million bits of information per square inch can be increased in the future. "The recorded data can be placed in archives for long periods of time without degradation; holograms are not affected

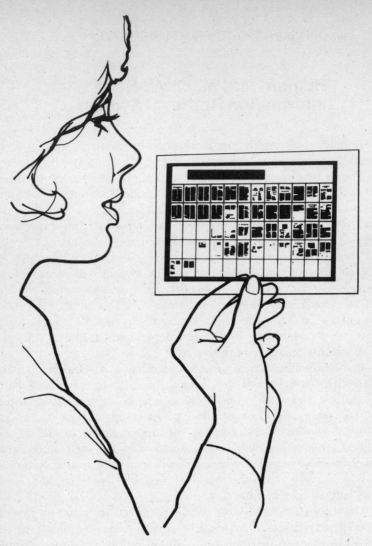

Standard four-by-six-inch microfiche card holds sixty pages of text. The upper black rectangle contains the same information, compressed by holography.

by dust or scratches. This is a significant feature since the new system will be used in an office environment by semiskilled personnel."

The system can store parts price books, mail order catalogs, newspaper files, library indices, scientific abstracts, past and future books—all at low cost. There will be a tremendous saving in time and money when a great deal of information must be stored, updated, added to or retrieved at a number of different locations. Future phone books, for example, may be stored on microfiche.

Personal and institutional libraries which suffer from lack of space will store many books and journals on systems like microfiche cards—more than their current capacities. Unlike paper, which undergoes deterioration with time and use, holograms won't disintegrate by rough handling.

Years from now, when information retrieval is voice-controlled (see page 355), we'll find future facts by phone without leaving our home or office. Libraries will become more and more like information-processing centers, rather than storage archives.

Spoken Print, Printed Speech

Ordinary books may soon become available to the blind with the help of a computer that converts printed English text into natural-sounding speech. Long-term objectives of synthetic speech: books that can read themselves aloud, and "automatic information" over the telephone.

At Haskins Laboratories, the key to synthetic speech is the sound spectrogram—a machine that analyzes spoken words for their frequency, time and energy. With the aid of a spectrogram, a trained observer can determine which patterns of sound are most crucial for communication to take place. These patterns—called acoustic cues—carry the essential information and meaning of spoken speech and must be reproduced to create synthetic speech.

Scientists at Bell Laboratories have programmed their computer with a description of the human tongue, lips, jaws and vocal cords. Then they gave the machine a dictionary of words and grammatical categories. Finally they fed in the complex rules of timing, pitch and stress.

vocal tract

The simulated vocal tract on the TV screen changes its shape with each sound generated by the computer's voice.

Synthetic speech could benefit the deaf as well as the blind, for by a similar process, speech can be converted directly into writing. Researchers foresee the day when a person could phone in a question and a computer would provide an articulate, clearly enunciated answer. It could recite a page from a medical text for a doctor, inventory status for a stock manager, or flight information for an airline clerk.

"People naturally change the sound of a word in speech when the meaning of the word changes, or when the word has a different position in the sentence," says Dr. Cecil Coker of Bell Labs.

"Conventional phonetic descriptions of words do not completely describe the pronunciation. We must provide timing cues that distinguish expressions such as 'a name/an aim,' and 'a nice man/an iceman.' We must program information about the separation of phrases and about the importance and function of words. In this way, we account for a number of factors that are normally thought of as 'style of speaking,' but in fact are important information for the understanding of a spoken message."

Imagine a computerized ask-it man. Phone in your question and the computer utters your answer in seconds. Converse with anyone in the world over the phone with a computer acting as translator.

What will happen to all the secretaries in five years when a system will convert speech to text *while you're talking?*

System Comprehends

A computer system capable of understanding and analyzing the sound and meaning of words and sentences spoken by a human operator, answering his questions and executing his instructions, is under development by Donald E. Walker at Stanford Research Institute in California.

Three major components make up the system. The first is *Pintle,* a complex computer "program" (or set of procedures) to analyze a sentence grammatically according to the meaning of its words, the syntax of its phrases, clauses and sentences, the parsing of nouns, verbs, adjectives, prepositions and so on. The second set of programs is based on the acoustics of the spoken word. It converts spoken words or voice input from analog (or proportional) signals to digital (or on-off) signals. These are then "filtered" into various classes of sound—voice or other turbulence, vowel sounds, silence and so on. The sounds are also analyzed for frequency and amplitude. Finally, a word verifier routine links the first two. It ensures the accuracy of the two analyses by testing parts of the Pintle speech against the acoustical program. This verifies the computer's "understanding" of the words.

The system whereby the computer demonstrates "understanding" isn't easy to explain. Imagine a table containing a box and several objects of different sizes, shapes and colors. Suppose a "robot" moves wooden blocks around to place them in a certain arrangement when commanded by a human voice. The computer being spoken to "hears" the first word of a sentence, for instance "Put." It immediately recognizes it as a verb and starts looking for a noun, preposition, adjective and others, to complete a gram-

```
. . .
PUT
THE
BLACK
BLOCK
IN
THE
BLACK
BOX

(CLAUSE MAJOR IMPER ACTV TRANSL)
     (VG IMPER)
          PUT (INF PAST VB TRANSL VPRT MVB)
     (NG OBJ OBJ1 NOLOC DET DEF NS)
          THE (DET NPL NS DEF)
          BLACK (ADJ)
          BLOCK (NOUN NS)
     (PREPG PLACE LOBJ)
          IN (PLACE PREP)
          (NG OBJ PREPOBJ DET DEF NS)
               THE (DET NPL NS DEF)
               BOX (NOUN NS)

*
MOVETO 472 192 128
GRASP :B3
MOVETO 448 448 129
UNGRASP
   OK.
NIL
—
```

A simple command sentence, "Put the black block in the black box," is analyzed for grammar by the Pintle computer program. First, it searches for a major clause, identifies an imperative class, looks for command verbs until it finds "Put." Then it searches for a noun group looking for a determiner until it finds "the." Next it seeks an adjective, verifying by rejecting red, green, blue and white that "black" is correct. To complete the noun group it identifies "block." Pintle continues in this manner until the entire sentence is identified as an active imperative involving the movement of an object to a location. The robot arm then obeys the command, with the numbers indicating the location coordinates.

matical sentence. In doing this, it employs a specially developed language called PROGRAMMAR that automatically instructs the computer to identify and process sentences as commands, statements or questions. The system is also programmed to take into consideration natural inconsistencies in spoken English, such as stress, accent, pronunciation and hesitation. To verify the accuracy of Pintle and the acoustical analysis, the system relates the sequence of words selected by Pintle to those picked by the acoustical process. A complex technique takes into account the minute time differences (thousandths of a second) between utterances, vowels, silences and turbulences in the speech, to arrive at a degree of consistency.

Future research will concentrate on a computer system capable of analyzing not only simple sentences but complex messages, multiparty conversations—and even continuous human speech. Ultimately, the system will engage a person in natural conversation on a specific subject.

Routine tasks, done today by hand, will be done tomorrow by voice. Already luggage is sorted by voice command (see page 420) and spoken inquiries are answered by synthetic speech (see page 353). Perhaps in five or ten years we'll see machines that "understand" continuous human speech and machines that convert speech into print instantly.

Synchronous Satellites Provide Global Communications

Synchronous satellites have been whirling in the sky for a decade, transmitting TV signals around the world. New uses are constantly being found for them—and soon countries around the world will have their own national communications satellites.

Synchronous satellites are so called because they travel through space in synchronization with the earth. While the earth spins with a velocity of about 1000 miles an hour at the surface to make a complete rotation every 24 hours, a satellite travels at about 7000 miles an hour to complete its rotation in the same period. If you could see one from earth (they're 22,300 miles up), it would seem to hover overhead. Because of its greater speed it stays "motionless" relative to a spot on the earth. The satellites receive and transmit TV, telegraph and other signals via ground stations around the world.

A new communications development is occurring as countries

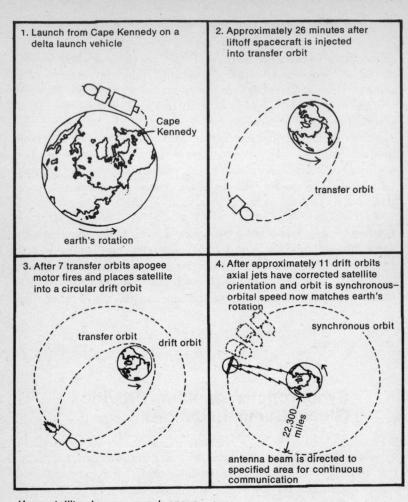

1. Launch from Cape Kennedy on a delta launch vehicle

Cape Kennedy

earth's rotation

2. Approximately 26 minutes after liftoff spacecraft is injected into transfer orbit

transfer orbit

3. After 7 transfer orbits apogee motor fires and places satellite into a circular drift orbit

transfer orbit

drift orbit

4. After approximately 11 drift orbits axial jets have corrected satellite orientation and orbit is synchronous—orbital speed now matches earth's rotation

synchronous orbit

22,300 miles

antenna beam is directed to specified area for continuous communication

How satellites become synchronous.

order their own "national" synchronous communications satellites, with the power of their antenna beams focused within the individual nation's borders. Canada was the first country to obtain its own national satellite. Today children in the remote North are learning their ABCs via satellite—and their parents are learning new techniques in homemaking, farming and cooking. The United States is next in line to obtain a national satellite system, and Brazil and Australia may follow.

Synchronous satellites have made possible a vast increase in the number of overseas phone calls, from under a million in 1950

358

to 35 million in 1972. About two thirds of all long-distance international calls now go via satellite, and not only do the calls cost less than they did some years ago, but they can be placed much faster than via cable. Another new communications technique called IDDD (International Direct Distance Dialing) enables a person to dial a certain code and talk directly with another per-

Two communications satellites. One (background) is already complete, the other (foreground) is still being assembled.

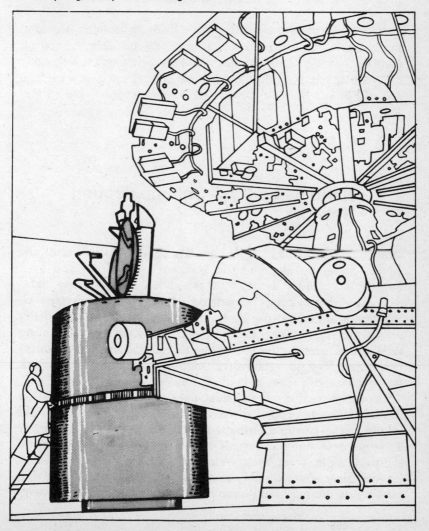

son in one of twenty countries without going through an operator. The satellites are manufactured by the Hughes Aircraft Company of El Segundo, California.

According to Dr. Harold A. Rosen, who developed the satellites, the surface has only been scratched in satellite communications. "I'm looking forward to community broadcasting. We'll have satellites beaming television direct to small communities or schools rather than to large ground stations. This will require ground stations that cost only a few thousand dollars."

Satellites can be lifesavers to people living in isolated areas. In emergencies, back-country physicians will be able to consult specialists in big cities and get guidance by making a telephone call via satellite. By 1980 there will be 200 million overseas calls annually to and from the United States—and more global shrinkage.

Nationwide Data-Communication Network

Oceans of business and technical data routinely flow across the United States by plugging two computers, hundreds and even thousands of miles apart, into two telephones. A new data-communication system, Telenet, conceived by Dr. Lawrence G. Roberts, is already in use by the Pentagon as the Advanced Research Projects Agency (ARPA) net. It employs earth-orbiting satellites in combination with radio and earthbound communication technology to establish a high-speed automatic network based upon the "packet-switching" concept.

The "packet" is a self-sufficient data package that "knows" its destination and is coded to "switch" to alternate routes it could follow. It also carries a format-conversion system if it's bound for a computer of different type. Once it enters the Telenet system, the packet goes from one computer to another, however dissimilar, via the quickest possible route among several paths involving satellite or ground-based equipment. Without clogging up tele-

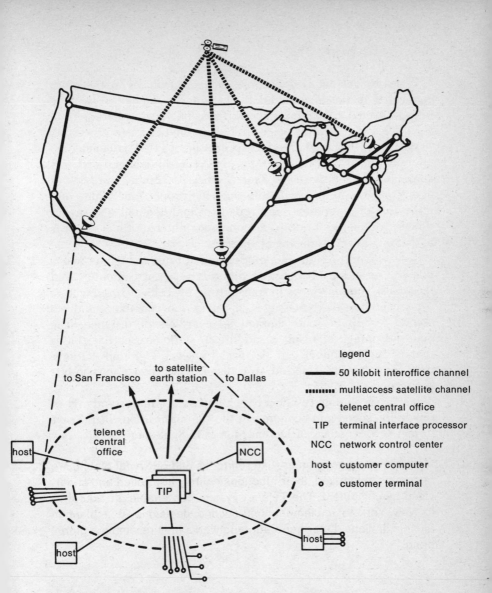

legend

——————	50 kilobit interoffice channel
▪▪▪▪▪▪▪▪	multiaccess satellite channel
O	telenet central office
TIP	terminal interface processor
NCC	network control center
host	customer computer
o	customer terminal

to San Francisco   to satellite earth station   to Dallas

telenet central office

host

NCC

TIP

host

host

The major elements of Telenet packet-switching network. Each participating computer, called a "host," is connected to the terminal interface processor (TIP) at a regional office.

phone lines at peak hours, it spreads the load, reduces transmission delays and transmits data accurately. Eighteen cities are to be hooked into Telenet by the end of 1975, and another 44 are expected to join the system by 1978.

Basically Telenet is a network of central offices in the cities connected to the system; all the customers' computers will be interconnected by high-speed transmission lines radiating from each office. The central offices have interface message processors (IMPs) and terminal interface processors (TIPs) connected to all operational offices. Two network control centers (NCCs) automatically supervise the central offices, receiving feedback at about one-minute intervals to ensure the proper functioning and utilization of equipment, and repairs of malfunctions and breakdowns. All one has to do to get one's computer on the Telenet is to dial into the nearest central office.

Telenet can transmit data on demand at rates as high as 80,000 bits per second, even between different types of computers and terminals. The time lapse in transmitting by Telenet is reduced to 0.3 second for short messages of up to 100 characters and 0.8 second for up to 1000 characters, regardless of distance. The main advantage of using a satellite in stationary earth orbit is that a single channel can be used by several ground stations, each for only a brief period, to transmit more than 1,500,000 bits per second.

It's "a revolutionary concept which has set new standards of reliability, speed and economy in the communications field," says former U.S. Secretary of Defense James R. Schlesinger.

More and more companies, like refineries and chemical plants, are becoming automated, their functions entirely controlled and supervised by computers. The Telenet system can enable an executive in New York to implement split-second decisions at a plant in Muncie, Indiana. Later generation networks may resemble a global brain.

8
Business and Work

To Improve Productivity

If American business is losing its competitive edge in the world marketplace, one remedy may be to improve productivity. Not through the old-fashioned time-and-motion studies of an earlier era, though. Organizations like the National Science Foundation, the National Productivity Commission, the Conference Board, the United Steelworkers of America, the United States Steel Corporation and others are looking into new ways to enhance national output per man-hour.

Suppose you could identify critical production bottlenecks in an industry or company—or even across industries, nationwide. Once these logjams were opened up, they would dramatically multiply the efficient flow in many related areas of manufactured goods and services. This multiplier or "ripple" effect would yield large productivity gains overall, as a result of relatively small gains in those important production bottlenecks, called "critical leverage points."

For example, suppose the task of joining two materials—by welding, sewing, gluing or bolting—is identified as a critical leverage point. This operation cuts across many key industries: automobile and garment manufacturing, publishing, home appliances, communications and so on. A high-priority effort by major companies or government agencies to attack critical leverage points could reap many benefits that would ripple throughout society: lower-price products, higher wages, shorter hours, increased profits, for example. Perhaps this explains why labor, management, universities and government appear to share genuine interest in productivity improvement.

Some of the sophisticated systems to improve productivity will incorporate automated equipment: to test manufactured goods for quality; to provide up-to-date diagnostic information or production-line trouble spots; to transport and distribute manufactured goods; to design and lay out new plants; to control the machining, cutting and fabrication of materials; to assemble, connect and transfer components of large systems; and to control inventories to properly supply spot consumer demands.

Other approaches will include expanded research on those productivity problems that are common denominators in many sectors of the U.S. economy. Among these are to create appropriate measurements of economic indicators (even on a microeconomic or functional level of detail), to signal productivity changes. Another goal is to set up worldwide data-banks on productivity and to disseminate this information through workshops and regional centers for the ultimate end user. The social consequences may be monitored to uncover any possible detrimental second-order effects of productivity changes—for instance, on morale, working conditions or profitability.

Studies indicate that the diffusion of innovation appears to be accelerated during times of rapid growth. Government assistance to potential adopters of new technologies is conducive to the diffusion of these innovations. And furthermore, personal experience with an innovation is the most significant factor in the promotion, adoption and continued use of that innovation. Because productivity improvements are innovative, these findings argue forcefully for calling productivity enhancement to the attention of the U.S. public.

Publicity and public relations efforts, begun recently on behalf of labor and management, will expand even further. A public interest campaign sponsored by United States Steel Corporation features notable community leaders like David Rockefeller, chairman of the board of Chase Manhattan Corporation, who says, "American business cannot afford the luxury of merely affirming its preeminence without improving its performance"; and I. W. Abel, president of the United Steelworkers of America, who says, "If we adopt a don't-give-a-damn attitude, we risk becoming a second-class power."

A critical minority of research and development furnishes important technological innovations. Some of these improve productivity, and thereby multiply their benefits throughout society. We need more—and better—ways to identify that critical minority to ensure a healthy future.

Eye Movements Command Machines

Eye trackers monitor eye position and movement. But ultimately they may find a far more exotic use, enabling man to control machines and equipment—simply by moving his eyes.

A variety of eye trackers currently exist; some employ contact lenses, others skin-mounted electrodes, and still others eyeglass-mounted photoelectric pickups. A sophisticated eye tracker is under development by Hewitt D. Crane and T. N. Cornsweet. It operates in infrared so as not to interfere with normal vision. needs no attachments to the eye, and can measure eye position with an astonishing accuracy of about one sixtieth of a degree (one minute of arc).

A highly focused, invisible infrared beam is directed at the eye of a subject, at an angle of about 20 degrees from his straight line of vision (see diagram). The eye reflects this beam much as a mirror reflects a flashlight beam. However, the eye, being more complex, contains four distinct reflecting surfaces: the front of the cornea, the rear of the cornea, the front of the lens and the rear of the lens. Thus four distinct images, known as Purkinje images, are reflected by the eye.

These images are in turn reflected by a special mirror angled across the subject's field of vision to reflect only infrared light without obstructing the subject's vision. Reflected light from this mirror is then divided by a beam splitter and directed toward various servo-controlled photocells and motion sensors. Through an analysis of the relative positions of the various Purkinje images, this mechanism tracks movement of the eye and even provides a graphic display of such movement (see diagram).

Despite its extremely high accuracy, the tracker is limited to a two-dimensional visual field of 10 to 20 degrees in diameter. It requires a subject's head to be positioned by a chin and forehead rest. This must be eliminated before dramatic applications become feasible, but these technical problems are soluble.

Since a tracker determines where the eye is looking, future man may guide and direct various operations of machines and equipment. A jet pilot or antiaircraft artilleryman could fix his

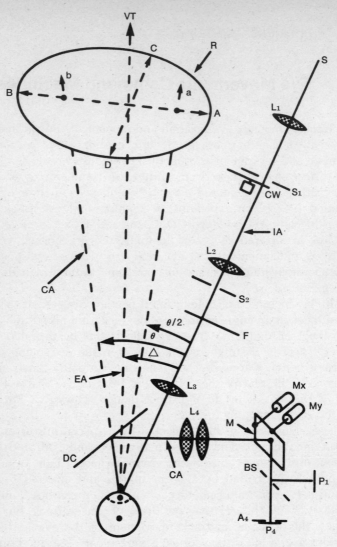

Schematic diagram of the eye-tracker optical system. The various symbols mean: VT, visual target; R, allowed range of eye movements; S, light source; L_1–L_4, lenses; DC, dichroic mirror; M, front surface mirror; M_x and M_y, motors that drive M in x and y direction; BS, beam splitter; P_1 and P_4, quadrant photocells.

eyes on a target enemy plane—and then fire away simply by blinking. A sports or news cameraman could film the action simply by looking at it, his cameras and microphones being shifted automatically by his eye movements. With an eye tracker, a crane operator at an industrial or construction site could direct his crane by looking first at what he wants to move and then at the location he wants it moved to.

Indeed, almost any operation in which the eyes are used to guide and control a system—typically your hands and feet—is open to direct manipulation with an eye tracker coupled to a robot.

Dr. Crane says the eye tracker "might well have impact on remote manipulation applications as well as many other areas—clinical testing, psychological testing, research in vision or perception."

Imagine operating a vacuum cleaner: simply *looking* at the dirt and dust directs the cleaner to its location.

How about a home camera automatically aimed and clicked by your eye movements.

A bike, car or plane could be rigged for eye control.

Graphic display recording eye movements over an 11 × 11 array of illuminated points. Adjacent points were separated by 1.8 degrees of arc. The subject's eye traced out the pattern, starting at the center point and then moving successively around each larger square. The random-looking motion about each point is the small hesitation that typically occurs.

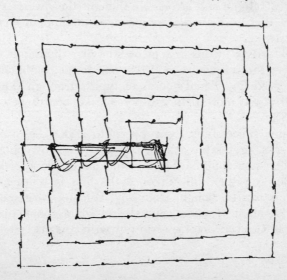

Qwerty Versus Aoeui

If you find "qwerty" unintelligible, try switching to "aoeui."

Though aoeui sounds like the call of the wild, it's also the first six keys in the middle (or home) row of an alternative to the conventional typewriter keyboard. The conventional keyboard is called qwerty, after the first six keys in its upper row. Known as the Dvorak Simplified Keyboard (or DSK for short) the "new" keyboard was invented in 1932 by August Dvorak. This followed twenty years of study financed by the Carnegie Corporation.

According to the Dvorak system, 70 percent of the finger work can be done in the home row (where the fingers rest), 22 percent in the row above and 8 percent below. This compares with 32, 52 and 16 percent (respectively) in the qwerty system. More work done in the home row conserves time and energy for the typist. In DSK, all vowels are in the home row. Qwerty, which was based on the letters and combinations appearing most frequently in the English language, places the most commonly used characters as far apart as possible in the type basket.

Most people are right-handed, so Dvorak gave the right hand a greater work load than the left—as opposed to qwerty which does the reverse. He also reduced the clumsy stroking that almost guaranteed fatigue and errors. He thought the qwerty system so imperfect that even the letters arranged at random would be a better system.

Dvorak arrived at his system by studying thousands of words to discover the frequency of letters and letter combinations. He also observed finger movements of typists through slow-motion films and tested more than 250 possible keyboards before arriving at DSK.

Switching successfully from qwerty to DSK takes a minimum of six weeks, preferably after a rest period from typing. Unlike bilinguality, switching back and forth from one kind of keyboard to another is rather difficult once the first is unlearned. DSK typewriters can be bought from any large typewriter company, along with an instruction manual, but some companies charge extra for it. Conversion of qwerty typewriters is also possible. For

370

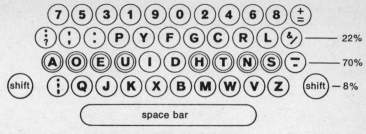

DVORAK SIMPLIFIED KEYBOARD

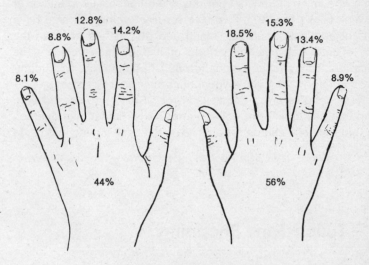

example, new type slugs can be resoldered on the old ones.

Promoters for DSK claim that it can be mastered in only a few weeks if a person is learning from scratch, and that fatigue and mistakes are greatly lessened.

Philip Davis of Irvington, New Jersey, heads a company that offers typewriters with the DSK keyboard. He would like to see DSK adopted by individual typists and by the printing industry, and expects a complete conversion to the new system eventually.

Tests done with navy women during World War II demonstrated that after a month, those who switched to DSK were turning out 74 percent more work and were 68 percent more accurate. Their fingers moved considerably less distance each day as well. Many DSK typists won typing competitions during the

1930s and 1940s, and other tests have shown that DSK typists can double their former speeds on conventional typewriters. Some even surpass the 100-word-a-minute mark.

By 1965, the U.S. Bureau of Standards said, "There is little need to demonstrate further the superiority of the Dvorak keyboard in experimental tests. Plenty of well-documented evidence exists."

Systems like DSK can increase office productivity (see page 365). Typists who finish more work per day will adjust easily to a shorter workweek (see page 397). Faster, error-free typing will also have important applications in publishing and printing—to shorten the length of time between the writing of a book or article and its publication. It may reduce typos in published material. Even computers fed information via keypunching may benefit someday.

Perhaps schools are a good place for DSK to be adopted first. Typing is a useful skill for college and the workaday world which many high school students don't have the time or inclination to learn.

Touch-Tone Shopping?

Since it was first initiated in 1872 by Aaron Montgomery Ward, catalog shopping has been a considerable convenience for families in small towns and rural areas far from the big-city department stores. Recently, Simpson-Sears Ltd. of Toronto introduced a "highly experimental" refinement in catalog shopping—an automated order system that will eventually permit telephone shopping day or night, every day of the week.

For the past year, selected customers have been able to place orders by communicating directly with the Simpson-Sears computer. The process is straightforward: A customer with a pushbutton phone calls a special ordering number and identifies himself by punching out his address and telephone number on the telephone buttons. In seconds, an on-line computer checks the keyed-in information against the customer's permanent record.

The computer then activates its tape-recorded speaking voice (see page 353) and asks the caller to tap in the catalog number of the item he is ordering. Upon receiving this information, the computer again searches its memory to find whether the ordered item is in stock. The computer's "voice" confirms availability or recommends the customer order again later. Finally, to guard against errors, the computer double checks the order while the customer is still on the line.

As of this writing, computer service is available to only about 500 customers for only a few hours per day. If the system proves successful, however, it could easily be extended to all 12-button telephones for round-the-clock shopping. In the experimental system, an operator automatically comes to the aid of a customer who is having difficulty; to date, only about 20 percent have required help.

The computerized system, believed to be the first of its kind in the world, cuts ordering time in half and at the same time reduces errors. The Simpson-Sears order service is a joint venture with IBM Canada Limited.

Computer ordering is intended to supplement regular mail and telephone orders, as Maurice Anderson, general manager of Methods Planning and Development, explains: "We are not contemplating in any way that this technique will become more than an alternate method of ordering. We will continue to need our . . . telephone sales clerks to handle the majority of orders that come from customers. We believe this automated order system will be an important step in providing greater convenience to many catalog shoppers."

Some theorists, like sociologist Philip Slater, would argue that the elimination of personal contacts via automation causes alienation and loneliness. Certainly computerized shopping is a long way from the personalized attention one received from the local tailor or dressmaker—and perhaps we are poorer for the loss.

In all likelihood, the notion of telephone transactions will catch on. Imagine, for instance, discussions and debates on the issues aired on television. People could vote yes or no via their push-button phones.

Future Retailing

Retailers predict cable TV merchandise orders, 24-hour-a-day store openings, and more specialty shops by the end of the century.

The Newspaper Advertising Bureau surveyed executives in department stores, chains and discount store organizations, and other experts in the retailing field. The retailers foresee a trend for new department store units to be located in geographic clusters, each within a few miles of other units of the same chain. There will be increased emphasis on boutiques and specialty shops within department stores to appeal to specific kinds of customers. Retailers will seek to individualize their store images, and stores will classify themselves more and more by *what* they sell. Advertising will change in this direction, and try to reach consumers in specific geographic areas or social strata.

A return of pleasant and social aspects of shopping, once associated with the marketplace, may occur. As stores move deeper into the suburbs, they may locate close to a variety of competitors within a single shopping complex. This will also lead to more large shopping centers.

According to both retailers and economists, customer services will represent an increased percentage of expenditures in the future. New personalized customer services will be made possible by new information technology and visual display techniques. Retailers believe more consumers are willing to pay a higher mark-up price in order to get more personalized service and a wider selection of individualized merchandise.

New technology will have other important effects on retailing. The spread of cable TV, for example, will have revolutionary impact, especially on promotion and sales methods. Over 50 percent of U.S. households will have cable TV by the end of the century, and nearly all homes on cable will be able to automatically order merchandise that has been displayed. An expansion of merchandise sale through the use of catalogs and through phone orders (see page 372) will probably also occur. Since many customer service problems are seen as resulting from the lack of coordination among individual store credit cards and accounts, the retailers expect these problems to be eliminated through a centralized, nationwide credit and banking system (see page 360).

Retailers believe, and industrial relations experts agree, that the four-day workweek (see page 397) will become standard by the late 1980s. Some speculate that this could lead to 365-day, 24-hour-a-day store openings. More women in the labor force will also encourage longer, and possibly Sunday, store openings.

According to Leo Bogart, executive vice president of the Newspaper Advertising Bureau, "No one can foretell the future. But people who exercise leadership and power are in the best position to translate their own assumptions about the shape of the future into decisions and actions that in turn affect the course of events."

Retailing in the future will be deeply affected by social and economic changes in other areas. The fate of downtown shopping, for example, will depend on coping with such urban problems as ghettos, crime, unemployment and drug addiction. The development of suburban and rural areas, on the other hand, will be deeply affected by large shopping centers with better merchandise moving into them. Further emphasis of retailing on customer services is compatible with our overall drift toward a service-oriented society. The retail market will be complex in the future: it will include both shopping at home and shopping in stores.

Forecast Storage and Retrieval

Forecasts of technological and consumer needs are essential for medium- and long-term planning of research, development and marketing activities in government and industry. Social, political, economic and population changes could be seen correctly. Although research projects future trends, organizations curious about trends in a particular field may have difficulty gaining

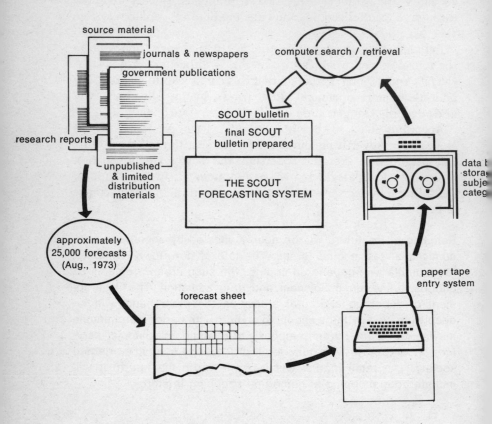

How the SCOUT forecast storage and retrieval system works.

access to relevant data because it comes from varied sources.

The Futures Group has developed a forecast storage and retrieval system called SCOUT. It's a large number of forecasts collected from "experts" in science, industry, the trades and professions, and government. The sources are academic journals, reports, books, newspapers and other publications. Because it's stored in a computer format, the SCOUT system can provide not only forecasts of specific events or phenomena, such as amounts of pollution in the Hudson River in 1980, but also forecasts of large-scale trends, such as the worldwide demand for wheat in 1982 or the state of international communism in 1984.

SCOUT provides the source of forecast and assesses its accuracy on a graded scale that runs from "inevitable" or "highly likely" through "unlikely" or "impossible." The methods the source used to arrive at particular forecasts are classified also. These include a "hunch," "individual genius," "polling," "mathematical and statistical trend projections," "game theory," and events that are "in motion" or already scheduled.

SCOUT forecasts are furnished to subscribers in subject areas from "aerodynamics" to "zoology."

Besides giving rapid access to computerized data, the SCOUT

A SCOUT energy forecast computer printout.

THE FUTURES GROUP		SCOUT BULLETIN 94-46-03	AUGUST 1973
		CATEGORY: SOCIO-ECONOMIC FACTORS--IMPORT/EXPORT	
SCOUT FILE NUMBER	SOURCE CODE	----FORECASTED EVENT----	PROB / YEAR
020108	01647	U.S. TRADE DEFICIT IN ENERGY REACHES $21 BILLION PER YEAR. CONSEQUENCES: 1. AGGREGATE DEFICIT FOR THE THREE MAJOR INDUSTRIALIZED AREAS OF THE WORLD $62 BILLION. 2. ALL DEFICIT COUNTRIES COULD BE FORCED TO ENGAGE IN A WILD SCRAMBLE OF VISCIOUS COMPETITION FOR BOTH ENERGY AND EXTERNAL EARNINGS TO PAY BILLS. SUBFORECAST: EUROPE AND JAPAN IN SIMILAR POSITION.	.50 / 1980
019915	03349	UNITED STATES SPENDS $21 BILLION ON IMPORTED PETROLEUM.	.50 / 1980
022653	03034	OIL IMPORTS PUSH NORTH AMERICA, EUROPE, AND JAPAN INTO PERMANENT BALANCE OF PAYMENTS DEFICIT TO OIL-PRODUCING NATIONS. SUBFORECASTS: 1. OIL IMPORT FOR DEVELOPED NATIONS INCREASES TO $75 BILLION. 2. NORTH AMERICA'S OIL IMPORT BILL INCREASES TO $20 BILLION.	.50 / 1980
015261	01507	UNITED STATES DEPENDS ON FOREIGN SOURCES FOR HALF OF ITS PETROLEUM NEEDS. SUBFORECAST: INCREASINGLY THIS WILL BE SUPPLIED BY THE MIDDLE EAST.	.50 / 1980

-220-

-16-

552

SAMPLE PAGE FROM ENERGY SCOUT

system also makes retrospective confirmation of predictions if
they prove correct—or otherwise.

A forecast is *not* a prediction. Forecasts assert a degree of likelihood to an anticipated event. Predictions assert the event will or
won't happen.

Pooled forecasts of a committee "dilute" the best—and worst—
of individuals' forecasts. Time will tell how well democracy-fore-
casts tell the future.

Speed Bagging at Supermarkets

A minor irritation, long checkout lines in grocery stores are the
cause of much grumbling from impatient customers. Relief may
be on the way. Amerplast, Inc., of Finland claims their Kviki
speed bagging system can hurry customers through cash register
queues up to 30 percent faster than the 13-year-old kid who
currently packs away your groceries.

Actually the system will not make the 13-year-old kid obsolete.
Someone still has to place each item in the sack, making sure the
eggs and bread are on top of the canned goods. Speed bagging's
primary function is to have the bag waiting wide open at an
efficient bagging angle.

When the customer arrives at the checkout counter, a jet of air
shoots up through two small holes in the bottom of a plastic bag.
The air flow separates each bag and keeps the mouth open as
wide as possible for easy filling. The packer no longer has the
opportunity to fiddle and fumble with a brown paper bag. When
one bag is removed, another is instantaneously inflated for the
next customer. They cost an estimated 1.1 cents apiece.

"Bagging purchases runs smoothly and the cashier's work is
speeded up," according to Amerplast spokesmen. "When the customer pays, his purchases are already packed and the cashier is
ready to serve the next customer."

Crowded supermarkets need ways to make shopping more pleasant, to unclog those bottlenecks at the checkout counter. Shopping at home (see page 372) is one way; gadgets like this are another one of several we'll see employed in supermarkets.

Post Office Data Management

An answer to those who complain there has not been an innovation in postal service since airmail: The RCA Corporation has installed an experimental data management system in San Jose, California, post offices. The system, which goes by the acronym POST (Point-Of-Sale Transactions), will assist clerks in selling stamps and money orders and in handling parcel post charges.

Essentially POST is a "thinking" cash register. It displays transactions on a TV-like screen and chronicles its thoughts with a printer and a tape recording device. When selling a ten-cent stamp (if such things exist in the future), the clerk taps the information on a keyboard similar to the array of buttons on an electronic calculator. The type of transaction, charges, money received, and change dispensed are automatically computed and flashed on the display screen.

Two paper copies of the sale are printed—one for the customer and one for Postal Service records. In addition, an electronic account of the sale is registered on magnetic tape for computerized bookkeeping. The system is intended to reduce the amount of time a clerk spends on paper work and correspondingly increase the amount of time he can spend serving customers.

The POST system also features an involved fail-safe mechanism designed to ensure that only an authorized clerk has access to the cash drawer. Both the supervisor's and the clerk's ID card must be inserted into the terminal before it will function.

If the system proves out, later models will include such extras as a postage meter stamp printer, an automatic parcel-post scale, a money-order printer, and change and stamp dispensers. The pilot program calls for RCA to set up twelve terminals in three San Jose offices.

"The POST system will bring postal clerks into the computer age and enable them to abandon certain time-consuming, pencil-and-paper record-keeping functions," according to Frederick H. Krantz, division vice president and general manager of RCA's Electromagnetic and Aviation Systems Division, Van Nuys, California. "Not only will it relieve the clerk of cumbersome book-keeping tasks, but it will provide greater internal control and accountability to the Postal Service."

The completely automated post office is far away. The Postal Service has to decide whether their future is to transport paper— or to transfer information. It makes a big difference (see page 357).

Fast Mail Sorting

A bull's-eye-shaped label can help packages sent parcel post reach their mark.

The labels are part of a new system developed by the RCA Corporation and known as "Parcel Post Coding Equipment." It produces address labels shaped like bull's-eyes which contain the ZIP code of the destination. Design of prototype equipment for the new system is now under way. It will work in conjunction with the automated bulk mail handling systems now being planned by the Postal Service. Together the new equipment and system will greatly speed up parcel sorting and decrease the possibility of packages being missent.

A small part of the package handling procedure is manual under the new system. After a parcel is stamped and paid for at the postal window, it's placed onto a conveyor by a clerk. It then passes a keying operator, who enters onto a keyboard the ZIP code where it's going. This ZIP code has usually been written in the destination address by the sender. The keying in of the ZIP code immediately activates a code print button. A computer verifies the ZIP code to see if it's valid—that is, if it actually exists and is correct for the destination. The computer then transmits the ZIP code to two label-producing machines. These machines each make one label and apply them to two different sides of the package. With this equipment, forty packages can be encoded a minute.

The package then continues along the conveyor to the "destination runout area." En route it passes through a "read station" where four electronic scanners, operated by lasers (page 329), help sort the packages. Using four scanners ensures that at least one of the two labels on each package is read. These scanners can read eighty packages a minute. At the same time, a second computer verifies the ZIP codes. Finally, the computer generates a command signal which routes the parcel by conveyor to the appropriate bin for its destination.

According to Paul Wright, director of RCA Corporation's Advanced Technology Laboratories, "With the Parcel Post Coding Equipment, the package will be handled when first received, encoded and permanently labeled. Then all subsequent sorting can be done automatically."

With mail, one approach is to transmit the information content electronically, rather than shipping paper back and forth across the country. Another approach delivers the information over lines to local offices where it's transferred to paper and then delivered. But packages are another matter—and here's one future solution.

File Management

A new records management and control system may someday largely replace conventional paper filing systems.

Banks first began to microfilm checks prior to further routing in the 1930s, and since then libraries routinely record such materials as newspapers and unpublished manuscripts on microfilm. During all of this time, however, one major drawback of microfilm systems has restricted their viability: the lack of an "add-on" capability. With traditional silver emulsion a microfilmed image

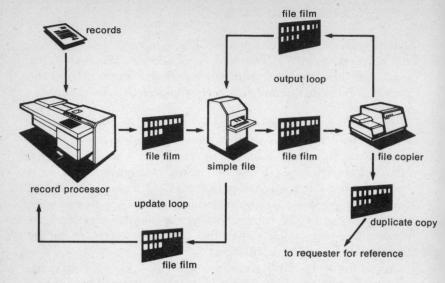

Business records are converted to postcard-size film (left) that can be updated or filed and copied (right).

once recorded was fixed (often in the middle of a long strip or tape); additions, deletions or annotations could not be made. As such, microfilming was best suited for what might be called "dead" files.

A new system, developed by Scott Graphics, a subsidiary of the Scott Paper Company, is especially designed to overcome this limitation. Utilizing transparent electrophotography, which forms images by depositing carbon particles onto a polyester film base, the Scott System 200 rapidly updates any record within its files.

Here's how it works. Incoming records are microfilmed in a desk-sized "record processor," which yields a filmed replica (in nine seconds) of a document one twenty-fifth of its original size. Up to sixty letter- or legal-size documents (related to a single subject, case or transaction) are recorded on one four-by-six-inch microfilm card. These cards are stored in a simple file and become the master or permanent record. Upon request, the record is quickly duplicated in a "file copier." To maintain the integrity of the original, a duplicate microfilm card, inserted in a "record display/printer," produces either a visual or a printed copy of the information sought.

In order to update a file, the master microfilm card is returned to the record processor; additional documents are recorded in the blank spaces on the card. Any one of the existing records can be annotated or voided by recording a control target over the previous image.

Besides the obvious saving in space (an eight-by-ten-foot work station can store and process records which in paper form would fill a hundred five-drawer filing cabinets), such a system may offer considerable savings in time, cost and manpower. At the same time it appears to provide file integrity, security and control.

Life insurance companies, financial institutions, health services, law enforcement agencies, businesses with large staff or extensive transactions, are likely beneficiaries of the record processing system.

According to Scott Graphics, "Geared to the requirements for a record management system which will accept the output of data processing and word processing systems as well as the information generated in the day-to-day conduct of business activities, the Scott Record Processing System 200 becomes the foundation for the total information systems of the future."

Conveyor Belt Banking

Workers at Chemical Bank's new operations center in downtown Manhattan don't have to walk farther than the water fountain during a day's work—their assignments come to them.

A vertical, mile-long conveyor system resembling a roller coaster distributes mail, interoffice communications and supplies to forty-eight stations located throughout the offices. The conveyor service stations on each floor can also send out materials to other floors. Items travel in special plastic containers, and a station can receive twelve containers a minute. This conveyor greatly cuts employee travel between floors and departments.

Employees control the conveyor system with a special panel located at each station. They enter instructions on mirrored slide tabs that break a beam of light, controlling an electrical circuit. The principle resembles that of automated doors used in super-

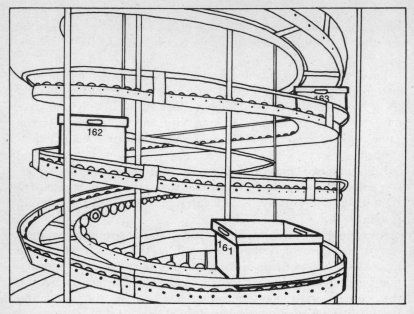

Conserv-a-trieve runs on tracks between rows of stored securities.

markets. If a station becomes full or breaks down, the exact location of the malfunction is pinpointed. A container passes through the entire system twice; should the problem at its destination station not be corrected by then, it returns to the central mail room.

Two other conveyor systems aid employees. The Central Funds Operation transfers the heavy load of checks from various departments to processing areas. Conserv-a-trieve, the trademark name for an elaborate securities retrieval system, also runs on a conveyor. A staff member enters his request for a specific securities file on a keyboard. This activates the conveyor which passes vertically and lengthwise between rows of metal file tubs in the securities storage vault. The conveyor mechanically removes the desired tub and delivers it to the work station which needs it. At the push of another button, Conserv-a-trieve automatically restores the tub to its assigned storage place.

Conserv-a-trieve is also designed to allow departments and windows dealing with securities to send and receive messages, whereas nonrelated departments can't. As a safety measure, if a station is full, a container returns immediately to the sender.

BUSINESS AND WORK

Chemical Bank reports, "The high-speed conveyor belts and the securities system are only a few of the modern features that make the center unique in the industry. Each day, the conveyor saves employees hundreds of work hours that would have been spent in nonproductive travel between floors."

Conveyors may help the productivity of bank workers to increase, the number of social visits to decrease. Both are important parts of the job, now and in the future. Success with these systems will determine how the balance will tip in future offices.

Vertical conveyor speeds work to and from service stations.

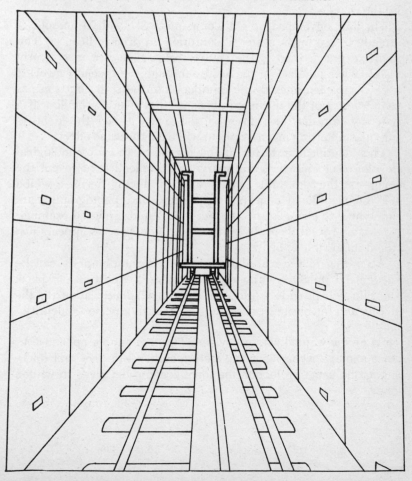

Fraud-Proof Documents

A transparent identification film, bonded as a covering to the face of documents, makes it easy to tell if and how they've been tampered with.

The film is covered with a reverse-printed image that's completely invisible under normal circumstances. However, the image shows up at once when the document is inserted in a specially designed viewer. If anyone has altered the document the change also shows up, since the film is destroyed or covered by the change.

The film, developed by 3M Company of St. Paul, Minnesota, is already in use in the state of California on drivers' licenses. The invisible image used is the state's seal, which becomes clearly visible when you look at the license through the special viewer. If a date has been altered, the numbers inserted stand out sharper than the rest of the document, because they overlay the film. If a new signature has been inserted, the area will lack the identifying image. Putting in a new photo will have the same effect.

This identification technique makes use of a new technological development known as transparent retroreflection to reveal the image on the film. Other methods of producing licenses, which rely on traditional concepts of printing and photography, are vulnerable to changes and counterfeiting, and a normal examination won't reveal them. By contrast, the new process appears just about impossible to beat.

According to the manufacturer, "Because authenticity can be recognized quickly, without great expense, education or space, the film will provide more secure personal identification for the public and for businesses seeking to establish a person's identity."

Next on the wanted list: an invisible film that can be applied over an audiotape when it's completely recorded—to give oral documents the same protection the identification film gives to written ones.

Computers Prevent Mine Disasters

In November 1968, in Farmington, West Virginia, 96 men were killed in a mine disaster. This tragedy mobilized a program to develop electronic monitoring equipment to measure the environmental conditions of coal mines and to prevent such mine disasters through technology. By tracking those conditions that lead to explosion, roof falls or fires, the program aimed at improving mine safety as well as operating efficiency.

A monitoring system was developed at the West Virginia University College of Engineering, in Morgantown, by a research team headed by Dr. M. Dayne Aldridge. Consisting of sensors placed at strategic locations within a mine, the system represents the first attempt in coal-mining history to simultaneously measure important environmental conditions in a mine. The seven environmental factors selected for analysis were methane, oxygen and carbon monoxide concentrations, the air flow, barometric pressure, temperature and relative humidity.

The first unit of the system was installed in a section of a mine in West Virginia in November 1972, and succeeded in performing its assigned tasks without any serious technical or operational difficulties during a two-month test period. Data from each sensor were transmitted to the data processing center at the Morgantown campus for computer analysis. The system's success encouraged the engineers that further improvement and wider application of it is possible.

Since most problems can occur anywhere in the mine and are not isolated to any one position, the research team decided to place the sensors at key positions throughout the mine. The positions chosen were major air splits, where air is supplied to each mine section and then fed back along nearby return airways. Each sensor is placed in such a way as to ensure exposure to a desired sample of the moving air.

Differences in the intake and return air circuits cause chemical changes in the sensors, which in turn trigger off an electric current. Power outputs from the sensors are fed into the telemetric equipment, and the signals are carried outside the mine by a

Researchers install and test sensor in mine.

telephone line. A circuit then provides communication to the central data processing and control center. Data can be processed by the computers to yield the maximum possible information. Not only mine conditions but also the condition of the sensors and electronic equipment themselves can be monitored from the outside. Abnormal changes can be detected within minutes of their occurrence, and when the output of all the sensors is processed, the general location of the problem can also be determined quickly.

For example, if a fire occurs in a section, the return air will contain carbon monoxide, which the intake air does not. The simultaneous measurement of air flow and pressure drops permits the calculation of the airway resistance. Inadequacy of air flow as well as a change of resistance in a section would indicate a partial blockage of the airway on that section.

All sensors and measuring instruments in the system are products commercially available to industrial plants.

Dr. Aldridge, head of the research team, says, "For the system to be useful, the data must be sufficiently trustworthy to permit important decisions to be made on their basis. Based on experience thus far, we conclude that such credibility can exist in an electronic coal-mine monitoring system. It is not clear how sensitive the system can be made, but it is obvious the occurrence of major problems can be detected quickly."

Mine disasters are among the most dreaded and horrible of all industrial accidents. Once men are trapped inside a mine, it can take hours or even days to rescue them. The anxiety caused to miners' families is intense, and human cost, if rescue doesn't come in time, is heavy.

Prevention of mine disasters is a wiser course than rescue operations. As the monitoring system is improved, disaster conditions, mine fires and explosions may eventually be eliminated if their causes can be accurately predicted. Improved mine safety will become especially needed as fuel shortages and coal gasification (see page 114) aid the growth of the mining industry.

Light Pulse Burglar Alarm

With practiced stealth, the man starts to raise the window. A bright light flashes a few inches from his eyes, and is immediately followed by what seems to be an answering flash from the other end of the room. Silence. Then an ear-splitting shriek of an alarm goes off. The man drops the window and runs. Sirens wind out as patrol cars full of policemen with drawn revolvers converge on the pharmaceutical company's factory-complex.

Alan L. Litman's light pulse burglar alarm system is both simple and economical. It eliminates the elaborate, expensive and easily tampered-with wiring required in electrical circuit burglar alarm systems, and the separate battery-powered radiowave or sonic transmitters for each window and door that are required in traditional radiant beam systems.

Each transmitter in Litman's system employs a cheap and disposable contact-activated photoflash unit that is self-energizable and does not require an electrical battery or other power source—a lightcube, for example. When triggered by the unauthorized opening of a window or door, the unit generates a high-intensity light pulse.

In optical communication with a series of such transmitters (one for each door or window) is a centralized detector photocell and electronic discriminator circuit that selectively responds to the alarm's light pulse: the circuit is insensitive to other light conditions, such as daylight or the lights ordinarily used in the room. This "receiver" activates the security device or devices in use—the bell, the camera, the radio signal.

If a multiroom, multilevel area is being protected, optical "relay units" are used: the first photoflash unit activates a second one, which activates a third one, and so on. This chain reaction leads from the activated transmitter through rooms and corridors, around corners and up and down stairs, to the central receiver.

Litman says, "In some applications it may be desired that the intruder not be made aware of the fact that his unauthorized entry, or triggering of the detector, has been discovered. This may be accomplished according to the invention by employing a wavelength of light, or radiant energy, falling outside of the visible bandwidth, such as the infrared or ultraviolet wavelengths."

Each year more than two million burglaries are committed in the United States alone. A cheaper and more effective burglar alarm system would save property owners hundreds of millions of dollars.

Intruder Tracking

Most burglar alarm systems detect the entrance of an intruder, and stop. An alarm sounds when a door is forced, when a window is broken, or when an infrared beam is interrupted. A new system detects the *presence* of an intruder—and keeps track of where he is.

The system uses *geophones,* vibration sensors used in oil prospecting and developed by the petroleum industry. Even a low-cost geophone detects vibrations of the floor or ground when anyone walks around in its vicinity. Electrical signals from geophones installed in a protected area are transmitted to a monitoring point and converted to visible or audible alarm-and-tracking signals. By observing the geophone signals, a plant watchman can tell how many intruders are present—and where they are.

Sophisticated intrusion-monitoring systems usually involve closed-circuit, low-light-level television installations. But the geophone system does almost the same job at a very much lower cost.

The inventor, Robert D. Lee, says, "an operator can identify the number of intruders, and also can identify the movements of the intruder or intruders, such as walking, running and the like."

The use of geophones is a good example of electronic cross-fertilization—from oil exploration to crime prevention. Modern police detection and deterrent systems are, and will continue to be, electronic. Already, computers correlate vast amounts of information on crimes and criminals, recognize patterns and furnish detectives with leads. Nonlethal weapons (see page 252) incapacitate offenders. Low-light surveillance TV cameras keep crime out of the streets. Even the Defense Department has technologies that will soon find their way into the local police departments.

Ultrasonic Dishwashing

A Swiss inventor has designed a dishwasher in which sound waves, above the range of hearing, take the place of mechanical agitators and jets of water. Dishes are placed in racks in the usual fashion, water and a mild detergent are added, and an ultrasonic generator is turned on. No drying is necessary.

Ultrasonic cleaning has been used for industrial purposes for a long time, but has not yet been applied to cleaning dishes. Delicate and complex devices, which would be damaged by scrubbing or agitation, are rapidly and easily cleaned. One company, for example, offers a small unit for cleaning jewelry and watch parts. But this design adapts the technique to the conventional kitchen dishwasher. The need for "aggressive" detergents is eliminated, and so is the requirement for hot-air drying. The complete wash-and-dry cycle will be only a few minutes instead of the usual hour.

The inventor, Max Thomen, points out that "strong detergents tend to bleach overglazes and other colored decorations on tableware, and attack certain types of glass."

Both energy and water are in short supply today. This dishwasher will use less energy than conventional units—hot-air drying is eliminated—and less water than it would take to wash the dishes by hand.

Life-Cycle Insurance

It's the business of insurance men to wager, and wager accurately, on the future of the statistically "average" policyholder.

Comprehensive insurance (see page 393) is a single policy to cover several areas of financial security, including needs that arise from death, disability, sickness and accidents, retirement, automobile accidents, fire and liability. Insurance companies are also showing an increased interest in savings and investment mechanisms. "Illustrative of this trend," according to Morton Darrow of Prudential, "will be the entrance of life insurance companies into the executor and estate settlement fields. The life-cycle client account will become a major sales vehicle."

Life-cycle insurance is a form of coverage that changes as a person reaches certain benchmarks in his life. The arrival of children, the purchase of a home, the education of the children, all require new insurance. But life-cycle insurance would embrace all these changes.

People will increasingly turn to their employer or the government to provide for their insurance needs, as the proportion of people relying primarily on themselves to meet their financial security needs will be much lower than today.

If the trend toward automation continues, mandatory cost comparisons will soon force insurers to sell similar policies at similar prices. Thus competition will shift to the area of customer service, where there will be more personalized relations between agent and policyholder.

"The general trend toward consumerist activities will increase," Mr. Darrow thinks, which will in turn force insurance companies to take "an active role in eliminating marketing practices contributing to negative public reactions. The conflicts, tensions and turmoil of modern societies will continue to create personal insecurity and markets for security products."

Consumerism is a force here to stay. Most businesses will feel opposing pressures: to streamline and automate operations, and at the same time to provide more personal services to the customer. The three-way struggle between government, industry and the public is likely to continue—particularly in services like insurance.

Comprehensive Insurance

The much-publicized "no-fault" automobile coverage was first initiated in Massachusetts in 1971. Since then, several other states have also adopted the system of one-person responsibility. With a no-fault policy, your insurance company pays you for damage to your car (and, in some states, for personal injury as well), no matter who was responsible for the accident. Likewise the other person's insurance company pays for his damage. This eliminates the suits and countersuits that clog the lower courts. Further, there is a reduction in legal fees incurred by the insurers, which is, in turn, passed on to the policyholder in the form of reduced premiums.

A new development in insurance is the comprehensive policy. Instead of taking out separate policies for home, automobile, life, medical, and disability income insurance, the consumer will soon be able to purchase a single all-inclusive policy.

There may be certain advantages to this kind of comprehensive protection plan (this is not an endorsement). The policyholder receives combined liability coverage. With separate policies, you might carry automobile liability insurance with an upper limit of $75,000 and homeowner's liability with a limit of $50,000. If the delivery man slips on a banana peel in your hallway and sues you for $75,000, you are in trouble; there is no way you can transfer your auto liability coverage. Under combined liability, in contrast, there is a single ceiling on your insurance no matter what you are being sued for.

A similar rule applies when you have separate coverage for your home and personal property. If your house is hit by a typhoon, and your household damages exceed the limit, you cannot resort to your personal property coverage. Again, with a comprehensive plan, you receive one overall amount of insurance, which serves as your limit no matter what form of loss you suffer.

Continental Insurance Companies of New York is already writing comprehensive policies in thirty states, and no doubt the program will soon be approved in other states as well. Other companies are developing comparable packages. An additional benefit of the Continental policy is inflation protection—the amount of coverage for one's house automatically increases as construction costs go up.

The primary advantage of comprehensive protection appears to be simplicity. There is one insurance company, one premium, one expiration date and one agent.

Continental President Milton W. Mays comments that personal comprehensive protection "offers a new and uniquely integrated form of protection. We consider it the most important development in personal-lines insurance since the introduction of the homeowner's concept."

Big changes in insurance will come if and when government moves in. Passage of some sort of nationwide health insurance might be a first step toward required life insurance, auto insurance and other kinds. "Life-cycle" insurance (see page 392) would cover a person from the cradle to the grave—with built-in modifications at critical turning points.

Market Limits and Prices

Pound for pound, coal, iron and autos are plentiful and cheap. Pound for pound hormones, platinum and electric switches are rare and expensive. This routine fact of economic life is not trivial, because it may help forecast future amounts and prices of chemical substances, materials, machinery and electrical appliances.

Suppose a new product or unsold commodity will be offered for sale. A businessman or corporation usually has a difficult time with two decisions: the quantity to manufacture and the price to charge.

Faced with this problem, Dr. L. G. Cook and General Electric Research Laboratories amassed data on the annual output in pounds per year versus the cost in dollars per pound for a variety of commodities and products. These included three groups: general chemicals (such as coal, gas, oil, sulfur, ammonia, caffeine, penicillins); metals (such as iron, copper, zinc, silver, mercury); and electrical machinery (such as TV sets, refrigerators, ranges, vacuum cleaners, steam irons, exposure meters).

Without regard to the complexity of different commodities, like computers and oil, a simple result emerged. Generally, a 1 percent drop (or rise) in price per pound was associated with a 2 percent rise (or drop) in the number of pounds produced per year.

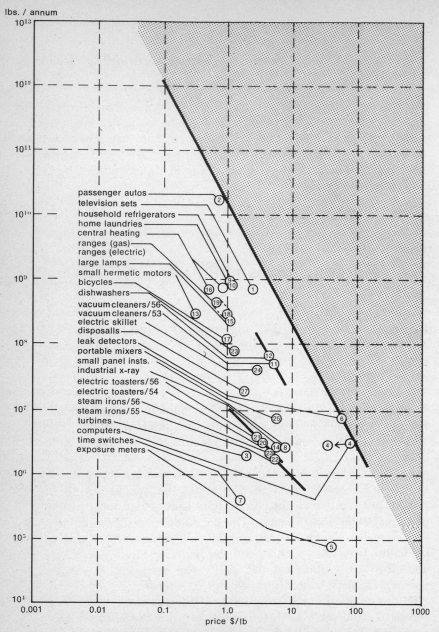

lbs. / annum

passenger autos
television sets
household refrigerators
home laundries
central heating
ranges (gas)
ranges (electric)
large lamps
small hermetic motors
bicycles
dishwashers
vacuum cleaners/56
vacuum cleaners/53
electric skillet
disposalls
leak detectors
portable mixers
small panel insts.
industrial x-ray
electric toasters/56
electric toasters/54
steam irons/56
steam irons/55
turbines
computers
time switches
exposure meters

price $/lb

The output in pounds per year versus the cost in price per pound (1957 prices) for a variety of machinery. The shaded area represents the market limits.

396

Because personal and national incomes are limited, and since the individual is the ultimate purchaser of all goods, there must be maximum limits to sales for any product. These limits would be set by the price—and the need—for the product.

Products go through a fairly predictable course. Early in their history, in the pilot plant stage, they are high in cost and low in production. As the production expands and demand exceeds it, the price doesn't drop much. Later, when demand and price are in balance, they are closely related. When obsolescence begins, the product usage decreases even as the price decreases. This period may extend over months or years. It and the price relationship will change according to the value of the dollar, the change in personal means, and the nationwide style of life.

According to Dr. Cook, prices for certain items could have been higher without decreasing sales. "Empirical estimates of maximum plausible sales," he says, are related to "a variety of established products and prices. How far this type of thinking can be properly refined—and at what point further refinement becomes unprofitable—only experience will tell."

A case in point—oil and fuel. A change in supply made the demand increase the price. But there are market limits to this process. As we shall see in the future, new sources (see Chap. 2) of energy and fuel will replace the old, causing the price of both to drop.

Flexible Working Hours

Time glides.

A system of flexible working hours allows employees to determine the number of hours they will work in any day. Begun in Germany in 1967, as the "Gleitzeit," it has seriously challenged the nine-to-five, five-day workweek in both Europe and Japan; and it presents an alternative to the four-day workweek which has been more popular in the United States. Here, the concept of flexible hours is known as "Flextime."

Under flexible working hours, a workday contains a number of fixed hours, arranged around the middle of the day, during which all employees must be present. Hours before and after this "core period" are voluntary, and employees can come and go as they please. An employee is required to put in a certain minimal number of hours during a time period the organization chooses—usually a week or a month. Generally, supervisors and employees decide together how many people are necessary to do the job during the flexible time period. They themselves split up the work load, but without imposing fixed, staggered hours.

The entire workday is thought of as a "bandwidth," and a typical bandwidth is from 8:30 A.M. to 5:30 P.M. Flexibility can be extended by broadening the bandwidth and thus give workers a wider range of choice in when to work. And when to eat lunch.

A "credit" and "debit" system permits employees to accumulate time off or owe time to be worked later. If the employee puts in more than the requisite number of hours, the extra hours are carried over as a bonus to the next time period. If he puts in fewer hours, it's a deficit which must be made up at a later time. The most flexible (but rare) form of Flextime is the variable hours system—where there's no core period and employees work whenever they choose, including evenings and weekends.

The Hengstler Company of Germany, a large manufacturer of electromechanical counters and controls, developed the concept of Flextime. It experimented with the concept on its own 1500 employees, and later set up a special division to counsel other organizations considering flexible hours. As of 1973, more than 5000 organizations in Europe were operating on Flextime. During the same year Hengstler formed a U.S. subsidiary, Flextime Corporation, to introduce this work concept into the United States and to counsel organizations here.

Standard time clocks can be used under Flextime to record employee hours, but Hengstler provides special automatic equipment to companies. Employees themselves can adjust their hours, and the equipment gives instantaneous totals of accumulated hours during any accounting period. It provides feedback to employees and record-keeping information to supervisors and management.

Studies in Europe and Canada have shown that lateness and

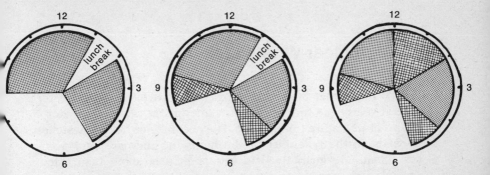

Typical bandwidth (left), stretched in the morning and afternoon (middle) to accommodate a long lunch break (right).

short-term absenteeism drop sharply with a flexible hours system. Productivity increases, but without the necessity of overtime. There is less turnover on jobs, and morale of workers improves.

According to the Flextime Corporation, "Using the flexibility allowed them, employees adjusted work schedules to their own personal rhythms and generally applied their most productive hours to the job. Flextime can help man maintain his individuality in this age of modernization, mechanization and automation."

Some have suggested that job boredom and malaise are increasing, accompanied by pandemic absenteeism. Perhaps giving people more control over their lives gives them more self-respect and sense of responsibility as well.

If both husband and wife wish to work, they can arrange for one of them to be home with young children during the day. People who want to work and go to school will be able to adjust their hours. And in big cities, of course, "glide time" will ease those lunch- and rush-hour crowds.

Nuclear Wristwatch

Wristwatches that hum rather than tick have been available for several years. The timing base is a tiny quartz crystal oscillator—a kind of miniature tuning fork. The accuracy of tickless watches depends on the reliability of the hum, and they are *very* accurate: Some are guaranteed to lose or gain no more than a few seconds each year.

If you strive to be perfectly punctual, however, there are still a few bugs that can cause your chronometer to err minutely. The oscillators are relatively fragile, and their hum can be thrown a bit off key by temperature changes. Moreover, the devices are not as small as watchmakers would like, and they aren't as cheap as watch wearers would like.

A timely solution: John Bergey, president of Pulsar Time Computer, Inc., has patented a nuclear-paced wristwatch which may prove cheaper, smaller and even more precise than crystal oscillator timepieces. A pinpoint source of radium-226 gives off alpha particles at a remarkably steady rate. A sensor then counts the particle rate and translates it into equally regular electrical impulses that keep time.

The present Pulsar system is the first to tell time in a ruby-red digital display, and the nuclear pacer could be integrated into this system. The principal remaining problem is to find materials for the alpha sensor that will not deteriorate under constant bombardment by the radioactive source.

The nuclear-paced watch would still depend on a now-conventional tiny three-volt battery to amplify the electrical pulse and to operate the digital display. But Mr. Bergey believes it would be a long step toward developing a completely nuclear-powered watch: "This would alleviate the need for frequent battery changes and add virtually a lifetime performance feature to one's personal timepiece."

And as Mr. Bergey explains—though the why is very difficult to fathom—the nuclear-paced watch actually increases in accuracy with use: "Since [nuclear-paced] time is calculated on a

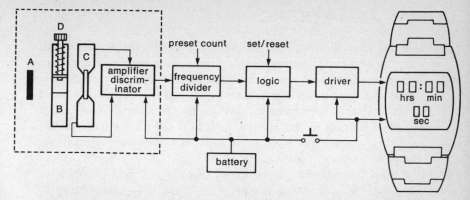

Schematically this is how the nuclear-paced watch would work. Everything outside of the dotted-line box is identical with the present Pulsar system. But the small chip (A) is radium-226. A window (B) permits alpha particles to pass through to the sensor (C). The watch can be adjusted to run faster or slower by opening or closing the window with an adjustable screw (D).

statistically random basis, it has the added advantage of achieving greater, rather than lesser, accuracy with time. Note: All other timebases accumulate a timing error since they work on a percentage basis."

The next logical step is to construct the power supply from a nuclear source. This would alleviate the need for frequent battery changes and add virtually lifetime performance to your personal timepiece. Not for a long time, though.

And while "real" time is being tracked ever more precisely, psychologists explore ways to modify subjective time (see page 235).

Employee Benefits and Portable Pensions

Employees tomorrow will enjoy an increasingly varied range of benefits—including capital accumulation plans, group auto and legal insurance, more Social Security aid, time off with pay, and company-financed tuition aid.

Working people of the future are likely to demand—and get—

benefits that their parents seldom if ever dreamed of. One of these is the capital accumulation plan. The employer provides dollar benefits each year, which are invested in the employee's name. It's like a savings account over which he doesn't have control. If the employee decides to change jobs, he can take a specified portion of this money with him—all of it after a period of years. These "portable pensions" may have a cost-of-living clause as a common feature.

Group benefits will also expand. Employees as a group have considerable purchasing power. Two ways they are starting to exercise it are in group auto insurance and group legal insurance. Group dental plans should be as widely used by the 1980s as group medical plans are today. Group travel plans, with employers sponsoring charter flights, are also likely to expand.

The workweek is shrinking. The four-day week, now starting to make headway, may eventually become standard. Flexible workweeks (see page 397), in which the individual has a certain amount of choice in his hours and days of work, are probable, too, according to experts. As both productivity (see page 365) and the work force continue to increase, workers will enjoy longer vacations. Sabbatical leaves, in which employees can pursue their personal interests, will spread.

Another important area of employee benefits is tuition aid. More and more corporations will institute and finance programs of lifetime learning for their employees.

"If other general increases are enacted," says Thomas H. Paine, a pension planner, "our future Social Security picture could be entirely different. . . . Exact predictions can't be made—our guesses range from 30 percent to over 40 percent—but I think it's safe to say that we will see some upward movement in the percentage of pay replaced by Social Security."

Compared with Europe, America is backward in providing benefits for workers. In a country like Germany, retired workers are maintained in dignity and comfort. They also live longer—thanks to a superior system of health benefits.

Employees of the future may be able to select the benefits they wish out of a number offered by employers. The scheme, already in practice in some places, is known as the "cafeteria approach to compensation."

9
Play
and
Pastime

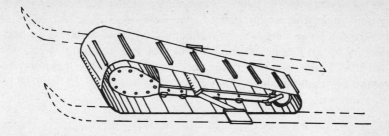

Downhill skiers no longer require ski lifts to take them to the top with this lift.

Mini-Tractor Hauls Skiers

Are you tired of waiting in line at the bottom of crowded ski lifts? Have you ever stood on a pair of skis and looked longingly at a high mountainside, only to realize that there was no way to reach it except by helicopter or an exhausting climb? Here's a possible solution to the problem of difficult winter travel in mountainous areas. Henri Gremeret has invented a collapsible motorized tractor that can carry a skier effortlessly to the top of a hill. The skier may then fold up the small lightweight machine and pack it on his back for the downhill run.

The tractor has a small gas engine set inside of an endless crawler belt. It's steered by shifting the weight from one footrest to the other, which tilts the track and causes the tractor to turn. Speed is controlled by a trigger-type throttle set in one ski pole. The tractor can be operated with or without skis. If it's used without skis, detachable stabilizers are provided for balance. Gremeret states that his intention is to provide "a tractor which leaves the skier completely independent . . . the range of the tractor is limited only by its fuel capacity."

These small tractors have many practical uses apart from their recreational value. They could be used for cheap, rapid, effective patrols of wilderness areas for purposes of rescue or game and forest management. Like cross-country skiing (see below) they would make the winter use of mountain areas practical without altering their wilderness environment. No longer would it be necessary to cut timber and construct steel and concrete towers for ski lifts. Large sleds could bring groups of tractors downhill, instead of "backpacking" them down.

Ski Spurs

Skiers employ several tactics in climbing up a slippery beginners' slope, in maneuvering their way to the tow line, or in "cross-country" skiing. Some sidestep, making a few awkward inches of headway at a time; others "herringbone" with a similar lack of progress—or grace. Backsliding and loss of balance are constant hazards, especially when crowds of fellow skiers have turned the powder base to ice.

Skiing is both a downhill and an uphill sport. So inventor Nathaniel Hawthorne (no relation to the writer) has devised ski spurs that may make climbing snowy hills and mountainsides considerably easier.

The spur is screwed onto the ski directly in front of the binding. With a gloved hand or the end of a ski pole, the skier rotates a simple lever that rocks two prongs outward and down so that they protrude slightly below the bottom of the ski. The prongs dig into the snow for sure footing and natural walking.

When he reaches the top of the slope, the skier trips the latch with his pole, and a torsion spring snaps the cleats up and out of the way. The prongs are safely contained on the top of the ski, so they offer no interference as the skier zips downhill.

Each unit weighs only three ounces, so it doesn't affect the balance of the ski. Mr. Hawthorne estimates the production cost at between three and four dollars per pair. For cross-country skiing, where you spend as much time going uphill as down, he has also designed a more streamlined set of spurs.

"I had done some skiing in California and noticed that control of skis is a problem when walking up a slope," Mr. Hawthorne

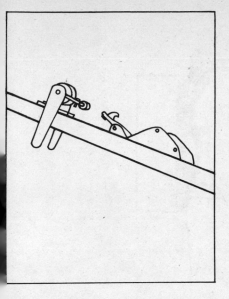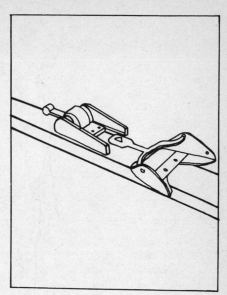

The ski spur, with prongs down, makes for easy climbing up icy slopes. For downhill skiing, the spurs snap up and out of the way.

says. "It seemed a device designed to prevent sliding would be of help . . . I tested the prototype at Alpine Meadows Ski Resort in California with excellent results."

Mechanized aids help skiers to avoid those long tow lines (see page 405). But cross-country skiing offers more and more people the opportunity to enjoy the peace and quiet of newly fallen snow, a walk through the woods. These spurs will spur cross-country skiing.

Embraceable Backpack

Hikers can readily imagine the twisting and contorting necessary to don a loaded backpack using only one hand. This is precisely the problem that would have faced astronauts preparing for a space walk or a hike on the moon. In low or zero gravity the

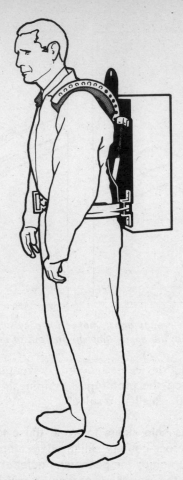

A pressure plate triggers the shoulder hooks and the waistbelts to spring into position on the quick-donning backpack. The wearer has only to fasten a simple buckle, which he can do with one hand, and the loaded pack is securely attached to his back.

backpacker must have at least one hand available to stabilize himself as he climbs into his gear or he will find himself doing inadvertent acrobatics.

NASA scientists anticipated this problem and invented a backpack harness one person can attach with one hand—even if he's wearing a bulky space suit. The backpack is stored with two shoulder hooks folded up and two rigid half belts folded to the sides. As the astronaut backs into the mounting frame, he makes contact with a sensitive pressure plate. The weight of his body against the plate triggers a spring mechanism causing the hooks to clamp down on his shoulders and the belts to swing around his waist. In short, the harness actively embraces the wearer. The extraterrestrial backpacker need only hook the two belts together with a simple buckle, then pack and back are securely joined.

NASA believes there may also be many earthly applications for the fast-donning harness. For instance, automobile and airplane seat belts could enfold the passenger automatically to make certain he's buckled up. Automatic patient restraints could be incorporated into litters and stretchers. Such devices would be particularly helpful to paraplegics, amputees and patients who are unable to hold themselves in wheelchairs.

Scientists foresee flatbed trailers and railway cars with spring-activated straps that would lock the loads in place. They also believe the folding design might become popular for ordinary hiking and scuba-diving equipment.

NASA says the quick-donning harness "could provide the means for a disabled person to experience the enjoyment of hiking even though a disability restricts his ability to get into and out of a pack with a conventional harness."

One example of valuable fallout from products originally designed for the space program (see also pages 199 and 204).

It demonstrates how a simple idea can have a wide variety of applications. Cargo nets could employ the spring-harness design. The net would be laid out flat and the weight of the material piled upon it would pop the load lines up into position where the hook could snatch it up.

Personal Underwater Propulsion

Fish-watching may soon become as popular as bird-watching. People may one day prefer to swim among coral reefs rather than hike in crowded national parks. Amid scenes of exotic beauty, fascinating varieties of animal life live underwater. If they are not fearful predators, people are accepted in the sea world; fish won't swim away from a diver the way birds fly at the approach

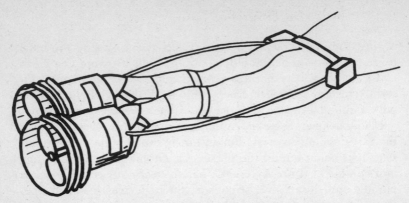

Propulsion units attached to feet free the hands and offer directional mobility.

of the most careful bird-watcher. Of course, man must adapt himself to this strange environment. To do so he must enable himself to see, breathe and move freely in the water.

In the 1930s, glass goggles were introduced to North America and Europe from the Pacific islands. Goggles enabled man to see underwater. He then developed air tanks and snorkel tubes. Once he could see and breathe, it became important for him to have his hands free—to collect fish, take photographs, make notes and so forth. Flippers gave man much of the same freedom and mobility he has when he walks on land. Unfortunately, flippers can be exhausting to use for extended periods of time. So the enjoyment of underwater recreation activities has been limited mainly to strong swimmers.

Joseph Rutkowski of San Diego, California, has created a propulsion system that eliminates the need to "swim" underwater. The diver wears a propeller and enclosed motor unit on the bottom of each foot. The propellers are powered by batteries or compressed air. Speed is controlled by a switch worn on the belt. The swimmer may change his direction simply by moving one or both legs, pointing the propulsion units in one direction—and himself in the opposite direction. The units will float if removed by the swimmer. They will also hinge back against the swimmer's legs so he can walk on land or on the floor of the ocean. The advantage these units have over minisubs and other hand-controlled propulsion machines is that they leave the hands free. Rutkowski says his intention is to provide "an underwater propulsion device which is inexpensive to manufacture and extremely convenient to use."

Undersea activities will adopt propulsion units, perhaps like this unit. Future uses might include these: In conjunction with floating offshore islands (see page 292), it's a personal conveyance to the mainland or an assist to underwater repairmen. It can hold a diver motionless in a current or propel him rapidly and tirelessly from place to place. It might open the seas to the elderly and others who don't swim strongly enough to enjoy diving with equipment presently available. It could facilitate the rescue of injured or incapacitated swimmers and divers, saving the rescuer's strength. And new sports or vacation pastimes may come from its compatibility with the common aqualung breathing apparatus.

Inflatable Suspenders

A West German, Walter Geier, has invented the world's first pair of inflatable suspenders. "Why?" one naturally asks. And Mr. Geier replies, when you are vacationing near the water, you strap them to your kid. Then, if junior should happen to fall in the lake, his suspenders will keep him bobbing with his head high and dry.

The "kinderbraces" contain two primary inflation chambers: the front straps, which provide some buoyancy, and the special oversize shoulder pads, which you blow up like water wings. The effect is to support the floundering child and to tilt his body upward slightly to keep his nose and mouth above the waterline. For formal wear, the suspenders deflate and the shoulder pads snap down, so the child can use the straps for their age-old purpose—to keep his pants up.

Mr. Geier's design calls for the suspenders to be inflated by lung power, but presumably a pump could also be used. Alternatively, a CO_2 charger, like those used for inflatable life rafts, might be incorporated for instant ballooning.

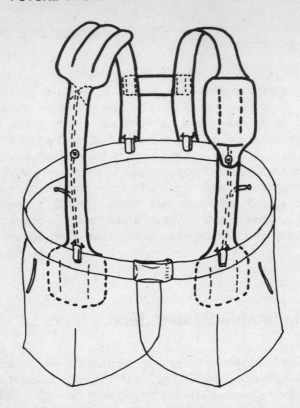

Inflatable suspenders, designed by Mr. Walter Geier, serve two purposes: They keep your child afloat if he falls in the water—and they keep his pants up.

In Mr. Geier's patent application he states, "Decorations may be applied to the back side of the inflatable chambers. . . . When the suspenders are used on small children, it is advantageous to sew the suspenders of this invention directly to the swim suit or play pants."

A new style at the beach: Children will wear inflatable suspenders to hold up their bathing suits—and to save the embarrassment of lost swim trunks and naked children. It will be easier to coax a kid into wearing suspenders than those bulky orange kapok life vests.

New Flames

Mr. Kyo-Bong Whang has solved a variety of ignition problems with three inventions: the self-lighting cigarette, waterproof matches, and waterproof charcoal.

In 1970 over 562 billion cigarettes and nearly 8 billion cigars were produced in the United States alone. Mr. Whang would like to see every future smoke outfitted with an "Insta-lite" combustion tip. The tip is ignited by striking the cigarette itself on an abrasive surface attached to the pack—no need for matches or a lighter.

Four millimeters long, the Insta-lite tip is a solid, spark-producing body enclosed in paper treated with an undisclosed (but reportedly harmless) chemical. Self-lighting cigarettes are windproof and waterproof, and they do not give off the sulfur stink of the traditional match.

But Mr. Whang is hedging his bets. He has also developed a waterproof safety match for outdoorsmen and people living in tropical climates. An odorless flame is produced by a head containing potassium chlorate and infusorial earths. The new match provides a reliable light even when the winter monsoons have made ordinary matches too soggy to strike.

A residual ember can rekindle the stem of a match if it's not dead-out. Many fires are caused by discarded matches that appear to be extinguished. To reduce the fire hazard, the stem of the waterproof match is chemically treated to deter the formation of coal embers.

Waterproof matches may be used to light Mr. Whang's waterproof charcoal briquettes. He has coated ordinary charcoal with a chemical that both repels moisture and eliminates the need for liquid lighter fluids. The briquettes start with a single match and do not flare up. They burn quickly, forming a hot bed of embers for additional regular charcoal. Like Mr. Whang's other products, waterproof charcoal emits no unsavory fumes that might affect the flavor of grilled foods.

Mr. Whang is from Seoul, Korea. He is vice chairman of the Korean Inventors Association and founder-president of Hanju

Enterprise Co., Ltd. The Korean government is supporting the development and marketing of his inventions.

Recreation on Mt. Trashmore

"Making a mountain out of a molehill" may be only a proverb. Making a mountain out of trash is a reality.

The city of Virginia Beach, Virginia, has created a mountain out of a swampy, fifty-acre garbage dump. The former trash heap is now being converted into a unique recreation area that will offer bicycle trails, riding paths, tennis courts, a 10,000-seat amphitheater, and two man-made lakes.

Dubbed "Mt. Trashmore," the project was first proposed by Roland Dorer, of the State Public Health Commission. Its intention was to find a substitute for the traditional ways of garbage disposal—burning, burying and dumping—which create pollution and health hazards. Dorer suggested dumping all the trash in one spot, covering it with dirt, and compacting it to form a solid "mountain."

Soap Box Derby on the slopes of Mt. Trashmore.

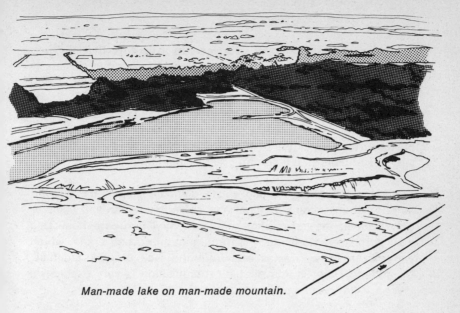

Man-made lake on man-made mountain.

Creating the mountain "resort" meant draining much of the swamp and building roads leading to and from the site. The garbage was then spread out over the entire site and covered with a layer of soil. The fresh soil helped decompose organic elements in the trash, eventually turning it into new soil. Alternate layers of soil and garbage formed building blocks. After a layer of garbage was laid, it was rolled over by mechanical compactors. Since the compactors exerted tremendous pressure on the garbage, all items, including auto parts and refrigerators, could be used. No sorting of the trash was necessary.

Mt. Trashmore was completed in 1972. It rises to a height of 65 feet and consists of 640,000 tons of garbage.

Phase II of the project, building a recreation area on the mountain, is now under way. Grass has been planted on a layer of topsoil, and the addition of two nearby lakes increases the size of the area from its original 50 acres to 125 acres. Eventually, the lakes will offer small paddle boats and fishing. An unusually heavy snowfall in the winter of 1973 gave Mt. Trashmore an added dimension. Residents were able to go sledding and skiing on its slopes. Earlier, during the summer, a Soap Box Derby was held at Mt. Trashmore, marking the first public event to take place in the park.

415

Mt. Trashmore has been so successful a venture that Virginia Beach has begun work on a second mountain project. This is scheduled to be a twenty-year undertaking, also based on a recreational concept.

The city of Virginia Beach reports, "A Mt. Trashmore type of project does not pollute the air or the land, as does burning or offshore dumping. Best of all, Mt. Trashmore will give the city and its residents an outstanding recreational facility."

Traditional methods of solid waste disposal pollute the air and land. Trash mountains may not only solve this health and ecological problem; they also offer great potential for recreation. This dual purpose is particularly advantageous in urban areas, which suffer from heavy wastes and from the lack of park facilities. Urban land either is unavailable or acquisition is very expensive.

Architectural Mobile Homes

Mobile homes, once synonymous with unattractive predictable "boxes," may turn into design-conscious and even simple-but-elegant houses.

The Frank Lloyd Wright Foundation has joined with the National Mobile Homes Corporation to produce inexpensive, architectural living units which combine the best elements of both mobile homes and modular housing. The "productive dwellings," as the foundation prefers to call them, will attempt to be innovative in their use of space and creative in design.

Since 1966 the foundation, students of Frank Lloyd Wright and heirs to his architectural concepts, has taken a second look at mobile and modular homes. Formerly the term "mobile home" referred to a unit with permanently attached wheels; "modular" referred to a house delivered on a chassis and dismounted on the spot. Homes designed by the foundation purposely blur the distinctions between these two categories: they are dedicated to the concept of improving the quality of design of low-cost housing.

The new units represent a departure from the "box" notion of

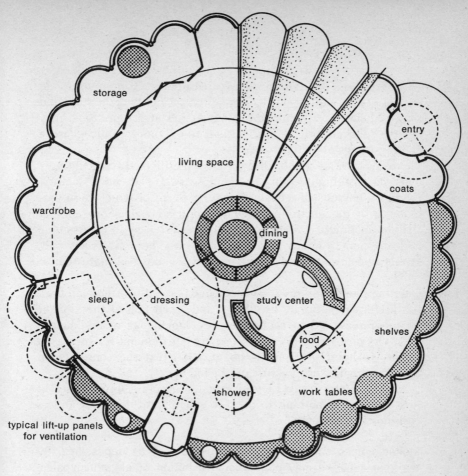

Like a soup dish upside down, this one has revolving inner walls.

housing and feature sloping and angular walls, ceiling-to-wall conservatory windows, and mirrors to enhance the feeling of spaciousness. Windows will have panes that open top and bottom for improved air circulation, and a porch will come as part of the house. Models in production now are 12 feet in width, and vary in length from 52 to 68 feet.

Although the units are made from aluminum, this will be disguised by baked-on enamel to harmonize with the colors found in nature. The inside color scheme coordinates with the exterior, blending the house with its environment.

Units can be attached side by side as with most modules to enlarge the size of the homes. The largest size now in production

417

will have three bedrooms and two bathrooms. "Communities" of mobile homes can be formed by adding a lightweight steel and plastic shelter to accommodate four homes at a time. Each may have a spacious private lot, but all four homes would share a central storage and utility area.

Previous homes of this kind have been criticized for being ugly and shoddy—blights on the landscape. The new factory-produced homes will reflect Wright's concept of structure in harmony with the environment. The emphasis is less on mobility than on modularity. Although the homes are easy to disassemble and transport from one place to another, the key idea is low-cost, attractive housing which may stay put a good deal more than it moves.

As the foundation says, "Seventy-five percent of American families prefer single-family dwellings, and about half of these, if for no other reason than economics, are looking at mobile homes . . . The next ten years will see a greater demand for increased quality in housing. There is no question that the consumerism movement will exert pressure on the industry."

And to quote Frank Lloyd Wright, "Simply selling houses at less cost means nothing to me. To sell beautiful houses at less cost means everything."

Mobile homes can serve as luxuries as well as necessities. By the year 2000 we may not become a nation of elegant gypsies. But any weekend we choose, in fair or foul weather, we can depart for the country in homes on wheels (fuel permitting), without sacrificing comfort. Those who don't like to "rough it" in tents and those without expensive country retreats can have a viable alternative. We will be able to save on travel fare and not impose on relatives, by traveling in our own homes to see them.

The "boredom" of suburban housing might even be alleviated by individually designed mobile homes. Low- and middle-income housing in already overcrowded cities takes a long time to build. Perhaps someday government may subsidize low-cost mobile homes outside central cities for easy transportation to work and services, or in planned growth communities in underpopulated areas—new towns.

Personal Space

Any subway rider knows the invasion of his "personal space" is an unpleasant experience.

"Personal space," a term used by psychologists and anthropologists, describes the area surrounding a person in which he carries out the majority of his interactions with others. Since the area moves with a person and changes according to varying conditions, it's not a space with fixed reference points. Personal space also varies from culture to culture. Frenchmen embrace when they meet; American men seldom do; Latin Americans probably view northern social distances as a sign of Yankee coldness; Englishmen see it as pushiness. Personal space is often unconsciously chosen. When people line up for a movie, for example, each time a new person joins the line, others shuffle sideways, uncomfortable about the lack of distance between them.

Recent studies on personal space show that the distance that two people assume is appropriate and comfortable between them varies with their relationship and the setting in which their interaction occurs. These results come from experiments conducted by Professor Kenneth Little of the University of Denver, with college students as subjects. The methods included projective techniques, not unlike Rorschach and thematic apperception tests, plus simultation of live situations.

In the projective part of the study, each subject was given line drawings of human figures the same sex as the subject. The experimenter placed a background setting in a slot in a box. Background settings were the inside of a living room, an office and a street corner. The experimenter told the subjects that the figures were either very good friends, acquaintances or strangers. He asked them to describe the interaction between them and place them in another slot in front of the background. Grid marks on the board spaced an eighth of an inch apart indicated what the distance was between the two figures. Later, this procedure was repeated with a blank background and plastic three-dimensional figures. Subjects had to imagine one of four possible settings—a street corner, the lobby of a public building, an office waiting room and an undefined location called simply "on campus."

The second part of the study simulated real "live" person interactions. Subjects were told to take the role of a director and arrange two female drama students in scenes. They placed the actresses face to face at any distance they chose and gave them poses. The same imagined four settings were used as in the first part of the study. A second experimenter watched through a one-way mirror and took a picture of the scene. He also estimated the nose-to-nose distances between the actresses based on a blackboard behind them on which vertical lines were drawn at four-inch intervals.

The results indicated that perceived interaction distances between both the figures and the actresses are very much affected by the degree of acquaintance between them. When they are seen as friends, they interact at closer distance than if seen as acquaintances; and if seen as strangers, at much farther distances. Interaction distance is also affected by setting. Maximum distances occur in an office, and minimal ones in the open-air settings.

According to Professor Little, "The determinants of personal space in man, its development, and the boundary variations under different settings and content-of-interaction have yet to be studied. The present project was designed to examine a restricted segment of these problems."

Future offices, public buildings and conveyances—even private homes—will incorporate these findings. "Good fences make good neighbors" is only part of a design for living that embodies social distances.

Sorting Airport Baggage by Voice Command

Vacation travelers fed up with baggage mixups at airports may find relief in a special communication system—the human voice. Both TWA and United Airlines have instituted voice encoding

Voice controlled supermarket checkout.

systems in which an operator tells your baggage where to get off simply by talking to a computerized conveyor belt.

Called the Voice Activating Encoding System (VAES), it was invented by Threshold Technology, Inc. With it, bags are checked and tagged as usual, but there's a complete transformation behind the scenes at the airport terminal.

Customers check in baggage either on the curb outside the terminal or at the ticket counter. There it's tagged normally with an identification number, flight number and destination. A conveyor belt then carries the baggage to a central automated sorting system, where it reaches an "induction station." The operator then speaks the digital code for the flight number and the city of destination into a microphone. The portable microphone leaves his hands free to direct the bags simultaneously into the sorter.

The system automatically decodes the spoken code into digital signals and forwards them to its computer memory. Then the conveyor sorter unloads the baggage at the computer's command into a loading area for the appropriate flight.

As the operator speaks, a visual display panel immediately flashes back the code assigned each piece of luggage, allowing him to verify machine recognition of the code. In case of error,

A secretary tells her typewriter to write.

the operator says "cancel" and the incorrect entry is erased.

VAES recognizes a vocabulary of twenty-one key words. These include all the numerical digits, names of eight key cities like Los Angeles and Philadelphia, and special control words. For example, the word "Go" is used when successive pieces of baggage are to go on the same flight. Since voices are permanently stored in memory, each operator has only to dial his assigned number when he comes on duty. The system identifies each speaker by his individual voice characteristics, accents and pronunciations.

With the voice input system, one man can orient a bag, find the tag and read the destination into the computer much faster than if he had to punch keys.

The first voice encoding system in the airline industry was installed at the United Airlines terminal in Chicago's O'Hare Airport. In 1973, the TWA terminal at New York's Kennedy Airport followed suit.

According to Threshold Technology, the voice encoding system "will provide improved customer service by permitting the present automated sorting systems to realize more of their automated baggage handling potential. The system should make baggage handling more efficient, accurate and productive."

Perhaps the voice command system can be incorporated into automated sorting systems in post offices (see page 380) or used in delicate assembly. Perhaps checkout in supermarkets will be done by voice control. Perhaps we'll eventually have robot servants that will obey our spoken words—a boon for people who have lost use of their limbs. Secretaries may dictate data into computer memories or letters into a typewriter.

Disposable Book on One Page?

A method has been invented to microfilm an entire book on a sheet of paper or film no bigger than a single one of its pages.

You'll need a viewer to bring those pages back up to reading size, but the viewer will bear no resemblance to the massive ones ordinarily used to read microfilm. It will be no bigger than a paperback book—small enough to carry in a pocket or handbag.

One of the significant advantages of books to be produced by the new microfilming method is price. It will cost only about 25 cents to manufacture each film copy. Total cost for recording an entire book of 625 pages on the master film from which the copies are made—about $600.

An unusual kind of lens makes the new microfilming technique

This simplified demonstration shows how words in two separate lines of two separate pages are fitted together on the film sheet.

```
HOW MICRO-IMAGE RECORDING IS DONE

Page 1 of                    The light
original text                brown fox

Page 2 of                    Now is the
original text                time for all

Page 1 as                    T h e   l i g h t
recorded in
micro-image                  b r o w n   f o x

Page 1 with addition         TN ho ew  li is g ht th  e
of page 2, as recorded
in micro-image               bt ri om  we  n f fo or xa l l
```

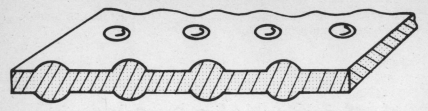

The microviewer or multilens, in which each of the 3500 tiny bubbles is spaced the same as the letters on the page.

possible. Normally a single lens is used, and each page of a book is photographed in miniature on film. The new system uses 3500 minute spheres, each of which functions as a lens. Each sphere captures the image of a single letter on the film sheet—at one twenty-fifth of the letter's normal size. Each letter is separated from the next letter by 24 additional printed characters, one from the first word of each of the next 24 pages. A slight shift rightward of the magnifying lens fills in the letters from the next page. The shrinkage works lengthwise as well, so a total of 625 pages is possible (25 horizontal characters times 25 vertical characters).

The film viewer also has 3500 lenses. As the reader moves the film, the lenses show him the letters of just one page at a time.

"The advantages of this arrangement become apparent," says Dr. Adnan Waly, the inventor, "if one considers the Manhattan telephone directory. It contained in a recent year 815,000 subscribers and ran 1890 pages, weighing 5 pounds. . . . But with the present invention, all entries in the Manhattan directory can be accommodated on a single fiche 8½ by 11 inches in size."

One answer to the paper shortage.

At last the promise of a solution for our overburdened libraries, which have had to add building after building to house the never-ending increase of knowledge. Libraries could issue microfilms of books at 25 cents a copy—and not require their return.

For the emerging nations, great libraries at a fraction of what they used to cost. For every scholar, a complete encyclopedia of the future he can carry around in his pocket. And at home, a thousand books on a single shelf a few inches wide.

Royalties for Artists

Artists are pressing for national legislation that will compel collectors who sell their work at a profit to pay them a percentage of that profit.

Practitioners in many branches of the creative arts are paid a basic fee for their efforts, plus a royalty or residual if their work is used again. Motion picture, television and radio artists generally work on such a basis, and so do composers and many writers. Moreover, they support guilds and unions that enforce their rights vigorously. By contrast, most visual artists are unorganized and their rights are unprotected. Sculptors, painters and printmakers, who sell their work to collectors, normally don't receive another cent, although the collectors may sell the work at substantial profits.

This inequitable situation is finally starting to change. A few artists, who hope for a percentage of any profit realized on resale of their work, are getting it. An advocate of the right of artists to subsequent payments is a New York accountant, Rubin Gorewitz. He and others have drawn up a bill for passage by Congress that would apply to all profits on the resale of work by living artists. Under this bill, whenever the artist's work is resold, the collector would pay him 15 percent of the profit. The artist would supply a certificate vouching for the authenticity of the work, and the seller would give a copy to the buyer. If the buyer wished to insure the work, he would present the certificate to his insurance company as proof of its origin. Legislators have indicated they will give this proposal their serious attention.

"All parties would profit to some extent," declares accountant Gorewitz. "The artist would receive his royalty; the buyer would be assured of the genuineness of the work; the insurance company's risk of theft would be reduced; and the seller's profit would be only a slightly reduced one."

Frequently, painters had to die before their paintings became valuable. After all these centuries, artists may finally get their due. But escalating prices in the art world will probably escalate still more as sellers add on to their sale price the percentage they will have to pay to artists.

Scoring on TV

A bowling system developed by RCA scores bowling automatically, and displays it on a console TV screen next to the player.

The system uses an electronic sensor located in front of the pins on each alley to record the number of pins left standing after each bowl. A computer converts this information into digits and displays it on the player's screen. One screen serves two lanes, and can keep score for up to six players per lane.

A special keyboard at the console logs in all the players' names before the game begins. The first player pushes the button next to his name, and it's illuminated at the console until his play has ended. If he scores a strike his name light goes out. Otherwise it remains on, indicating another ball must be bowled. When he's finished, a light saying "Next Player" is illuminated until the second player pushes his name button. A flag mechanism in front of the pinsetter will remain down if he fails to do this. The system scores single players or running team scores in league and open play.

Besides the console display for the players, a larger overhead display unit can be installed for spectators. Another console, located at the proprietor's desk, makes it easy for him to keep track of the games played. By merely pushing a button on it he's provided with the same information that appears on the screen in any lane. It calculates the cost of the game (not including practice bowling) and prints up score sheets for the leagues.

In a semiautomatic version, the bowler himself feeds pinfall information to the computer simply by pressing appropriate buttons on a scoring panel.

RCA vice president Frederick H. Krantz said the automated bowling system would have a major impact on the bowling market. "It will relieve veteran bowlers of the task of keeping score,

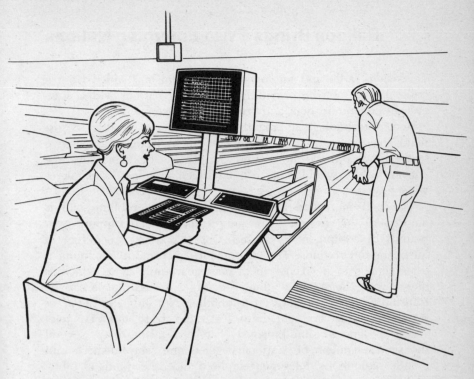

The console used in the automatic bowling score system.

allowing them to concentrate more on improving their games. At the same time, it will eliminate the discouraging prospect that scorekeeping sometimes presents to the beginning bowler."

So accustomed are we to a television screen that even out for a night of bowling we may soon find ourselves watching a TV screen. But it helps improve scores to concentrate on what you are doing rather than the scoring. More and more, other sports too are finding ways to increase an athlete's concentration, such as practice sessions video taped for instant playback to see errors, scientific muscle training—and even meditation.

427

Balloon Brings TV to Emerging Nations

Television, radio and microwave equipment suspended from a balloon may soon be providing developing nations with a low-cost telecommunications and broadcasting system.

Recent technological breakthroughs make it possible to suspend electronic communications equipment from a balloon two to three miles above the ground. To provide the same coverage conventionally would require over fifteen broadcast and microwave towers.

The balloon, called an aerostat, looks like a blimp and is moored to the ground by a long cable. It can support 3500 pounds of equipment at altitudes of 10,000 to 15,000 feet in hurricane-force winds. The equipment can provide communications signals to a 50,000- to 70,000-square-mile area, which is bigger than the state of Ohio. For larger areas, signals can be transmitted from one aerostat to another. Not only can the aerostat broadcast several AM radio, FM radio, UHF and VHF television programs simultaneously, it can also relay several thousand channels of stationary telephone, ship-to-shore and mobile radiophone, teletype, telephoto and other kinds of information.

The transmitting and receiving equipment gets its electric power from a lightweight Wankel-engine-driven generator. The aerostat can carry over a week's supply of gas for the engine. A second aerostat maintains uninterrupted service during the two hours it takes to haul the aerostat down and refuel it.

The airborne telecommunications concept was developed by TCOM (Tethered Communications) Corporation, a Westinghouse Electric subsidiary. Westinghouse first experimented with a tethered-balloon broadcast system in 1920, when radio station KDKA in Pittsburgh used a balloon to support a broadcast antenna during the Harding-Cox presidential election. However, stability problems held up the use of tethered balloons for communications until recent developments in aerodynamic design, electronics miniaturization, and materials technology made it possible.

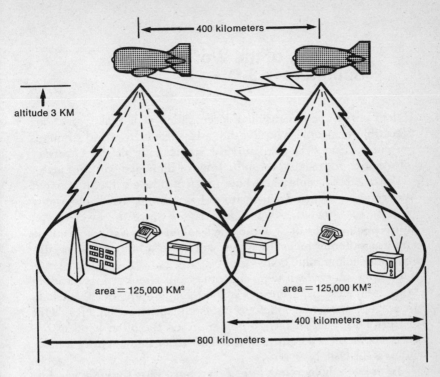

altitude 3 KM

area = 125,000 KM²   area = 125,000 KM²

400 kilometers

800 kilometers

Two communities are linked by a multiple aerostat system.

According to Richard S. Cesaro, head of TCOM, "An aerostat-borne communications system will initially cost about 20 percent of a conventional microwave and broadcast tower system and will have less than 10 percent of the operating costs. In addition, the initial aerostat system can be installed in less than half the time necessary for a conventional network."

Less expensive than synchronous communications satellites (see page 357), aerostats will be a hazard to aircraft, so a three-mile restricted flight zone must be declared around them. But they'll do fliers more good than bad: the aerostats and their tethers, clearly lighted, can serve as an aid to air navigation.

A Library of the World's Sculpture in 3-D

Holograms—three-dimensional laser slides—will make great art accessible to people who live far away from the world's famous museums. They will also provide artists with all the necessary information for making reproductions of damaged works of art.

What is holography, and how can it produce a lifelike image? Writer and scientist Isaac Asimov has written that "holography may be the greatest advance in imaging since the eye." If you study photographs of a statue, each taken from a different angle and at a different focus, then you will have "a hint of the versatility of the holographic image."

Photography, which takes its name from Greek words meaning "the light message," requires a lens; holography, or "the whole message," doesn't. A photograph is the intersection of a light pattern and a flat surface; a hologram, on the other hand, is the intersection of two light patterns. The major ingredient of a hologram is the laser beam.

To create a hologram a laser beam must pass through a beam-splitting mirror, which separates it into two parts. The light reflected off the mirror illuminates the object to be holographed; the other part becomes the "reference beam." When these two halves are reunited, they form a new pattern of light and dark, called the "interference pattern." A hologram is the recording of this interference pattern on film. Directing a laser beam at the hologram will bring the image back to life.

Holography was invented by Dennis Gabor, who received a Nobel Prize in 1971. That same year, Walter Munk suggested a series of laser experiments to reproduce art objects. Because 35 percent of the art of Venice is in a state of decay, F. Valcanover, superintendent of the galleries of Venice, worked with the American scientists to produce holograms of various Venetian statues. From these holograms copies may someday be made—reconstructions of those statues that will have disintegrated owing to the ravages of weather, pollution or vandalism.

A collection of holograms, which are relatively easy to display, could be brought together in a touring museum, or permanent library, of the world's great monuments. Moreover, holography can restore art as well as reproduce it: Laser beams can clean art objects and "deblur" photographs.

Artists like Bruce Nauman have already begun to incorporate holograms in their work. And Salvador Dali has reportedly made a 3-D portrait of rock star Alice Cooper. As for commercial displays—in November 1972, a hand seemed to extend from the windows of Cartier's on Fifth Avenue, offering a diamond ring and bracelet to passers-by.

Three-dimensional movies (see page 433) or television (see below) in color are years away, but coming. And so are holographic museums of statues.

It has been suggested that holograms be made of Mayan art in the Yucatan, which is fast disappearing into private collections.

Some sculptors are worried that the hologram will lead to the appearance of many pirated copies of their work.

One elderly shopper was seen swatting at the Cartier's display with her umbrella; she was convinced it was "the devil's work."

Three-Dimensional TV

Scientists at Bell Laboratories have demonstrated a method for producing three-dimensional television images that can be viewed directly—without special glasses. Like the illusions of the stage magician, they do it with mirrors.

The key to the process is a varifocal mirror—one with an adjustable focus. The mirror is used to convert a three-dimensional object into a series of 15 two-dimensional images. Each 2-D picture is a different depth plane, and all 15 are flashed in rapid sequence on a screen being televised by an ordinary camera.

A second varifocal mirror is connected to the TV receiver. It flashes in rhythm with the mirror at the point of broadcast, focus-

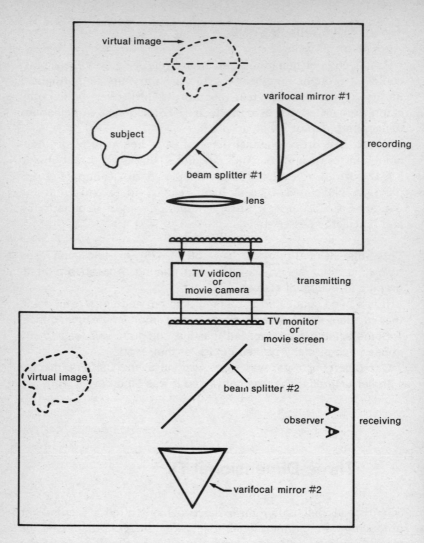

The subject is recorded (above) with one adjustable-focus mirror and reproduced (below) with the second such mirror synchronized with the first.

ing the 2-D images one in front of the other. It is like a scene painted on 15 panes of glass stacked in a row. The foreground is on the first few panes, the background on the back panes—the overall effect is that of a 3-D painting. Similarly, the different depth planes of the Bell system flash so fast that the eye perceives a single, convincing 3-D image.

Unfortunately, the picture suffers from phantom imaging—solid objects in the foreground do not block out the objects behind them. In other words, a viewer might be able to see a ghostly image of John Wayne right through a stage coach parked in front of him. This incurable shortcoming makes it unlikely that this system will ever be used for commercial TV programming, but it could have applications in science and medicine where phantom images would present no particular problem. Bell has already demonstrated how the process could be used to produce a 3-D microscope.

The inventors say, "We have . . . a novel approach to three-dimensional image transmission. The technique described is a simple and economical method for transmitting three-dimensional visual information in real time. . . . The system is autostereoscopic, requiring no external viewing devices such as glasses, and does not restrict the observer to critical viewing positions. . . . Phantom imaging will always be present so that application will only be found in areas where this is not important."

Someday, objects may be visible in their entirety. Imagine 3-D x-rays of the human body. Or teaching perspective to beginning art students. This system may be limited to technical applications now, but other systems will present large TV images (see page 437), 3-D movies (see below), and holographic reconstructions of the world's great statues (see page 430).

Three-Dimensional Movies by Holography

For years Hollywood filmmakers have dreamed of producing three-dimensional movies. Decades ago, they outfitted audiences with red and blue glasses to give a primitive illusion of depth, as well as a peculiar purple tinge, to the Saturday matinee. More recently a polarized light process has been used to make a few (mostly X-rated) films in 3-D. Wearing polarized "sunglasses,"

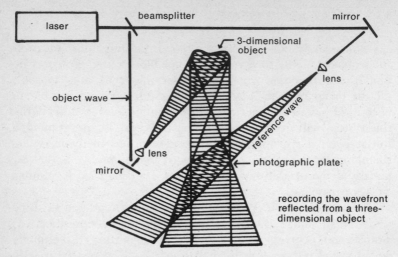

The conventional holography configuration is triangular. The focus is stationary, making it impossible to capture a moving object on film.

the audience can indeed perceive a third dimension, but the effect is marred by frequent blurring and double imaging.

The invention of holography, which made it possible to reproduce three-dimensional images of stationary objects, represented a significant breakthrough. But it was not until late 1972 that Dr. Robert Kurtz of NASA's Marshall Space Flight Center successfully reconfigured the holographic apparatus to produce the first 3-D motion picture that can be viewed without special glasses.

To take a still holograph, a laser beam is "split" by a half-silvered mirror. Half the light passes through the mirror and shines directly on photographic film; the other half is reflected onto the subject, then in turn reflected onto the film. The rejoining of the two beams produces an "interference pattern," which is recorded on the film. When laser light is beamed back through the film, the original image is reconstructed with remarkable realism in three dimensions.

Taking a holograph of a moving object, however, presents a very difficult problem. Conventionally there is a one-point focus; it would be virtually impossible to train the laser on a subject in motion. But Dr. Kurtz rearranged the laser beam so it reflects from the object and a mirror both mounted on an ellipse. Its special properties make possible a rapid sequence of holographs of an object moving parallel to the axis of the ellipse.

434

There are still many problems. For example, as the speed of the target increases, the size of the object appears to decrease. Then too, moving holographs are thus far limited to very small subjects. "We have barely scratched the surface," Dr. Kurtz says. "This is just a glimmer of what can come in the future."

The holographic image must be viewed by looking directly through the film. Consequently the size of the film limits the size of the audience that may view it at one time. "At first, [holographic movies] will conceivably be only for small groups, like watching television," Dr. Kurtz notes. Later, scientists may develop a method for enlarging and projecting a 3-D image.

Alternatively, Dr. Kurtz conceives of a theater design in which a continuous length of holographic film, illuminated by a laser, would pass directly in front of each member of the audience. Each member of the audience would see a given scene slightly later than the person to his left, due to the finite line of film progression. The sound could be synchronized for each viewer. "This technique has been demonstrated successfully for an audience of ten people viewing simultaneously," Kurtz says.

Once perfected, the applications for holographic movies would be manifold. In addition to 3-D motion picture and television shows, Dr. Kurtz conceives of 3-D advertising and educational visual aids. In sports, a holograph could "automatically define the strike zone for umpires."

Dr. Robert Kurtz rearranged the apparatus so that the laser beam reflects from an object and mirror along an ellipse. This configuration enabled him on October 19, 1972, to take the first three-dimensional motion pictures which can be viewed without the aid of special glasses.

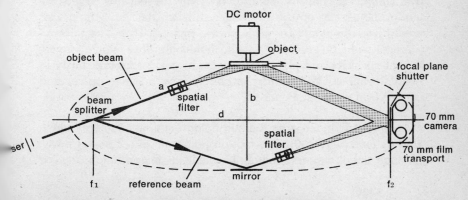

3D MOTION PICTURE ARRANGEMENT

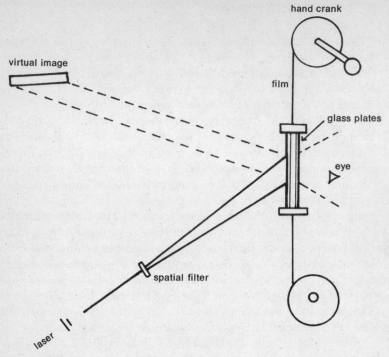

Motion holograms, as of now, must be viewed by looking directly through the film. Dr. Kurtz has developed this system in which a continuous holographic film passes in front of each viewer.

Dr. Kurtz speculates: "Large-scale motion holograms of outdoor scenes would be employed inside windowless buildings to relieve worker stress. Exotic locations, waterfalls, etc., could be displayed in restaurants, air terminals, and so on. Large industrial complexes could be beautified by the presence of large-scale motion holograms on the periphery. In the arts . . . a hologram would free the model from the sitting process. . . . The teleconference could be replaced by the holoconference where projection of speakers and presentations could occur simultaneously in many locations. We could thereby reduce business travel and conserve much needed energy."

In science and in the arts, the still hologram is already very much with us (see page 430). The motion hologram is not so far away. Science fiction writers frequently speak of teleportation devices

436

that "dematerialize" a person, carry him across space and time, and rematerialize him. The motion hologram—and 3-D TV that will soon follow—could bring teleportation closer to reality someday. It is indeed hard to believe.

Wall-Size Flat Panel TV Screen

For years, the television industry has been stymied by the lack of a large-scale but compact display system. The cathode-ray picture tube used in current television sets is too awkward, bulky and heavy to provide the wide screen. Projection systems, besides being optically inefficient, also consume excessive space. The solution may lie in what is known as the gas-discharge panel.

A gas-discharge panel employs an array of pinhead-size neon-filled cells, arranged in columns and rows, each about one thirty-second of an inch from the next. A square inch of the panel, for example, contains about one thousand cells. By changing the neon gas inside, variable amounts of current flowing through the cell produce variable amounts of brightness. The composite effect of these pinpoints of varying intensity over the entire panel of cells resembles a newspaper photograph built up of many dots. As a television picture its quality is equivalent to or surpasses that of the traditional television image. Color is possible, and the picture is pleasing to the eye, especially at close range.

The panel itself is a mere five-eighths of an inch thick; with the circuitry needed to deliver the proper voltage to each cell, the entire display ensemble is about three and a half inches deep. A home movie screen rolls onto a cylinder about this size.

While technical problems remain, recent advances in the art of large-scale integrated circuits make it possible that large, even wall-size television sets utilizing gas-discharge panels can be produced at modest costs in the near future.

According to Zenith engineers working with the panels, "Large TV pictures are pleasant to look at from surprisingly close viewing distances such that the picture subtends a horizontal angle of

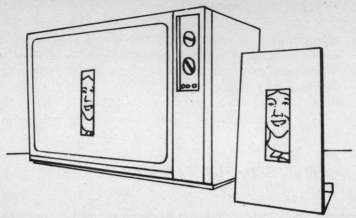

Compare the regular 25-inch color TV set and a thin Burroughs "Self-Scan" gas-discharge panel. The standard set is masked to give the same picture size as the panel. Most of the electronics for the panel are out of view.

30 to 60 degrees [at the viewer's eye] rather than 10 degrees conventional with cathode-ray tubes." The gas-discharge panel, they say, "must be considered as a good starting point for large thin matrix TV displays."

"Television" literally means "seeing from afar." And because current television sets are in small boxes, a viewer often feels very distant from where the action is—like the light at the end of the tunnel, or looking through the wrong end of a telescope.

This visual barrier denies us the emotions of "total immersion" in a spectacular experience. The marketing of wall-size TV's may overcome this obstacle.

Like moving from the back of the bleachers to a box seat, or from the balcony right onto the stage itself.

Video Cassettes

Video cassettes fit in the historical continuum that began in ancient times with the introduction of writing, continued in the early Renaissance with the invention of the printing press, and accelerated more recently with the appearance of radio, film, tape recorders and TV.

Similar in format to an audio cassette and in size to a book, a video cassette is a self-contained, sealed tape package. Inserted into a playback machine, it can produce a video and audio program on any standard TV set. The unit is self-threading and can be started, stopped, rewound or removed at any point. Running time can be from 10 to 60 minutes, and the program may be in color or black and white. Video tapes are long-lasting, readily produced and inexpensively duplicated. Video cassette systems are likely to become economical and widespread in the fields of education, communications and business.

The greatest initial impact of video cassettes and films will probably be in the area of independent study. Since programs can be easily filmed in any location using a minimum of equipment, can be prepared for a select and interested audience, and are viewer-controlled in their playback, they are ideally suited for individual instruction in virtually any subject. Law students can observe courtroom procedures, business students can learn about management problems, labor students can dissect a lengthy negotiation, and budding chefs can study pastry making—all using video cassettes. Anyone wanting to learn about Peruvian Indians, embroidery, the solar system, indoor gardening, Roman architecture or thousands of other subjects may someday have not just books, but video cassettes, at his disposal.

Within the domain of business, video cassette programs could augment such traditional forms of communication as management memos, conference summaries, codified training procedures, interoffice and interbranch correspondence, and trade journals—wherever the printed word is insufficient or too readily ignored.

A New York firm, Playback Associates, already provides video cassette services to such clients as museums, multinational corporations, foundations, government agencies, financial institutions, universities and medical agencies. One example is the assistance they rendered to a large construction and development corporation. Meetings with subcontractors, architects, engineers and inspectors were videotaped and on-site progress recorded. This direct and graphic information, provided to supervisory personnel in regional and home offices, allowed them to keep abreast of a remote project, anticipate problems and suggest solutions. As a result of this more efficient communication and coordination, swift and orderly progress was made, leading to the completion of the project well ahead of schedule.

According to Playback Associates, "The video cassette's flexibility and portability, its more practical production costs, and its ability to be stored and reviewed at will make it an ideal instrument for providing information. . . . In short, the video cassette is a new kind of book; only it is more vivid, lively, motivating . . ."

Today's young people are avid moviegoers—cinema as art form—perhaps because they grew up watching television. Video cassettes would tap their heavily visual orientation. But very few books make it to the screen. Only if the conversion is inexpensive, like cassettes may become, will we "watch" books.

Remote Cassette Vendors

Music lovers may soon buy their "records" from vending machines, linked to master tape stations, as easily as they buy candy.

A vending system for purchasing remotely stored information has been patented by Robert Lightner. It includes a central tape station where commercial recordings are stored on master tapes, and a number of peripheral vending machines distributed around the market area served by the master tapes.

Each vending machine offers the consumer a selection of recordings stored in the master tape center. The data selected by the consumer are transmitted from the master tape center to the remote vending machine, where they are copied by a built-in duplicator onto one of the cassettes stored in the machine. The

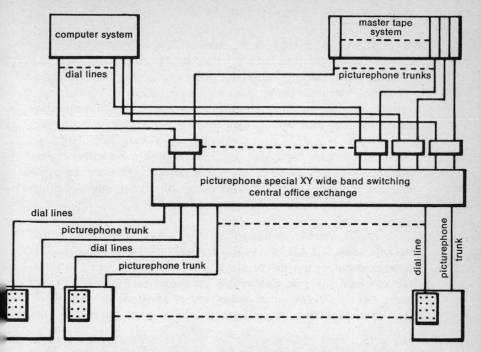

Block diagram of the system to sell remotely recorded cassettes from master tapes (above) to remote locations (below). This requires the special broad band equipment used for video telephones or "picturephones."

machine ejects the cassette into the waiting hands of the consumer. Cassettes are purchasable in currency, tokens or credit cards, if the consumer maintains an account kept current by a computer at the master tape center.

The master tapes contain complete albums of recordings, which are automatically reproduced on the cassette as is, or a variety of solo recordings which can be individually selected to create a new album "menu" of the purchaser's choice. With the remote cassette vendor, a person doesn't have to buy a complete record just to get to hear one or two songs.

Cassettes are magnetic tape cartridges, playable on regular tape-deck equipment owned by the purchaser. Once ejected from the machine they become permanently his. This frees consumers from the need to wait for reshipments if the retailers are temporarily out of supply of a very popular recording. Record companies can produce a relatively small number of recording copies before placing a product on the market. These lower production costs will allow them to have a larger selection.

Though originally intended for commercial audio recordings, the cassette vending system can also be applied to the distribution and sale of almost any stored information, including audio and video. Mr. Lightner would like to see the system extended even farther. He says, "In a more preferred embodiment of the system, the master tape system includes multiple endless tapes which are arranged to be continuously driven by a common capstan. Each tape is individually accessible from *any* vending machine serviced by the master tape center."

In the future, your local supermarket or record store may vend remotely recorded cassettes. The frustration of a wanted record being sold out or out of "print" will be alleviated. And you may also buy completed movies or old TV shows on video tape cassettes. Perhaps they would "self-destruct" after one or two showings—to protect the author's rights.

Tiny TV Camera

Solid-state TV cameras the size of a cigarette pack have been developed by General Electric, Fairchild Camera and Instrument Corporation, and Bell Laboratories.

Miniaturization was feasible through the replacement of the large video vacuum tube basic to conventional TV cameras by an imaging device the size of a penny. The device, a metal-oxide semiconductor, utilizes the photosensitive properties of a tiny silicon chip to create an electrical video signal from an optical image. As light strikes the chip, thousands of minute specially treated regions in the chip collect electrical charges proportional to the intensity of light received. Miniaturized integrated circuits surrounding the chip register these charges and produce an output which is then converted into a standard TV signal.

Provided with a small video tape recorder, a family can use

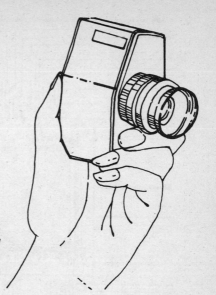

The Fairchild solid-state TV camera measures 3½" × 1½" × 2¼" and weighs 6 ounces. It operates under a wide dynamic range of light levels and has low power consumption.

this new solid-state camera to make home "movies" for instant replay on the household TV set. The portability, compactness, long life and low power required for such a video system also make it very suitable for applications in law enforcement, security surveillance, space systems and related fields.

Equally significant advances featuring the data handling, rather than the optical, capacities of metal-oxide semiconductors can be expected. These miniature devices will someday serve as the memory components in computers; other possibilities are just beginning to emerge.

According to Dr. G. F. Amelio of Fairchild Camera and Instrument Corporation, one of the companies producing the new camera, the technology of the miniature sensor "has created an impact on the field of imaging, especially TV cameras, comparable to that of the transistor on vacuum tubes. It is opening up major and revolutionary new applications for silicon semiconductors . . ."

Tiny video phones are possible—but expensive. And even when their cost comes down, many people may still shun video phones. Their reasons: desire for privacy, force of habit. In his novel *1984*, George Orwell imagined video "bugs" in citizens' homes. But tiny

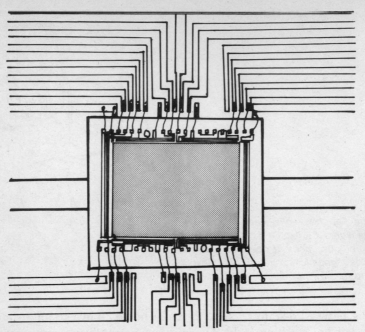

The heart of the tiny TV camera senses images with this flat chip of oxidized silicon.

TV cameras could dot our roads for highway surveillance and safety. Or probe our bodies to facilitate exploratory operations.

Remember how the price of radios plummeted after the transistor made them pocket-sized? Miniaturization may do the same for compact, portable video systems. TV movies could be made at home and replayed on the household set or mailed to distant relatives.

Personalized Vacations

"Driving alone at night scares the hell out of me." "I sound like a leaf blowing in the wind." "I would rather be a teddy bear than a duck." "Even though I enjoy good food I am quite conscious of

444

my weight." Your reaction to statements like these may begin your next vacation.

The recent population in America grows by about 2 million a year. So whatever you decide to do on your vacation, or wherever you decide to go, it's likely someone else has the same good idea. The travel industry encourages all of us to travel. And aside from tour packages and group travel bargains, they offer other less direct inducements. For example, banks give free travel coupons for specified airlines to attract depositors. To alleviate crowding at resort areas, travel agencies, railroads, bus and shipping lines are attempting to provide ready access to alternative vacation choices.

A portion of the personality profile test; computer dovetails the results to a personalized vacation.

Column A Statement	Column B — Phrase				
	Strongly Agree (1)	Tend to Agree (2)	Hard to Decide (3)	Tend to Disagree (4)	Strongly Disagree (5)
22. I believe in giving children lots of help and advice.	☐	☐	☐	☐	☐
23. I admire big spenders.	☐	☐	☐	☐	☐
24. I have never been on a diet.	☐	☐	☐	☐	☐
25. I usually make decisions on my own.	☐	☐	☐	☐	☐
26. I am almost never late for an appointment.	☐	☐	☐	☐	☐
27. I am quite active in the PTA.	☐	☐	☐	☐	☐
28. I like my house to look spotless when people visit.	☐	☐	☐	☐	☐
29. When I was young, I learned the value of money.	☐	☐	☐	☐	☐
30. I'd like to try living in a commune.	☐	☐	☐	☐	☐
31. Children should never be spanked.	☐	☐	☐	☐	☐
32. I would like to be a fashion model.	☐	☐	☐	☐	☐
33. Blue jeans are all the clothes I want.	☐	☐	☐	☐	☐
34. I like to walk around in strange cities.	☐	☐	☐	☐	☐

2. What sounds like you? Please put a check mark underneath the one you pick.

3. Which one would you like to be? Please put a check mark underneath the one you pick.

Suppose you plan a trip. You may want to do too many things all at once. Perhaps conventional ideas leave you restless. You may not wish to take a chance with an unfamiliar area. Some of us already know what vacations make us happy. But few things are more disappointing than planning a vacation that would have been perfect . . . for someone else. Now agencies and airlines are beginning to make use of personality profiles and computers to design a "foolproof" vacation. A computer tells you where in all the world to go and what you would like to do there, even though you may never have heard of the place.

The new variety of custom-tailored vacation areas makes it simple to find one's own special "place in the sun." Costs and attractions of each area, stored in the computer, are matched with individual likes, dislikes, budgets and dreams. Like computerized dating, your fantasies are matched to the available alternatives with the flexibility of modern technology. The computer's choice of a "perfect" vacation may even surprise you. But Eastern Airlines, who offers this concept to its travelers, says "ideally you should end up with a unique vacation experience that's a reflection of your own inner reality. Don't take someone else's vacation."

We've always personalized our vacations—but not by computer. It becomes necessary because of the increasingly rich choices we face. Not only where and when to vacation, but what goods and services to buy. What careers to choose.

It's both bad and good. Bad, because we're increasingly ignorant of all the possible alternatives. Good, because technology recaptures personal choice. We will see more of both.

Computers Teach Fun and Games

Computers aren't only serious business. Children are now using them to draw figures, learn the principles of juggling, and play tic-tac-toe.

A computer program, developed at the Artificial Intelligence Laboratory at MIT, teaches children to manipulate their words and concepts—and enjoy the process. Unlike preprogrammed computer-assisted instruction, the MIT computer allows children to create their own programs. It's been found to be helpful for normal children as well as for those with learning disabilities.

The equipment consists of a screen, a typewriter keyboard, and attachments. The children learn a simplified language of the computer, called LOGOS, from trained teachers. This language, easily understood even by students with learning problems, is made up of simple instructions: examples are "forward," "right" and "print." "To riddle" may instruct the keyboard to type out the old joke, "What has four wheels and flies?" The program will congratulate students who answer "Garbage truck," and ask others to keep trying.

Children feed information into the computer by typing out

Turtle wanders around classroom directed by girl at computer terminal.

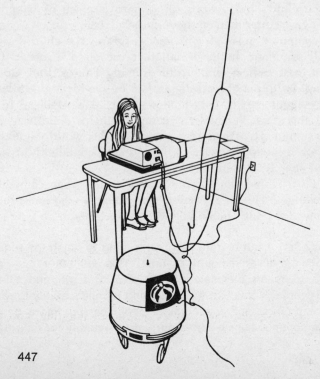

instructions on a keyboard. They work on the computer one at a time. The instructions of the children are turned into figures, letters, words and even musical notes on the screen.

If a child misuses LOGOS, the figure, letter or drawing he wishes to make will come out wrong. Such mistakes are called "bugs." Since the child can see his mistake printed in front of him, he can also visualize the fault in his logic. The computer breaks down each program into procedures and smaller subprocedures. This process helps the child understand that a complex whole is really made up of small, simpler parts. When the child understands his mistake, he doesn't make wild guesses at random just to get the right answer, but guesses logically. He can then "debug" or correct his procedure step by step.

One of the computer attachments is called the "turtle." Shaped like the cannister of a large vacuum cleaner and propelled by an electric motor, it is wired to the computer terminal. It's mounted on three wheels and can be directed by the child via the terminal to move in different directions. The turtle holds a pen which can, upon the child's instructions, drop onto a piece of paper and draw a figure larger than on the terminal screen.

The computer stores all previous programs the child designed and will print out this information if the child wants it. Once children master the technique of drawing figures, they can use the computer to play board games like tic-tac-toe and battleship.

Dr. Seymour Papert, coordinator of the MIT Artificial Intelligence Laboratory, believes the computer helps children gain "a greater and more articulate mastery of the world, a sense of power of applied knowledge and a self-confidently realistic image of oneself as an intellectual agent."

The idea behind the computer and its language comes from the thinking of Piaget, a learning psychologist who looks for the logic, however faulty, behind children's concepts.

Schools often teach by rote learning, racing to finish the required material in a given amount of time. This computer may allow children to teach themselves principles of logic and thinking applied gradually to any area. Improving a child's ability to reason may not produce more scholastic geniuses, but more children will gain common sense—an important commodity for their future.

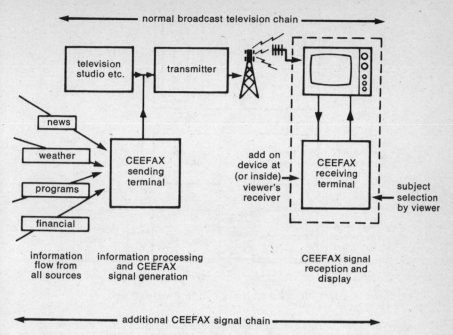

The signal chain from studio to home.

Instant Information

Television programs are on the air virtually twenty-four hours a day, but anyone who wants to know the weather forecast or commuter-traffic conditions has to wait until six or eleven P.M. to get that information on TV. A new receiving system, called CEEFAX, invented by engineers at the British Broadcasting Corporation in London, has changed this.

A CEEFAX broadcasting station transmits up to thirty-two "pages" of up-to-the-minute information in addition to its usual programs. This could include immediate and predicted weather conditions, for example, or the latest stock-market quotations, sports forecasts and scores in London, Tokyo and Oakland; or even the movies being shown in various parts of Manhattan.

The CEEFAX information magazine is inserted by the broadcasting station into the regular TV line transmissions. At the

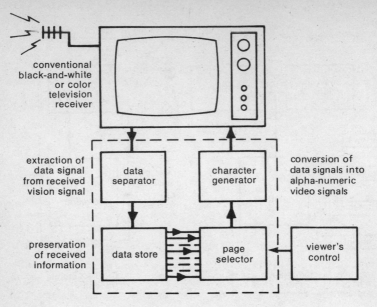

conventional
black-and-white
or color
television
receiver

extraction of
data signal
from received
vision signal

data
separator

character
generator

conversion of
data signals into
alpha-numeric
video signals

preservation
of received
information

data store

page
selector

viewer's
control

The control system attached to the viewer's television set.

receiving end, a device attached to the conventional TV receiver contains elaborate circuits. These do the job of data-extracting, decoding, storage, and alpha-numeral character-generating. The viewer has a push-button page selector on which he can pick any one of the thirty-two pages of information, and this will be displayed on the TV screen and the viewer can read the page against a blank screen or superimposed on a regular program. Image storage is necessary because it takes about fifteen seconds to transmit thirty-two pages, and information can be added or edited at any time during transmission.

A person going to the office in the morning can be sure of getting the 11:30 A.M. Tokyo closing prices by pressing 32.11.30 on his push-button selector. This will mean that the storage circuit will record page 32, broadcast at 11:30, and display the page when he comes home in the evening.

The deaf can watch TV with the script superimposed on the video picture. Connected to a telephone circuit the system can call upon a central computer on the other side of the United States (see page 360) for vital data to display on the home screen. Telegrams and telex messages piped into the viewer's home by the phone company will await his arrival.

Programs in foreign languages can be watched, with translation into English subtitles—as they happen.

The viewer, heretofore a passive witness, can play a vigorous and selective role in choosing his TV "menu."

Slowing Down Live Action

It is possible to slow the action on your own television screen, when *you* want to. A new device lets you watch the critical few seconds of a game-deciding football play in slow motion, a stunning tennis return or high jump—while it's actually taking place without missing anything.

Television pictures don't really move (neither do "moving" pictures). The television receiver builds up a sequence of images on the screen, point by point, and produces a complete image every one thirtieth of a second. Because our eyes possess something called "persistence of vision" the set of points look like a sequence of images in an uninterrupted changing scene.

Motion pictures are slowed by speeding up the camera and running it through the projector at regular speed, thus capturing more frames per movement or "slow motion."

However, live action is slowed for television by recording a changing scene as a succession of images, and then broadcasting a played-back version in which each normal image is transmitted for more than the standard one thirtieth of a second. The extra time is used up by transmitting each image, or part of each image, more than once. The viewer still sees thirty images each second—but not thirty different images. If each image is transmitted for slightly *more* than a thirtieth of a second, a ten-second action sequence is stretched out to, say, twelve seconds; the scene appears to unfold more slowly than in the real world.

In a conventional playback system, if a ten-second sequence is stretched out to twelve seconds, two seconds of *something* are lost when the television producer returns to live action. But in the new scheme the lost time may be broken into small segments which are dropped, say, once each second. Out of every second of live action, ten-twelfths appear in slow time and two-twelfths are lost.

While watching a pole vaulter, for example, the new device may be operated like existing replay equipment to deliver a long action sequence in slow-time, and then drop several seconds (in one chunk) when it returns to live action at normal speed. The system has a modified video tape recorder with a number of playback heads. Switching from real-time to the first playback head introduces a small delay and causes a portion of the image sequence to be repeated. Switching to the second introduces an additional delay, and so on. The heads are switched automatically (in sequence), and the return to real-time from the last playback head drops the lost-time segment.

The inventor, Herbert Lehmann, says his device is an improvement over available "instant replay" equipment. While existing techniques "have enhanced interest in football and the enjoyment of the game by the television audience," he explains, "it is still difficult to clearly follow all of the players' movements when an especially rapid play occurs."

Instant replay often makes sports events more exciting to watch on television than in the stadium. Certainly true for football. It's so true that the forthcoming New Orleans Superdome (and others) will have a giant screen so the *stadium* audience can see replays at quarter and half time.

Electronic aids to sports popularize them—and will continue to do so. They also help keep them honest. When a laser beam calls the strikes better than an umpire, or an instant replay refutes an unfair decision, that's progress. But something else is happening, too. Television creates athletic stars and heroes. Not only the game itself but the players, and even the announcers, become cultural heroes.

Playbacks also improve sports performance. Watching reruns of the big game (minutes after the play) expands an athlete's experience, concentration and understanding of the opponents' weaknesses. Athletic training will become increasingly more intuitive—and more "scientific."

A futuristic approach to body cleanliness also helps provide beauty care, physical therapy and relaxation.

A "People Washer" Egg

It's a clean trip. It's an adventure in personal hygiene and comfort. It's an ultrasonic bath developed by the Sanyo Electric Company of Japan. This machine showers and bathes the body, cleans the skin, massages the muscles and dries you. All you do is lift a finger.

The people washer looks like a large dinosaur egg. Except for your head (which sticks out of the egg) the entire body is cleaned. The round shape permits free, rapid circulation of water and air. It's easier to use than a dishwasher, clothes washer-drier, or even a tub-and-shower combination. There's no need to wait for a tub to fill, and no need to take a shower after a tub bath. Because the unit is sealed, there are no puddles on the floor—and no more steam to peel the paint from the ceiling. Because the air-bubbled water is in constant motion and because the bath uses sound waves for cleaning instead of soap, there are no messy rings.

It's simple to operate. Just select the water temperature, climb inside the egg and start the machine. It goes through these cycles automatically: First you are enveloped by a warm shower. Two minutes later, the ultrasonic washing begins with bubbly warm water. The bubbles are activated by ultrasonic sound waves, which cleanse you. Gradually the bath fills after five minutes with warm water. At a set level the water intake automatically shuts off and the hot water begins to whirl, cleaning your body even more thoroughly. The ultrasonic sound waves continue. While the water whirls around and over you, small rubber balls float in the water and massage your skin and relax your muscles.

After seven minutes of washing and rubber-ball massage, the bath water drains from the sphere and the body is reshowered for two minutes. The shower and ultrasonic waves cease and all the water is drained out. Now for the dry cycle: low moisture air circulates through the chamber. Five minutes later you are ready for the office, dinner—or just plain sleep. The entire cycle takes only fifteen minutes.

For relaxation, massage and sheer pleasure.

Another luxury that will drift down to the average citizen. Physical therapy and athletics are booming, and systems like this may be just what the doctor ordered.

Longevity Quotient

If you're educated, stay fit, quit smoking and keep working, you're likely to live longer than if you're not and don't.

Studies show behavior and health are very important in predicting longevity. But physical, mental and social examinations improve the accuracy of longevity predictions by about one third over predictions based on actuarial life expectancy alone. (Actuarial tables, the kind used by life insurance companies to calculate the risk of a prospective client, indicate life expectancies for a person based on the averages for his age, sex, race and occupation.)

Interviews with elderly people were followed up after a lapse of over a decade. Dr. Erdman Palmore at Duke Medical Center devised a longevity quotient, or LQ, as the measure of longevity rather than actuarial life expectancy. The LQ is similar to the Intelligence Quotient, or IQ: It's the observed number of years a person survived after the initial interview, divided by the actuarially expected number of years based on age, sex and race. For example, an LQ of 1.0 means the person survived exactly as long as expected. An LQ of 1.5 means he survived 50 percent longer than expected, while an LQ of 0.5 means he survived half as long as expected. For those who were still living at the time of the follow-up studies, the number of years they will survive was estimated by adding the present number of years they have already survived (since the initial interview) to the expected number of years now remaining according to the life expectancy tables.

LQ equalizes the known general effects of age, sex and race on longevity by concentrating on the less understood factors of health and mental and social variables.

Among 268 community volunteers aged 60 to 94 in Durham, North Carolina, and in a follow-up study some fifteen years later, Palmore used the LQ as the predicted measure. He found that the four strongest predictors of longevity were work satisfaction, happiness rating, physical functioning and tobacco use. Apparently, psychological factors were even more important than health in predicting longevity.

In 1958 and 1971, Dr. Virginia Stone, an associate, conducted a similar study in Chapel Hill and Carboro, North Carolina, with a typical population. Four variables significantly predicted longevity: physical mobility, education, occupation and employment. However, education and occupation taken together were even more important in predicting longevity than physical mobility.

The researchers believe education reflects the underlying dimensions of mental ability and socioeconomic status. Intelligence increases longevity since it promotes problem solving and crisis adaptation. Higher work status provides healthier working conditions, more income to spend on health care and housing, and the intangible rewards that come from performing a meaningful role in society.

Palmore and Stone conclude, "These findings suggest that, in general, the most important ways to increase longevity are: (1) maintain a useful and satisfying role in society; (2) maintain a positive view of life; (3) maintain good physical functioning; (4) avoid smoking."

If jobs, education, happiness and no tobacco are associated with extended life, then a person may have some control over how long he lives. A good education, a good job and staying happy are intrinsically important. They add depth—and perhaps length—to life. All the more reason to pursue them.

Dietary restriction may be the simplest way to prolong life (see page 72), simply because it's under our conscious control day by day.

10
Environment

Sonic-Boom Softener

A simple means of reducing the sonic booms caused by super-sonic planes has been patented.

At *sub*sonic speeds an aircraft creates pressure waves in front of itself which cleave the air, clearing a "path." These pressure waves travel only as fast as the speed of sound—about 760 miles per hour. But a plane flying at *super*sonic speeds gives no ad-vance warning to the air molecules ahead to yield the space they occupy to oncoming aircraft. The resulting collision or pileup of

The aircraft flying at supersonic speed and the propagation of the major shockwaves to ground level. The antiboom jet weakens the wing shock, separating it from the nose shock.

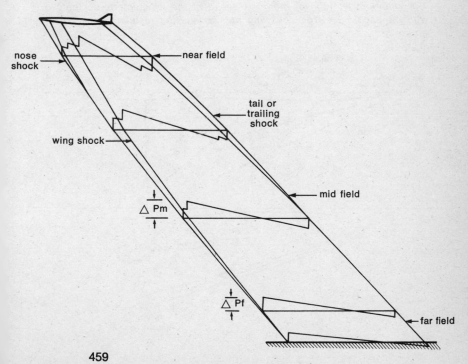

air molecules, while invisible, is pronounced. Shockwaves—a wall of increased air density, temperature and pressure—radiate from the aircraft. The impact of these waves upon the ground is accompanied by an explosive noise known as the sonic boom. It's sometimes intense enough to shatter windows or even eardrums.

Sonic booms are so objectionable that military jets, when flying over populated areas, normally ascend to extremely high altitudes before surpassing the speed of sound. Since such altitudes are beyond the capability of the supersonic transport (SST), supersonic flights of these planes have been banned over land.

The character and contour of the relevant shockwaves reveal that a single sonic boom is actually a product of the merging and mutual reinforcement of distinct shockwaves leaving the nose and wings of an aircraft. Taking this into account, Sin-I Cheng and the Research Corporation of New York City have patented a

The antiboom jet (above) mounted ahead of the wing interferes (below) with the shockwave from the wing and softens the resulting sonic boom on the ground.

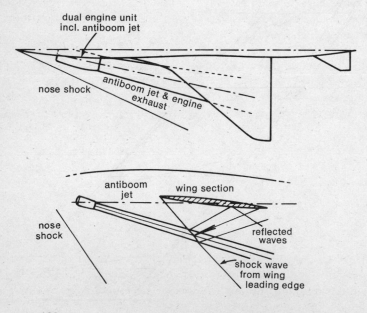

way to deflect the shockwaves proceeding from the wings, thereby altering their "boom signature"—the characteristic way the shockwaves strike the ground.

Cheng's idea is to produce a supersonic stream of air, directed below the wing's leading edge. One way is to install a separate "antiboom jet" on the fuselage forward of the wing. Another method is to relocate one or more of the main thrusting jets to such a position, modifying it to produce the additional supersonic stream. This auxiliary jet stream intercepts and weakens the wing shockwave. Thus diffused the sonic boom is softened to a tolerable level by the time it reaches the ground.

Fortunately, existing SSTs can incorporate antiboom equipment without major design changes or excessive penalties in fuel consumption and weight. Preliminary findings suggest that valuable advantages of such incorporation will be greater lift and improved maneuverability of the aircraft.

According to Sin-I Cheng, "It is presently feasible, using existing technology, to create an antiboom jet . . . to be used satisfactorily for boom reduction on the Boeing prototype 2707-300 SST. . . . In fact, in view of its improved control capability, this jet interacting device may find wide application in connection with unmanned supersonic vehicles, such as drone aircraft, rockets and missiles . . ."

We have banned the boom by restricting overland supersonic flights of the SST.

If an innovation is important and useful enough for our future, technological "fixes" are often made to the social objections.

Space-Garbage Collector

Several thousand man-made objects are now whirling around in earth orbit, not counting the nut-and-bolt-sized scraps too small for radar-tracking stations to detect. There may soon be enough

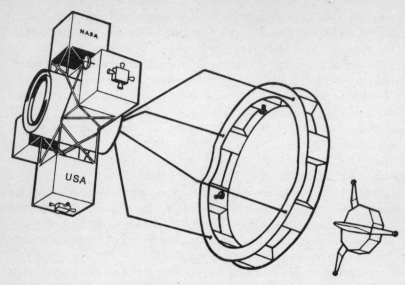

The model space mitt. TV cameras (upper left) guide the radar-located "junk" (lower right) into spinning ring (center) attached to satellite.

dead satellites, discarded rocket stages, and other space junk to jeopardize future space flights. Any collision at orbital speeds—in the vacuum of space—would be deadly to a space traveler.

Most of the orbiting objects are what Dr. Marshall Kaplan of Pennsylvania State University calls "garbage"; it's useless clutter. But some old satellites contain expensive equipment that could be reused if salvaged, and future satellites will be built with replaceable components so they can be easily repaired "on location."

Under a grant from NASA, Dr. Kaplan has designed a remote-controlled space retriever to clear the space traffic lanes and to capture reusable payloads. He has named his concept "the space mitt."

Many of the artificial moons are spinning very rapidly, which makes retrieval tricky. For a safe catch, the mitt must be spinning at exactly the same rate as the object. Dr. Kaplan's solution is to build a large ring—fourteen feet in diameter—mounted on a rocket-powered tender. The ring begins spinning until it is synchronized with the spinning object. The four telescoping arms clamp down on the space junk and make the catch. Finally, brakes are applied to the ring, and the spinning is gradually brought to a halt.

The whole process is to be monitored by TV cameras and controlled by astronauts aboard a nearby space station. If a satellite is captured, it can then be brought into the station, repaired and returned to orbit. If it is space junk, small retrorockets are attached and fired, causing it to fall back into the atmosphere and burn up.

Dr. Kaplan also hopes to rescue astronauts from space stations tumbling out of control. He explains the problem: "Since these craft may be as big as a 747 jet, the problems of docking a rescue craft are enormous. It would be a little like mooring a tug to an ocean liner in the middle of a typhoon. The craft must be de tumbled before docking can be attempted." One suggested solution is a kind of orbiting hose that shoots out jets of water to stop the tumbling. Then the rescue craft could safely dock and remove the crew.

Dr. Kaplan says, "There are two basic schools of thought on the solution: You could have an arm attached to the shuttle which would reach out and grab objects, or you could use a separate vehicle for retrieval. The arm approach is more difficult and dangerous if the object is spinning. I think our idea is a little more versatile."

The space mitt could deactivate enemy missiles or spy satellites, and save stranded future astronauts.

Solar Flare Warning

An alarm system, which warns of fires and burglaries on earth, gives advance notice of solar flares in space. Together with a radiation detection device, it allows space and air travelers sufficient time to take precautions against lethal solar flares.

FUTURE FACTS

Solar flares are intense, temporary outbursts of gases and nuclear particles from small areas of the sun's surface. They produce radiation potentially dangerous to men traveling in space or flying at high altitudes in airplanes. The radiation can cause severe burns and cellular damage. Solar flares can also disrupt radio, TV and shortwave communications.

The radiation detection device is selectively sensitive to the initial surge of a solar flare. But the peak in radiation intensity

The iron and manganese filters are in front of a pair of radiation detectors, called scintillation counters. When the signals from each are equal, they cancel; when unequal, they signal the onset of a solar flare.

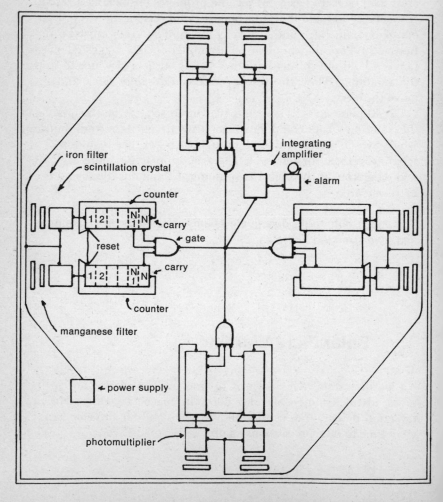

occurs about 20 minutes after this initial surge. At the first appearance of intense radiation, the device activates an alarm. Since a significant part of an hour still remains before the onset of the solar flare, the alarm gives early—and sufficient—warning.

Space travelers could then seek shelter within those areas of the spacecraft especially shielded for this purpose; interiors of spacecraft are normally shielded by light structural materials only. Upon warning, aircraft flying at high altitudes can descend quickly to altitudes of 50,000 feet or less. At that level, the upper atmosphere absorbs enough radiation to give travelers adequate protection.

The radiation detector unit is exposed to the environment, mounted outside the spacecraft or aircraft. It has two selective radiation filters, one of manganese and one of iron, and a radiation detector is placed behind each filter. The electrical outputs of the two detectors are combined in such a way that at wavelengths outside the early-sensitive portion of the solar radiation, both detectors produce equal signals which cancel each other out. Inside the specified wavelength band, the detector behind the iron filter will produce a larger output than the detector behind the manganese filter. The net output from the two opposing detectors produces enough electricity to trigger an alarm device.

According to the inventor, Andrew Sterk, "While the hazard of radiation from solar flares during space travel has been recognized, no prior-art solution to the problem it creates is known."

Is there any question that a device of this sort will be needed in the future as we expand our exploration of outer space? Vacation trips to the moon advertised by a major airline already have a waiting list. When they become commonplace, the need to forewarn space travelers of solar flares will be much greater than now. But even while space travel is limited to a handful of astronauts only, we have to protect them, military flights, airline passengers and our delicate communications systems between earth and the planets.

465

Modifying Weather and Climate

Experiments in modifying the weather have been going on for twenty-five years with inconclusive results. Now the National Academy of Sciences has set up a timetable to get weather modification on a sound basis within the next decade.

A recent study by the National Academy's Panel on Climate and Weather Modification sums up what's been learned so far and what still remains to be learned. The panel also proposes a program to fill in vague areas of knowledge so weather can be modified effectively.

One problem area is rainfall control. Many of us assume man-made rainfall is well established, but the panel finds the facts are far from clear-cut. Cloud-seeding can increase rainfall—but sometimes it actually decreases it. Sometimes it does nothing at all, or it changes the rainfall amounts in nearby areas. A lot, apparently, depends on meteorological conditions at the time. In a long-term cloud-seeding project involving orographic (mountain region) winter clouds, precipitation was increased substantially.

Airport fogs are another concern. Several U.S. and foreign airfields routinely dissipate cold fogs and low stratus clouds by seeding them with solid carbon dioxide or silver iodide. Unfortunately, about 95 percent of fogs over American airports are warm ones, and a procedure for dissipating warm fogs still remains to be found.

Other meteorological areas in which the panel calls for continued research are hail, hurricanes and tornadoes. Experiments are under way in the U.S.S.R. and elsewhere to suppress hail or mitigate its damages, and results are reported to be encouraging. There is also promise that seeding can reduce the force of hurricane winds. Other experiments have suggested it may be possible to control tornadoes and the destruction they cause.

A little-understood area for which the panel has proposed intensified research is the inadvertent damage that man is doing to the atmosphere by pouring pollutants into it. The panel calls for the findings to be in by 1980.

According to Thomas F. Malone of the Review Panel on Weather and Climate Modification, "That man *can* modify the weather consciously has been determined. That man is *likely* to modify climate inadvertently is a valid judgment that can be made. The gaps and deficiencies in our knowledge are known, as are the measures required to remedy them."

Like nuclear energy, weather modification can be used for war or peace. But we have to know more about the effects of poking around in the atmosphere this way. "Weather engineering" will be a routine occupation *only* when we're sure that our intervention will make the rain fall over drought areas, the fog dissipate at airports, the tornadoes and hurricanes vanish.

Turning the Lightning Off

Tiny fibers released into thunderclouds can turn the lightning off. Scientists at the Environmental Research Laboratories believe that the suppression of lightning for forest fire prevention and other purposes is at hand.

In a six-week experiment in northeastern Colorado, metallized nylon fibers—called chaff—were seeded into menacing thunderhead clouds. Scattered by an aircraft, the chaff consistently neutralized the electrical fields building in the storm.

How lightning is produced is not fully understood. One theory says that collisions of cloud particles electrically charge them. The clouds become polarized, that is, positive charges go to the top and negative charges to the bottom. Since air is a poor conductor, these charges accumulate until they reach 500,000 volts per meter. At that electrical strength the insulating effect of the air is overcome, and a lightning bolt cuts across the sky.

But the metal fibers depolarize the charges inside the clouds. This makes the air a better conductor, as the powerful charges are dissipated before they reach lightning strength.

Alan R. Taylor of the Northern Forest Fire Laboratory has

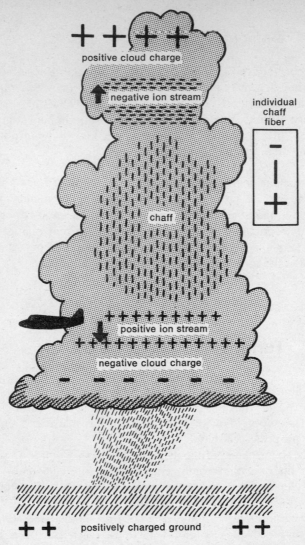

positive cloud charge

negative ion stream

individual chaff fiber

$-$
$|$
$+$

chaff

positive ion stream

negative cloud charge

positively charged ground

The electrically conducting "chaff" (center) provides a pathway to neutralize the buildup of charge above and below.

estimated that if all lightning were suppressed, there would be 70 percent fewer forest fires in the western United States. However, some researchers maintain that lightning, and even the fire it causes, are necessary to preserve an ecological balance.

For instance, the heat of small forest fires causes lodgepole pine cones to drop their seeds, which can only germinate at a temperature of 113° F. For this and other reasons, foresters will probably never want to eliminate lightning-caused fires completely. But lightning suppression may permit the forest rangers of the future to choose where and when to have fires, so they can be easily controlled.

Dr. Heinz Kasemir, director of the experiments, says, "Our limited previous experiment indicated that, indeed, we could suppress the lightning mechanism in thunderstorms. This summer's study has reaffirmed our belief."

Stored in satellites, the metallized chaff could be released upon command.

This is a benign example of weather control. Clouds are sapped of their electrical charges, suppressing lightning.

But all weather control is not so benign. There have been reports that the U.S. government was "making weather" over Laos to control strategic situations. Weather-making could be a powerful, unconventional weapon in future conventional wars. We might wage thunderbolt warfare, like Zeus.

Static Electricity Clears the Air

Static electricity is already being used in household filtration units to remove dust, pollen and odors from the air. Now a Japanese company has put the same principle to work clearing smoke and dust during tunnel construction. Scientists at Nippon Kogei Kogyo believe that electrostatic equipment can be used on a larger scale to clear fog from airport runways—or even to disperse city smog.

The most ambitious use of electrostatic clean-up so far has been to remove lung-damaging dust caused by boring and blasting operations in mines and tunnels. A system of positively and negatively charged electrodes is connected to an electrostatic generator. Particles around the negative pole are pushed toward

Electrostatic "dusters" at work in tunnel construction (above) and highway tunnels (below).

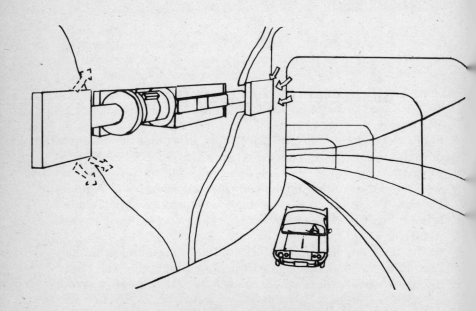

the positive pole, where they are collected by high-volume fans. The dust is filtered out, and the clean air is recirculated.

A similar unit can be used in a highway tunnel to collect noxious auto fumes. An alternative system, where good housekeeping is unnecessary, uses only positive electrodes. The pollutants collect along the walls of the tunnel, which are naturally "grounded."

In some underground malls and skyscrapers, closed ventilation systems continue to circulate the air during fires, carrying smoke to all parts of the building. In such an emergency, an electrostatic filtration system can be a lifesaver. By simply connecting a smoke sensor, an electrostatic system can be automatically activated at the first sign of a blaze. Constant filtration keeps the interior of the building relatively smoke-free, reducing the loss of life from smoke inhalation.

At an inventors' convention in New York City, scientists from Nippon Kogei Kogyo demonstrated the potential use of static electricity to clear fog and smog. Fog was artificially generated over a scale model of San Francisco. When static was discharged from two structures resembling radio towers, the fog was removed within seconds.

"We believe," say Japanese scientists who tested the system, "that this device will make a great contribution to the health of workers and the improvement of working efficiency according to the increase of sight distance when a tunnel is excavated. This device has been used in many fields to remove the smoke in case of fire or to remove the dust in a cement works."

Suppose the Empire State Building were the positive pole and the World Trade Center the negative pole. An electrostatic "wind" between the two buildings could sweep away the bad air over Manhattan. But the extra electricity needed to do the job itself would generate smog elsewhere, unless antipollution devices were used.

Forecasting Quakes

Within a few years it may be possible to forecast the time, place and magnitude of earthquakes. When rock formations begin to swell, according to geophysicist Dr. J. Theodore Cherry, it's time to be on the alert.

Under the tremendous subterranean pressure that leads to a rupture or fault, rock formations are compressed. But, curiously, sometime before the actual quake the volume of rock begins to expand. This is the tipoff.

The expansion, known as "rock dilatancy," was first observed in the laboratory. While studying computer data on California's San Andreas Fault, Dr. Cherry and Dr. James Savage of the National Center for Earthquake Research confirmed that dilatancy occurs in natural rock formations.

As the rocks are swelling, they become anisotropic: their properties vary with direction or orientation. In this case, the speed of sound through the rocks varies according to the direction the sound wave travels. The behavior of these sound waves "may well be the key to earthquake prediction," Dr. Cherry reports.

Sound equipment used in oil prospecting could easily be adapted for quake forecasting. Sound-wave data, along with conventional seismic measurements, would be analyzed by a computer, which could reliably predict when, where and how violent a quake might take place.

Dr. Cherry of Systems, Science and Software, La Jolla, California, recently testified before Senators Alan Cranston and Ernest Hollings on proposed new earthquake legislation. He stated that his company has also developed computer simulation techniques that can predict ground motion resulting from quakes. "Such calculations," he said, "are essential in developing standards and design criteria for major land improvements (buildings, utility networks, transportation facilities, reservoirs, dams, etc.), and for determining the potential hazards to existing structures."

Citizens of major quake-prone cities, like Tokyo and San Francisco, will benefit from early warnings—not only when and where the quakes will occur, but how much movement to expect.

Air Monitoring Analysis and Prediction

An "advance air warning system" advises major fuel users when weather conditions will not disperse high-sulfur emissions. Users can quickly switch to low-sulfur fuels or curtail operations to protect threatened air quality.

Health experts are deeply concerned about the enormous quantities of pollutants, including compounds of sulfur, that industry discharges into the air. However, industry can avoid this only at a heavy cost, which it will pass along to consumers because low-sulfur fuels are in short supply, whereas high-sulfur fuels are more abundant. It's a problem to which there is no cheap and easy answer.

Now a company named Environmental Research and Technology, Inc., of Lexington, Massachusetts, has come forward with a compromise solution. It has developed a system it calls AIRMAP—an acronym of *air monitoring analysis and prediction*. AIRMAP provides sophisticated hardware that gives constant reports on air quality. It analyzes all combinations of meteorological conditions, identifies those that may cause emissions from a source to threaten air quality standards, and produces a recommendation for emission reduction based on air quality forecasts up to thirty hours in advance. Thus, declares ERT, industry can use high-sulfur fuels whenever the warning system indicates the emissions will be thoroughly dispersed.

AIRMAP uses networks of field instruments, telecommunications, computers and data analysis programs which continuously monitor air quality, smokestack emissions and weather quality. It has been providing reports in Massachusetts and New York State, since December 1971, to industry, utilities and government agencies, so they can comply with air quality standards.

"Information obtained from the AIRMAP system," says Dr.

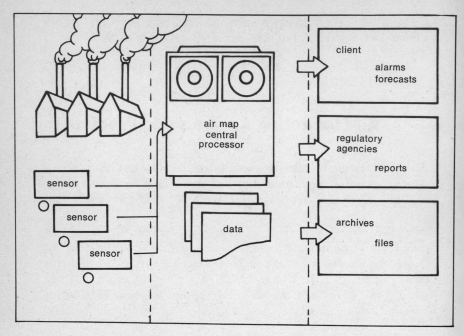

The sensing elements (left) feed information on air quality to the central processor, where it's relayed (right) to clients, regulatory agencies and files.

Norman Gault of ERT, "has clearly shown that high-sulfur fuels can be burned at many locations as much as 85 to 90 percent of the time without exceeding Environmental Protection Agency ambient standards, and highly dependable forecasts can indicate just when low-sulfur fuels must be used to protect the community."

Algae "Polish" Water and Make Paper

Algae grown abundantly in fish tanks, sewage pools and the sea can reclaim waste water as well as becoming fibers in paper.

474

ENVIRONMENT

Conventional sewage treatment, which involves removal of suspended solids and microorganisms, doesn't adequately prepare sewage effluent for direct discharge into oceans, lakes or streams. It fails to remove many chemical compounds from the process water. Certain of these compounds promote dense algae growth, indicating pollution or organically enriched conditions.

Using algae to treat wastes has been suggested before, but the one-celled varieties under study proved too difficult to remove from the water when the cleaning was completed. Biologist Peter Benson of the Lockheed Ocean Laboratory proposes to use multicellular green algae to reclaim waste waters. These simple water plants feed on pollutants, and could be harvested and used in place of wood fibers to manufacture paper.

Cladophora, multicellular algae, tend to form large, detached, free-floating masses naturally which facilitate removal from water. *Cladophora* tolerates high levels of organic or toxic pollutants and grows rapidly in municipal waste water. The algae can digest many different pollutants—nitrates, phosphates, DDT and even radioactive isotopes. Because of their large size and ability to form masses, the algae are easily filtered from the clean water, unlike smaller and simpler forms.

Particularly suitable for water renovation systems, they grow very rapidly under municipal waste water conditions, and are found worldwide.

Algal fibers harvested from waste water treatments may find

The biological reclamation of waste water with algae.

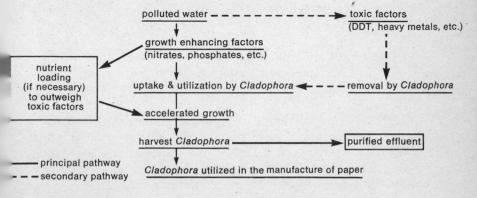

475

use in paper manufacture. This has a dual advantage. Paper-making demands for natural fibers, like wood, are exceeding current supplies. In addition, turning wood into paper generates wastes that choke the streams surrounding paper mills. Algal fibers would significantly cut down on this pollution problem. Algae have a natural stripping process whereby their cell division separates the protein and cellulose-rich cell wall from the intracellular contents. Consequently cell walls are available as fibers.

Dr. Benson notes that algae are a high-protein source. *Cladophora* might someday be grown and harvested as a food supplement.

He says, "The idea occurred to me when I was conducting some research on *Cladophora,* a multicellular algae which exhibits explosive growth under municipal waste water conditions. At this time, I uncovered an obscure Russian reference to the algae being utilized during the manufacture of a high-grade paper. Putting both observations together led to the proposed system."

The three-birds-with-one-stone syndrome is common enough nowadays to prove that even pollution has technological solutions. This one (or systems like it) shows that ingenuity and patience will help clean our future environment.

Clean Cars

Four men from California have put together a totally pollution-free car. In their spare time, and with their own funds, they converted a regular automobile engine to burn a mixture of hydrogen and oxygen.

This is very timely research because the premise on which it's based is that the future of fossil fuels, like oil and gasoline, is limited. In fact, hydrogen is the only substance known that can release energy chemically without pollutants. When hydrogen is burned with oxygen it produces energy and water.

476

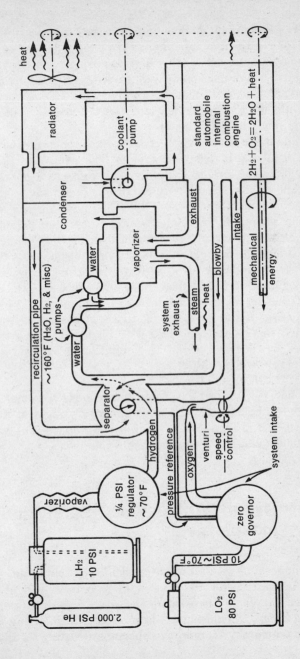

Flow diagram for hydrogen-oxygen intake (left) to a standard internal-combustion engine (right).

After pilot experiments demonstrated the feasibility of this type of engine, they modified an old Model A Ford pickup truck. The engine ran well and with great efficiency: it got 10 miles per pound of hydrogen compared to only 2.5 miles per pound of gasoline. The next vehicle to be modified was another Ford pickup, but a 1960 model; and this worked as well as, in fact better than, the older model.

The engine loses no power by the conversion from gasoline to hydrogen, and it runs totally clean. The two major problems are storage space for the hydrogen and oxygen, and what the inventors call the Hindenburg Syndrome (referring to the German zeppelin of that name which, filled with hydrogen, exploded one day in a gigantic fire). The United States uses helium to fill its zeppelins to avoid such disasters. However, the inventors contend that the public is slightly hysterical on the subject, and also ignorant. The dangers of using hydrogen as a fuel, they say, although different, are no worse than those involved with gasoline; in fact, they consider them not as great. At this point they are looking for companies or the government—that is, for some institution with money, time and sophisticated technology to take their home-made product and make it safe, economical and completely acceptable to the consumer.

Although the back of the pickup truck looks extremely unwieldy, future technology may find ways of packing gases at much higher pressures and therefore in much smaller space. The vehicle that is totally pollution-free is an ultimate solution.

Ozone Purifies Water Safely and Inexpensively

Recent technological advances make it possible to produce ozone (a form of oxygen) practically and economically right where it's needed—in plants where water and waste water are treated.

Traditionally, chlorine has been used in disinfecting water. But it's a potentially dangerous substance because it's delivered in

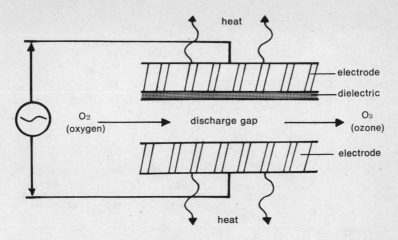

The electric field (left) is applied to the upper and lower electrode through the dielectric or insulator. Oxygen (O_2) at left enters between the discharge gap and leaves at the right as ozone (O_3).

pressurized cylinders or tank cars, and accidents happen with it. When used, chlorine produces compounds harmful to aquatic life.

By contrast, safety problems with ozone are few, since it must be produced when and where needed because it isn't stable. But it's more effective than chlorine in destroying viruses and is a quicker bacterial disinfectant. Moreover, ozone produces no residuals that are dangerous to life.

The problem has always been to generate ozone economically. In 1968 Frank E. Lowther, an engineering physicist, became interested in finding a solution. Ozone is produced by the reaction of an oxygen-containing feed gas in an electric discharge called a corona. Starting from scratch, Lowther derived the physics of corona generation and then reduced the equations to a practical piece of equipment that can produce the ozone at reasonable cost. Now he is pioneering in devising systems that increase the efficiency of water and sewage treatment.

According to Lowther and his associates, "Ozonation for wastewater disinfection is a rapidly emerging technology. Ozone eliminates the basic problems associated with chlorine while offering a number of advantages. High cost has been a problem in the past,

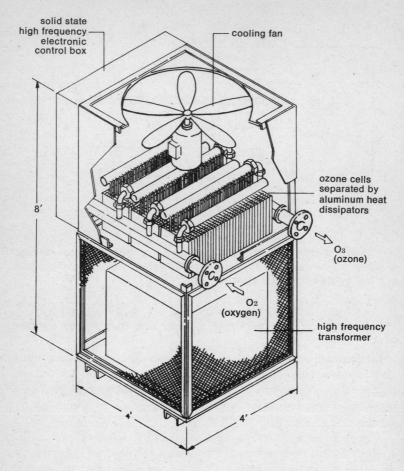

This basic module will produce 300 pounds of ozone a day.

but new ozone generation and application technology is overcoming this liability."

Electric power is used to convert oxygen into ozone. Ozone generators of the future will doubtless switch to nuclear power—and, eventually, probably to solar energy.

Deodorizing Olfactory Offenders

Sewage plants stink. So do animal and industrial wastes. And though these organic wastes can be recycled for use as fertilizers, the manufacturing process and end products are also offensive to the nose.

As waste products proceed through the various stages of decomposition, their chemical makeup changes. This natural process has made it difficult to develop a single substance that will deodorize wastes once and for all. But by carefully researching the chemical source of odors, Josef Weiss of Stockholm, Sweden, has developed a number of chemicals he believes can neutralize olfactory offenders.

After several years of testing, Mr. Weiss developed a fine

The production of food and the production of wastes is an elaborate cycle. The heavy black arrows indicate those processes in the cycle in which the application of odor-removing chemicals would make for a more pleasant environment.

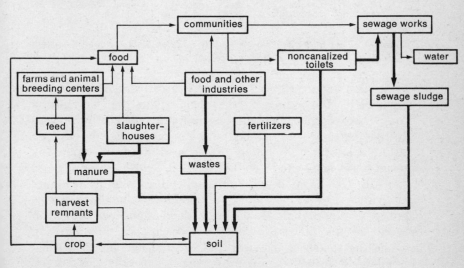

ODOR REMOVAL
FROM HUMAN, ANIMAL, AND ORGANIC INDUSTRIAL WASTES

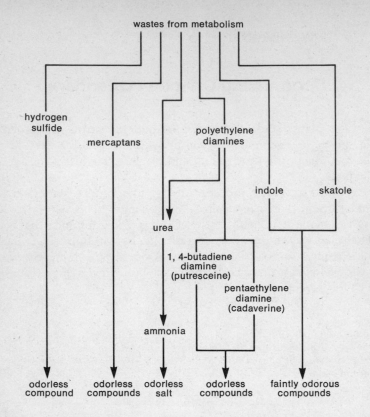

Treatment of organic wastes by a variety of chemicals reduces a variety of olfactory offenders to odorless compounds.

powder that apparently counteracts fetid smells immediately and permanently. Depending on the chemistry of the wastes, the formula varied somewhat, but overall the powders were very effective even when applied to notoriously malodorous pig wastes. Unfortunately, after extensive testing, the powders proved too expensive to be commercially practical.

So Mr. Weiss searched for other chemicals offering a higher reactivity at a lower cost, and developed a new line of chemicals applied in liquid form. The liquid "deodorants" cost about 10 percent of the powders. About two parts per thousand can change the stench of manures and factory effluents to a smell resembling well-treated garden compost.

The odor pollution of sewage plants and other industrial facilities can be noticeably reduced. (The results of a seven-week test at the Stockholm sewage works "exceeded all expectations.") Further, chemical treatment may make it feasible to use animal fertilizers in parks, on lawns, and in other locations where it was formerly impractical. In fact, the additives decrease the phosphorus content in sludge by up to 90 percent, and they actually increase the effectiveness of wastes as fertilizer.

"Regarding sewage works," Mr. Weiss explains, "questions arise not only about the odor in and around the works themselves, but also about disposal. Drying the sludge with heat exchangers or burning it is expensive and consumes a lot of energy. The cheapest approach is to recirculate wastes, as recommended by all experts concerned (who, at the same time, recommend certain limitations in the use of human wastes). If the disgusting odor can be removed, the reuse of wastes as manure or as soil conditioner would be facilitated."

To neutralize offensive odors will take considerable research and development. And most of us will welcome useful results as another form of pollution abatement. In a few years, perhaps, we'll have food additives that deodorize pets—and maybe people.

Electric Toilet

Electric bills may one day include the costs of operating an anti-pollution electric toilet in private homes. Toilet waste water is incinerated at a temperature of 1000° C., leaving no bad odors and no sludge to transport through the sewage pipes. The system, designed by the AB Allonette Company in Sweden, can also handle all other household water waste.

The Allonette system is a compact unit with an ordinary toilet seat on top. All household waste waters are collected into a tank, and then pumped over to a boiler for incineration. Water other than toilet waste water is distilled for recirculation in the toilet and other units in the house, such as a washing machine. Or it can be led directly out into ditches. Since it contains no sludge, there's no need for sewers or waste water treatment plants.

The impure matter that rises to the surface of the waste waters (called scum) is led over a scum-separating device and then burned, together with the toilet waste water. A sterile white ash remains from the scum, and it's easily emptied from the ash box with a vacuum cleaner. The steam from the incinerator is used to heat the house or the water system.

Average incinerating time of wastes is fifteen minutes. The incinerator runs on oil, electricity or gas, so it can be integrated with the heating system already in the house.

A large working model of the Allonette toilet has been made for a Swedish oceanliner with a capacity of 1400 passengers.

According to Goran Langstrom, manager of the Allonette Company, "The Allonette system is the only fully integrated water and waste water treatment system for single houses. It's easy to install and easy to use."

A fully integrated waste system for homes will be more important than one might at first imagine. To the extent that your privacy is voluntary isolation or autonomy from society, a home garbage incinerator or an electric toilet is merely another privacy-enhancing "instrument." It frees your regular (or weekend) house from dependence on municipal garbage disposal. This trend will accelerate as homes will begin to have their own power sources.

Gelling and Dispersing Oil Spills

Oil pollution is one of the ecological problems of our times. With multitudes of big tankers plying the oceans of the world, there's always a danger of collision, grounding or sinking—with the possibility that vast quantities of oil may pour into the sea.

One process, developed by Exxon engineers, is now available to prevent the spills. It's based upon the release into the ship's oil

Workboat sprays dispersant, cutting oil slick.

tank of two organic chemicals. When they meet, the reaction produces molecules that gel the oil. One version creates a gel in 14 to 45 minutes, the other in periods of 3 to 18 hours. Only small concentrations of the chemicals are needed and the gels are stable.

The gelled oil helps a stricken vessel retain some degree of buoyancy, since it keeps water from leaking into the tank. If the vessel breaks up, the gelled oil floats as a coherent mass and does not cause the wide degree of pollution that liquid oil does.

According to one of the inventors, Gerald Canevari of Exxon, "Raising the temperature up to about 135–145 degrees F. will reconvert the gel back to liquid form. The recovered oil could be used or processed in a normal manner."

In another process, a chemical dispersant, Corexit 7664, developed by Enjay Chemical Company of New Jersey, an Exxon subsidiary, appears to work safely and effectively. When oil spills on water, it forms a film. This not only contaminates shore property and beaches—it kills fowl, fish and other marine life. It also apparently forms a barrier that prevents oxygen, essential to the life processes of marine plankton and other species, from reaching the water.

One of the key components in the new dispersant is a surfactant (or surface-active agent) that thins the oil. It does this by forming tiny oil droplets when it's mixed with the oil. It also keeps the droplets from coalescing, which would restore the oil film. Dispersed oil droplets won't adhere to beaches or birds and they're biodegradable. Microorganisms in the water can get at them, using them as food, dispersing the oil slick. The surfactant in the new dispersant is also biodegradable. Tests are continuing to determine the long-range safety of the dispersant.

"When exposed to Corexit 7664 at 10,000 parts per million for 24 hours," the manufacturer says, "the mortality level for shrimp was not significantly different from the mortality of shrimp in untreated seawater. Similar results were obtained for test fish."

Magnetic Fingerprints Trace Oil Polluters

Oil tankers often flush or "clean" their tanks offshore and discharge oil into the ocean. Magnetic dust added to tankers' bulk liquid cargoes can be given a distinctive "fingerprint." In case of an oil spill, as little as a half-pint of recovered oil is enough to trace the offending vessel.

The technique depends on the magnetic properties of ferrites—compounds that contain iron, nickel and zinc. A ferrite is magnetic below a critical temperature (called the Curie point), and *non*-magnetic above that temperature. By varying the relative amounts of iron, nickel and zinc in the ferrite, the Curie point can be shifted over a wide range. Relatively simple tests allow one to determine the Curie point of a ferrite, or the several Curie points of a mixture of ferrites.

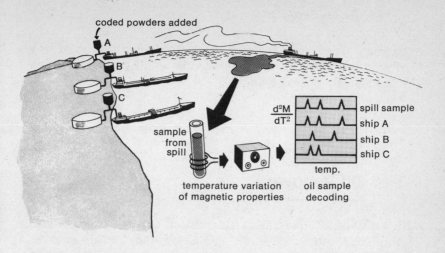

coded powders added

A

B

C

sample
from
spill

$\dfrac{d^2M}{dT^2}$

spill sample

ship A

ship B

ship C

temp.

temperature variation
of magnetic properties

oil sample
decoding

*The magnetic dust, added to ships during fill-up, is traced by noting the
critical (Curie point) temperature.*

A mixture of powdered ferrites is added to the bulk liquid cargo of a tanker, perhaps ten gallons of powder for each million gallons of liquid. Eleven different ferrites can be used, and each of eleven different Curie points is present or absent in the mixture. Therefore more than 2000 different identifying tags are available.

Any desired mixture of powdered ferrites can be added to the liquid when a tanker is loaded. The powder is readily recovered by a simple magnetic separator when the vessel is unloaded. The recovered mixture of ferrites requires no processing, and can be used to tag another cargo.

According to General Electric, who developed the technique, ". . . 2000 tankers are estimated to make about 10,000 calls annually on U.S. ports." On the Northeast seacoast during a recent six-month period "an average of three and a half oil spills a day were reported." With ferrite tagging, "in the event of an oil spill, the magnetic 'tags' in the petroleum could be analyzed and the source vessel quickly identified. The responsible party would then be assigned the cleanup cost."

Tags, like radar speed indicators, make us obey the rules better when we know we might be caught. Cleaning up the spills (see page 488) could be done by an offshore "coast guard" type of operation. Equipped with the tracer instruments, they could levy the fine and clean up the spill—on the spot. Oil traffic to the United States ought to be watched.

Oil Recovery

The Lockheed Corporation has developed a device called "Clean Sweep" to scoop up giant oil slicks before they can do environmental damage. Under ideal conditions, the floating skimmer can recover as much as 12,000 gallons of spilled oil in one hour.

The unlovely craft looks like a riverboat paddlewheel riding between two pontoons. As the paddles dip into the slick, oil clings to the honeycomb of metal surfaces inside the wheel. A series of wipers scrape the oil from the metal and channel it into a large storage drum. For big cleanups, the oil is pumped into a 2500-gallon floating plastic bag and stored there until bag and oil can be towed to shore.

As the drum rotates, oil adheres to the discs. It is then wiped off by metal wipers and guided to a storage tank.

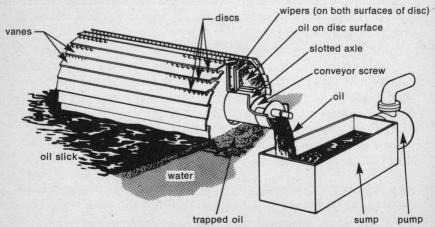

vanes — discs — wipers (on both surfaces of disc) — oil on disc surface — slotted axle — conveyor screw — oil — oil slick — water — trapped oil — sump — pump

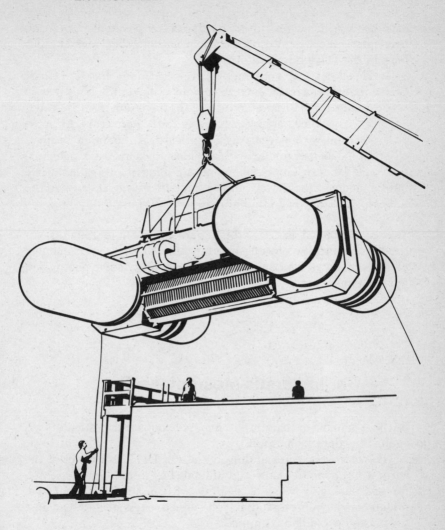

Large version of the oil recovery device has two huge tanks for storage of recovered oil.

The skimmer is readily transportable; it can be powered into position with an outboard motor or towed by a small craft. Recently, when there was an oil spill in the remote Utah wilderness, a Clean Sweep was airlifted to the cleanup site by an Army helicopter. One was also used to help battle a slick several miles long in the Oakland (California) Estuary.

Lockheed is now constructing a larger unit for the Coast Guard that is seaworthy enough to fight spills on the high seas.

According to the manufacturer, "The inventor, Robert Yates, has been a Lockheed engineer for over thirty-four years. At home on a weekend several years ago, he heard of the Santa Barbara oil spill and began toying with an idea for a recovery machine that would be an improvement on anything then available. He built a model of the device in his garage that weekend and on the following Monday had something to show his boss."

The oil reclaimed is 95 percent pure—enough to refine it for profitable reuse. Future oil supertankers will carry vast amounts of oil; recovery of their spilled cargo will help conserve energy and the environment.

Garlic Versus Mosquitoes

Garlic, common to many a kitchen, is a powerful pesticide used against the durable mosquito.

The controversy surrounding the use of DDT as a result of the harm it has done to plants and animals has stimulated the search for less damaging ways of dealing with insect pests. In India, researchers have been studying the effectiveness of garlic against the mosquito and find it impressive.

Garlic oil, according to the researchers, not only is a medical stimulant and an antibacterial agent, but is also a useful pesticide. Earlier research showed that it could destroy aphids, cabbage white butterfly, caterpillars, and Colorado beetle larvae. The Indian researchers isolated the active principles in garlic oil, which they identified as diallyl disulfide and diallyl trisulfide and tested these on mosquito larvae. In the tests, a concentration of 4 parts per million of these substances killed 76 percent of the mosquito larvae. A 5-parts-per-million dose killed 100 percent of the test population. The experimenters used both natural and synthetic samples of these substances in the tests.

In other experiments the researchers found the substances effective against other pests such as potato tuber moth, red palm weevil, red cotton bug, mosquitoes and houseflies.

According to A. Banerji and S. V. Amonkar, the researchers, "The nontoxic nature of garlic to higher animals has been established on the basis that it has been used for edible purposes for a long time. This, together with the wide range of activity of the oil, suggests that garlic oil or its active principle, whether natural or synthetic, could be used as a pesticide."

Vampires suck blood. So do mosquitoes. An old wives' tale says garlic wards off vampires. Now, research says that garlic keeps away mosquitoes. What will future research say about other ancient wives' tales?

Zoo Animals Provide Early Warning System

It may be possible to detect dangerously high levels of lead in the atmosphere by keeping an eye on zoo animals.

While death as a result of simply breathing may seem like an alarming prediction, researchers at New York Medical College have discovered that a large number of animals at the Staten Island Zoo are suffering from lead poisoning, the main source of which seems to be polluted air.

After two leopards at the zoo died of lead poisoning, the researchers decided to check other species at the zoo. They found that animals ranging from reptiles to primates had high concentrations of lead in their bodies—often in amounts far exceeding those considered toxic in man. While it's true that some of the lead contamination came from paint on the animals' cages, those kept in outdoor cages, some of which were unpainted, showed the highest amounts of lead.

The amounts of lead found in the grass, leaves and soil around the zoo grounds were unusually high, equivalent to the amounts found along the sides of major highways where automobile exhausts build up.

Dr. Ralph Strebel, the pathologist who directed the study, said, "The findings have ominous implications for the people who live in that area of the city." The rest of the city, however, had no reason to breathe easily, for the same problem was found at the Bronx Zoo.

According to *Science* magazine, "One of the difficulties in detecting widespread lead poisoning is the lack of specific symptoms. For many years, the headaches and listlessness experienced by slum children who were suffering from subclinical cases of lead poisoning were overlooked by doctors—simply because they were unaware of the problem."

Domestic cats may provide a more accurate barometer of pollution than large zoo cats, since they share their owners' environment. Like canaries in the coal mines—a domestic early warning system. But if the cities are becoming coal mines, will future city dwellers resemble coal miners?

Hormone Sprays Disrupt Insect Life Cycles

Synthetic juvenile hormones—which mimic hormones actually found in insects—may soon be widely used against harmful insects to keep them from growing and reproducing.

Natural juvenile hormones are secreted in tiny glands in the insect's head. These hormones play a major part in the insect's development in both the egg and adult stages (much less so in

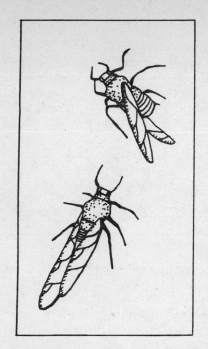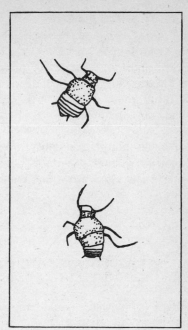

At right is a black bean aphid treated with hormones. Its body is abnormal and it has no wings. At left is the normal untreated adult, which is fully winged.

the larval stage). If extra amounts are absorbed at critical times they play havoc with the insect's life cycle. For example, when excessive juvenile hormone is administered to a larva or a pupa it cannot metamorphose into the next stage, or it grows into a sterile adult.

Synthetic juvenile hormones, applied at the right moment, are thus a powerful insecticide, in effect. Not only will they deform larvae or make adults unable to reproduce, they will also prevent eggs from hatching. Moreover they are extremely specific. Unlike ordinary pesticides, they attack only the insects they're intended for. Beneficial insects, such as ladybugs, can be spared.

Extensive tests with the hormones are being conducted and results look encouraging. Many manufacturers of chemicals are now experimenting with brands of their own. They are optimistic that the hormones will be free of one of the basic shortcomings of pesticides like DDT—insects won't develop resistance to them.

493

According to Dr. Barry M. Trost of the University of Wisconsin, "Enormous doses [of juvenile hormone] have been fed to laboratory animals without toxic effects showing up. As far as we can tell, they are some of the safest compounds for mammals that one could imagine."

Juvenile hormones—environmentally neutral and toxic only to destructive insects—are a "compromise" pesticide that both ecologists and plant growers have been looking for.

An Ultrasonic Rat Contraceptive?

After copulation, a male rat sings an ultrasonic song with the message, "I've had it. . . . Leave me alone." By playing continuous recordings of these songs, it might be possible to discourage rat reproduction, or at least chase them away.

Two Rutgers University biologists, Ronald Barfield and Lynette Geyer, were making "a standard observation of sexual behavior" when they found that the postejaculatory male emits a high-frequency sound. Apparently this call functions as a signal of social withdrawal (or contentment?) while the male is recuperating. During this period, the male dozes or quietly grooms himself, and the females refrain from the hopping, darting and ear wiggling that are considered sexually provocative among rats.

The signals, at a frequency of 22 kilohertz, accompany the rat's long, sighlike breathing. This antisocial song continues throughout most of the male's refractory period—when he is incapable of sexual responses.

The signal is also characteristic of males that have been defeated in a fight or females who are trying to discourage the unwanted advances of rodent romeos. Barfield and Geyer speculate that 22 kilohertz may be a general carrier frequency for rats who want to avoid social contacts.

But ultrasound may also have a positive role in the sex life of rodents. Dr. Barfield is now investigating the possibility that another song may be used to woo the female and ensure a fruitful coupling.

Dr. Barfield cautions: "The sound apparently does *not* retard fertility—my guess is that it may serve just the opposite function. That is, the vocalization as an integral part of the copulatory pattern of the male may influence the physiological response of the female so as to ensure a successful pregnancy. We are currently investigating the latter possibility but cannot say anything further at this time. As far as the efficacy of ultrasound to repel rats, it can work in open areas. Loud noises are aversive; but ultrasounds attenuate markedly and can be masked effectively by rather thin barriers. Clearly rats could have peace and quiet once within the walls."

Rats carry plague, rabies and other diseases, and cause extensive damage to property.

A Pied Piper to remove these pests would be most welcome.

Bad Blood Between Bats

Deadly rabies-carrying vampire bats are highly susceptible to anticoagulant drugs (drugs that prevent the blood from coagulating). Small doses of the drugs spread on the back of one bat affect dozens more as they lick and groom one another in the roost.

Vampire bats kill countless cattle in Latin America each year despite cattle vaccination, electric night lighting, fumigation and the use of strychnine poison. But now a new technique, developed jointly by the U.S. Department of Interior, the Agency for International Development, and the Mexican government, offers a practical and inexpensive solution to the problem.

In experiments, scientists spread a mixture of petroleum jelly and anticoagulant on the backs of a small number of captured bats. When released, the bats flew to their roosts, where the drugs were spread among fellow bats by licking and grooming. For every treated bat, two to three dozen died. Within two weeks there was a 96 to 100 percent reduction in bat bites among livestock.

Anticoagulants were also injected directly into the cattle's stomachs. The cattle were unaffected because of their bulk, but the tiny bats(three inches in length, one ounce in weight) died off quickly because they fed on cattle's blood that contained anticoagulants. They died of hemorrhage, hematoma or starvation because they were too weak to search for nourishment once they ingested the anticoagulants.

The technique costs one to two cents per bat killed and should be repeated only once every three to eight years. The $800,000 cost of the project research is an estimated 0.3 percent of the $250 million annual loss in meat and milk attributed to blood-sucking bats.

"The bats in question are *Desmodus rotundus,* one of three major types of bats," says a report on the experiments. "Unlike the other species, which are, respectively, insectivorous and frugivorous, and unlike the vampire bats that prey on birds, the *Desmodus rotundus* likes mammalian blood, particularly that of docile and easy-to-locate cattle. The territory of these bats stretches from Mexico to northern Argentina . . ."

Future pest control will carefully exploit newfound weaknesses, without bad side effects, because every pest has a weak link in its life cycle. So bats, who live by blood, will die by blood.

Birth Control for Pets

Cats and dogs have a population explosion of their own. To combat this growing problem, a recent Senate proposal offers a low-cost birth control plan for stray animals, like the planned parenthood programs for human beings.

Senator Birch Bayh of Indiana has introduced legislation to

regulate stray cat and dog populations. His plan calls for the Department of Health, Education and Welfare to lend municipalities and counties the funds to establish nonprofit spaying and neutering clinics.

The bill would authorize HEW to loan up to $200,000 to any municipality or county with a population of at least 500,000 persons according to the 1970 U.S. census. At least one trained veterinarian will be employed to supervise the spaying or neutering, but a qualified paraprofessional may perform the actual operation. HEW will also be authorized to make grants to qualified individuals or institutions to set up short courses for training paraprofessionals in these procedures.

Strays create serious problems for a community. They damage property, disturb sleep, bite, spread disease, pollute the streets, kill other animals (and sometimes children), and cause traffic accidents in which people are maimed and killed. In any given town, the incidence of rabies tends to be directly related to the size of its stray pet population. The more dogs registered and hence vaccinated, the lower the incidence of both rabies and distemper.

Humane and animal protective societies have not been totally successful in dealing with this problem. In 1970, in Los Angeles alone, animal shelters handled more than 120,000 stray dogs and cats. In Indianapolis, where pets are half as numerous as people, 50,000 stray cats and dogs are killed by the humane society each year. Another 20,000 are removed by the sanitation department after death from starvation or accidents. One Los Angeles study of pet overpopulation showed that since 1963 dogs have increased at a 40 percent rate—more than double the rise in human population.

Senator Bayh's program is modeled after the successful animal control clinic opened in Los Angeles in February 1971. It demonstrated that the long-term savings in a city's animal control costs more than offset the initial costs of establishing and operating a public spay and neuter clinic, and that a properly run clinic need not drain public funds. Senator Bayh believes that most pet owners are willing to pay for spaying or neutering at a reasonable fee if sufficient facilities are available and accessible.

According to the senator, "When an opportunity presents itself to advance the public health and, at the same time, save the community direct costs in currently operating programs, it is an opportunity which should not be permitted to slip by. When that same opportunity presents the chance to eliminate the suffering of hundreds of thousands, if not millions, of displaced animals, it must be seized."

In mainland China, pets are banned.

But here spaying and neutering clinics will hold back the tide of pet overpopulation; they will provide humane treatment to animals and health for human communities. They will also prevent those clashes between pet owners and non-pet owners from escalating into major warfare.

Ceramics from Waste

A UCLA professor has developed two new home construction products and in the process helped solve three major waste disposal problems. Out of a mixture of glass bottles and cow manure, Dr. John Mackenzie created Ecolite, a foamed, lightweight ceramic substitute for brick or shingle. And from a mixture of glass bottles and dried sewage sludge, he's created a new kind of slate and tile.

Waste disposal, quite literally, is an enormous problem. Consider glass bottles: Californians alone discard some 50 million a week; only 1 percent of these are recycled.

Consider cow manure: an estimated one million tons is produced each year in the state of California. And since farmers prefer to use commercial manure, it goes unused, accumulating in the fields and occupying an estimated 100 million cubic feet. (Burning manure, incidentally, creates pollution problems.)

Consider sewage sludge: 1500 tons are produced every day in Los Angeles and Orange County alone. And where does all this treated human waste wind up? In our proud Pacific Ocean.

Ecolite, the glass and manure mixture, resembles styrofoam in

Ordinary brick (on right balance pan) is heavier than lightweight materials (left). They are a composite of cow manure and powdered glass.

weight and appearance. It's odorless, fire-resistant, water- and gas-impermeable, plus being an excellent heat and noise insulator. It's also cheap to produce: The inventor, Dr. John Mackenzie, estimates the cost at 3 cents per board foot (that's 1 ft by 1 ft by 1 inch). Potential uses: a replacement product for bricks and shingles, in wall and roof insulation, water pipes, acoustic tiles and wall partitions. In its denser form, Ecolite is competitive in cost with brick, but it weighs only one fifth as much.

The production process utilizes 5–10 percent manure as a foaming agent to 90–95 percent finely powdered glass. The manure itself is converted into a fine black powder and mixed with the powdered glass. The mixture is then placed in a mold or tray and heated for varying time periods (at relatively low temperatures) to produce products of different shapes and densities. Density can be controlled from one tenth to twice that of water; so the final product may either float or sink in water.

The bottle-sludge mixture, as yet unnamed, can be used as roofing material or as a replacement for bath or kitchen tiles. It's also odorless, fire-resistant and water-impermeable. A mixture of 50 percent glass and 50 percent sludge, its production technique is basically the same as that for Ecolite.

Dr. Mackenzie says his tiles are up to 50 percent lighter than existing products; they also have greater tensile strength, are thinner and cheaper; and the tiles can easily be decorated in different colors and patterns.

Dr. Mackenzie has discovered a surprising by-product to his extraction process: he found that for every 100 pounds of raw manure, he could produce roughly 15 pounds of crude man-made oil, resembling natural oil. This oil, running through the country's sewer pipes as sludge, can be recovered, he thinks, at an even greater volume.

A trend: making wastes usable. Food from oil (see page 145), beaches from bottles (see below), and now construction materials—or oil—from sewage.

Beaches from Bottles

Old bottles, broken windows, and worn-out light bulbs could be ground into artificial sand, solving two ecological problems: waste glass disposal and the erosion of beaches. This sand, frosted white, would resemble natural sand.

Shore communities spend millions each year to replace sand swept away from beaches by ocean currents. Most of the new sand is dredged from bays behind barrier islands, with disastrous environmental consequences for the bay clams, flounders and migratory waterfowl living there. Using artificial sand for beach fills would leave their breeding areas undisturbed.

Artificial sand would also be less vulnerable to erosion than natural sand. Most natural sand is too fine to withstand the ocean's current, but glass can be ground as coarsely as necessary for maximum beach stability.

New York City alone generated 320,000 tons of waste glass in one recent year. Since the use of glass containers is rapidly increasing while fewer of them are being returned to stores by consumers, the supply of glass is certain to grow larger.

The Army Corps of Engineers calculates that after an initial massive beach fill, the entire 130 miles of New Jersey coastal beach could be stabilized by an annual addition of one to two million tons of sand. The waste glass of greater New York and Philadelphia would probably be sufficient for the project.

The use of artificial sand would raise the cost of beach replenishment from the current two or three dollars per linear foot to five or ten dollars per linear foot. But this cost might be defrayed by selling scrap metal and paper collected with the bottles.

According to Michael Piburn in *Natural History* magazine, "Land disposal sites adjacent to urban centers are nearly exhausted. Even if cities like New York and Philadelphia start reclaiming solid waste, they will still have to dispose of recycled material, such as glass, for which the supply will exceed the demand. The only place to dump these unwanted materials will be the oceans."

Is this a trend? Old tires are reprocessed into road surfaces (see page 299). Wastes are converted into food (see page 149). And now glass bottles may be ground into sand.

The cost of sorting reusable scrap would be outrageous—unless it were done by volunteers. It's not a new idea. The French utopian socialist, Fourier, suggested more than one hundred years ago that children, who like playing in dirt, handle garbage detail. How about hordes of scavenging Boy and Girl Scouts?

Acid Digestion of Nuclear Wastes

Operation of a nuclear power plant produces radioactive by-products which must be captured and stored to prevent contamination of the environment. This problem, which has been with us since World War II, is well understood. A new problem is that of

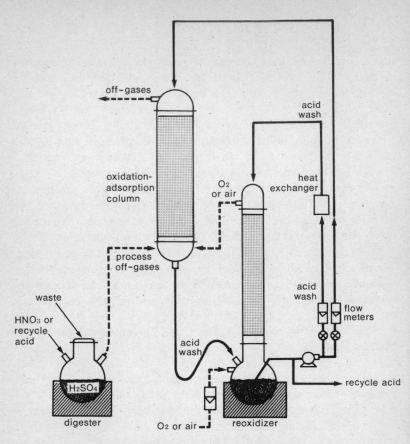

The acid digestion cleanup process consists of a digester (left), an oxidation-adsorption column (center) and reoxidizer (right). Gases from the digester are "scrubbed" by acid as they enter the reoxidizer. Nitrogen oxides and sulfur dioxide are removed from these gases by the acid, before leaving the system. The acids are recycled.

handling large amounts of *secondary* nuclear waste—contaminated laboratory and industrial materials.

In the past, the problem of handling secondary nuclear waste was relatively unimportant. The immediate question was what to do with primary waste—radioactive by-products. Now, though, the sheer volume of secondary waste has brought the problem into prominence. For example, a large nuclear plant may use more than five hundred 55-gallon drums of water-treatment material in its cooling systems each year. When this is exhausted, it can't be treated as conventional industrial waste. Contaminated by radioactive material it's too "hot" to leave at the local dump. Other secondary waste is generated when nuclear fuel is processed.

Westinghouse, a major supplier of nuclear reactors, has developed a process for treating secondary waste with acid and then isolating the radioactive portion. Five hundred drums of contaminated water-treatment material are processed to yield about six drums of radioactive waste. The residue isn't radioactive and is disposed of conventionally.

Westinghouse points out, "The process appears readily usable" in small-scale versions "at the point of waste generation, thereby improving fissile material accountability and eliminating excessive waste handling and storage." They expect a fifty-to-one compaction of radioactive waste, and "greater than 95 percent recovery for recycle" of the acids used in the digestion process.

It looks as though we're going to learn how to live with nuclear power. Anything that reduces the volume of radioactive waste—which must be stored for a long time—will make nuclear power easier to use.

Disappearing Plastic

A process developed by Professor Gerald Scott of the University of Aston, Birmingham, England and others decomposes plastic containers through the use of sunlight. A nontoxic additive makes the plastics decay and disintegrate after disposal.

Plastic containers represent only one part of the total litter problem. A plastic bottle on a beach might be as strong as new after a decade of being washed over by ocean waves. The durability of plastics, so valuable as packaging materials, ironically also protects them from degradation by bacterial microorganisms.

However, a chemical additive introduced into the structure of the plastic during manufacture will absorb ultraviolet radiation once the plastic container is exposed to sunlight. The absorbed radiation then causes the molecular chain, or polymer, to break down. This is called "photodegradation." The plastic remains stable in *visible* light, so there's no danger a container will fall apart indoors when still in use; window glass filters out most ultraviolet radiations.

The strength of plastics depends on long molecular chains. As soon as these are broken, the plastic becomes fragile and brittle. Rain and wind will break it up into small, sandlike particles. When the chains of molecules get small enough, the plastic becomes susceptible to biodegradation by bacteria.

Scientists are able to control the rate of photodegradation by varying the amounts of the compounds used to modify the plastic. Articles of short-term use, such as plastic cups, can be made to disintegrate quickly; but heavy-duty industrial plastics are given a much longer life.

The photodegradation process has been tested successfully on several different kinds of plastic, and licensed for use in a number of countries, such as Japan and some in Africa. A Finnish company began commercial production of photodegradable plastic shopping bags in 1972.

Professor Scott says, "The commercial and technical arguments in favor of plastics are overwhelming and the retailing industries will not be persuaded readily to give up the advantages they have gained . . . while potential solutions to the problem of plastic pollution exist. . . . What the public does not realize is that the pollution problems which scientists have produced can often be reversed just as readily if the public is prepared in the end to pay for that improvement."

The development of containers was essential for the development of civilization. It gave man the important civilizing ability—to carry food and other necessities from one place to another. But now there's a danger we may be discomforted by the wastes of our civilization. The *destruction* of containers we no longer need is probably as important as their *development* for future civilization.

Litter Gulper Cleans Up Roadsides

Highway motorists who drop beer cans and popcorn containers out of their car windows may see them gobbled up by the "Litter Gulper."

"Litter Gulper" is a vehicle resembling a fire truck with a long, snakelike collecting chute mounted on top. Controlled from the cab of the truck, the chute can reach out eighteen feet. A mechanical snout at the end of the chute picks up bottles, cans, paper and other litter with hydraulically powered rotating steel fingers.

Blasts of compressed air blow the litter up the chute into the truck's compactor unit, but blow out nonlitter items like stones and grass. The compactor unit can hold up to eight cubic yards of litter. Trash barrels from highways and rest areas can be emptied by hand directly into the compactor.

On gulping runs, one man operates the collecting arm, or boom, while another picks up large items by hand. The Gulper and attendants move along at about two miles an hour in heavily littered areas, covering three to four times as much ground as the conventional patrol of four men and a pickup truck. It cleans an average of twenty-five lane miles a day, and operates on all kinds of terrain—hills, shoulders, flat roadside areas, and even construction ditches.

The thirty-foot truck on which the chute is mounted has dual controls. This gives the driver great operating flexibility. During normal highway travel, he can drive from the left side of the cab, with the pickup apparatus nested overhead. During cleanup operations, he can sit on the right side, gaining better visibility of the work area as well as simultaneous control of both truck and pickup functions.

Invented by Jerry Fleming, the "Litter Gulper" is one of an increasing number of mechanical, mobile devices used to pick up roadside litter. A second prototype model developed by the American Can Company was successfully demonstrated in a dozen cities across the country in 1972.

All that's litter is picked up by the long arm of the Litter Gulper.

The American Can Company reports, "The prototype Litter Gulper is a unique mobile device designed to increase the efficiency and reduce the cost of highway litter pickup. Our interest is in developing technical and market data which would make the concept commercial."

Roadside litter isn't only a blight on our national scenery, its collection is a $500 million burden on the taxpayer and growing frustration for highway departments.

One solution to roadside litter is to educate or fine the public out of their careless habits. A more practical, immediate way is to make its removal less costly and more efficient with mechanical equipment.

Waterweed Harvester

A strange contraption may soon be plying its way across this country's lakes and streams, harvesting the water plants that often choke them. The aquatic vegetation harvester, as it's called, could play a highly significant role in keeping our waters clean and pure.

Time was when plants in a lake were simply an inconvenience to the swimmer or boatman. Now they are recognized as a sign of eutrophication, a term that makes ecologists see red. Eutrophication means that the water is overnourished—it's extremely rich in dissolved nutrients that cause plants to grow superabundantly. But the excess of nutrients means that industrial or agricultural wastes or other pollutants are being poured into the water. Even-

The harvester in operation. This one is a small experimental model.

tually the plants clog the water, disturb its natural balance, and cause the death of fish.

The harvester, essentially a self-propelled barge with a difference, was developed by the Clark Equipment Company of Buchanan, Michigan. Using a sickle bar, it cuts the plants at depths to five feet. A conveyor belt then carries them aboard the vessel. When the harvester has a full load, it goes to the shore and deposits the crop in a waiting truck with the help of an elevating conveyor. The contraption can cut two and a half tons of plant material in an hour, and only two men are required to operate it.

Researchers at the University of Wisconsin are now making a long-term study of the harvester. There's every indication it will be successful—certainly much more so than attempts to kill the plants with chemicals, which have only resulted in increased amounts of weed at the bottom of lakes and eventually increased eutrophication.

"The concept of mechanical removal of nuisance waterweeds is entirely valid," says W. P. Gregory, a Clark official, "and is looked upon by ecologists as eminently safe. I believe this method of waterweed management will become widely used in time."

Removal of water plants may keep some of our greatly endangered bodies of water, like the Great Lakes, or fish from going down the drain. Moreover, the operation might pay for itself: the plants brought ashore by the harvester could be processed into fertilizer and livestock feed.

Satellite to Monitor Oceans from Space

A comprehensive new satellite monitoring system has been developed by the National Oceanic and Atmospheric Administration. It combines the data-gathering ability of orbiting satellites with earth-based research stations, ships, aircraft and buoys to make precise studies of ocean and undersea conditions—for example, the direction and strength of current flow, fishing conditions, tides and tidal waves, icebergs, marine pollution, coastal erosion and so on.

Among the instruments to be carried by the satellites for marine surveillance are a scanning camera to make infrared and regular photographs of ocean surfaces. These indicate the flow and temperature of cold and warm currents, the presence of fish, shrimp, algae, icebergs, and also the pollution level or oil spills in the oceans and coastal areas. A high-precision radar altimeter measures the distance of the satellite from the ocean surface, and the waves, tides, and storm or calm conditions of the sea.

A side-looking radar uses microwaves to measure ocean-surface conditions from several angles, giving the precise height and nature of ship wakes and wave formations, tides and icebergs, and the wind and oil-pollution conditions. A multifrequency imaging microwave radiometer "looks" through a cloud cover and even light rainfall.

A device measures surface windspeed by the energy scattered back from microwaves. A transmitter-receiver system uses a buoy or a ship equipped with a medium and high-frequency transmitter and a receiver on the satellite to confirm ocean-surface data. A laser altimeter supplements the functions of the radar altimeter. Vertical tropospheric and ionospheric sounders determine the water vapor, atmospheric pressure and electron density in the ionosphere (25 to 250 miles high) and troposphere (up to 10 miles from the earth's surface).

These advanced marine monitors are several years away. But similar land-surveillance satellites already yield valuable information on new mineral deposits, crop diseases and other geographic features. Some important oceanographic data are obtainable only from high altitudes.

Keeping pace with improvements in our scientific equipment, the accuracy of long-range weather forecasts improves yearly. And so will the prediction of tornadoes, hurricanes, tidal waves, and other storm conditions on land, in the air—and on the sea.

We can expect better safety and navigation of ships at sea. Marine resources are only beginning to demand our attention.

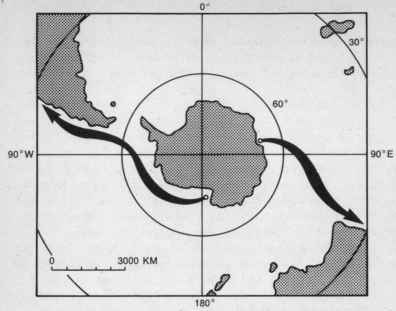

A view of the Antarctic Continent showing the preferred towing paths from the Ross Ice Shelf to the South American Atacama Desert (left), and from the Amery Ice Shelf to Australia (right).

Fresh Water from Icebergs

According to a recent study it is economically feasible to tow icebergs from the Antarctic to Africa, Australia and the United States, where they can be melted to supply fresh water.

In a world that suffers perennial shortages of fresh water for drinking and agriculture, icebergs are a precious renewable resource that has long been going to waste. Ninety-seven percent of the earth's water is salt water. Only 3 percent is fresh water, and three fourths of that is locked in ice, much of it in the Antarctic.

A recent study carried out by the U.S. Army indicates that icebergs of substantial size can be towed long distances without excessive loss by melting. Delivery from the Antarctic ice shelf to the West Coast of the United States will take the best part of a year, but even on this long-haul basis it appears that fresh water can be delivered to arid regions at competitive prices. The required supertugs are no larger than ice-breakers now being designed.

Waste heat from fossil-fuel or nuclear generating plants could be used to melt the ice—which would improve the efficiency of the generating plants and also reduce thermal pollution. Solar energy could also melt the ice.

Small icebergs were towed to Callao, Peru, before 1900—presumably to be used as a source of ice—but since then little use has been made of them.

As the Army study points out, "The water delivered by the operation of one supertug alone could irrigate 16,000 square kilometers"—an area five times the size of Rhode Island.

Is water scarcity next? In some places, of course, it's existed for thousands of years.

We can make fresh water by desalting seawater, but that process uses large amounts of energy—already in short supply. To tow Antarctic ice, a renewable resource, requires a relatively small amount of energy. And the energy needed to melt the ice would cost society very little. At present it is largely wasted.

Putting Smoke Rings to Work

The principle of the smoke ring may be used to clear polluted skies, make rain, and bring dead lakes back to life.

When a cigarette smoker purses his lips and puffs out a ring of smoke, he's actually producing a small vortex ring—a whirling donut of vapor and smoke. Other familiar vortex rings include the mushroom-shaped cloud of the atomic bomb and the circles of smoke produced by heavy artillery guns.

Dr. George Mattingly of Princeton's School of Engineering and Applied Science has found that vortex rings of one substance can be transmitted without dissipation through another substance. A ring may change shape, but it will not mix with the surrounding substance until its internal energy is used up. Dr. Mattingly has several ideas on how to put mechanically produced vortices to work.

A thermal inversion occurs when a layer of cold air gets trapped under higher, warmer air. Normal circulation is interrupted, and air pollutants are trapped near the ground. Ring vortices could be used in two different ways to prevent these pollutants from collecting in dangerously high levels. First, the effluents from factory smokestacks could be puffed out in giant smoke rings. These would rise through the stagnant air into the freely circulating air above, preventing the smog from becoming even more noxious. More ambitiously, Dr. Mattingly theorizes that by sending up vortex rings of clear air, we could agitate the inversion layer above so much that it would break up altogether.

Another environmental problem is the thermocline—a dividing line in water where temperatures change drastically. Thermoclines are also a matter of poor circulation. Warm surface water rich in oxygen cannot penetrate below the line; plants and fish are starved for oxygen, and the bottom of the lake dies. But periodic vortex rings of aerated water forced down into the lake could destroy the thermocline and keep the lake alive. Similarly, the streams discharged from high dams are oxygen poor; the same process could be used to aerate the deep water behind the dams before it is released.

As far back as the Civil War, artillery fire was tried as a rainmaking technique. The idea was to shock the clouds into action. Dr. Mattingly has proposed a vortex gun, a refinement of that old idea, which may prove much more reliable. Vortices filled with silver iodide crystals would be fired into rain clouds from the ground, instead of the present airplane seeding approach. The turbulence of the vortex combined with the condensing effect of the crystals may be an effective means of artificial rainmaking.

Space-Age Sails to Fight Forest Fires

A California truck driver and ex-firefighter has devised a new way to fight forest fires. When high winds keep tree-spraying planes grounded, he suggests surrounding an advancing fire with huge barriers of lightweight fire-resistant fabrics.

The project calls for huge panels of the metallized fabrics (aluminized Beta Cloth, Nomex, and Refrisil) used in astronauts' space suits. Two long and continuous walls of this fabric, each as high as the treetops, would be erected in front of an advancing fire. Converging in a V shape, the walls would funnel the fire into a narrow area where it could be stopped.

The fabric would be hung along a metal cable, which in turn would be suspended by tall metal rods driven into the ground and clamped to nearby trees. Guy lines and stakes would further stabilize the barrier. More fancifully, the inventor suggests supporting the walls with hot-air balloons built into the fabric.

The technique appears particularly suitable for containing fires in brush or scrub tracts. In densely forested areas, however, erection of the barriers would be a formidable problem; furthermore, a raging fire in such an area, which can readily hurl burning logs hundreds of feet into the air, would probably continue on its course by burning over the barrier.

James L. Schneider, who devised the systems, says, "This idea occurred to me while I was stationed at Camp Pendleton, California, as a marine recruit. The year was 1953, and a very dry year for southern California. . . . When a fire would break out somewhere in the reserve, volunteers were picked to help contain the fire. The only tool we would be given consisted of a small GI shovel, and we would use our field jackets to beat out spot fires. I remember the helpless feeling I would have when completely encircled by large fires, the visibility too low to determine which way to safety."

Someday, this layman's imaginative application of space-suit materials may save thousands of acres of woodland.

An enormous fireproof tent, draped over a single structure or small settlement, could even ward off flying cinders.

Afterword

> . . . in the Bolivian Quechua language it is quite pos-
> sible to speak of the future, even as it is in any language,
> but one speaks of the future as "behind oneself" and the
> past as "ahead of one." When pressed for an explanation
> of such an expression, Quechuas have insisted that be-
> cause one can see "in the mind" what has happened such
> events must be "in front of one," and that since one can-
> not "see" the future such events must be "behind one."
> Such a perspective of the past and the future is every bit
> as meaningful as our own, and it can certainly not be con-
> demned as distorted. It is simply different from ours.
> —Eugene A. Nida, 1966

So here in an afterword, I look backwards at the future with
some perspectives on what it will bring. Behind us, this mosaic of
facts presents a detailed panorama of the future. Trends, thread-
ing their way through the facts that create them, are visible:

In health and medicine we'll see more efficient use of available
medical equipment, facilities and all personnel, particularly tech-
nicians and paramedics. Also coming is the potential resolution,
convergence or unification of *physical medicine* (like drugs and
organ transplants) with *behavioral sciences* (like biofeedback,
learning and psychology).

In power and energy, we'll see the growth of new *sources* and
new *shortages*. Scientists and engineers will scavenge old sources
and systems of energy (like the sun and steam engines). And
we'll see many new means of energy storage and transmission
like reservoirs, batteries and light beams.

In food and agriculture, we'll see more movement toward consumption "high" on the food-ecology chain (like animals), and
also more toward "low" on the cycle (like microorganisms). Im-

proved storage methods are coming, along with better distribution, packaging and preparation. Yet at the same time that new artificial foods will appear, we'll also see more gourmet cuisine—with improved combinations, variety and tastes.

Where possible, communications will replace transportation. We will see more efficient use of private and public transportation, diminishing the costs of shipped goods. We may also see more speed—coupled with more safety.

Society and personal behavior are almost impossible to summarize in simple trends. Nevertheless, we will probably see more privacy-enhancing habits, patterns and "instruments" (like telephones, weekend homes and television); at the same time, and perhaps because of these patterns, people may perceive more assaults on their privacy (computerized credit checks and personal data banks). More and more we'll see multipolar and nuclear centers of advocacy—forming and dissolving. We'll probably see both more tradition-oriented values (like the Puritan ethic) and more freedom or liberation from it (like relaxed taboos). People will probably change careers once or maybe twice in a lifetime, aided by less formal open-ended educational institutions. Compared with the present, more teamwork (corporate-government style) and more solitary work (in research, the arts and small business) will prevail.

Construction and materials will use and conserve more "natural" substances. There will be both more synthetics *and* less synthetics. Man-centered building methods and materials will be employed.

Communication and information will become more efficient. Also in store is more precise information delivered on target. Thus, "less" will often mean "more." The information or communications "explosion" will be manageable, helping other trends in society: in science, knowledge, privacy and commerce.

As our economy gets more service-oriented, businesses will continue to be increasingly capital-intensive. But fewer large corporations will take risks. Conceiving new services will be more the province of small entrepreneurial organizations or innovative individuals, operating as autonomous profit centers. The large organizations will enjoy increasing productivity, and consequently more "fat," more "art," and more "the public interest."

Entertainment will flourish in direct proportion to the availability of leisure and affluence. There will be more spectator and participator activities in sports and the arts, along with widespread use of existing and new facilities. Middle-class people will increasingly do more of what the wealthy once did, in skiing, tennis and vacations.

And in the short term, activities aimed at cleaning up the environment will hold even, or at least won't be pushed much more vigorously. In the long term, man's place and efforts in the total ecological scheme of things will achieve a delicate balance.

Recurrent *leit-motifs* appear among the facts. Privacy, leisure, productivity, freedom are issues—rather than directions—of the future. "If you want to know what people will be doing in twenty-five years," says Richard Farmer, "see what the top 5 percent of income earners are doing now. They are the group everyone emulates." I think that's true. Shorter and shorter time-lags elapse before these issues and new things from science and technology drift down from the rich to the rest of us.

But science and technology have suffered a "bad press," particularly during the later 1960s. Perhaps this was a reaction against the promised "miracles" during the golden age of science that followed Sputnik in 1958. Because this can (and probably will) happen again, it's worth a closer look at public attitudes *against* science and technology:

—Science and technology fuel and lubricate our military engines, and are therefore antilife and intrinsically evil.

—Science and technology manipulate our personal lives and society, and can no longer be controlled.

—Other projects deserve higher priority than the luxury of basic research: repairing the human environment, strengthening social welfare, reducing poverty, enriching our lives.

—Science and technology seem to threaten our command over our lives, perhaps making visible our own impotence.

—The momentum of the scientific and technological enterprise, and the enthusiasm of its advocates, carry the enterprise toward its own abstract (and consequently antihuman) goals.

—Any increase in productivity due to science and technology comes at substantial costs: of exhausting our natural resources; contaminating our environment; causing social ills and economic inequities (like the coexistence of a large GNP per capita with extreme poverty).

—Synthetic desires are created (rather than satisfied) by increased productivity from science and technology.

—Even scientific priorities are so inverted that research on high-publicity glamour projects (like heart transplants) appears to have gained at the expense of important low-profile efforts (like reduction of infant mortality rates).

—Science has lost its revolutionary flavor. In the Middle Ages, science was an underground, clandestine activity (the "invisible college") engaged in surreptitiously by intellectual adventurers. Science, like bureaucracy, is now a target—not an agent—of revolution.

—Science and technology are no longer exciting, since the fields are overcrowded, and discoveries are increasingly difficult and expensive to make. Few elegant, dramatic or low-budget-but-rewarding theories (like relativity) await our discovery these days.

—The United States cannot afford to lead the world in every sphere of scientific and technological activity.

—"Science illuminates part of our experience with such glaring intensity that the rest remains in even deeper darkness. The part in darkness," says Victor Weisskopf, "is the irrational and the affective in human behavior, the realm of the emotional and instinctive world."

But there is another side—and other voices—in the continuing dialogue that pits the "culture" of science against the "culture" of art. These are the public attitudes *for* science and technology:

—Scientific research and technological development assist (or ensure) productivity, economic growth and the general well-being and welfare of society. The total cost of all basic research, from Archimedes to the present, is less than the value of ten days of the world's current industrial production.

—Basic science, technology, research and development provide a natural national resource of ideas, a talent pool of leaders, a mobilization base for defense, and thus insurance for the future.

—Scientific research improves the mental, conceptual and philosophical climate of our times, as a side effect of the continuous accumulation and ordering of new knowledge.

—Research and development tell us what we *can* do, and consequently what other countries can do, thereby improving our intelligence estimates.

—National morale and pride are at stake in the competitive arena of international science and technology.

—The United States is a major exporter of advanced technology. Over half of our exports have a high-technology component. Our balance of payments and balance of trade benefit.

—Research and development activities provide employment on a vast scale for scientists and engineers, whose skills might otherwise remain unused.

—Pure science, research and development are the seeds from which technology and growth are the harvest to sustain future generations.

—Research and development in pursuit of one set of goals yield special side benefits (often unwittingly), "colonizing" areas of scientific ignorance with scientific research activities.

—Research and development, science and technology potentially improve interpersonal communication, and actually improve personal, national and global exchange.

—Accomplishing the extraordinary makes the difficult easy. It is much simpler to orbit a satellite after developing the technology for a lunar landing, rather than before.

The tension or polarity between these "two cultures" appears to wax and wane. But although I often find my sympathies are planted firmly on *both* sides of this dialogue, I enjoy the fruits of science and technology.

The United States was settled by immigrants fleeing the past, determined to excise history from their lives. "With their minds fixed upon the future," says Richard Hofstadter, "they set a premium upon technical knowledge and inventiveness which would unlock the riches of the country and open the door to an opulent future."

This heritage created a special tradition—the American "tradition of the new." It's often expressed in other forms: the wish to locate perfection in the future and to identify it with the successive achievements of mankind; the doctrinaire assertion that *change* is *in itself* a sufficient validation of our activities; that novelty is a virtue; that change is progress.

Indeed, one of the more journalistic and vulgar notions of our time is that we live in an age of unprecedented and ubiquitous change. But every age does. And yet what is most important in our lives is precisely what does *not* change through the ages—the "eternal verities"—our familiar quests for love, justice, comfort, truth, order, nourishment, integrity, beauty, honesty . . . the human constants.

Courtesy of science and technology, we'll find more anthropocentric goods, services and activities. These will come from those "nuclear centers of advocacy" which include corporations (large and small), foundations and educational institutions, government agencies dedicated to special missions, and individuals. They will continue servicing the human organism, in all its glory. Health and medicine will service the human body. Communication and information, the human mind. Agriculture, the human mouth and guts; transportation, the human feet. Entertainment and the environment, the human eyes, ears and senses. Man is, and will continue to be, the measure of all things.

Acknowledgments

The talents of many people appear in this book. It would have been impossible to put together without the research and editorial skills of a conscientious staff: Dinesh Agrawal, James Alexander, Alan Bloch, Tony Chiu, Frederick Drimmer, Paul Flannery, Mark Fowler, Don Harris, Ron Horning, Cliff James, Gara La Marche, David Lehman, Alan Lipschitz, Deonanan Oodit, Ashak Rawji and Barbara Trainin. My assistants Gail Rosenberg and Jay Cooke (plus Anne, Jennifer and Whitney) were invaluably helpful. Fay Brugger typed a difficult manuscript to high standards.

The venture capital and investment banking communities, among others, furnished useful leads and ideas: Robert Buescher, Bessemer Securities Corporation; Peter O. Crisp, Rockefeller Associates; Bruce Dahlbo, Dr. Dvorkovitz and Associates; William Draper, Sutter Hill Ventures; Daniel Gregory, Graylock Corporation; Ken Kovaly, Technical Insights, Inc.; James F. Morgan, American Research and Development; Jack McKitterick, General Electric Company; Kenneth W. Rind, Oppenheimer & Company; and W. Hardie Shepard, Payson & Trask.

Peter Schwed, Emily Boxer, Gypsy da Silva, Dan Green, Emily Gwathmey, Eve Metz and Kathy Walukevich at Simon and Schuster and Peter Matson at Harold Matson Company deserve my thanks and respect for their professional efforts.

I am gratefully indebted to a host of friends and advisers, my comrades-in-arms, for superior counsel and support: Henry A. Alker, Cornell University; Barbara Bauer, The Rowland Company; Winston Franklin, Charles F. Kettering Foundation; Richard Fryklund, Rand Corporation; Banesh Hoffman, City University of New York; Joseph S. Iseman of Paul, Weiss, Rifkind, Wharton & Garrison; Arnold Lieber; Tom Lincoln; Ephraim London of London, Buttenweiser, Bonem and Valente; Rodney W. Nichols, The Rockefeller University; Raymond Ripper; and

ACKNOWLEDGMENTS

David Z. Robinson, Carnegie Corporation of New York; and Nancy Hechinger Vlack.

Paul Greenfield, in particular, believed in the project when a friend counted most. And Sherri Zitron helped make it all come together.

This book is for my mother Emma Katznelson Rosen, my father Morris Rosen, my son Daniel Marc Rosen, and my daughter Lisa Jo Rosen.

Stephen Rosen

Index

INDEX